The Theory of Decorative Art

Suzanne M Parker
101 Paisley Court
apt 'A'
Bozeman, MT 59715

re'vd from Amazon
by post on Thussday,
January 29, 2009
I am @ MSU's
Todd Larkins class

THE THEORY OF

DECORATIVE

ART

AN ANTHOLOGY OF
EUROPEAN & AMERICAN
WRITINGS, 1750–1940

EDITED BY ISABELLE FRANK

with translations by David Britt

Published for The Bard Graduate Center

for Studies in the Decorative Arts, *New York,*

by Yale University Press, *New Haven & London*

Designed by Richard Hendel.
Set in Minion type by B. Williams & Associates.
Printed in the United States of America by
Thomson-Shore, Inc.

Library of Congress Cataloging in Publication Data
The theory of decorative art : an anthology of
European and American writings, 1750–1940 / edited
by Isabelle Frank ; with translations by David Britt.
    p. cm.
  Includes bibliographical references (p.).
  ISBN 0-300-07551-0 (cloth : alk. paper)
  —ISBN 0-300-08805-1 (pbk. : alk. paper)
  1. Decorative arts. I. Frank, Isabelle, 1959–
NK25.T48 2000
745′.01—dc21   00-042881

A catalogue record for this book is available from the
British Library.

The paper in this book meets the guidelines for
permanence and durability of the Committee on
Production Guidelines for Book Longevity of the
Council on Library Resources.

10 9 8 7 6 5 4 3 2 1

To my parents, with love and gratitude

Contents

A Note on the Selection and Organization of the Writings

The writings on the theory of decorative art in this anthology span roughly two centuries, from the mid-eighteenth to the mid-twentieth century. The use of the term decorative arts is a shorthand way of referring to all arts that, under various labels from the eighteenth century on, were excluded from the category of the fine arts (music, poetry, architecture, painting, and sculpture) but were nonetheless seen to possess their own distinctive artistic properties. Thus, although the terminology fluctuates by country and by period, it is clear that such labels as *arts decoratifs, Angewandtekunst,* applied arts, *Kunstgewerbe,* and *arts mineurs* were all understood to refer to the same category of objects. As the authors themselves make clear, the abundance of different labels was confusing, but they were more or less interchangeable.

The selections are intended to introduce the reader to a debate about the nature of decorative arts that occurred in Europe and the United States from approximately the mid-eighteenth century to the 1940s, and they have been chosen to represent the most influential theoretical positions in this debate. In some cases, excerpts are taken from relatively well-known works by major historians, designers, and craftsmen, while others are by minor figures chosen to provide contrasting opinions. The selections also represent a sampling of writings such as historical studies, learned treatises, public lectures, and manuals of instruction. However, it is important to remember that the aim of the anthology is not to document the emergence of all categories of writings about decorative art but only those directed at theoretical investigations of its artistic and practical nature. Space limitations have restricted the contents to what are considered the most significant contributions to this wide-ranging debate among designers, historians, and art theorists.

The writings presented here will introduce the reader to the history of the theory of what were, and sometimes still are, called the decorative arts. They fall within clear chronological and geographical boundaries based on the general development of the debate. As I shall argue, a specific tradition of writing about the theory of decorative arts developed between the late-eighteenth and the early-twentieth centuries in Western Europe (notably in Britain and German-speaking countries), which then spread to the United States. All selections are therefore written by European and American authors and are mostly about Western art. However, the American contributions are few, consisting of texts known either to have to have been influential or to have represented typical attitudes of the late-nineteenth century. Although the writings span a two-hundred-year period, the majority date from the nineteenth century when the crisis of the decorative arts truly came to the fore. The anthology ends with the demise of a consensus about the properties and even the existence of a "decorative art," and the emergence in its stead of new, related, notions of material culture, folk art, craft, and contemporary design. Indeed, I hope that another historian will be inspired to complete this overview, in an anthology focusing on a twentieth-century debate.

The excerpts are organized into three main parts. Instead of presenting the writers in chronological order, I have highlighted certain themes and approaches to the theory of decorative art. Most important, I felt, was the unspoken agreement among authors about the nature of the decorative arts, which they believe are characterized by three key elements: function, technical production and material, and ornamentation. Although many writers attempt to account for all three of these defining features, most tend to privilege one in their theories. For this reason I have divided the anthology into parts that bring together writings focusing, first, on the function of decorative art objects; second, on the techniques and materials employed; and, third, on their ornamental qualities. Each part is preceded by a brief introduction that points out some of the relations linking the various texts.

The ordering of these three parts also underlines a shared method of analyzing and discussing the decorative arts common to most of the participants in this debate. Thus, the authors often move from the question of their utility, to a discussion of their material production, and finally to an analysis of their ornamental detail. In addition, the sequence of the three parts is loosely based on the chronological order in which these questions arose within the history of the theory of decorative arts. That is, some of the earliest writers on decorative art focus on their practical uses, whereas some late-nineteenth-century writers concentrate on problems of mechanized production. And though discussions of ornament also began relatively early, they survive in contemporary architectural debates (not included in the anthology). However, it is important to note that the distinction between function and technique, or ornament and technique, was not rigid in the eyes of the authors. Several selections could fit in any of the various parts, and their placement results from an assessment of their central arguments and influence on other writers.

Each part on function, technique, and ornament is, in turn, divided into two sections. This division reflects the difference between authors intent on improving current production of decorative art and those interested in understanding the stylistic or aesthetic principles of decorative arts from a historical perspective. This important distinction is intended to highlight the common roots of what became two completely distinct ways of writing about the decorative arts: that of art critics and reformers, on the one hand, and of art historians, on the other. Until the early-twentieth century, writers in both groups shared a similar interest in decorative art's function, technical production, and ornamentation, and were influenced by each other's writings. However, the tradition of historical, scholarly interpretations of decorative art emerged after that of the reform-minded ones, and I have therefore placed the reform-oriented group of writings first. Of course the relation between these two modes of artistic writing is such that at times it is difficult to distinguish between the two; a theorist and designer such as Owen Jones and Gottfried Semper could write in both modes. Within each of these sub-sections, the selections appear in chronological order.

Finally, most chapters in the anthology are excerpts from longer texts. In some cases the selections are condensed versions, with text deleted from the original work; omission of text within the excerpt is indicated by an ornament between paragraphs.

Acknowledgments

It is with great pleasure that I express my debt to those who shared their ideas about decorative art with me. Because this project began as a seminar on the theory of decorative art, taught at the Bard Graduate Center for Studies in the Decorative Arts, I would first like to thank my students and colleagues at the Bard Graduate Center. Once the anthology took shape, it benefited from suggestions by James Ackerman, Norton Batkin, Richard Brilliant, Richard Etlin, Oleg Grabar, Rochelle Gurstein, Karsten Harries, Pat Kirkham, Jeanne-Marie Musto, Nancy Troy, and readers at Yale University Press; unfortunately only a two-volume publication would do justice to their pertinent and thoughtful ideas. On a more personal note, I would like to express my deepest gratitude to my husband, Mark Lilla; the volume as a whole owes much to his penetrating observations and careful readings.

Finally, the anthology could not have come together without the assistance of Heather Jane McCormick, who zealously assembled various parts of the anthology, from researching little-known authors to handling publication permissions. The production of the volume was greatly aided by Judy Metro and Margaret Otzel at Yale University Press, who patiently waited, advised, and edited, and by the Bard Graduate Center and Edward Lee Cave, who helped defray research and publication costs.

Introduction
The History of the Theory of Decorative Art

What are the decorative arts?[1] For over two centuries historians, artists, and philosophers alike have tried to answer this seemingly innocent question. Finding a satisfactory and durable answer has turned out to be surprisingly elusive, and the attempt was more or less abandoned in the first part of the twentieth century.[2] One superficial reason for the difficulty of defining the nature and character of the decorative arts must surely arise from the variety of activities and objects to which the term now applies and has referred to in the past. For instance, weaving, pottery, metalwork, glass work, and woodworking were (and often still are) considered to be decorative arts, though some or all of these could be labeled mechanical arts, minor arts, applied arts, industrial arts, or craft, depending on the historical period. Even more problematic, the term indicates an artistic activity (weaving) as well as a product of an activity (pottery). Confusion therefore surrounds both the label decorative arts and the type of artistic expression it is supposed to designate.

Between the late-eighteenth and early-twentieth centuries, however, there was a clear, if fragile, consensus about the nature of the decorative arts. This consensus becomes apparent when one looks more closely at a group of writings focused on examining the artistic merits, status, and features of the decorative arts. During this period, the decorative arts were situated somewhere between the domain of the fine arts and the non-arts (to the latter group most eighteenth- and nineteenth-century writers would have consigned undecorated utensils, tools, construction blocks, and so on). In the eighteenth century, when the decorative arts first attracted the interest of writers and philosophers, their artistic realm was already difficult to circumscribe. But by the mid-nineteenth century, industrial materials and methods gave this issue new urgency. Faced with new forms and types of objects, consumers and theorists alike searched for a way to evaluate the economic as well as aesthetic value of such protean arts.

Philosophers, historians, artists, and designers attempted to resolve this issue, producing a rich literature that has been forgotten by all but a handful of specialists.[3] Despite the variety of opinions, most writers agreed that the decorative arts (however they referred to them) possessed their own distinctive, artistic nature. Moreover, this artistic nature could be understood and analyzed by focusing on the relations among three principal features: function, material and production, and ornamentation. The result was a stimulating array of theories of decorative art that attempted to explain these relations in terms of a single principle or set of principles. These principles varied widely from author to author and, in some instances, even from text to text of any given author. Some were linked to theories of historical evolution, some reflected certain beliefs about social and economic development, and others were directed at improving contemporary artistic practice. But regardless of differences in approach, all the contributors to this debate endeavored to fashion comprehensive theories to explain the particular nature of decorative art, theories that responded to other related theories as well as to more wide-ranging ideas about the nature of art, design, history, and visual perception. This debate, whose participants include Denis Diderot, John Ruskin, Gottfried Semper, William Morris, Le Corbusier, and Alois Riegl, began in the mid-eighteenth century and died out in the early-twentieth. Despite a few contributions to the theory of ornament in the second half of the twentieth century, notably by E. H. Gombrich and Oleg Grabar, this debate was never truly revived, presumably because no such consensus about the nature of decorative art could exist after the Modernist criticism of ornament and decoration.[4]

This anthology is the first attempt to reconstruct the history of this debate, which focuses on arts situated between the fine arts and the non-arts and occurred within specific chronological limits. I hope to dispel some of the confusion surrounding the notion of the decorative arts by demonstrating the existence, for a time, of a shared, evolving understanding of their artistic nature. At first glance these earlier writings on the decorative arts might seem too historical to many involved in the contemporary debate about art and artistic practice.[5] At best, contemporary historians might concede that these writings contain a few precocious thoughts on, for instance, ornament's abstract forms, artistic pleasure, or artistic process.[6] Such an impression would be misleading, for these writings represent something far more ambitious. What one finds throughout these earlier writings are bold attempts to elaborate new, overarching aesthetic theories capable of encompassing both the fine and the decorative arts. Although these attempts are fragmentary, many of them delve into the nature of artistic creativity and perception precisely in order to challenge the aesthetic canon developed by writers from the Renaissance to the eighteenth century. John Ruskin, Owen Jones, Karl Philipp Moritz, and Alois Riegl, to name but a few, questioned the validity of an aesthetic hierarchy dominated by the fine arts. But they did so by arguing that the decorative arts possessed both visual, sensual, or perceptual significance as well as functional, historical, or social meaning. The ultimate failure of such writers to shake the foundations of eighteenth-century aesthetics should not obscure the fact that we have to a certain degree inherited their fight. We too are now busily engaged in demolishing this same aesthetic tradition, much more successfully than they ever did. But as we look at the results, both at the shrinking, entrenched realm of "high painting and sculpture," holding its own against the encroaching claims of all other human artifacts, we would perhaps do well to study these earlier writings. Their imaginative and perceptive characterization of human creativity and artistic appreciation could offer us theoretical alternatives to the *aut/aut* (either/or) confronting the notion of art and artistic creativity today.

This anthology is intended for readers interested in art theory and decorative art, as well as for those concerned with the issues of aesthetic appreciation. The following introduction is a brief account of the development of the theory of decorative arts to help place the writings in context. Such a survey might seem overly ambitious, yet a synthetic overview of the theory of decorative arts must be attempted for the simple reason that none exists. This is all the more surprising given the numerous recent studies of the theory of fine arts and of the history of art history.[7] Such a survey can only try to present the highlights of this theoretical debate, and must leave to others the narration of the fascinating social and economic history of the decorative arts. Fortunately, this is the aspect of the decorative arts attracting scholarly attention today, and the interested reader can now consult several studies of the social and political significance of French, English, and American decorative arts.[8]

FROM *ARS* TO DECORATIVE ART

The idea of the decorative arts slowly developed out of classical and medieval concepts of art.[9] Greek and Latin writers did not distinguish between the fine and the decorative arts, using the word art in a general fashion to refer to a skilled craft or science rather than to an inspired creative activity. Poetry, painting, and music were considered arts that had to be learned, like weaving and geometry. However, by the medieval period two complementary groups of arts were distinguished: the liberal versus the mechanical. The conceptual labor of the liberal arts was placed above the physical labor of the mechanical. The liberal arts encompassed intellectual activities and skills, such as grammar, rhetoric, astronomy, as well as the affiliated disciplines of music and poetry. The mechanical arts, on the other hand, included manual activities, ranging from weaving, wood carving, pottery, and navigation to armament, in which subgroup were also found painting, sculpture, and architecture.[10]

The medieval classification of the arts is a distant ancestor of our contemporary one. During the intervening centuries there grew up yet another notion of art that bound painting, sculpture, and architecture together with music and poetry. Medieval theorists had originally separated the three visual arts (as they are commonly called today) from poetry and music by assigning the former to the mechanical arts and the latter to the more highly regarded liberal arts. However, Italian Renaissance artists and humanists challenged this medieval classification, claiming for the visual arts the same intellectual status as that of poetry and music, and leaving behind among the mechanical arts what would become known as the decorative arts. Renaissance theorists reinforced the intellectual and artistic claims of the visual arts by establishing academies devoted exclusively to painting, sculpture, and architecture, the three "arts of design" (*arti del disegno*).[11] With the help of these academies, the visual arts acquired an identity distinct from that of the mechanical arts, one that paved the way for the later notion of the fine arts.

The changes in art theory initiated by Renaissance writers culminated two centuries later in the full acceptance of the fine arts as an artistic group possessing its own theoretical principles. Renaissance art theorists had furthered the conceptual, and even imaginative, claims of visual artists, but had not linked these claims to a concept of beauty in art. A theory of fine arts proper, one that tied the theory of beauty to the visual as well as to the literary and musical appreciation of art, emerged clearly only in the eighteenth century, when such thinkers as Shaftsbury, Burke, Baumgarten, and Kant developed new philosophical principles for judging artistic beauty. The new theories of aesthetics in turn provided the conceptual framework within which to establish a separate notion of art applicable only to painting, sculpture, architecture, poetry, and music.[12] As activities devoted to the creation of beauty, the fine arts were theoretically absolved from the moral and practical demands still placed on the other arts and sciences.

This transformation in eighteenth-century thought introduced a theoretical border between the fine arts and all other arts. Although this distinction may have helped to clarify the nature of those activities now considered the fine arts, it left behind an ill-assorted group of activities under the medieval term mechanical arts. In the eighteenth century, art theorists began turning their attention to these as well, on the presupposition that they were arts, but of a lower kind. The growing theoretical interest in the mechanical arts was also stimulated by the expanding social and economic role of manufactured goods.[13] By the end of the eighteenth century, practitioners and critics alike were struggling to understand the artistic nature of such manufactured, machine-made products, and they recognized the absence of a suitable definition for artistic activities outside the realm of fine arts.

These initial eighteenth-century explorations of the nature of decorative art were so perceptive that they set the groundwork for future discussions. The German historian Friedrich August Krubsacius, for instance, developed the first history of decoration, which despite its title, *Reflections on the Origin, Growth, and Decline of Decoration in the Fine Arts* (Gedanken von dem Ursprung, Wachstum und Verfall der Verzierungen in den schönen Künsten [1759]), was in fact more pertinent to the decorative than to the fine arts.[14] Around the same time Denis Diderot and Jean Le Rond d'Alembert stressed the beneficial and practical role of the mechanical arts, praising them at the expense of the fine arts in their *Encyclopedia* (1751). A few decades later, the German philosopher Karl Philipp Moritz attempted to tie a theory of ornament to a general concept of artistic beauty in his remarkable *Preliminary Ideas on the Theory of Ornament* (Vorbegriffe zu einer Theorie der Ornamente [1793]). Influenced by Moritz's theories, and reacting to the rapid growth of mechanized production, even Goethe took up the question of the relative merits of hand-made and machine-made decorative art in his writings, arguing that only the human touch could endow a work with true artistic worth. These few works reflect a shared concept of decorative art based on three main elements: utility, materials and production, and decoration. Whereas eighteenth-century writers were content to explore these features individually, nineteenth-century theorists focused on the relation of these constituent elements, in order to grasp the workings of decorative art's nature as a whole.

THE NINETEENTH CENTURY

The London Great Exhibition of 1851 (popularly known as the Crystal Palace exhibition) was the first international display of decorative art and as such became the focus of much European and American writing on decorative art.[15] Of course, interest in the production of contemporary decorative art and, to a lesser degree, curiosity about its theoretical nature existed well before this event.[16] But the Crystal Palace exhibition helped transform decorative art from a domain of relatively limited interest into one of public consequence, exposing for all to see the relative merits and weaknesses of national products. The exhibition sharpened competition among European nations vying to dominate a rapidly expanding market of goods ranging from household furnishings to practical appliances and machines. In the wake of the 1851 exhibition, the British, followed most notably by the Austrians, Germans, and French, implemented a national policy of arts education intended to improve the application of art to manufacture.[17] This policy, in turn, led to the founding of the first decorative art museums, schools, and publications throughout Europe, and later in the United States.[18] The new journals and institutes devoted to decorative art actively engaged designers and historians in discussions of its past development, as well as in debates about its industrial, economic, and artistic future.

Practitioners—including architects, artists, and designers—were most concerned with what decorative art would and should become. From an examination of its fundamental elements, they extracted principles to guide both its present and future course. Historians and art theorists, on the other hand, were intent on reconstructing the origins of decorative art and discovering the principles enabling it to mix utility and beauty so effortlessly in past artifacts. This division in approach also seems to fall along national lines. The British dominated the theoretical writing about contemporary practice throughout the nineteenth century; such writers as A. W. N. Pugin, John Ruskin, Owen Jones, and later William Morris initiated reform movements influencing others in the rest of Europe and the United States. By contrast, German-speaking writers produced the more scholarly theories and were the first to develop historically grounded interpretations of the nature of decorative art.

THE BRITISH REFORM OF THE DECORATIVE ARTS

In the 1840s and 50s, the writings of Pugin and Ruskin set the terms of debate for both scholarly and practical examinations of the decorative arts. Both authors were initially inspired to write on the theory of decorative art by what they regarded as the confused state of contemporary building style. Promoting an eclectic style in treatises and actual designs, architects throughout Europe championed the revivals of specific historical forms of decoration, from Gothic and Romanesque to Egyptian and Moorish. Even Pugin and Ruskin intervened in these debates in favor of a particular style (Gothic and Italian Romanesque, respectively), but they supported their arguments with influential explanations of what constituted beauty in the decorative arts.

Pugin's writings offered rules about the relation of ornament to function and material that were almost immediately incorporated into new theories for contemporary practice. An architect himself, Pugin saw ornament as the primary expression of beauty in architecture and the decorative arts because it carried a specific style. Though Pugin was partial to the Gothic style, identifying it as *the* style of Catholicism, he was also well aware of the dangers of reviving a historical style only through ornament, which, he explained, could result in the promiscuous application of ornament to surfaces and forms in all materials. He instead encouraged architects and craftsmen, first, to choose the form most suited to the object's function, and then to decorate it in a way that revealed the form itself. For Pugin, the greatest threat to the organic creation of form and decoration lay in mechanized production, the use of which he sharply condemned on both artistic and moral grounds. Cast iron, he argued in a famous passage, only simulated stone or wood carvings in a deceitful and mechanical manner, losing all visual beauty in the process. Pugin's precepts today seem self-evident, but this is only because his concept of the function of decoration lay at the heart of more radical theories developed by Ruskin and Morris.

Ruskin, often seen as the intellectual source of late nineteenth-century re-form movements, offered perhaps the subtlest analyses of ornament's relation to function and material production.[19] For Ruskin, an object's function included not only its intended use but a host of other unexpected factors. These features were both external as well as intrinsic to the decoration itself, such as the character of the wall surface or object (secular or religious), its degree of utility (a fresco versus a scarf), the frequency of its physical use (a scarf versus the handle of a cup), and even its relative visibility (the lower edge of a surface as opposed to its center). The status of an object and of its decoration was established by means of this pyramid of functions, in which the pinnacle was occupied by the most visible and protected surfaces in religious or dignified edifices. Ruskin expected the designer-craftsman to adjust the level of artistic forms, the richness of materials, the type of decoration, and even the amount of labor involved, to the object's relative status. The principles governing the relation between an object's artistic and material features and its functional status were moral ones, presented most clearly in the *Seven Lamps of Architecture* (1849). There Ruskin applied his own notion of Christian virtues to the making of art. In his view, art had to be truthful, a belief that led Ruskin to condemn all falsifications of materials as well as all machine-made decoration. Similarly, rules of decorum and suitability determined Ruskin's notion of beauty. According to such rules, an artist-designer should expend the greatest skill and invention on representational subjects placed only on the most visible surfaces (the ones at the top of his pyramid of functions), and in surroundings favoring artistic contemplation. In contrast, where decoration cannot be admired in a state of repose, such as in railroad stations or on objects of daily use (the ones at the base of the pyramid), the artist should use more stylized decoration, less skill, and less costly materials. Hence for Ruskin, each level of function possesses its own level of beauty, enjoyable on its own terms. The success of this beauty depends on the ability of the designer-craftsman to adapt his invention, materials and execution, and representational content to Ruskin's theoretical hierarchy of functions.

Ruskin's writings yielded principles by which to analyze and even judge successful decorative art. Although he intended these principles to encourage designers-craftsmen to follow the right moral and artistic path, he never desired these principles to be mistaken for academic rules of design.[20] Ruskin always firmly maintained that true beauty, in both the fine and the decorative arts, could emerge only from the creative imagination of a maker inspired by nature; beauty could not be learned, only helped to fruition.[21] In contrast, the generation of British writers active during Ruskin's lifetime, particularly Owen Jones and Christopher Dresser, were dedicated to establishing fixed principles of instruction to govern the production of contemporary decorative art.

According to the principles Jones presented in the introduction to his famous *Grammar of Ornament* (1856), "True beauty results from that repose which the mind feels when the eye, the intellect, and the affections, are satisfied from the absence of any want."[22] Unlike Ruskin, for whom repose was the *precondition* for the appreciation of fine art alone, Jones identified repose as the *result* of contemplating successful art. Moreover, the notion that beauty resides in the absence of want (nothing to be removed or added) was itself a well-established definition of beauty, first formulated by the Renaissance architect Leon Battista Alberti in relation to architecture.[23] An important feature of Jones's text is that he applies this definition to ornament itself, claiming for decoration the same ability to achieve perfect beauty on its own as that of the fine arts—a statement perhaps intended to shock those who saw ornament precisely as that which could be added or removed at will. To support this claim, Jones uses the rest of the introduction to offer his theory of beauty, now reduced to a set of self-sufficient, teachable, and potentially universal rules for the decorative arts. What is striking about these rules (aside from their rigidity) is their treatment of ornament design as an independent creative act, detached from the intended function of the surface and object to be decorated. This sense of abstractness is heightened by Jones's apparent lack of interest in problems of material and execution, ones that had so preoccupied Pugin and Ruskin. In effect, by giving decoration specific rules for the stylization of natural forms, for the use of certain geometric proportions, and for the combination of certain colors—rules that prepared decoration for application to a variety of surfaces—Jones was liberating ornament from the fluctuating pressures of functional and material requirements.

William Morris, the founder of the Arts and Crafts movement, redirected late-nineteenth-century theoretical debates about the decorative arts back to the issue of artistic production.[24] Unlike his predecessors, Morris focused his polemical writings exclusively on *how* decorative art should be made and used, rather than on its principles of ornamentation. Morris's artistic ideas are difficult to extract from his writings, on the one hand, because his public lectures often presented impassioned exhortations rather than cogent arguments and, on the other, because so many of his convictions were embodied in his own artistic activities. Nonetheless, from the perspective of decorative art theory, it is possible to distill three main ideas that were important for his followers: his concept of decorative art as a democratic art, responsive to the needs of the people; his vehement defense of handiwork and craft; and the related concept of collaborative artistic production.

To a certain extent Morris radicalized Ruskin's views, analyzing decorative art not only in terms of a functional and artistic hierarchy but also as a social hierarchy as well. In his public lectures Morris spoke of future decorative art by and for the people, insisting that it retain contact with traditional hand-made craft. Drawing on Ruskin, he argued that only objects made with pleasure and imprinted with the human spirit could in turn bring pleasure to those using the objects in their daily, and often dreary, lives.[25] The political message of Morris's writings had a great influence not only on many British followers, including Walter Crane and William Richard Lethaby, but also on a generation of designers and theorists on the Continent and in the United States.[26] This influence often stemmed less from the distinctly socialist ideas infusing Morris's writings than from his sharp criticism of new modes of production and his condemnation of the artistic hierarchy that these modes seemed to reinforce.

By Morris's lifetime, industrial producers of decorative art had little use for skilled handicraft, many requiring a designer only at the top end of the production line and mechanical laborers at the bottom. The new academies and schools of design, founded throughout Europe from the mid-1850s on, also contributed to the growing marginalization of skilled craftsmen.[27] Just as in the seventeenth and eighteenth centuries, when the new academies of fine art established the distinction between artist and craftsman, so too did these academies and schools of decorative art now help to eliminate the craftsman by creating the professional designer.[28] By the end of the nineteenth century, the designer had in many ways become an independent artistic professional, situated somewhere between artist and craftsman.[29] Graduates of these new schools of design were supposedly taught to work in all media and techniques, but more often their training focused exclusively on producing drawings and models for industrial manufacturing. The designer was in charge of creating the new forms, and the industrial worker and his machine executed them in various media. Between these two, the skilled craftsman was made obsolete.

Morris objected to the emergence both of the industrial worker and of the designer in the art world, lamenting their dire influence on handicraft. However, he focused his criticisms on the sorry plight of the worker, which Morris described from the political vantage of socialism. He recognized that the working conditions of those employed in the production of furnishings and decoration were no worse than those in other types of industries. But the use of such workers in art manufacturing brought out his distaste for machine production in general. If industrial workers derived no pleasure from their labor on the assembly line, how could decorative art objects in turn be expected to evoke pleasurable, human qualities in others?

Morris built his reform movement in part around this very issue. In his lectures "The Lesser Arts"(1878), "The Revival of Handicraft" (1888), and "The Arts and Crafts of To-day" (1889), he declared that industry was incapable of producing art objects. He believed that only by destroying the traditional system of industrial production and replacing it with collaborative enterprises could individuals participate willingly and happily in the creation of art that would impart pleasure to others. Rejecting a mode of production that separated designer from artist, craftsman from designer, and worker from object, Morris proposed instead that art-makers band together in artists' associations, modeled on the medieval guild system. Only by reviving such collaborative enterprises, Morris argued, could all art-makers protect themselves from the pernicious pressures of commerce, mechanical production, and enforced division and denigration of labor.

Morris's writings struck a responsive chord among several generations of artists and designers. Although Morris's vision of an ideal medieval past left little room for industrial production, his dreams of a utopian future included the machine as a liberating tool, capable of freeing society from the drudgery of physical labor. It was precisely Morris's blend of Socialist utopianism and Ruskinian artistic idealism that proved to be irresistible. Not only did it capture his contemporaries' disillusionment with a capitalist economy, it also spoke to their growing distaste for modern technology. Morris's theories (and his practice) fueled art reform movements in Europe as well as in the United States. And in a strange twist of fate, some of these reform groups were, a few decades later, to promote undecorated industrial production in the name of Morris's own principles.[30]

THE EMERGENCE OF THE HISTORY OF DECORATIVE ART

The writings of such reformers as Pugin and Morris encouraged not only transformations within artistic production but also more researched, historical analyses of decorative art. The greatest contribution to the development of a proper "history of decorative art" came from scholars allied to the emerging academic discipline of art history. Naturally the writings of reformers and scholars overlapped—Ruskin, for instance, was also the first Slade Professor of

Art History at Oxford University.[31] However, historical studies of decorative art written by reformers remained fundamentally different both in character and approach from the slightly later ones by German-language architects and historians. Whereas the British writers used history as ammunition to defend the use of a specific historical style, the more historically minded Germans examined the past in order to gain perspective on the present.

The most influential history of the decorative arts of this period was written by the German architect and historian Gottfried Semper.[32] Tellingly, Semper's own interest in decorative art and ornament was stimulated by the Great Exhibition of 1851, whose widespread repercussions he witnessed both in Britain and in German-speaking countries. Semper contributed not only to the planning of the 1851 exhibition, designing the Swedish, Canadian, Danish, and Egyptian displays, but also, a few decades later, to the founding of the Austrian Museum of Art and Industry, modeled after the South Kensington museum—the first British museum of decorative arts.[33] Semper shared his contemporaries' interest in improving the decorative arts, believing that their decay stemmed essentially from the increasing alienation between technique and material, fueled by the developing industrialization of art manufacturing. However, rather than focusing on problems of contemporary production, Semper searched instead for fundamental principles of evolution that could explain the development of all decorative arts. According to his unfinished magnum opus *Style in the Technical and Tectonic Arts* (Der Stil in den technischen und tektonischen Künsten [1860]), these principles depended not only on an interpretation of the object's function but also on an analysis of the materials and technique used in production.[34] For Semper, the historical emergence of an ornamental motif, such as the criss-cross pattern, was often determined by the chance meeting of a certain technique, like weaving, with a certain material, like straw, at a given historical moment. The resulting, fortuitous pattern was then appreciated for its own sake and adapted to ornamental purposes in other media. Semper's aim was to expose the greater role played by these external factors in the history of ornament, tracing their influence on the creation of certain patterns and shapes. Though Semper did admit the additional influence of artistic imagination into his history of formal patterns, his followers tended to focus exclusively on function, technique, and material, overlooking the role of human creativity.

Semper's "materialist" theory of ornament was so successful that it inspired technical and functional analyses of decorative art until the end of the nineteenth century, especially in German-speaking countries.[35] It was these technical interpretations that so aroused the fury of the Viennese art historian Alois Riegl in the 1890s, provoking him to champion the artistic and conceptual origins of ornament instead. Within the fields of art and design history, Riegl's early writings represent the most ambitious attempts to join the fledgling studies of decorative art with the slightly older discipline of art history.[36] In his early *Problems of Style* (Stilfragen [1893]), Riegl freed decorative art from the Semperian straitjacket of function, material, and technique. To achieve this, he endowed ornament with a continuous stylistic history that was now almost exclusively generated by human artistic intent, or *Kunstwollen,* to use his famous term.[37] In these early studies of ornament, Riegl even argued that ornament was a more direct expression of artistic creativity than narrative painting and sculpture, because it offered a pure visual play of form and color in space (a worrisome claim for later abstract artists).[38]

But Riegl's ambitions were different from those of his contemporary Viennese Secessionist colleagues. Rather than elevating decorative art to the level of fine art, he tried first to redefine the two notions of art themselves. Riegl recognized the influence of external factors on the artist's fashioning of ornament and included them in his explanation of stylistic development. But he also believed that these, or similar pressures, were at work in the fine arts. Thus for him the political, religious, or secular functions of the fine arts paralleled the technical and practical ones of the decorative arts.[39] To a certain degree, therefore, Riegl did recognize the impact of external factors on artistic production, but he did so for all the arts. In so doing, he was equating what until then had been considered completely different types of artistic constraints: religious, spiritual, or political with mechanical or technical ones. Yet, in the final analysis, all of these external factors remained subordinate to the maker's artistic will [*Kunstwollen*].[40]

From the Secessionist's and reformers' perspective, therefore, Riegl can be seen as championing the equality of the arts.[41] However, Riegl's defense of decorative art was a corollary to a larger endeavor rather than an end in itself. This larger endeavor, simply put, was to discover the principles guiding the synchronic development of style in all the arts of a given culture. In his *Late Roman Art Industry* (Spätrömische Kunstindustrie [1901]), Riegl thought he had found such principles. That he was mistaken can be gathered from the conspicuous absence of most decorative arts in *Late Roman Art Industry* and in his subsequent writings.[42]

Independent of one's assessment of Riegl's success or failure, his early studies mark the climax of nineteenth-century enthusiasm for ornament and the decorative arts. Interestingly, they also point to telltale fissures in nineteenth-century writers' concept of the nature of decorative art. Although many practitioners still argued for a way of establishing a new harmony between function, material and technique, and ornamentation, Riegl privileged ornament over the other two. In turn, Riegl's faith in the aesthetic significance of decoration and ornament was to be challenged by the next generation of reformers, who promoted function, materials, and techniques at the expense of ornament and decoration. The story of Modernism is the story of the final dismemberment of the concept of decorative art.

MODERNISM

William Morris's writings raised a question that continued to plague artists, designers, and manufacturers in subsequent decades: Could a capitalist society that favored machine production, division of labor, and cheap imitations produce decorative art worthy of the name? Though Morris himself answered the question in the negative, dreaming of the rebirth of hand-made art in a utopian, socialist future, his younger admirers could no longer postpone their final assessment of industrialization and art. This next generation of writers thus had to take seriously the possibility of adapting industrial means to artistic ends. And naturally, those who embraced this fusion, including theorists like the German Samuel Bing, the French Rioux de Maillou and Le Corbusier, and the American Frank Lloyd Wright, were in turn countered by others, like the British Walter Crane, the Belgian Henry van de Velde, and the American August Stickley, who were skeptical of a machine aesthetic.[43]

At the core of these increasingly polemical debates about machine production lay the unresolved problem of decoration itself. By the nineteenth century, the extent to which the designer could treat ornament as an independent feature, divorced from the object itself, was undermining its artistic value. The problem of ornament was of course not a new one. Rococo ornament had been bitterly attacked in the 1750s, and by the nineteenth century the question of ornament's style and production had become a familiar leitmotif in European debates about design.[44] The success of mechanized production (and reproduction) of ornament, however, transformed discussions about ornament's style and placement into debates about its very existence.

Early theorists of Functionalism, including Louis Sullivan and the young Le Corbusier, at first only subordinated ornament to the stringent demands of function and materials without rejecting it completely.[45] Slightly later, more radical designers, like Adolf Loos, W. R. Lethaby, and L. Mies van der Rohe, were prepared to discard ornament altogether from the process of design.[46] Though ornament survived in practice, it was shorn of aesthetic significance and of its independent artistic principles.[47] Giving themselves up to the enchantment of industrial materials and technological structures, Modernist theorists proclaimed that only purified forms should be used to express function in the most limpid and luminous way. By excluding ornament from the ideals of a new, modern design, the proponents of the Modern movement effectively destroyed the notion of decorative art that had emerged over the past two centuries.

The success of the Modern movement and its architectural tenets naturally dampened the interest of artists-designers and art historians in the significance of decorative art. Curiosity about ornament and decoration survived only among sociologists and social historians, who were more removed from the direct influence of contemporary artistic practice and study. In the first few decades of the twentieth century, such German scholars as Georg Simmel, Ernst Bloch, and Norbert Elias explored the differing ways in which decorative art's function, material make-up, and even ornament could make any object into a carrier of social meaning. Like nineteenth-century designers and theorists, these sociologists were fascinated by decorative art's seemingly effortless ability to synthesize aesthetic and utilitarian demands. Moreover, their studies revealed that the utilitarian aspect of decorative art was an asset rather than a liability, enabling these objects to reflect more vividly than the fine arts the history of religious and social practices, and even of psychological attitudes.[48] However these studies did not inspire imitation, perhaps because young scholars were less interested in the possible meanings of ornament than in the significance of objects as a whole, especially those shorn of decorative appeal.

By World War II, the theoretical debate about decorative art had in fact come to an end among Modernist designers and artists. Decorative art (or its equivalent denomination) had vanished from their vocabulary, replaced by such terms as industrial art, industrial design, or simply design, which clearly referred to a different type of artistic creation free of ornamental accretions.[49] Art historians soon followed suit, abandoning the study of style and meaning in the decorative arts. In large part, historians and even sociologists were simply responding to the mood of current artistic practice. The questions that had moved Riegl and Secessionist artists in fin-de-siècle Vienna no longer seemed central once the Modernists had revealed ornament to be a frivolous, shallow, and deceptive feature of design. Moreover, historians themselves began studying the Modern movement as a historical style, sometimes promoting its anti-ornamental tenets.[50] Thus, as in the world of artistic practice, scholars restricted their use of the term decorative art mainly to objects of the past, and instead spoke in the new vocabulary of "design" and "material culture."[51] The disappearance of the term decorative art from art theory and its almost simultaneous banishment to the margins of academic study signaled the end of the lively debate about the nature of decorative art. Only in the 1990s have we seen a small renascence of theoretical writing about ornament, mainly due to the demise of Modernist architectural theory. And, perhaps not coincidentally, a few art historians and social historians are once again taking seriously the artistic and social significance of ornament as well.[52]

These faint stirrings are encouraging but so far fail to match the breadth and depth of eighteenth- and nineteenth-century theoretical writings about the decorative arts. Having lost sight of our ancestors' intellectual achievements, we are less prepared than they to tackle the thorny question of decorative art's relation to the fine arts, on the one hand, and to non-art, on the other. In fact we would have trouble acknowledging the existence of such a tripartite division of the artistic realm. Yet, if we believe that artistic creations can be classified at all, we must also be prepared not only to apply but also to defend principles of evaluation—be they artistic, practical, social, ethnic, or political. There is no better place to learn about the flaws and strengths of such principles than in the writings of authors who, like us, puzzled over the protean nature of artistic creation and aesthetic response.

NOTES

1. See my definition of decorative art in the Note on the Selection; the anthology ends at a point in time when I believe the idea of such an artistic category was exhausted and replaced by a variety of new labels, such as folk art and material culture.

2. It is difficult to find a contemporary definition of decorative art. The most recent I have seen is in *The Oxford Companion Guide to the Decorative Arts*: "those arts which are made to serve a practical purpose but are nevertheless prized for the quality of their workmanship and the beauty of their appearance."

3. Historians who do pay attention to it have done so only according to their specializations. Thus architectural historians have collected writings on architectural theory that include pieces by designers who have influenced the Modern movement; see Benton, *Form and Function*, and Hermann's *In What Style Should We Build? The German Debate on Architectural Style*.

4. See Gombrich, *The Sense of Order*, and Grabar, *The Mediation of Ornament*. Both offer an explanation of ornament's overarching appeal to different cultures in different periods. In *Das Ornament in der Kunsttheorie*, Kroll points out as well that writing on ornament ended with Modernism.

5. Looking at writings of Arthur Danto, Hans Beltung, Rosalind Krauss, and Norman Bryson, to name but a few, one is struck by how the current artistic debate restricts itself to the traditional high arts, especially painting, although artists themselves seem to have abandoned the notion of the division of the arts and of aesthetic worth. In turn historians of decorative art are concerned with social, economic, and political meaning, even as designers and craftsmen are heightening the formal, sensual appeal of their work.

6. K. P. Moritz, Semper, and Riegl are being rediscovered in German-speaking countries as well as in Anglo-Saxon ones, though only some of their writings appeal to contemporary art historians—usually those applicable to painting or modern art.

7. It is impressive to see the number of anthologies on the theory of fine arts that con-

tinue to emerge: Harrison, ed., *Art in Theory: 1900–1990* and Preziosi, ed., *The Art of Art History: A Critical Anthology,* (see his note 1, which lists many others). In contrast there is one on the decorative arts: Greenhalgh's compendium of *Quotations and Sources on Design and the Decorative Arts.* As I argue here, the term design or craft, has come to replace decorative art, as seen in the titles of anthologies like *Design Discourse, History, Theory, Criticism,* Margolin, ed.; *Design History: An Anthology,* Doordan, ed.; and *The Culture of Craft,* Dormer, ed. But the decorative arts fall by the wayside in these works.

8. Studies by art historians are Troy, *Modernism and the Decorative Arts in France;* Snodin and Howard, *Ornament: A Social History;* Kirkham, *Ray and Charles Eames;* Scott, *The Rococo Interior;* and by historians: Auslander, *Taste and Power: Furnishing Modern France;* Fumerton, *Cultural Aesthetics;* Silverman, *Art Nouveau in Fin-de-Siècle France.*

9. See Kristeller, "The Modern System of the Arts," for information on the emergence of the fine arts.

10. The two groups were still fluid categories in the Middle Ages, but the liberal arts usually consisted of the trivium (grammar, rhetoric, and dialect) and the quadrivium (arithmetic, astronomy, geometry, and music). The seven mechanical arts, fashioned as a manual counterpart to liberal arts, usually included *lanificium, armatura, navigatio, agricultura, venatio, medicina,* and *theatrica.* The visual arts were included in the art of *armatura* (Kristeller, "Modern System of the Arts," p. 175).

11. The first academy of art was founded by Giorgio Vasari; on the history of academies, see Pevsner, *Academies Past and Present* and Goldstein, *Teaching Art.*

12. Baumgarten coined the term aesthetics and Kristeller clarifies Baumgarten's influence on French philosophers, especially Diderot and d'Alembert; see their selections from the *Encyclopedia* in this anthology, where they apply aesthetics exclusively to the fine arts.

13. Hume, in "On the Rise and Progress of the Arts and Sciences," and Diderot and d'Alembert, in the selections here, all stress the importance of manufactured goods and their economic and social benefits.

14. See in this anthology Krubsacius, *Reflections on the Origin, Growth, and Decline of Decoration in the Fine Arts* (Gedanken von dem Ursprung, Wachstum und Verfall der Verzierungen in den schönen Kunst). This pamphlet attacked the then prevalent style of the Rococo; it is still relatively unknown, mentioned briefly by Gombrich, *The Sense of Order,* p. 25.

15. The exhibition was planned for what was called industrial art, but was understood to be decorative art, including hand-made products as well. See ffrench, *The Crystal Palace Exhibition: An Illustrated Catalogue,* and for an extremely critical account of Victorian taste, see Pevsner, *Studies in the Art, Architecture, and Design.*

16. In Britain there was already government interest in funding art for manufacture in order to improve the national economy. This interest came to the fore around 1830, when the British noticed the relative inferiority of their products compared to those of the French; see Bell, *The Schools of Design.*

17. Documentation about this intense economic competition surrounding decorative art in France is in the first chapter of Troy, *Modernism,* and in Silverman, *Art Nouveau.*

18. On the history of academies of design in general see Pevsner and Goldstein, and see Bell for those in Britain; for their development in Germany see Mundt, *Die deutschen Kunstgewerbemuseen.*

19. Ruskin's influence on Morris and his circle are explicitly acknowledged by the latter in his various writings.

20. See selection from *The Two Paths* in this anthology, where Ruskin makes clear his antipathy for principles of art in general.

21. The importance of nature is clear in Ruskin's writings in this anthology.

22. Jones, *Grammar of Ornament,* p. 5.

23. *Leon Battista Alberti on the Art of Building,* Rykwert et al., p. 156.

24. See two publications: Parry, *William Morris* and MacCarthy, *William Morris.* For his entire corpus see the *Collected Works* and Lemire's *Unpublished Lectures of William Morris.*

25. See his two lectures in this anthology, as well as "The Lesser Arts," in *William Morris, News from Nowhere,* pp. 84–105.

26. Morris's influence is visible in the selections by Crane, Bing, Wright, Van de Velde, to name a few. See also MacCarthy, *William Morris,* and Naylor, *Bauhaus Revisited.*

27. On the academies of design see note 11 above.

28. Of course artists had always produced designs, and in the eighteenth century there were designers for the various Royal manufacturers in France. The difference is that it then became an acknowledged profession, with its own training schools.

29. Pevsner in *Studies in Art* briefly discusses the cross-over between artists and designers in relation to the 1851 exhibition. See also Stansky's introduction to his *Redesigning the World,* where he discusses the rise of the new designer. Architects and artists, such as Pugin and Morris, remained at the top of this new artistic profession, while the graduates of schools of design remained at the lower end.

30. The connection between Morris and Modernism has been overstressed, by Pevsner in particular. This, in turn, should not blind us to the influence that did exist, see Wright's "The Art and Craft of the Machine" in this anthology, where he argues that Morris misunderstood his own principles.

31. See the chapter "The Professor," Kemp, *The Desire of My Eyes,* pp. 336–391.

32. See Börsch-Supan et al., *Gottfried Semper* as well as Mallgrave, *Gottfried Semper.*

33. Pevsner, *Studies in Art,* p. 90, and Mallgrave, *Gottfried Semper.*

34. See Semper, *Style in the Technical and Tectonic Arts* (Der Stil in den technischen und tektonischen Künsten), only parts of which have been translated by Herrmann and Mallgrave in *Gottfried Semper: The Four Elements of Architecture.*

35. For a concise summary of the historians influenced by Semper, see Bazin, *Histoire de l'histoire de l'art,* pp. 134–37, who points out the contemporary materialist or "determinist" theories of Viollet-le-Duc (excerpt in this anthology), and also Mallgrave, *Gottfried Semper.*

36. For a brief overview of his work, see Pächt, "Alois Riegl," and for two in-depth studies see Iversen, *Alois Riegl,* and Olin, *Forms of Representation.*

37. *Kunstwollen* is notoriously difficult to translate; see Pächt, "Art Historians," and Panofsky, "The Concept of Artistic Volition."

38. For such claims see Riegl's introduction to his *Late Roman Art Industry* (Spätrömische Kunstindustrie), in the English translation by R. Winkes (Rome, 1985).

39. This is most clearly visible in the excerpt from Riegl's *Historical Grammar of the Visual Arts* (Historische Grammatik) in this anthology.

40. For Riegl the notion of "artistic drive" could be that of an individual, a region, or of an entire society, stated in its most radical form in *Late Roman Art Industry*.

41. See Hofmann, "L'Emancipation des dissonances," and Sauerländer, "Alois Riegl und die Entstehung der autonomen Kunstgeschichte," in *Fin-de-siècle: Zur Literatur und Kunst der Jahrhundertwende* who both make these connections, though it was Franz Wickhoff, Riegl's colleague, who publicly defended Secessionist art. Iversen, in her *Alois Riegl*, rights the balance, arguing that he was not necessarily a champion of current ornament and decorative arts.

42. For a lengthier interpretation, see Frank, "Alois Riegl." After this publication Riegl turned to painting, with *The Group Portraiture of Holland*, tran. E. Kain, intr. W. Kemp (Santa Monica, 2000), and to architecture with the posthumously published *Die Entstehung der Barockkunst in Rom*, ed. by A. Burda and M. Dvorka (Vienna, 1908).

43. See selections in this anthology as well as Benton, *Architecture and Design 1890–1939*.

44. For its early beginnings see Harries, *The Bavarian Rococo Church*, as well as Kroll, *Das Ornament in der Kunsttheorie*. For nineteenth-century debates see Hermann's introduction to *In What Style Should We Build?* and Part III in this anthology.

45. See the relevant selections in the anthology; Sullivan is famous for coining the phrase "form follows function," in "The Tall Office Building Artistically Considered" (1896), now in *Kindergarten Chats*.

46. See Mordaunt Crook, *The Dilemma of Style*, pp. 225–50, for an overview of the role of decoration and ornament in early twentieth-century debates about architecture; he points out that many writers and architects waffled on the issue of ornament.

47. The Eameses offer a good example of the problem facing architects who used ornament but did not want to call it that; instead they dubbed it functional decoration, as described in Kirkham, *Ray and Charles Eames*, pp. 164–99.

48. This is especially evident in Elias's writings, see his excerpt in this anthology.

49. Design and even craft are the terms whose boundaries are debated, see for instance a colloquium about the definition of design and design history, published in vol. 11, no. 1 of *Design Issues*, 1995, as well as the books cited in note 7.

50. A good example of this is Pevsner's *Pioneers of Modern Design*.

51. The term survives in the United States, though with pejorative connotations. In Britain the term design is also being used for objects of the past.

52. Criticism of the Modernist movement starts as early as Robert Venturi, and becomes mainstream by the 1980s, as argued by Jencks in *What Is Post-Modernism*, and Mordaunt Crook in *The Dilemma of Style*. See as well Harries, *The Ethical Function of Architecture*, part of which offers a vigorous defense of ornament. See note 8 for examples of a revival of interest in ornament and decoration.

I

THE
FUNCTIONS
OF THE
DECORATIVE
ARTS

INTRODUCTION

The first part of the anthology brings together writings concerned above all with the *function* of decorative art. The authors here consider the practical role of decorative art as its defining characteristic, that which distinguishes it from the fine arts. In the eighteenth century, before the concept of "applied" or "decorative" art emerged, useful objects were automatically classified as mechanical art. And it is precisely the usefulness of these objects that first attracted the attention of Diderot and d'Alembert. In the prologue to the *Encyclopedia* (1751), d'Alembert articulates what is probably the earliest defense of the mechanical arts while explaining the overall classification of human knowledge.

In his prologue, d'Alembert praises the mechanical production of goods, stressing the material benefits it represents not only for society but for the nation's economy. At the same time, although d'Alembert appreciates the financial, political, and human advantages to be gained from the mechanical arts, he assumes that they have little to offer in the way of mimetic, visual pleasure. He believes that we should admire the ingenuity of those who invented the mechanical objects and the machines used to make them, and he advises us to appreciate these products as art because they have been created by human intelligence, not because of their representational qualities. The term art, for these mid-eighteenth-century *philosophes,* was still tied to its medieval significance, encompassing the areas of human knowledge derived from skill and labor.

Only a few decades later, however, Karl Philipp Moritz discusses the "useful" arts from an aesthetic point of view. In his essay "On the Concept of Self-Sufficient Perfection" (1785), Moritz separates the fine and the useful arts according to their respective aims. He explains that most people believe the purpose of fine arts is to please whereas that of the practical arts is to be useful, a distinction that seems to justify the former's greater value.[1] He, however, disagrees with this traditional explanation. As he puts it, if the aim of fine art is to please, then such an art can find completion only outside of itself, that is, in the eyes of the beholder. But for Moritz, true fine art must be complete in and of itself, independent of the viewer, because dependency would place it at the level of practical art. Foreshadowing Kant's famous definition of disinterested beauty, Moritz here suggests that beauty in the fine arts must have no purpose, even that of pleasing. And in an almost proto-romantic variation, Moritz concludes that true fine art must express only the inner aim (*Zweck*) of the artist. In contrast, practical art finds fulfillment in the hands of the user. Its beauty, clearly dependent upon function, becomes what Moritz terms "decoration" (discussed in Part III).[2]

Moritz's theories represent an exception within the development of writing on decorative art by taking for granted the existence of decorative art's own form of beauty. But despite Moritz's auspicious beginnings, a proper theory of decorative art and its beauty was never truly developed. The growing industrialization of production galvanized designers and reformers to focus on the quality of contemporary decorative art instead, distracting even those interested in an aesthetic theory of ornament and decoration. British designers and theorists like Pugin and Ruskin, wrote specifically on the production of ornament and on its ideal relation to the object's function.[3] Unlike Moritz, they were concerned with the contemporary problem of creating a practical object that retained some claim to beauty—though its type of beauty remained undefined.

In the selection of 1841 presented here, Pugin first explains that ornament should express the object's mechanism, tying visual form to physical functioning. Aesthetic pleasure results from the most perfect merging of form and function. Ruskin, on the other hand, offers an alternative vision of the ideal relation between the decoration and the object's intended purpose in these two selections (1849 and 1859).[4] Decorative features, he explains, should not simply be a visual expression of an object's use, as Pugin would have it; rather, decorative features must be suited to the *status* of the object or surface.

To explain his evaluation of beauty in applied art, Ruskin first establishes a hierarchy of function, ranked according to the object's or surface's relative mobility, visibility, and utility (with wall-frescoes at the top and dishes at the bottom). He then introduces a corresponding hierarchy of artistic form, running in decreasing order from figurative painting to inanimate, geometric ornament, reminiscent of the traditional hierarchy of genres in painting, descending from mythological canvases to still life. To be called beautiful, the type of decoration used must correspond to the level of use; thus immobile, well-protected wall surfaces should be frescoed with figurative forms, whereas dados hidden behind furniture, or handled utensils, should have simple geometric ornament. In an important departure from Pugin, Ruskin frees decoration from the necessity of having to express function visually, allowing it instead to match intended function with appropriate visual forms.

In a similar vein, William Morris also assumes the visual independence of decoration from function—the former does not have to express the latter. In his lecture "The Arts and Crafts of To-day" (1889), Morris wonders why craftsmen add beauty (that is decoration) to objects of utility, concluding that they do so because it provides pleasure both to the user and to themselves. For Morris, function and beauty remain two completely separate elements, which somehow, miraculously, come together in the hands of a good craftsman. Although dismayed at contemporary misuses of ornament, Morris, like Ruskin, is here less concerned with decoration's ability to represent function than with the pleasure to be derived from decoration itself. In order for this pleasure to survive, the fine artist—not the craftsman or designer—must come to the aid of ornament. As Morris explains in "The Lesser Arts" the divorce of artists from craftsmen has impoverished ornament, which is now left solely to artisans.[5] Only with the reunion of artists and craftsmen will decoration again become a source of beauty and pleasure.

A few decades later, it is precisely the artist's lack of understanding for functional objects that irritates the designer and reformer Samuel Bing. In an interesting reversal, Bing complains that the fusion of the arts, and artistic collaborations, so desired by Morris, has only worsened the situation. In "Where Are We Going?" (1897), Bing includes a heartfelt plea to designers and artists that they reinstate the traditional division of the arts. Contemporary painters and sculptors, he explains, aspire only to create art for art's sake, and are ill-suited to design decoration for functional objects. As a result, contemporary ornament suffers from an excess of artistic inspiration, whereas concern for function and comfort has all but vanished. Like Moritz and Pugin before him, Bing concludes that the visual forms of decorative art must originate in the object's function, rather than in an abstract beautiful visual form added on at a later moment.

By the early-twentieth century, designers and architects like Hermann Muthesius, Walter Gropius, and Charles-Edouard Jeanneret (Le Corbusier) were developing the artistic implications of such criticism in different directions. Muthesius, initiator of the German Werkbund, declares in "The Meaning of Applied Art" (1907) that the form of decorative art should be determined by function alone, resulting in the creation of pure, unburdened objects. In contrast, Gropius calls for the union of arts and crafts in the famous Bauhaus manifesto (1919). Yet Gropius is not simply repeating the ideals of the Arts and Crafts, as expressed first by Ruskin and then Morris. Rather, he places decorative as well as fine art in the service of architecture, whose form and function they must both embellish. The union of fine and decorative art occurs because they now share a *decorative* function within architecture. Gropius thus establishes a new artistic hierarchy that not only privileges architecture but also reduces all the other arts to pure decoration.

Le Corbusier's writings of 1925 seem all the more radical when read after Gropius's early manifesto. Whereas Gropius stresses the decorative role of all the arts, Le Corbusier argues that the decorative nature of decorative art has vanished. As Le Corbusier explains, decorative art now responds to concrete human needs in the most direct and useful way. In so doing, decorative art eliminates useless ornament, and accepts functional form as the only type of decoration. To achieve this end, Le Corbusier is prepared to embrace the traditional hierarchy of the arts, acknowledging that beauty is now the property only of higher spheres of artistic creativity.

Le Corbusier's harsh and provocative definition of decorative art provides a fitting conclusion to writings directed at contemporary production in this chapter, by introducing the main theoretical tenets of what came to be called "Functionalism." At the same time, his text allows one to notice a certain circularity within the trajectory of these writings. D'Alembert begins with a celebration of the practical benefits of the mechanical arts, which Moritz, in turn, abandons in his musings about a theory of ornament and decoration loosely related to function. This relation then becomes the main subject of the writings of reformers, who advocate some sort of visual correspondence between the object's use and its decoration. The early Modernist movement, instead, returns to a single-minded focus on decorative art's usefulness; form is evaluated *only* as a visual expression of that function, which ultimately leads, as Moritz predicts (in his essay in Part III), to the appreciation of undecorated form as the pure expression of function.

THE THEORY OF FUNCTION

By the middle of the nineteenth century there had also begun to emerge another type of writing about decorative art. Unlike the essays by the reformers (loosely speaking), these other writings explored the notion of beauty in functional art of the past. Moritz is a precursor of this, though he stops short of offering a historical account of the relation between function, form, and ornament. The first writer to do so was the German architect Gottfried Semper, author of *Style in the Technical and Tectonic Arts* (discussed in Part II). The writing selected here is a lesser-known lecture on adornment of 1856, in which Semper offers a sociological explanation for three forms of ancient jewelry, which, he argues, have remained relatively constant over time and across cultures. According to Semper, these three forms of ancient ornament are used, intentionally or not, to enhance the wearer's movement and form. Thus high head-gear increases the vertical direction of the wearer, earrings emphasize movement as well as bodily weight, while encircling bands stress the static, horizontal forms of the human body. Semper believes that the expression of human axial direction and movement is a shared universal need, one most visible in jewelry of less civilized, ancient cultures. Later cultures, he explains, have lost sight of these earlier, empathetic functions, according clothing and ornament a purely symbolic role.

At the turn of the century, the Viennese art historian Alois Riegl challenged Semper's influential, functional interpretation of form in an unfinished manuscript entitled *A Historical Grammar of the Visual Arts* (1897–99). Of special interest here is that Riegl openly acknowledges that all art has a function or purpose (*Zweck*), something he minimizes in his other writings. Yet Riegl has done so only in order to transfer function from the practical to the artistic realm. The acknowledged aims of art described by Riegl range from the useful and religious, as in utensils and statues, to the representational, as in portraiture. Yet none of these, Riegl points out, can fully explain the specific aesthetic choices made by the artist. These, he suggests, must stem from an even deeper necessity: that of creativity itself. Like Semper, Riegl believes the source of artistic form is an inner, universal drive, but, unlike Semper, one dedicated to art alone. Both historians use function to explain the form of decorative art, and both assume that it is partially determined by culture, capable of reflecting political, religious, social, and artistic beliefs. In so doing, they are using the new idea of "historicism," developed by late-nineteenth-century historians. But, they fundamentally disagree over the character of that human drive, and the meaning of function itself.

In the first few decades of the twentieth century, sociologists Georg Simmel and Norbert Elias took up questions similar to those raised by Semper and Riegl. However, as sociologists, neither was concerned with the artistry of decorative art—an issue of prime importance to art historians. Rather, their concern was to see how certain types of decorative art not only functioned in society but could also reveal otherwise hidden changes within it. Simmel, for instance, offers an excursus on jewelry in his monumental work *Sociology* of 1908. Focusing on jewelry's ability to dazzle and impress, Simmel suggests that such luxuries do not simply signal status, but are worn for the viewer, whose admiring gaze jewelry's glitter will attract. Simmel goes on to explain that such jewelry must be *impersonal* in order for it to possess a social style, one instantly understood by the viewer. The more personalized and artistic a luxury item becomes, the weaker it is as a conveyor of intended social meaning. Only the characterless, sparkling jewel can adapt itself to the wearer's own style while simultaneously reflecting that of society at large. Simmel's conclusion challenges cherished beliefs of such designers as Morris as well as of historians like Riegl by revealing that contemporary society now requires objects devoid of the maker's individuality and creativity.

Elias, writing between the two world wars, devotes his magnum opus to a history of manners and comportment in early modern Europe. In *The Civilizing Process* (1939), Elias offers a worm's-eye view of the court of Louis XIV among others, seeing how the handling of forks, knives, spoons, handkerchiefs, and toilets established social hierarchies and expressed social relationships. Like Simmel, Elias explores how an object's function is determined by cultural beliefs, but even more than Simmel, he reduces the object to the level of a variable, which mirrors changing human attitudes toward propriety and civility. As these attitudes evolve they engender new needs, which in turn stimulate the creation of new objects to answer those needs. For these two sociologists, the relation of function to form, which remained so problematic both for reformers and art historians alike, is neatly resolved by a mediating, connecting force: changing cultural beliefs about self-presentation.

NOTES

1. This is similar to Diderot's definition of beaux-arts, in the *Encyclopedia*, but Diderot adds that the aim of the fine arts is to imitate nature, which Moritz says is no longer an operative definition.

2. Kant's notion of disinterested beauty as it applies to fine art is most helpfully discussed by Scheffer, *L'Art de l'âge moderne*, pp. 27–84. As Scheffer points out, Kant's model of beauty seems to be nature, not the fine arts at all. Moritz was indirectly aware of Kant's theories through Salomon Maïmon; in his own work Moritz perhaps comes closer to Romantic theories of art, as argued by Todorov, *Thèories du symbole*, pp. 179–260. For a complete edition of Moritz's work see Günther's *Karl Philipp Moritz. Werke*.

3. The relative meaning of decoration and ornament is extremely problematic. These authors tend to see ornament as the sculpted detail of architecture or metalwork, and decoration as a larger, painted surface. For other definitions see Grabar, *Mediation of Ornament*, p. 5.

4. Much has been written about Ruskin's aesthetics in terms of painting and architecture; it is almost impossible to find writings focusing exclusively on his notion of beauty and ornament in decorative arts. One exception is a section in Kemp, *The Desire of My Eyes*.

5. In *William Morris: News from Nowhere*.

JEAN LE ROND D'ALEMBERT

Preliminary Discourse to the *Encyclopedia*

In general the name *Art* may be given to any system of knowledge which can be reduced to positive and invariable rules independent of caprice or opinion. In this sense it would be permitted to say that several of our sciences are arts when they are viewed from their practical side. But just as there are rules for the operations of the mind or soul, there are also rules for those of the body: that is, for those operations which, applying exclusively to external bodies, can be executed by hand alone. Such is the origin of the differentiation of the arts into liberal and mechanical arts, and of the superiority which we accord to the first over the second. That superiority is doubtless unjust in several respects. Nevertheless, none of our prejudices, however ridiculous, is without its reason, or to speak more precisely, its origin, and although philosophy is often powerless to correct abuses, it can at least discern their source. After physical force rendered useless the right of equality possessed by all men, the weakest, who are always the majority, joined together to check it. With the aid of laws and different sorts of governments they established an inequality of convention in which force ceased to be the defining principle. Even though they united with good reason to preserve this inequality of convention once it was well established, men have not been able to resist complaining against it secretly because of that desire for superiority which nothing has been able to destroy in them. Thus, they have sought a sort of compensation in a less arbitrary inequality. Since physical force enchained by laws is no longer capable of offering any means of superiority, they have been reduced to seeking a principle of inequality in the difference of intellectual excellence—a principle which is equally natural, more peaceful, and more useful to society. Thus the most noble part of our being has in some measure taken vengeance for the first advantages which the basest part had usurped, and the talents of the mind have been generally recognized as superior to those of the body. The mechanical arts, which are dependent upon manual operation and are subjugated (if I may be permitted this term) to a sort of routine, have been left to those among men whom prejudices have placed in the lowest class. Poverty has forced these men to turn to such work more often than taste and genius have attracted them to it. Subsequently it became a reason for holding them in contempt—so much does poverty harm everything that accompanies it. With regard to the free operations of the mind, they have been apportioned to those who have believed themselves most favored of Nature in this respect. However, the advantage that the liberal arts have over the mechanical arts, because of their demands upon the intellect and because of the difficulty of excelling in them, is sufficiently counterbalanced by the quite superior usefulness which the latter for the most part have for us. It is this very usefulness which reduced them perforce to purely mechanical operations in order to make them accessible to a larger number of men. But while justly respecting great geniuses for their enlightenment, society ought not to degrade the hands by which it is served. The discovery of the compass is no less advantageous to the human race than the explication of its properties would be to physical science. Finally, considering in itself the principle of the distinction about which we are speaking, how many alleged scholars are there for whom science is in truth only a mechanical art? What real difference is there between a head stuffed with facts without order, without utility, and without connection, and the instinct of an artisan reduced to mechanical operation?

The contempt in which the mechanical arts are held seems to have affected to some degree even their inventors. The names of these benefactors of humankind are almost all unknown, whereas the history of its destroyers, that is to say, of the conquerors, is known to everyone. However, it is perhaps in the artisan that one must seek the most admirable evidences of the sagacity, the patience, and the resources of the mind. I admit that most of the arts have been invented only little by little and that it required a rather long sequence of centuries to bring watches, for example, to their present point of perfection. But is not the same true of the sciences? How many of the discoveries that have immortalized their authors had been prepared by the works of preceding centuries, sometimes being already brought to their maturity, to the point where they required just one step more to be accomplished? And not to leave watchmaking, why are not those to whom we owe the fusee, the escapement, the repeating-works[1] of watches equally esteemed with those who have worked successively to perfect algebra? Moreover, if I may believe a few philosophers who have not been deterred from studying the arts by the prevailing contempt for them, there are certain machines that are so complicated, and whose parts are all so dependent on one another, that their invention must almost of necessity be due to a single man. Is not that man of genius, whose name is shrouded in oblivion, well worthy of being placed beside the small number of creative minds who have opened new routes for us in the sciences?

Among the liberal arts that have been reduced to principles, those that undertake the imitation of Nature have been called the Fine Arts because they have pleasure for their principal object.[2] But that is not the only characteristic distinguishing them from the more necessary or more useful liberal arts, such as Grammar, Logic, and Ethics. The latter have fixed and settled rules which any man can transmit to another, whereas the practice of the Fine Arts consists principally in an invention which takes its laws almost exclusively from genius. The rules which have been written concerning these arts are, properly speaking, only the mechanical part. Their effect is somewhat like that of the telescope; they only aid those who see.

NOTES

1. These are all technical watchmakers' terms whose definitions can be found in the *Encyclopedia* or in an unabridged dictionary. [R. Schwab]

2. Eloquence, poetry, music, painting, sculpture, architecture, and engraving are in this category. [R. Schwab]

KARL PHILIPP MORITZ

from *Preliminary Ideas on the Theory of Ornament*

ON THE CONCEPT OF SELF-SUFFICIENT PERFECTION

To Mr. Moses Mendelssohn:[1]

The principle of the *imitation* of nature has been abandoned as the central purpose of the fine arts (*die schöne Künste*) and sciences, and subordinated to that of *pleasure,* now set up as the fundamental law of the fine arts. The only goal of those arts is pleasure, it is said, just as that of the mechanical arts is utility. And yet we derive pleasure both from the beautiful and from the useful; so where lies the distinction between the two?

Where a thing is purely useful, I take pleasure not so much in the object itself as in the notion of the convenience or comfort that I or another will derive from its use. I make myself, as it were, into the central focus to which I relate every part of the object: that is, I regard the object simply as a means to an end, that end being myself (or the perfecting of myself). The purely useful object is therefore not whole or perfect in itself but becomes so only on accomplishing its purpose, or its perfection, in me.

When I contemplate the beautiful, however, the purpose lies not in me but in the object itself, which I regard as perfect not in me but in itself: *something that constitutes a whole in itself,* and gives me pleasure *for its own sake.* I do not so much relate the beautiful object to myself, as relate myself to it. And so, since the beautiful is pleasing to me for its own sake, and the useful solely for my sake, the beautiful affords me a higher and more unselfish pleasure than does the purely useful. The pleasure of the purely useful is comparatively commonplace and crude; the pleasure of the beautiful is rare and refined. The former we share, in a sense, with the beasts; the latter elevates us above them.

Since the useful serves a purpose *outside,* rather than inside, itself, and thereby enhances something else's perfection, anyone desirous of producing something useful must keep this *external* purpose constantly in mind as he works. If the object serves its external purpose, it does not matter what it looks like; to the extent that it exists purely in order to be useful, this is immaterial. Just so long as a clock keeps good time, and a knife cuts well, I care nothing, from the viewpoint of strict utility, for the preciousness of the clock case or of the knife handle. Nor do I notice whether the works of the clock, or the blade of the knife, please my eye or not. The clock and the knife have their purpose outside themselves, in the person who uses them for his convenience; they are therefore not perfect in and of themselves, and have themselves no value aside from the potential or actual attainment of their external purpose. Only in conjunction with this external purpose do they give me pleasure; isolated from this, they leave me utterly indifferent. I look at the clock and the knife with pleasure only in so far as I need them: I do not need them in order to look at them.

With the beautiful, the reverse is true. The beautiful has no purpose outside itself, and does not exist for the sake of perfecting something else, but for the sake of its own intrinsic, inner perfection. It is not that we look at it in so far as we need it: we need it in so far as we look at it. It is not so much that we need the beautiful in order to delight in it: the beautiful needs us in order to be apprehended. We can survive perfectly well without looking at beautiful works of art; but they cannot well exist, as such, without us to look at them. And so, the more dispensable they are to us, the more we look at them for their own sake. By looking at them, we give them their full measure of existence. For, through our growing recognition of beauty in a beautiful work of art, we in a sense increase that beauty and invest it with greater value.

This explains, once we have recognized something as beautiful, why we are so impatient to have everyone else pay homage to it. For, the more generally it is recognized and admired as beautiful, the more value it acquires even in our own eyes. Hence, the displeasure we feel in an empty theater, however magnificent the performance. If we took pleasure in the beautiful for our own sake rather than for its sake, why should we care whether anyone else recognized it or not? We exert ourselves, we wax zealous in the service of the beautiful; we recruit admirers for it, wherever we find it; indeed, we feel a kind of pity at the sight of a beautiful work of art that gathers dust and is viewed with indifference by passers-by.

Even the sweet astonishment, *the pleasurable forgetfulness of self,* which overcomes us at the sight of a beautiful work of art, is proof that our pleasure is one of self-subordination. For the moment, we willingly allow our pleasure, which beauty defines for us, to take precedence over all our other feelings. By attracting our attention entirely to itself, beauty diverts us for a while from ourselves, so that we seem to lose ourselves in the beautiful object; and this loss of self is the supreme degree of pure and unselfish pleasure that beauty can afford us. In that moment we offer up our individual, limited existence to a type of higher existence. To be genuine, our delight in beauty must approximate ever more closely to selfless *love.* If a beautiful work of art contains a personal reference to me, this adds to my pleasure something that is lost on anyone else. For me, however, the beauty of the work is never pure and unalloyed until I dismiss the personal from my mind and regard the work as something created solely for the sake of its own perfection.

Love and benevolence may, so to speak, become inner exigencies to the noble philanthropist without his thereby becoming self-serving. Similarly, to the man of taste, the delight in beauty may become a necessity by force of habit, without its losing any of its original purity. We need a beautiful thing, simply because we desire the opportunity to pay homage to it by acknowledging its beauty.

It follows that an object cannot be beautiful purely because it gives us pleasure; for otherwise everything that is useful would also be beautiful. The thing that gives us pleasure without being of any real use to us is what we call beautiful. But anything that is useless, or unfit for its purpose, cannot possibly give pleasure to a rational being. Where an object lacks an external use or purpose, it can never give me pleasure, unless the purpose lies within the object itself. Or, alternatively, *I must discover in the individual parts of the object so much fitness for purpose that I forget to ask what the whole is actually for.* In other words, I must take pleasure in a beautiful object only for its own sake; to that end, its internal purpose must compensate for its lack of external purpose. The object must be something perfect in itself.

If the internal purpose of a beautiful work of art is not sufficient to make me forget its external purpose, I naturally ask: "What is the object as a whole for?"

If the artist gives me the answer, "In order to give you pleasure," I then ask him:

"What grounds have you for giving me pleasure rather than displeasure through your work of art? Is my pleasure so important to you that you would deliberately make your work more imperfect than it is, in order to appeal to my possibly corrupted taste? Or do you not rather care so much for your work that you will try to attune my taste to it, so that its beauties may not be lost on me? If the latter, I cannot see how my fortuitous pleasure in your work could ever be its true purpose, since that pleasure exists only if stimulated and defined by your work. My pleasure is agreeable to you only in so far as you know that I have learned to take pleasure in that which is truly perfect in itself. This would not be the case if my pleasure were your sole concern; your concern is to see the perfection of your work confirmed by my interest in it. Pleasure is a *subordinate purpose,* or rather a mere natural consequence, of the fine arts. Otherwise, would not the true artist seek to please as many people as possible, instead of sacrificing to the perfection of his work, as he often does, the pleasure of many thousands who have no feeling for the beauties he creates?

Says the artist: "But if my work is liked, or gives pleasure, I have surely achieved my purpose."

To which I reply: "On the contrary! Your work gives pleasure because you have achieved your purpose; or else the fact that your work gives pleasure *may possibly be a sign* that you have achieved your purpose in the work itself. But if the true purpose of the work is the pleasure you intend it to give, rather than the perfection of the work in itself, then this in itself makes me suspicious of the applause it has received from this or that person."

"But I strive only to please noble minds."

"Good! But this is not your ultimate purpose; for may I ask why you strive to please those noble minds rather than any others? Surely because they have learned to take the greatest pleasure in that which is most perfect? You refer their pleasure back to your work, whose perfection you hope to see reaffirmed thereby. Take heart from the thought that noble minds will approve your work; but never let their approval be your supreme and ultimate purpose, or you will never receive it. Even the most gratifying applause is not to be hunted down, but must be garnered in passing. Let the perfection of your work fill your whole soul as you work; let it overshadow even the sweetest thought of fame, which must surface only at intervals, to renew your vigor when your spirit begins to flag. Then you will receive, unsought, what thousands labor for in vain. But if applause be your principal concern; if you value your work only for the fame that it earns for you; then you need no longer to expect applause from noble minds. You are pursuing a selfish end; the focus of the work will lie outside the work itself; you are not producing it for its own sake alone, and so you are not producing a whole that is perfect in itself. You will pursue a false brilliance, which may well dazzle the mob for a while, but which in the eyes of the wise will vanish like a mist."

The true artist will seek to infuse his work with the highest sense of inner purpose or perfection. If it is then applauded, he will be glad; but his true purpose is already attained through the perfection of the work. In the same way, the truly wise man seeks to infuse all his actions with the highest sense of purpose, in harmony with the course of events; he regards the purest happiness and lasting feelings of pleasure as a clear consequence of this, but not as its goal. For even the purest happiness can only be *garnered* in passing, along the road to perfection: it cannot be hunted down. The line of happiness runs parallel with the line of perfection; as soon as happiness becomes a goal in itself, the line of perfection must inevitably run askew. Where individual actions are directed solely to the aim of pleasurable sensation, this may well constitute a sense of purpose, but they never combine to form a harmonious whole. So it is with the fine arts, wherever the idea of perfection—of the thing that is perfect within itself—is subordinated to the idea of pleasure.

"So is pleasure not a purpose at all?"

My answer is this: "What is pleasure, or what is its source, if not the contemplation of fitness for purpose? If there were a thing made with pleasure as its sole purpose, then I could judge its fitness for purpose by the pleasure that I derive from it. But my pleasure in itself must derive from that judgment, and so the latter must exist before the former. Again, the end must always be simpler than the means used to reach it; yet the pleasure derived from a beautiful work of art is as much a composite as the work itself. How, then, can I regard this pleasure as something simpler than that toward which the individual parts of the work are striving? I cannot, any more than I can regard the image of a painting in a mirror as the purpose of its composition: that image will always be there, of its own accord, without the slightest effort on my part. Similarly, the more perfect my work is, the more imperfectly will it appear in a clouded mirror. But surely, I am not going to make that work more imperfect only so that fewer of its beauties may be lost in the clouded mirror?—"

NOTES

This piece, as the others in the anthology, became part of Moritz's *Preliminary Ideas on the Theory of Ornament* (Vorbegriffe zu einer Theorie der Ornamente [1793]), though written prior to it. Here, as in all extracts in this volume, the emphases are authorial.

1. Moses Mendelssohn (1729–1781) was a German Jewish philosopher and a close friend of the German dramaturgist Gotthold Ephraim Lessing.

A. WELBY PUGIN

On Metal-work

We now come to the consideration of works in metal; and I shall be able to show that the same principles of suiting the design to the material and decorating construction were strictly adhered to by the artists of the middle ages in all their productions in metal, whether precious or common.

In the first place, hinges, locks, bolts, nails, &c., which are always *concealed in modern designs,* were rendered in pointed architecture, *rich and beautiful decorations;* and this not only in the doors and fittings of buildings, but in cabinets and small articles of furniture.

The early hinges covered the whole face of the doors with varied and flowing scroll-work. Of this description are those of Notre Dame at Paris, St. Elizabeth's church at Marburg, the western doors of Litchfield Cathedral, the Chapter House at York, and hundreds of other churches, both in England and on the continent. [Plate 1, figs. 1 and 3]

Hinges of this kind are not only beautiful in design, but they are *practically good.* We all know that on the principle of a lever a door may be easily torn off its modern hinges by a strain applied at its outward edge. [fig. 2] This could not be the case with the ancient hinges, which extended the whole width of the door, and were bolted through in various places. In barn-doors and gates these hinges are still used, although devoid of any elegance of form; but they have been most religiously banished from public edifices as unsightly, merely on account of our present race of artists not exercising the same ingenuity as those of ancient times in rendering the *useful* a vehicle for the beautiful: the same remarks will apply to locks that are now concealed and let into the styles of doors, which are often more than half cut away to receive them. [Plate 1, fig. 4]

• • •

In all the ancient ornamental iron-work we may discern a peculiar manner of execution, admirably suited to the material, and quite distinct from that of stone or wood. For instance, tracery was produced by different thicknesses of pierced plates laid over each other. [Plate 1, fig. 6]

Leaves and crockets were not *carved or modelled,* and *then cast,* but cut out of thin metal plate, and twisted up with pliers [Plate 2, figs. 1, 2], and the lines of stems either engraved or soldered on. By these simple means all the light-

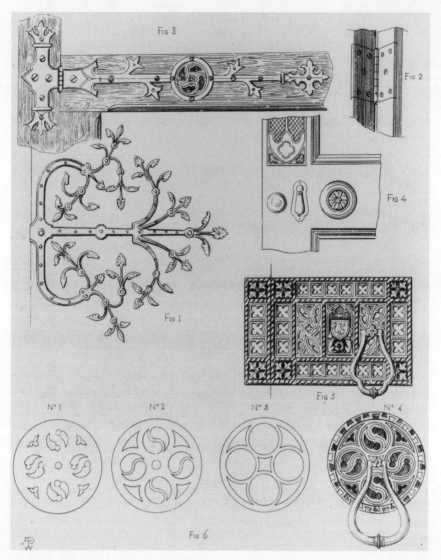

Plate 1. Hinges

ness, ease, and sharpness of real vegetation is produced at a much less cost than the heavy flat foliage usually cast and chased up. It is likewise to be remarked, that the necessary fastenings for iron-work were always shown and ornamented. Bolts, nails, and rivets, so far from being unsightly, are beautiful studs and busy enrichments, if properly treated. [Plate 2, fig. 3]

. . .

It is impossible to enumerate half the absurdities of modern metal-workers; but all these proceed from the false notion of *disguising* instead of *beautifying*

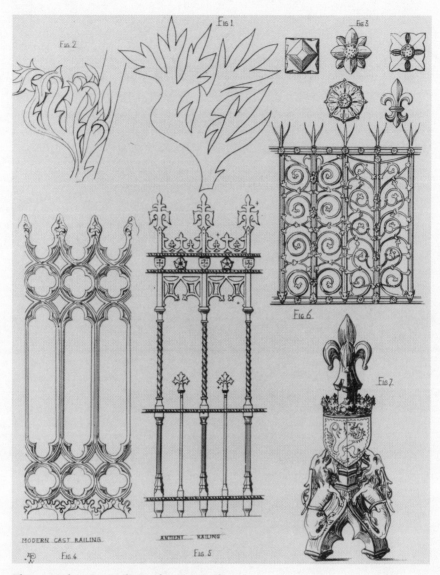

Plate 2. Modern Cast Railing and Ancient Railing

articles of utility. How many objects of ordinary use are rendered monstrous and ridiculous simply because the artist, instead of seeking the *most convenient form,* and *then decorating it,* has embodied some extravagance *to conceal the real purpose for which the article has been made!* If a clock is required, it is not unusual to cast a Roman warrior in a flying chariot, round one of the wheels of which, on close inspection, the hours may be descried; or the whole front of a cathedral church reduced to a few inches in height, with the clock-face occupying the position of a magnificent rose window. Surely the inventor of this

A. Welby Pugin {37}

patent clock-case could never have reflected that according to the scale on which the edifice was reduced, his clock would be about two hundred feet in circumference, and that such a monster of a dial would crush the proportions of almost any building that could be raised. But this is nothing when compared to what we see continually produced from those inexhaustible mines of bad taste, Birmingham and Sheffield; staircase turrets for inkstands, monumental crosses for light-shades, gable ends hung on handles for door-porters, and four doorways and a cluster of pillars to support a French lamp; while a pair of *pinnacles* supporting an arch is called a Gothic-pattern scraper, and a wiry compound of quatrefoils and fan tracery an abbey garden-seat. [Plate 3, fig. 2] Nei-

Plate 3. French Lamp and Abbey Garden Seat

ther relative scale, form, purpose, nor unity of style, is ever considered by those who design these abominations; if they only introduce a quatrefoil or an acute arch, be the outline and style of the article ever so modern and debased, it is at once denominated and sold as Gothic.

While I am on this topic it may not be amiss to mention some other absurdities which may not be out of place, although they do not belong to metalwork. I will commence with what are termed Gothic-pattern papers, for hanging walls, where a wretched caricature of a pointed building is repeated from the skirting to the cornice in glorious confusion,—door over pinnacle, and pinnacle over door. [Plate 4] This is a great favourite with hotel and tavern keepers. Again, those papers which are shaded are defective in principle; for, as a paper is hung round a room, the ornament must frequently be shadowed on the light side.

The variety of these miserable patterns is quite surprising; and as the expense of cutting a block for a bad figure is equal if not greater than for a good one, there is not the shadow of an excuse for their continual reproduction. A moment's reflection must show the extreme absurdity of *repeating a perspective* over a large surface with some hundred different points of sight: a panel or wall may be enriched and decorated at pleasure, but it should always be treated in a consistent manner.

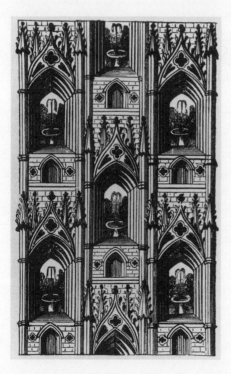

Plate 4. Pattern of Modern Gothic Paper

Flock papers are admirable substitutes for the ancient hangings, but then they must consist of a pattern *without shadow,* with the forms relieved by the introduction of harmonious colours. [Plate 5] Illuminated manuscripts of the thirteenth, fourteenth, and fifteenth centuries would furnish an immense number of exquisite designs for this purpose.

These observations will apply to modern carpets, the patterns of which are generally *shaded.* Nothing can be more ridiculous than an apparently *reversed groining* to walk upon, or highly relieved foliage and perforated tracery for the decoration of a floor.

The ancient paving tiles are quite consistent with their purpose, being merely ornamented with a pattern not produced by any apparent relief, but only by *contrast of colour* [Plate 6]; and carpets should be treated in precisely the same manner. Turkey carpets, which are by far the handsomest now manufactured, have no shadow in their pattern, but merely an intricate combination of coloured intersections.

Modern upholstery, again, is made a surprising vehicle for bad and paltry taste, especially when any thing very fine is attempted.

To arrange curtains consistently with true taste, their use and intention should always be considered: they are suspended across windows and other openings to exclude cold and wind, and as they are not always required to be drawn, they are hung to rings sliding on rods, to be opened or closed at pleasure: as there must necessarily be a space between this rod and the ceiling through which wind will pass, a boxing of wood has been contrived, in front of which a valance is suspended to exclude air.

Now the materials of these curtains may be rich or plain, they may be heavily or lightly fringed, they may be embroidered with heraldic charges or not, ac-

Plate 5. Ancient Pattern for a Flock Paper   *Plate 6. Pattern of Ancient Paving Tiles*

cording to the locality where they are to be hung, but their real use must be strictly maintained. Hence all the modern plans of suspending enormous folds of stuff over poles, as if for the purpose of sale or of being dried, is quite contrary to the use and intentions of curtains, and abominable in taste; and the only object that these endless festoons and bunchy tassels can answer is to swell the bills and profits of the upholsterers, who are the inventors of these extravagant and ugly draperies, which are not only useless in protecting the chamber from cold, but are the depositories of thick layers of dust, and in London not unfrequently become the strong-holds of vermin.

The Lamp of Beauty

XVI. What is the place of ornament? Consider first that the characters of natural objects which the architect can represent are few and abstract. The greater part of those delights by which Nature recommends herself to man at all times, cannot be conveyed by him into his imitative work. He cannot make his grass green and cool and good to rest upon, which in nature is its chief use to man; nor can he make his flowers tender and full of colour and of scent, which in nature are their chief powers of giving joy. Those qualities which alone he can secure are certain severe characters of form, such as men only see in nature on deliberate examination, and by the full and set appliance of sight and thought: a man must lie down on the bank of grass on his breast and set himself to watch and penetrate the intertwining of it, before he finds that which is good to be gathered by the architect. So then while Nature is at all times pleasant to us, and while the sight and sense of her work may mingle happily with all our thoughts, and labours, and times of existence, that image of her which the architect carries away represents what we can only perceive in her by direct intellectual exertion, and demands from us, wherever it appears, an intellectual exertion of a similar kind in order to understand it and feel it. It is the written or sealed impression of a thing sought out, it is the shaped result of inquiry and bodily expression of thought.

XVII. Now let us consider for an instant what would be the effect of continually repeating an expression of a beautiful thought to any other of the senses at times when the mind could not address that sense to the understanding of it. Suppose that in time of serious occupation, of stern business, a companion should repeat in our ears continually some favourite passage of poetry, over and over again all day long. We should not only soon be utterly sick and weary of the sound of it, but that sound would at the end of the day have so sunk into the habit of the ear that the entire meaning of the passage would be dead to us, and it would ever thenceforward require some effort to fix and recover it. The music of it would not meanwhile have aided the business in hand, while its own delightfulness would thenceforward be in a measure destroyed. It is the same with every other form of definite thought. If you violently present its expression to the senses, at times when the mind is otherwise engaged, that expression will be ineffective at the time, and will have its sharpness and clearness destroyed for ever. Much more if you present it to the mind at times when it is painfully affected or disturbed, or if you associate the expression of pleasant thought with incongruous circumstances, you will affect that expression thenceforward, with a painful colour for ever.

xviii. Apply this to expressions of thought received by the eye. Remember that the eye is at your mercy more than the ear. "The eye it cannot choose but see." Its nerve is not so easily numbed as that of the ear, and it is often busied in tracing and watching forms when the ear is at rest. Now if you present lovely forms to it when it cannot call the mind to help it in its work, and among objects of vulgar use and unhappy position, you will neither please the eye nor elevate the vulgar object. But you will fill and weary the eye with the beautiful form, and you will infect that form itself with the vulgarity of the thing to which you have violently attached it. It will never be of much use to you any more; you have killed, or defiled it; its freshness and purity are gone. You will have to pass it through the fire of much thought before you will cleanse it, and warm it with much love before it will revive.

xix. Hence then a general law, of singular importance in the present day, a law of simple common sense,—not to decorate things belonging to purposes of active and occupied life. Wherever you can rest, there decorate; where rest is forbidden, so is beauty. You must not mix ornament with business, any more than you may mix play. Work first, and then rest. Work first, and then gaze, but do not use golden ploughshares, nor bind ledgers in enamel. Do not thrash with sculptured flails: nor put bas-reliefs on millstones. What! it will be asked, are we in the habit of doing so? Even so; always and everywhere. The most familiar position of Greek mouldings is in these days on shop fronts. There is not a tradesman's sign nor shelf nor counter in all the streets of all our cities, which has not upon it ornaments which were invented to adorn temples and beautify kings' palaces. There is not the smallest advantage in them where they are. Absolutely valueless—utterly without the power of giving pleasure, they only satiate the eye, and vulgarise their own forms. Many of these are in themselves thoroughly good copies of fine things, which things themselves we shall never, in consequence, enjoy any more. Many a pretty beading and graceful bracket there is in wood or stucco above our grocers' and cheesemongers' and hosiers' shops: how is it that the tradesmen cannot understand that custom is to be had only by selling good tea and cheese and cloth, and that people come to them for their honesty, and their readiness, and their right wares, and not because they have Greek cornices over their windows, or their names in large gilt letters on their house fronts? How pleasurable it would be to have the power of going through the streets of London, pulling down those brackets and friezes and large names, restoring to the tradesmen the capital they had spent in architecture, and putting them on honest and equal terms, each with his name in black letters over his door, not shouted down the street from the upper stories, and each with a plain wooden shop casement, with small panes in it that people would not think of breaking in order to be sent to prison! How much better for them would it be—how much happier, how much wiser, to put their trust upon their own truth and industry, and not on the idiocy of their customers. It is curious, and it says little for our national probity on the one hand, or prudence on the other, to see the whole system of our street decoration based on the idea that people must be baited to a shop as moths are to a candle.

xx. But it will be said that much of the best wooden decoration of the middle ages was in shop fronts. No; it was in *house* fronts, of which the shop was a part, and received its natural and consistent portion of the ornament. In those days men lived, and intended to live *by* their shops, and over them, all their days. They were contented with them and happy in them: they were their palaces and castles. They gave them therefore such decoration as made themselves happy in their own habitation, and they gave it for their own sake. The upper stories were always the richest, and the shop was decorated chiefly about the door, which belonged to the house more than to it. And when our tradesmen settle to their shops in the same way, and form no plans respecting future villa architecture, let their whole houses be decorated, and their shops too, but with a national and domestic decoration. (I shall speak more of this point in the sixth Chapter [in *The Seven Lamps of Architecture*].) However, our cities are for the most part too large to admit of contented dwelling in them throughout life; and I do not say there is harm in our present system of separating the shop from the dwelling-house; only where they are so separated, let us remember that the only reason for shop decoration is removed, and see that the decoration be removed also.

xxi. Another of the strange and evil tendencies of the present day is to the decoration of the railroad station. Now, if there be any place in the world in which people are deprived of that portion of temper and discretion which are necessary to the contemplation of beauty, it is there. It is the very temple of discomfort, and the only charity that the builder can extend to us is to show us, plainly as may be, how soonest to escape from it. The whole system of railroad travelling is addressed to people who, being in a hurry, are therefore, for the time being, miserable. No one would travel in that manner who could help it— who had time to go leisurely over hills and between hedges, instead of through tunnels and between banks: at least those who would, have no sense of beauty so acute as that we need consult it at the station. The railroad is in all its relations a matter of earnest business, to be got through as soon as possible. It transmutes a man from a traveller into a living parcel. For the time he has parted with the nobler characteristics of his humanity for the sake of a planetary power of locomotion. Do not ask him to admire anything. You might as well ask the wind. Carry him safely, dismiss him soon: he will thank you for nothing else. All attempts to please him in any other way are mere mockery, and insults to the things by which you endeavour to do so. There never was more flagrant nor impertinent folly than the smallest portion of ornament in anything concerned with railroads or near them. Keep them out of the way, take them through the ugliest country you can find, confess them the miserable things they are, and spend nothing upon them but for safety and speed. Give large salaries to efficient servants, large prices to good manufacturers, large wages to able workmen, let the iron be tough, and the brickwork solid, and the carriages strong. The time is perhaps not distant when these first necessities may not be easily met: and to increase expense in any other direction is madness. Better bury gold in the embankments, than put it in ornaments on the stations. Will a single traveller be willing to pay an increased fare on the South Western, because the columns of the terminus are covered with patterns from Ninevah?—he will only care less for the Ninevite ivories in the British Museum: or on the North Western, because there are old English-looking spandrils to the roof of the station at Crewe?—he will only have less pleasure in their prototypes at Crewe House. Railroad architecture has, or would have, a dignity of its own if it were only left to its work. You would not put rings on the fingers of a smith at his anvil.

XXII. It is not however only in these marked situations that the abuse of which I speak takes place. There is hardly, at present, an application of ornamental work, which is not in some sort liable to blame of the same kind. We have a bad habit of trying to disguise disagreeable necessities by some form of sudden decoration, which is, in all other places, associated with such necessities. I will name only one instance, that to which I have alluded before—the roses which conceal the ventilators in the flat roofs of our chapels. Many of those roses are of very beautiful design, borrowed from fine works: all their grace and finish are invisible when they are so placed, but their general form is afterwards associated with the ugly buildings in which they constantly occur; and all the beautiful roses of the early French and English Gothic, especially such elaborate ones as those of the triforium of Coutances, are in consequence deprived of their pleasurable influence: and this without our having accomplished the smallest good by the use we have made of the dishonoured form. Not a single person in the congregation ever receives one ray of pleasure from those roof roses; they are regarded with mere indifference, or lost in the general impression of harsh emptiness.

XXIII. Must not beauty, then, it will be asked, be sought for in the forms which we associate with our every-day life? Yes, if you do it consistently, and in places where it can be calmly seen; but not if you use the beautiful form only as a mask and covering of the proper conditions and uses of things, nor if you thrust it into the places set apart for toil. Put it in the drawing-room, not into the workshop; put it upon domestic furniture, not upon tools of handicraft. All men have sense of what is right in this manner, if they would only use and apply that sense; every man knows where and how beauty gives him pleasure, if he would only ask for it when it does so, and not allow it to be forced upon him when he does not want it. Ask any one of the passengers over London Bridge at this instant whether he cares about the forms of the bronze leaves on its lamps, and he will tell you, No. Modify these forms of leaves to a less scale, and put them on his milk-jug at breakfast, and ask him whether he likes them, and he will tell you, Yes. People have no need of teaching if they could only think and speak truth, and ask for what they like and want, and for nothing else: nor can a right disposition of beauty be ever arrived at except by this common sense, and allowance for the circumstances of the time and place. It does not follow, because bronze leafage is in bad taste on the lamps of London Bridge, that it would be so on those of the Ponte della Trinita; nor, because it would be a folly to decorate the house fronts of Gracechurch Street, that it would be equally so to adorn those of some quiet provincial town. The question of greatest external or internal decoration depends entirely on the conditions of probable repose. It was a wise feeling which made the streets of Venice so rich in external ornament, for there is no couch of rest like the gondola. So, again, there is no subject of street ornament so wisely chosen as the fountain, where it is a fountain of use; for it is just there that perhaps the happiest pause takes place in the labour of the day, when the pitcher is rested on the edge of it, and the breath of the bearer is drawn deeply, and the hair swept from the forehead, and the uprightness of the form declined against the marble ledge, and the sound of the kind word or light laugh mixes with the trickle of the falling water, heard shriller and shriller as the pitcher fills. What pause is so sweet as that—so full of the depth of ancient days, so softened with the calm of pastoral solitude?

JOHN RUSKIN

Modern Manufacture and Design

LECTURE III

A Lecture Delivered at Bradford, March, 1859

It is with a deep sense of necessity for your indulgence that I venture to address you to-night, or that I venture at any time to address the pupils of schools of design intended for the advancement of taste in special branches of manufacture. No person is able to give useful and definite help towards such special applications of art, unless he is entirely familiar with the conditions of labour and natures of material involved in the work; and *in*definite help is little better than no help at all. Nay, the few remarks which I propose to lay before you this evening will, I fear, be rather suggestive of difficulties than helpful in conquering them: nevertheless, it may not be altogether unserviceable to define clearly for you (and this, at least, I am able to do) one or two of the more stern general obstacles which stand at present in the way of our success in design; and to warn you against exertion of effort in any vain or wasteful way, till these main obstacles are removed.

The first of these is our not understanding the scope and dignity of Decorative design. With all our talk about it, the very meaning of the words "Decorative art" remains confused and undecided. I want, if possible, to settle this question for you to-night, and to show you that the principles on which you must work are likely to be false, in proportion as they are narrow; true, only as they are founded on a perception of the connection of all branches of art with each other.

Observe, then, first—the only essential distinction between Decorative and other art is the being fitted for a fixed place; and in that place, related, either in subordination or command, to the effect of other pieces of art. And all the greatest art which the world has produced is thus fitted for a place, and subordinated to a purpose. There is no existing highest-order art but is decorative. The best sculpture yet produced has been the decoration of a temple front— the best painting, the decoration of a room. Raphael's best doing is merely the wall-colouring of a suite of apartments in the Vatican, and his cartoons were made for tapestries. Correggio's best doing is the decoration of two small church cupolas at Parma; Michael Angelo's, of a ceiling in the Pope's private

{47}

chapel; Tintoret's, of a ceiling and side wall belonging to a charitable society at Venice; while Titian and Veronese threw out their noblest thoughts, not even on the inside, but on the outside of the common brick and plaster walls of Venice.[1]

Get rid, then, at once of any idea of Decorative art being a degraded or a separate kind of art. Its nature or essence is simply its being fitted for a definite place; and, in that place, forming part of a great and harmonious whole, in companionship with other art; and so far from this being a degradation to it— so far from Decorative art being inferior to other art because it is fixed to a spot—on the whole it may be considered as rather a piece of degradation that it should be portable. Portable art—independent of all place—is for the most part ignoble art. Your little Dutch landscape, which you put over your sideboard to-day, and between the windows to-morrow, is a far more contemptible piece of work than the extents of field and forest with which Benozzo has made green and beautiful the once melancholy arcade of the Campo Santo at Pisa;[2] and the wild boar of silver which you use for a seal, or lock into a velvet case, is little likely to be so noble a beast as the bronze boar who foams forth the fountain from under his tusks in the market-place of Florence. It is, indeed, possible that the portable picture or image may be first-rate of its kind, but it is not first-rate because it is portable; nor are Titian's frescoes less than first-rate because they are fixed; nay, very frequently the highest compliment you can pay to a cabinet picture is to say—"It is as grand as a fresco."

Keeping, then, this fact fixed in our minds,—that all art *may* be decorative, and that the greatest art yet produced has been decorative,—we may proceed to distinguish the orders and dignities of Decorative art, thus:—

I. The first order of it is that which is meant for places where it cannot be disturbed or injured, and where it can be perfectly seen; and then the main parts of it should be, and have always been made, by the great masters, as perfect, and as full of nature as possible.

You will every day hear it absurdly said that room decoration should be by flat patterns—by dead colours—by conventional monotonies, and I know not what. Now, just be assured of this—nobody ever yet used conventional art to decorate with, when he could do anything better, and knew that what he did would be safe. Nay, a great painter will always give you the natural art, safe or not. Correggio gets a commission to paint a room on the ground floor of a palace at Parma: Any of our people—bred on our fine modern principles— would have covered it with a diaper, or with stripes or flourishes, or mosaic patterns. Not so Correggio:—he paints a thick trellis of vine-leaves, with oval openings, and lovely children leaping through them into the room; and lovely children, depend upon it, are rather more desirable decorations than diaper, if you can do them—but they are not quite so easily done. In like manner Tintoret has to paint the whole end of the Council Hall at Venice. An orthodox decorator would have set himself to make the wall look like a wall—Tintoret thinks it would be rather better, if he can manage it, to make it look a little like Paradise;—stretches his canvas right over the wall, and his clouds right over his canvas; brings the light through his clouds—all blue and clear—zodiac beyond zodiac; rolls away the vaporous flood from under the feet of saints, leaving them at last in infinitudes of light—unorthodox in the last degree, but, on the whole, pleasant.

And so in all other cases whatever, the greatest decorative art is wholly unconventional—downright, pure, good painting and sculpture, but always fitted for its place; and subordinated to the purpose it has to serve in that place.

II. But if art is to be placed where it is liable to injury—to wear and tear; or to alteration of its form; as, for instance, on domestic utensils, and armour, and weapons, and dress; in which either the ornament will be worn out by the usage of the thing, or will be cast into altered shape by the play of its folds; then it is wrong to put beautiful and perfect art to such uses, and you want forms of inferior art, such as will be by their simplicity less liable to injury; or, by reason of their complexity and continuousness, may show to advantage, however distorted by the folds they are cast into.

And thus arise the various forms of inferior decorative art, respecting which the general law is, that the lower the place and office of the thing, the less of natural or perfect form you should have in it; a zigzag or a chequer is thus a better, because a more consistent ornament for a cup or platter than a landscape or portrait is: hence the general definition of the true forms of conventional ornament is, that they consist in the bestowal of as much beauty on the object as shall be consistent with its Material, its Place, and its Office.

Let us consider these three modes of consistency a little.

(A.) Conventionalism by cause of inefficiency of material.

If, for instance, we are required to represent a human figure with stone only, we cannot represent its colour; we reduce its colour to whiteness. That is not elevating the human body, but degrading it; only it would be a much greater degradation to give its colour falsely. Diminish beauty as much as you will, but do not misrepresent it. So again, when we are sculpturing a face, we can't carve its eyelashes. The face is none the better for wanting its eyelashes—it is injured by the want; but would be much more injured by a clumsy representation of them.

Neither can we carve the hair. We must be content with the conventionalism of vile solid knots and lumps of marble, instead of the golden cloud that encompasses the fair human face with its waving mystery. The lumps of marble are not an elevated representation of hair—they are a degraded one; yet better than any attempt to imitate hair with the incapable material.

In all cases in which such imitation is attempted, instant degradation to a still lower level is the result. For the effort to imitate shows that the workman has only a base and poor conception of the beauty of the reality—else he would know his task to be hopeless, and give it up at once: so that all endeavours to avoid conventionalism, when the material demands it, result from insensibility to truth, and are among the worst forms of vulgarity. Hence, in the greatest Greek statues, the hair is very slightly indicated—not because the sculptor disdained hair, but because he knew what it was too well to touch it insolently. I do not doubt but that the Greek painters drew hair exactly as Titian does. Modern attempts to produce finished pictures on glass result from the same base vulgarism. No man who knows what painting means, can endure a painted glass window which emulates painter's work. But he rejoices in a glowing mosaic of broken colour: for that is what the glass has the special gift and right of producing.

(B.) Conventionalism by cause of inferiority of place.

When work is to be seen at a great distance, or in dark places, or in some other imperfect way, it constantly becomes necessary to treat it coarsely or severely, in order to make it effective. The statues on cathedral fronts, in good times of design, are variously treated according to their distances: no fine execution is put into the features of the Madonna who rules the group of figures above the south transept of Rouen at 150 feet above the ground: but in base modern work, as Milan Cathedral, the sculpture is finished without any reference to distance; and the merit of every statue is supposed to consist in the visitor's being obliged to ascend three hundred steps before he can see it.[3]

(C.) Conventionalism by cause of inferiority of office.

When one piece of ornament is to be subordinated to another (as the moulding is to the sculpture it encloses, or the fringe of a drapery to the statue it veils), this inferior ornament needs to be degraded in order to mark its lower office; and this is best done by refusing, more or less, the introduction of natural form. The less of nature it contains, the more degraded is the ornament, and the fitter for a humble place; but, however far a great workman may go in refusing the higher organisms of nature, he always takes care to retain the magnificence of natural lines; that is to say, of the infinite curves, such as I have analyzed in the fourth volume of "Modern Painters."[4] His copyists, fancying that they can follow him without nature, miss precisely the essence of all the work; so that even the simplest piece of Greek conventional ornament loses the whole of its value in any modern imitation of it, the finer curves being always missed. Perhaps one of the dullest and least justifiable mistakes which have yet been made about my writing, is the supposition that I have attacked or despised Greek work. I have attacked Palladian work, and modern imitation of Greek work. Of Greek work itself I have never spoken but with a reverence quite infinite: I name Phidias always in exactly the same tone with which I speak of Michael Angelo, Titian, and Dante. My first statement of this faith, now thirteen years ago, was surely clear enough. "We shall see by this light three colossal images standing up side by side, looming in their great rest of spirituality above the whole world horizon. Phidias, Michael Angelo, and Dante,—from these we may go down step by step among the mighty men of every age, securely and certainly observant of diminished lustre in every appearance of restlessness and effort, until the last trace of inspiration vanishes in the tottering affectation or tortured insanities of modern times." (*Modern Painters*, vol. ii., p. 63.)[5] This was surely plain speaking enough, and from that day to this my effort has been not less continually to make the heart of Greek work known than the heart of Gothic: namely, the nobleness of conception of form derived from perpetual study of the figure; and my complaint of the modern architect has been not that he followed the Greeks, but that he denied the first laws of life in theirs as in all other art.

The fact is, that all good subordinate forms of ornamentation ever yet existent in the world have been invented, and others as beautiful *can* only be invented, by men primarily exercised in drawing or carving the human figure. I will not repeat here what I have already twice insisted upon, to the students of London and Manchester, respecting the degradation of temper and intellect which follows the pursuit of art without reference to natural form, as among the Asiatics: here, I will only trespass on your patience so far as to mark the inseparable connection between figure-drawing and good ornamental work, in the great European schools, and all that are connected with them.

Tell me, then, first of all, what ornamental work is usually put before our students as the type of decorative perfection? Raphael's arabesques; are they not? Well, Raphael knew a little about the figure, I suppose, before he drew them. I do not say that I like those arabesques; but there are certain qualities in them which are inimitable by modern designers; and those qualities are just the fruit of the master's figure study.[6] What is given the student as next to Raphael's work? Cinquecento ornament generally. Well, cinquecento generally, with its birds, and cherubs, and wreathed foliage, and clustered fruit, was the amusement of men who habitually and easily carved the figure, or painted it. All the truly fine specimens of it have figures or animals as main parts of the design.

"Nay, but," some anciently or mediævally minded person will exclaim, "we don't want to study cinquecento. We want severer, purer conventionalism."

What will you have? Egyptian ornament? Why, the whole mass of it is made up of multitudinous human figures in every kind of action—and magnificent action; their kings drawing their bows in their chariots, their sheaves of arrows rattling at their shoulders; the slain falling under them as before a pestilence; their captors driven before them in astonied troops; and do you expect to imitate Egyptian ornament without knowing how to draw the human figure? Nay, but you will take Christian ornament—purest mediæval Christian—thirteenth century! Yes: and do you suppose you will find the Christian less human? The least natural and most purely conventional ornament of the Gothic schools is that of their painted glass; and do you suppose painted glass, in the fine times, was ever wrought without figures? We have got into the way, among our other modern wretchednesses, of trying to make windows of leaf diapers, and of strips of twisted red and yellow bands, looking like the patterns of currant jelly on the top of Christmas cakes; but every casement of old glass contained a saint's history. The windows of Bourges, Chartres, or Rouen have ten, fifteen, or twenty medallions in each, and each medallion contains two figures at least, often six or seven, representing every event of interest in the history of the saint whose life is in question. Nay, but, you say those figures are rude and quaint, and ought not to be imitated. Why, so is the leafage rude and quaint, yet you imitate that. The coloured border pattern of geranium or ivy leaf is not one whit better drawn, or more like geraniums and ivy, than the figures are like figures; but you call the geranium leaf idealized—why don't you call the figures so? The fact is, neither are idealized, but both are conventionalized on the same principles, and in the same way; and if you want to learn how to treat the leafage, the only way is to learn first how to treat the figure. And you may soon test your powers in this respect. Those old workmen were not afraid of the most familiar subjects. The windows of Chartres were presented by the trades of the town, and at the bottom of each window is a representation of the proceedings of the tradesmen at the business which enabled them to pay for the window. There are smiths at the forge, curriers at their hides, tanners looking into their pits, mercers selling goods over the counter—all made into beautiful medallions. Therefore, whenever you want to know whether you have got any real power of composition or adaptation in ornament, don't be content with sticking leaves together by the ends,—anybody can do that; but try to conventionalize a butcher's or a greengrocer's, with Saturday night customers buying cabbage and beef. That will tell you if you can design or not.

I can fancy your losing patience with me altogether just now. "We asked this fellow down to tell our workmen how to make shawls, and he is only trying to teach them how to caricature." But have a little patience with me, and examine, after I have done, a little for yourselves into the history of ornamental art, and you will discover why I do this. You will discover, I repeat, that all great ornamental art whatever is founded on the effort of the workman to draw the figure, and, in the best schools, to draw all that he saw about him in living nature. The best art of pottery is acknowledged to be that of Greece, and all the power of design exhibited in it, down to the merest zigzag, arises primarily from the workman having been forced to outline nymphs and knights; from those helmed and draped figures he holds his power. Of Egyptian ornament I have just spoken. You have everything given there that the workman saw: people of his nation employed in hunting, fighting, fishing, visiting, making love, building, cooking—everything they did is drawn, magnificently or familiarly, as was needed. In Byzantine ornament, saints, or animals which are types of various spiritual power, are the main subjects; and from the church down to the piece of enamelled metal, figure,—figure,—figure, always principal. In Norman and Gothic work you have, with all their quiet saints, also other much disquieted persons, hunting, feasting, fighting, and so on; or whole hordes of animals racing after each other. In the Bayeux tapestry, Queen Matilda gave, as well as she could,—in many respects graphically enough,—the whole history of the conquest of England. Thence, as you increase in power of art, you have more and more finished figures, up to the solemn sculptures of Wells Cathedral, or the cherubic enrichments of the Venetian Madonna dei Miracoli.[7] Therefore, I will tell you fearlessly, for I know it is true, you must raise your workman up to life, or you will never get from him one line of well-imagined conventionalism. We have at present no good ornamental design. We can't have it yet, and we must be patient if we want to have it. Do not hope to feel the effect of your schools at once, but raise the men as high as you can, and then let them stoop as low as you need; no great man ever minds stooping. Encourage the students, in sketching accurately and continually from nature anything that comes in their way—still life, flowers, animals: but, above all figures; and so far as you allow of any difference between an artist's training and theirs, let it be, not in what they draw, but in the degree of conventionalism you require in the sketch.

For my own part, I should always endeavour to give thorough artistical training first; but I am not certain (the experiment being yet untried) what results may be obtained by a truly intelligent practice of conventional drawing, such as that of the Egyptians, Greeks, or thirteenth century French, which consists in the utmost possible rendering of natural form by the fewest possible lines. The animal and bird drawing of the Egyptians is, in their fine age, quite magnificent under its conditions; magnificent in two ways—first, in keenest perception of the main forms and facts in the creature; and, secondly, in the grandeur of line by which their forms are abstracted and insisted on, making every asp, ibis, and vulture a sublime spectre of asp or ibis or vulture power. The way for students to get some of this gift again (*some* only, for I believe the fulness of the gift itself to be connected with vital superstition, and with resulting intensity of reverence; people were likely to know something about hawks and ibises, when to kill one was to be irrevocably judged to death) is never to pass a day without drawing some animal from the life, allowing themselves the fewest possible lines and colours to do it with, but resolving that whatever is characteristic of the animal shall in some way or other be shown.*[8] I repeat, it cannot yet be judged what results might be obtained by a nobly practised conventionalism of this kind; but, however that may be, the first fact,—the necessity of animal and figure drawing, is absolutely certain, and no person who shrinks from it will ever become a great designer.

One great good arises even from the first step in figure drawing, that it gets the student quit at once of the notion of formal symmetry. If you learn only to draw a leaf well, you are taught in some of our schools to turn it the other way, opposite to itself; and the two leaves set opposite ways are called "a design:" and thus it is supposed possible to produce ornamentation, though you have no more brains than a looking-glass or a kaleidoscope has. But if you once learn to draw the human figure, you will find that knocking two men's heads together does not necessarily constitute a good design; nay, that it makes a very bad design, or no design at all; and you will see at once that to arrange a group of two or more figures, you must, though perhaps it may be desirable to balance, or oppose them, at the same time vary their attitudes, and make one, not the reverse of the other, but the companion of the other.

I had a somewhat amusing discussion on this subject with a friend, only the other day; and one of his retorts upon me was so neatly put, and expresses so completely all that can either be said or shown on the opposite side, that it is well worth while giving it you exactly in the form it was sent to me. My friend had been maintaining that the essence of ornament consisted in three things:— contrast, series, and symmetry. I replied (by letter) that "none of them, nor all of them together, would produce ornament. Here"—(making a ragged blot with the back of my pen on the paper)—"you have contrast; but it isn't ornament: here, 1, 2, 3, 4, 5, 6,"—(writing the numerals)—"you have series; but it isn't ornament: and here,"— (sketching this figure at the side)—"you have symmetry; but it isn't ornament."

My friend replied:—

*Plate 75 is Vol. V. of Wilkinson's "Ancient Egypt" will give the student an idea of how to set to work.

"Your materials were not ornament, because you did not apply them. I send them to you back, made up into a choice sporting neckerchief:—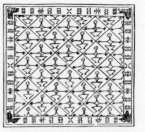

Symmetrical figure . .   Unit of diaper.
Contrast . . . . .   Corner ornaments.
Series . . . . .   Border ornaments.

Each figure is converted into a harmony by being revolved on its two axes, the whole opposed in contrasting series."

My answer was—or rather was to the effect (for I must expand it a little, here)—that his words, "because you did not apply them," contained the gist of the whole matter;—that the application of them, or any other things, was precisely the essence of design;—the non-application, or wrong application, the negation of design: that his use of the poor materials was in this case admirable; and that if he could explain to me, in clear words, the principles on which he had so used them, he would be doing a very great service to all students of art.

"Tell me, therefore (I asked), these main points:

"1. How did you determine the number of figures you would put into the neckerchief? Had there been more, it would have been mean and ineffective,—a pepper-and-salt sprinkling of figures. Had there been fewer, it would have been monstrous. How did you fix the number?

"2. How did you determine the breadth of the border and relative size of the numerals?

"3. Why are there two lines outside of the border, and one only inside? Why are there no more lines? Why not three and two, or three and five? Why lines at all to separate the barbarous figures; and why, if lines at all, not double or treble instead of single?

"4. Why did you put the double blots at the corners? Why not at the angles of the chequers,—or in the middle of the border?

"It is precisely your knowing why *not* to do these things, and why to do just what you have done, which constituted your power of design; and like all the people I have ever known who had that power, you are entirely unconscious of the essential laws by which you work, and confuse other people by telling them that the design depends on symmetry and series, when, in fact, it depends entirely on your own sense and judgment."

This was the substance of my last answer—to which (as I knew beforehand would be the case) I got no reply; but it still remains to be observed that with all the skill and taste (especially involving the architect's great trust, harmony of proportion), which my friend could bring to bear on the materials given him, the result is still only—a sporting neckerchief—that is to say, the materials ad-

dressed, first, to recklessness, in the shape of a mere blot; then to computative-
ness, in a series of figures; and then to absurdity and ignorance, in the shape of
an ill-drawn caricature—such materials, however treated, can only work up
into what will please reckless, computative, and vulgar persons,—that is to say,
into a sporting neckerchief. The difference between this piece of ornamentation and Correggio's painting at Parma lies simply and wholly in the additions
(somewhat large ones), of truth and of tenderness: in the drawing being lovely
as well as symmetrical—and representative of realities as well as agreeably disposed. And truth, tenderness, and inventive application or disposition are indeed the roots of ornament—not contrast, nor symmetry.

It ought yet farther to be observed, that *the nobler the materials, the less their
symmetry is endurable.* In the present case, the sense of fitness and order, produced by the repetition of the figures, neutralizes, in some degree, their reckless
vulgarity; and is wholly, therefore, beneficent to them. But draw the figures
better, and their repetition will become painful. You may harmlessly balance a
mere geometrical form, and oppose one quatrefoil or cusp by another exactly
like it. But put two Apollo Belvideres back to back, and you will not think the
symmetry improves them.[9] *Whenever the materials of ornament are noble, they
must be various;* and repetition of parts is either the sign of utterly bad, hopeless, and base work; or of the intended degradation of the parts in which such
repetition is allowed, in order to foil others more noble.

Such, then, are a few of the great principles, by the enforcement of which
you may hope to promote the success of the modern student of design; but remember, none of these principles will be useful at all, unless you understand
them to be, in one profound and stern sense, useless.*

That is to say, unless you feel that neither you nor I, nor any one, can, in the
great ultimate sense, teach anybody how to make a good design.

If designing *could* be taught, all the world would learn: as all the world
reads—or calculates. But designing is not to be spelled, nor summed. My men
continually come to me, in my drawing class in London, thinking I am to teach
them what is instantly to enable them to gain their bread. "Please, sir, show us
how to design." "Make designers of us." And you, I doubt not, partly expect me
to tell you to-night how to make designers of your Bradford youths. Alas! I
could as soon tell you how to make or manufacture an ear of wheat, as to make
a good artist of any kind. I can analyze the wheat very learnedly for you—tell
you there is starch in it, and carbon, and silex. I can give you starch, and char-
coal, and flint; but you are as far from your ear of wheat as you were before. All

*I shall endeavour for the future to put my self-contradictions in short sentences and di-
rect terms, in order to save sagacious persons the trouble of looking for them.

that can possibly be done for any one who wants ears of wheat is to show them where to find grains of wheat, and how to sow them, and then, with patience, in Heaven's time, the ears will come—or will perhaps come—ground and weather permitting. So in this matter of making artists—first you must find your artist in the grain; then you must plant him; fence and weed the field about him; and with patience, ground and weather permitting, you may get an artist out of him—not otherwise. And what I have to speak to you about, to-night, is mainly the ground and the weather, it being the first and quite most material question in this matter, whether the ground and weather of Bradford, or the ground and weather of England in general,—suit wheat.

. . .

We are about to enter upon a period of our world's history in which domestic life, aided by the arts of peace, will slowly, but at last entirely, supersede public life and the arts of war. For our own England, she will not, I believe, be blasted throughout with furnaces; nor will she be encumbered with palaces. I trust she will keep her green fields, her cottages, and her homes of middle life; but these ought to be, and I trust will be enriched with a useful, truthful, substantial form of art. We want now no more feasts of the gods, nor martyrdoms of the saints; we have no need of sensuality, no place for superstition, or for costly insolence. Let us have learned and faithful historical painting—touching and thoughtful representations of human nature, in dramatic painting; poetical and familiar renderings of natural objects and of landscape; and rational, deeply felt realizations of the events which are the subjects of our religious faith. And let these things we want, as far as possible, be scattered abroad and made accessible to all men.

So also, in manufacture: we require work substantial rather than rich in make; and refined, rather than splendid in design. Your stuffs need not be such as would catch the eye of a duchess; but they should be such as may at once serve the need, and refine the taste, of a cottager. The prevailing error in English dress, especially among the lower orders, is a tendency to flimsiness and gaudiness, arising mainly from the awkward imitation of their superiors.* It should be one of the first objects of all manufacturers to produce stuffs not

---

*If their superiors would give them simplicity and economy to imitate, it would, in the issue, be well for themselves, as well as for those whom they guide. The typhoid fever of passion for dress, and all other display, which has struck the upper classes of Europe at this time, is one of the most dangerous political elements we have to deal with. Its wickedness I have shown elsewhere (Polit. Economy of Art, p. 62, *et seq.*); but its wickedness is, in the minds of most persons, a matter of no importance. I wish I had time also to show them its danger. I cannot enter here into political investigation; but this is a certain fact, that the

only beautiful and quaint in design, but also adapted for every-day service, and decorous in humble and secluded life. And you must remember always that your business, as manufacturers, is to form the market, as much as to supply it. If, in shortsighted and reckless eagerness for wealth, you catch at every humour of the populace as it shapes itself into momentary demand—if, in jealous rivalry with neighbouring States, or with other producers, you try to attract attention by singularities, novelties, and gaudinesses—to make every design an advertisement, and pilfer every idea of a successful neighbour's, that you may insidiously imitate it, or pompously eclipse—no good design will ever be possible to you, or perceived by you. You may, by accident, snatch the market; or, by energy, command it; you may obtain the confidence of the public, and cause the ruin of opponent houses; or you may, with equal justice of fortune, be ruined by them. But whatever happens to you, this, at least, is certain, that the whole of your life will have been spent in corrupting public taste and encouraging public extravagance. Every preference you have won by gaudiness must have been based on the purchaser's vanity; every demand you have created by novelty has fostered in the consumer a habit of discontent; and when you retire into inactive life, you may, as a subject of consolation for your declining years, reflect that precisely according to the extent of your past operations, your life has been successful in retarding the arts, tarnishing the virtues, and confusing the manners of your country.

But, on the other hand, if you resolve from the first that, so far as you can ascertain or discern what is best, you will produce what is best, on an intelligent consideration of the probable tendencies and possible tastes of the people whom you supply, you may literally become more influential for all kinds of good than many lecturers on art, or many treatise-writers on morality. Considering the materials dealt with, and the crude state of art knowledge at the time, I do not know that any more wide or effective influence in public taste was ever exercised than that of the Staffordshire manufacture of pottery under William Wedgwood;[10] and it only rests with the manufacturer in every other business to determine whether he will, in like manner, make his wares educational instruments, or mere drugs of the market. You all should be, in a certain sense, authors: you must, indeed, first catch the public eye, as an author must the public

---

wasteful and vain expenses at present indulged in by the upper classes are hastening the advance of republicanism more than any other element of modern change. No agitators, no clubs, no epidemical errors, ever were, or will be, fatal to social order in any nation. Nothing but the guilt of the upper classes, wanton, accumulated, reckless, and merciless, ever overthrows them. Of such guilt they have now much to answer for—let them look to it in time. [J. Ruskin, *The Political Economy of Art* (London, 1857)]

ear; but once gain your audience, or observance, and as it is in the writer's power thenceforward to publish what will educate as it amuses—so it is in yours to publish what will educate as it adorns. Nor is this surely a subject of poor ambition. I hear it said continually that men are too ambitious: alas! to me, it seems they are never enough ambitious. How many are content to be merely the thriving merchants of a state, when they might be its guides, counsellors, and rulers—wielding powers of subtle but gigantic beneficence, in restraining its follies while they supplied its wants. Let such duty, such ambition, be once accepted in their fulness, and the best glory of European art and of European manufacture may yet be to come. The paintings of Raphael and of Buonaroti gave force to the falsehoods of superstition, and majesty to the imaginations of sin; but the arts of England may have, for their task, to inform the soul with truth, and touch the heart with compassion. The steel of Toledo and the silk of Genoa did but give strength to oppression and lustre to pride: let it be for the furnace and for the loom of England, as they have already richly earned, still more abundantly to bestow, comfort on the indigent, civilization on the rude, and to dispense, through the peaceful homes of nations, the grace and the preciousness of simple adornment, and useful possession.

NOTES

1. Ruskin refers to the most famous fresco painters of sixteenth-century Italy—Raphael (1483–1520), Michelangelo (1475–1564), Correggio (1489–1534), Titian (1487/88–1576), Veronese (1528–1588), and Tintoretto (1519–1594)—to argue that even masterpieces were originally suited to a purpose.

2. Benozzo Gozzoli (1420/22–1497) was a follower of Fra Angelico whose most famous frescoes were done to complete the fourteenth-century decoration of Camposanto, Pisa.

3. The neo-Gothic façade of the Milan Cathedral was built between 1806–13 by Carlo Amati.

4. J. Ruskin, *Modern Painters*, 5 vols. (London, 1846–1860).

5. Ibid.

6. See K. P. Moritz's excerpt on Raphael's arabesques in Part III.

7. The examples are meant to show an increasing complexity of figurative and narrative style. The Bayeux Tapestry, an embroidered strip of linen telling the story of the Norman Conquest of England in 1066, is now presumed to have been made for Odo, Bishop of Bayeux (1030–1097), and was previously thought to have been embroidered by Queen Matilda; Wells Cathedral contains the largest body of early Gothic sculpture in England; and the Venetian church of the Madonna dei Miracoli has a tympanum façade, showing a Virgin and Child by Pyrgoteles, c. 1510.

8. Ruskin is referring to Plate 75, "Birds, snakes, and some insects from the sculptures." John Gardner Wilkinson's book *Manners and Customs of the Ancient Egyptians* (London, 1837) was initially published as three volumes. Later, two volumes of text were published as

the *Second Series*; when referring to "Volume 5," Ruskin undoutedly meant volume 2 of the second volume of the second series in which the birds and animals illustrated in Plate 75 are discussed.

9. The Roman sculpture, the Apollo Belvedere (in the Belvedere Courtyard of the Musei Vaticani, Rome), was discovered in the late fifteenth century, and until the late nineteenth century was believed to be a Greek original.

10. Ruskin probably means Josiah Wedgwood (rather than William Wedgwood—who cannot be identified), who founded the famous English ceramic company in 1759.

WILLIAM MORRIS

The Arts and Crafts of To-day

AN ADDRESS DELIVERED IN EDINBURGH BEFORE
THE NATIONAL ASSOCIATION FOR THE ADVANCEMENT
OF ART IN OCTOBER, 1889

"Applied Art" is the title which the Society has chosen for that portion of the arts which I have to speak to you about. What are we to understand by that title? I should answer that what the Society means by applied art is the ornamental quality which men choose to add to articles of utility. Theoretically this ornament can be done without, and art would then cease to be "applied"—would exist as a kind of abstraction, I suppose. But though this ornament to articles of utility may be done without, man up to the present time has never done without it, and perhaps never will; at any rate he does not propose to do so at present, although, as we shall see presently, he has got himself into somewhat of a mess in regard to his application of art. Is it worth while for a moment or two considering why man has never thought of giving up work which adds to the labour necessary to provide him with food and shelter, and to satisfy his craving for some exercise of his intellect? I think it is, and that such consideration will help us in dealing with the important question which once more I must attempt to answer, "What is our position towards the applied arts in the present, and what have we to hope for them and from them in the future?"

Now I say without hesitation that the purpose of applying art to articles of utility is twofold: first, to add beauty to the results of the work of man, which would otherwise be ugly; and secondly, to add pleasure to the work itself, which would otherwise be painful and disgustful. If that be the case, we must cease to wonder that man should always have striven to ornament the work of his own hands, which he must needs see all round about him daily and hourly; or that he should have always striven to turn the pain of his labour into a pleasure wherever it seemed possible to him.

Now as to the first purpose: I have said that the produce of man's labour must be ugly if art be not applied to it, and I use the word ugly as the strongest plain word in the English language. For the works of man cannot show a mere negation of beauty; when they are not beautiful they are actively ugly, and are thereby degrading to our manlike qualities; and at last so degrading that we are not sensible of our degradation, and are therefore preparing ourselves for the next step downward. This active injury of non-artistic human work I want especially to fix in your minds; so I repeat again, if you dispense with applying art to articles of utility, you will not have unnoticeable utilities, but utilities which will bear with them the same sort of harm as blankets infected with the small-pox or the scarlet-fever, and every step in your material life and its "progress" will tend towards the intellectual death of the human race.

Of course you will understand that in speaking of the works of man, I do not forget that there are some of his most necessary labours to which he cannot apply art in the sense wherein we are using it; but that only means that Nature has taken the beautifying of them out of his hands; and in most of these cases the processes are beautiful in themselves if our stupidity did not add grief and anxiety to them. I mean that the course of the fishing-boat over the waves, the plough-share driving the furrow for next year's harvest, the June swathe, the shaving falling from the carpenter's plane, all such things are in themselves beautiful, and the practice of them would be delightful if man, even in these last days of civilization, had not been so stupid as to declare practically that such work (without which we should die in a few days) is the work of thralls and starvelings, whereas the work of destruction, strife, and confusion, is the work of the pick of the human race—gentlemen to wit.

But if these applied arts are necessary, as I believe they are, to prevent mankind from being a mere ugly and degraded blotch on the surface of the earth, which without him would certainly be beautiful, their other function of giving pleasure to labour is at least as necessary, and, if the two functions can be separated, even more beneficent and indispensable. For if it be true, as I know it is, that the function of art is to make labour pleasurable, what is the position in which we must find ourselves without it? One of two miseries must happen to us: either the necessary work of our lives must be carried on by a miserable set of helots for the benefit of a few lofty intellects; or if, as we ought to do, we determine to spread fairly the burden of the curse of labour over the whole community, yet there the burden will be, spoiling for each one of us a large part of that sacred gift of life, every fragment of which, if we were wise, we should treasure up and make the most of (and allow others to do so) by using it for the pleasurable exercise of our energies, which is the only true source of happiness.

Let me call your attention to an analogy between the function of the applied arts and a gift of Nature without which the world would certainly be much unhappier, but which is so familiar to us that we have no proper single word for it, and must use a phrase; to wit, the pleasure of satisfying hunger. Appetite is the single word used for it, but is clearly vague and unspecific: let us use it, however, now we have agreed as to what we mean by it.

By the way, need I apologize for introducing so gross a subject as eating and drinking? Some of you perhaps will think I ought to, and are looking forward to the day when this function also will be civilized into the taking of some intensely concentrated pill once a year, or indeed once in a life-time, leaving us free for the rest of our time to the exercise of our intellect—if we chance to have any in those days. From this height of cultivated aspiration I respectfully beg to differ, and in all seriousness, and not in the least in the world as a joke, I say that the daily meeting of the house-mates in rest and kindness for this function of eating, this restoration of the waste of life, ought to be looked on as a kind of sacrament, and should be adorned by art to the best of our powers: and pray pardon me if I say that the consciousness that there are so many people whose lives are so sordid, miserable, and anxious, that they cannot duly celebrate this sacrament, should be felt by those that can, as a burden to be shaken off by remedying the evil, and not by ignoring it. Well now, I say, that as eating would be dull work without appetite, or the pleasure of eating, so is the production of utilities dull work without art, or the pleasure of production; and that it is Nature herself who leads us to desire this pleasure, this sweetening of our daily toil. I am inclined to think that in the long-run mankind will find it indispensable; but if that turn out to be a false prophecy, all I can say is that mankind will have to find out some new pleasure to take its place, or life will become unendurable, and society impossible. Meantime it is reasonable and right that men should strive to make the useful wares which they produce beautiful just as Nature does; and that they should strive to make the making of them pleasant, just as Nature makes pleasant the exercise of the necessary functions of sentient beings. To apply art to useful wares, in short, is not frivolity, but a part of the serious business of life.

Now let us see in somewhat more detail what applied art deals with. I take it that it is only a matter of convenience that we separate painting and sculpture from applied art: for in effect the synonym for applied art is architecture, and I should say that painting is of little use, and sculpture of less, except where their works form a part of architecture. A person with any architectural sense really always looks at any picture or any piece of sculpture from this point of view; even with the most abstract picture he is sure to think, How shall I frame it, and where shall I put it? As for sculpture, it becomes a mere toy, a tour de force, when it is not definitely a part of a building, executed for a certain height from the eye, and to be seen in a certain light. And if this be the case with works of art which can to a certain extent be abstracted from their surroundings, it is, of course, the case a fortiori with more subsidiary matters. In short, the complete work of applied art, the true unit of the art, is a building with all its due orna-ment and furniture; and I must say from experience that it is impossible to or-nament duly an ugly or base building. And on the other hand I am forced to say that the glorious art of good building is in itself so satisfying, that I have seen many a building that needed little ornament, wherein all that seemed needed for its complete enjoyment was some signs of sympathetic and happy use by human beings: a stout table, a few old-fashioned chairs, a pot of flowers will ornament the parlour of an old English yeoman's house far better than a wagon-load of Rubens will ornament a gallery in Blenheim Park.[1]

Only remember that this forbearance, this restraint in beauty, is not by any means necessarily artless: where you come upon an old house that looks thus satisfactory, while no conscious modern artist has been at work there, the result is caused by unconscious unbroken tradition: in default of that, in will march that pestilential ugliness I told you of before, and with its loathsome pretence and hideous vulgarity will spoil the beauty of a Gothic house in Somersetshire, or the romance of a peel-tower on the edge of a Scotch loch; and to get back any of the beauty and romance (you will never get it all back) you will need a conscious artist of to-day, whose chief work, however, will be putting out the intrusive rubbish and using the white-washing brush freely.

Well, I repeat that the unit of the art I have to deal with is the dwelling of some group of people, well-built, beautiful, suitable to its purpose, and duly ornamented and furnished so as to express the kind of life which the inmates live. Or it may be some noble and splendid public building, built to last for ages, and it also duly ornamented so as to express the life and aspirations of the citizens: in itself a great piece of history of the efforts of the citizens to raise a house worthy of their noble lives, and its mere decoration an epic wrought for the pleasure and education, not of the present generation only, but of many generations to come. This is the true work of art—I was going to say of genuine civilization, but the word has been so misused that I will not use it—the true work of art, the true masterpiece, of reasonable and manly men conscious of the bond of true society that makes everything each man does of importance to every one else.

This is, I say, the unit of the art, this house, this church, this town-hall, built and ornamented by the harmonious efforts of a free people: by no possibility could one man do it, however gifted he might be: even supposing the director or architect of it were a great painter and a great sculptor, an unfailing designer of metal work, of mosaic, of woven stuffs and the rest—though he may design all these things, he cannot execute them, and something of his genius must be in the other members of the great body that raises the complete work: millions on millions of strokes of hammer and chisel, of the gouge, of the brush, of the shuttle, are embodied in that work of art, and in every one of them is either intelligence to help the master, or stupidity to foil him hopelessly. The very masons laying day by day their due tale of rubble and ashlar may help him to fill the souls of all beholders with satisfaction, or may make his paper design a folly or a nullity. They and all the workmen engaged in the work will bring that disaster about in spite of the master's mighty genius, unless they are instinct with intelligent tradition; unless they have that tradition, whatever pretence of art there is in it will be worthless. But if they are working backed by intelligent tradition, their work is the expression of their harmonious co-operation and the pleasure which they took in it: no intelligence, even of the lowest kind, has been crushed in it, but rather subordinated and used, so that no one from the master designer downwards could say, This is my work, but every one could say truly, This is our work. Try to conceive, if you can, the mass of pleasure which the production of such a work of art would give to all concerned in making it, through years and years it may be (for such work cannot be hurried); and when made there it is for a perennial pleasure to the citizens, to look at, to use, to care for, from day to day and year to year.

Is this a mere dream of an idealist? No, not at all; such works of art were once produced, when these islands had but a scanty population, leading a rough and to many (though not to me) a miserable life, with a "plentiful lack" of many, nay most, of the so-called comforts of civilization; in some such way have the famous buildings of the world been raised; but the full expression of this spirit of common and harmonious work is given only during the comparatively short period of the developed Middle Ages, the time of the completed combination of the workmen in the gilds of craft.

And now if you will allow me I will ask a question or two, and answer them myself.

1. Do we wish to have such works of art? I must answer that we here assembled certainly do, though I will not answer for the general public.

2. Why do we wish for them? Because (if you have followed me so far) their production would give pleasure to those that used them and those that made them: since if such works were done, all work would be beautiful and fitting for its purpose, and as a result most labour would cease to be burdensome.

3. Can we have them now as things go? Can the present British Empire, with all its power and all its intelligence, produce what the scanty, half-barbarous, superstitious, ignorant population of these islands produced with no apparent effort several centuries ago? No; as things go we cannot have them; no conceivable combination of talent and enthusiasm could produce them as things are.

Why? Well, you see, in the first place, we have been engaged for at least one century in loading the earth with huge masses of "utilitarian" buildings, which we cannot get rid of in a hurry; we must be housed, and there are our houses for us; and I have said you cannot ornament ugly houses. This is a bad hearing for us.

· · ·

This parenthesis, to the subject of which I shall presently have to recur, leads me to note here that I have been speaking chiefly about architecture, because I look upon it, first as the foundation of all the arts, and next as an all-embracing art. All the furniture and ornament which goes to make up the complete unit of art, a properly ornamented dwelling, is in some degree or other beset with the difficulties which hamper nowadays the satisfactory accomplishment of good and beautiful building. The decorative painter, the mosaicist, the window-artist, the cabinet-maker, the paper-hanging-maker, the potter, the weaver, all these have to fight with the traditional tendency of the epoch in their attempt to produce beauty rather than marketable finery, to put artistic finish on their work rather than trade finish. I may, I hope, without being accused of egotism, say that my life for the last thirty years has given me ample opportunity for knowing the weariness and bitterness of that struggle.

For, to recur to my parenthesis, if the captain of industry (as it is the fashion to call a business man) thinks not of the wares with which he has to provide the world-market, but of profit to be made from them, so the instrument which he employs as an adjunct to his machinery, the artisan, does not think of the wares which he (and the machine) produces as wares, but simply as livelihood for himself. The tradition of the work which he has to deal with has brought him to this, that instead of satisfying his own personal conception of what the wares he is concerned in making should be, he has to satisfy his master's view of the marketable quality of the said wares. And you must understand that this is a necessity of the way in which the workman works; to work thus means livelihood for him; to work otherwise means starvation. I beg you to note that this means that the realities of the wares are sacrificed to commercial shams of them, if that be not too strong a word. The manufacturer (as we call him) cannot turn out quite nothing and offer it for sale, at least in the case of articles of utility; what he does do is to turn out a makeshift of the article demanded by the public, and by means of the "sword of cheapness," as it has been called, he not only can force the said makeshift on the public, but can (and does) prevent them from getting the real thing; the real thing presently ceases to be made after the makeshift has been once foisted on to the market.

Now we won't concern ourselves about other makeshifts, however noxious to the pleasure of life they may be: let those excuse them that profit by them. But if you like to drink glucose beer instead of malt beer, and to eat oleo-margarine instead of butter; if these things content you, at least ask yourselves what in the name of patience you want with a makeshift of art!

Indeed I began by saying that it was natural and reasonable for man to ornament his mere useful wares and not to be content with mere utilitarianism; but of course I assumed that the ornament was real, that it did not miss its mark, and become no ornament. For that is what makeshift art means, and that is indeed a waste of labour.

Try to understand what I mean: you want a ewer and basin, say: you go into a shop and buy one; you probably will not buy a merely white one; you will scarcely see a merely white set. Well, you look at several, and one interests you about as much as another—that is, not at all; and at last in mere weariness you say, "Well, that will do"; and you have your crockery with a scrawl of fern leaves and convolvulus over it which is its "ornament." The said ornament gives you no pleasure, still less any idea; it only gives you an impression (a mighty dull one) of bedroom. The ewer also has some perverse stupidity about its handle which also says bedroom, and adds respectable: and in short you endure the said ornament, except perhaps when you are bilious and uncomfortable in health. You think, if you think at all, that the said ornament has wholly missed its mark. And yet that isn't so; that ornament, that special form which the ineptitude of the fern scrawl and the idiocy of the handle has taken, has sold so many dozen or gross more of that toilet set than of others, and that is what it is put there for; not to amuse you, you know it is not art, but you don't know that it is trade finish, exceedingly useful—to everybody except its user and its actual maker.

But does it serve no purpose except to the manufacturer, shipper, agent, shopkeeper, etc.? Ugly, inept, stupid, as it is, I cannot quite say that. For if, as the saying goes, hypocrisy is the homage which vice pays to virtue, so this degraded piece of trade finish is the homage which commerce pays to art. It is a token that art was once applied to ornamenting utilities, for the pleasure of their makers and their users.

Now we have seen that this applied art is worth cultivating, and indeed that we are here to cultivate it; but it is clear that, under the conditions above spoken of, its cultivation will be at least difficult. For the present conditions of life in which the application of art to utilities is made imply that a very serious change has taken place since those works of co-operative art were produced in the Middle Ages, which few people I think sufficiently estimate.

Briefly speaking, this change amounts to this, that Tradition has transferred itself from art to commerce—that commerce which has now embraced the old occupation of war, as well as the production of wares. But the end proposed by commerce is the creation of a market-demand, and the satisfaction of it when created for the sake of the production of individual profits: whereas the end proposed by art applied to utilities, that is, the production of the days before commerce, was the satisfaction of the genuine spontaneous needs of the public, and the earning of individual livelihood by the producers. I beg you to consider these two ideas of production, and you will then see how wide apart they are from one another. To the commercial producer the actual wares are nothing; their adventures in the market are everything. To the artist the wares are everything; his market he need not trouble himself about; for he is asked by other artists to do what he does do, what his capacity urges him to do.

The ethics of the commercial person (squaring themselves of course to his necessities) bid him give as little as he can to the public, and take as much as he possibly can from them: the ethics of the artist bid him put as much of himself as he can in every piece of goods he makes. The commercial person, therefore, is in this position, that he is dealing with a public of enemies; the artist, on the contrary, with a public of friends and neighbours.

Again, it is clear that the commercial person must chiefly confine his energies to the war which he is waging; the wares that he deals in must be made by instruments—as far as possible by means of instruments without desires or passions, by automatic machines, as we call them. Where that is not possible, and he has to use highly-drilled human beings instead of machines, it is essential to his success that they should imitate the passionless quality of machines as long as they are at work; whatever of human feeling may be irrepressible will be looked upon by the commercial person as he looks upon grit or friction in his non-human machines, as a nuisance to be abated. Need I say that from these human machines it is futile to look for art? Whatever feelings they may have for art they must keep for their leisure—that is, for the very few hours in the week when they are trying to rest after labour and are not asleep; or for the hapless days when they are out of employment and are in desperate anxiety about their livelihood.

Of these men, I say, you cannot hope that they can live by applying art to utilities: they can only apply the sham of it for commercial purposes; and I may say in parenthesis, that from experience I can guess what a prodigious amount of talent is thus wasted. For the rest you may consider, and workmen may consider, this statement of mine to be somewhat brutal: I can only reply both to you and to them, that it is a truth which it is necessary to face. It is one side of the disabilities of the working class, and I invite them to consider it seriously.

Therefore (as I said last year at Liverpool), I must turn from the great body of men who are producing utilities, and who are debarred from applying art to them, to a much smaller group, indeed a very small one. I must turn to a group of men who are not working under masters who employ them to produce for the world-market, but who are free to do as they please with their work, and are working for a market which they can see and understand, whatever the limitations may be under which they work: that is, the artists.

They are a small and a weak body, on the surface of things obviously in op-position to the general tendency of the age; debarred, therefore, as I have said, from true co-operative art; and as a consequence of this isolation heavily weighted in the race of success. For co-operative tradition places an artist at the very beginning of his career in a position wherein he has escaped the toil of learning a huge multitude of little matters, difficult, nay impossible to learn otherwise: the field which he has to dig is not a part of a primeval prairie, but ground made fertile and put in good heart by the past labour of countless gen-erations. It is the apprenticeship of the ages, in short, whereby an artist is born into the workshop of the world.

We artists of to-day are not so happy as to share fully in this apprenticeship: we have to spend the best part of our lives in trying to get hold of some "style" which shall be natural to us, and too often fail in doing so; or perhaps oftener still, having acquired our "style," that is, our method of expression, become so enamoured of the means, that we forget the end, and find that we have nothing to express except our self-satisfaction in the possession of our very imperfect instrument; so that you will find clever and gifted men at the present day who are prepared to sustain as a theory, that art has no function but the display of clever executive qualities, and that one subject is as good as another. No won-der that this theory should lead them into the practice of producing pictures which we might pronounce to be clever, if we could understand what they meant, but whose meaning we can only guess at, and suppose that they are in-tended to convey the impression on a very short-sighted person of divers ugly incidents seen through the medium of a London fog.

Well I admit that this is a digression, as my subject is Applied Art, and such art cannot be applied to anything; and I am afraid, indeed, that it must be con-sidered a mere market article.

Thus we artists of to-day are cut off from co-operative tradition, but I must not say that we are cut off from all tradition. And though it is undeniable that we are out of sympathy with the main current of the age, its commercialism, yet we are (even sometimes unconsciously) in sympathy with that appreciation of history which is a genuine growth of the times, and a compensation to some of us for the vulgarity and brutality which beset our lives; and it is through this sense of history that we are united to the tradition of past times.

· · ·

In short, we artists are in this position, that we are the representatives of craftsmanship which has become extinct in the production of market wares. Let us therefore do our very best to become as good craftsmen as possible; and if we cannot be good craftsmen in one line, let us go down to the next, and find our level in the arts, and be good in that; if we are artists at all, we shall be sure to find out what we can do well, even if we cannot do it easily. Let us educate ourselves to be good workmen at all events, which will give us real sympathy with all that is worth doing in art, make us free of that great corporation of creative power, the work of all ages, and prepare us for that which is surely coming, the new co-operative art of life, in which there will be no slaves, no vessels to dishonour, though there will necessarily be subordination of capacities, in which the consciousness of each one that he belongs to a corporate body, working harmoniously, each for all, and all for each, will bring about real and happy equality.

NOTE

1. Morris is here referring to the British tradition of filling palaces, like Blenheim Palace (completed c. 1725), with paintings by such Renaissance and Baroque Continental painters as Rubens and Titian. Peter Paul Rubens (1577–1640), a leading Flemish painter, was especially patronized by English royalty such as Charles I (1625–1649).

SAMUEL BING

Where Are We Going?

In the great crises of history, when we are shocked into realizing the decadence into which we have fallen, and the source of the ills that have sapped our former strength, remedies emerge in the form of new theories, which we instantly turn into immovable principles. Nothing is more dangerous than the abuse of such universal remedies. We have already seen, in my article in the second number of this journal, the consequences of the misguided notion that we can rejuvenate our art by going back to Nature.[1] Another, no less dangerous theory asserts that all artistic activities belong to one family, denounces the division of art into separate fields, and takes particular exception to the view that a distinction exists between high and low arts.

The principle that all arts are equal in value and are connected with each other has led to the conclusion that all must pursue one and the same goal, and that they enshrine one common ideal. Finally, from the supposition that the most disparate talents are all equally suited to any artistic activity, it was but a step to the encroachment of one art upon another.

We have all welcomed, as a happy and progressive event, the liberation of painters and sculptors from their hierarchical prejudices; and we are grateful to them for using their influence to foster the elevation of handicraft, and for extending a helping hand to save it from foundering. A host of artists—highly respected artists—have turned aside from abstract contemplation and have not only created forms and models but made utilitarian objects with their own hands. Now that a number of years have passed since the inception of this tendency, it is already possible to discern the nature of its consequences.

We must confess that the results fall far short of our early expectations. This tendency, which filled all our hearts with the hope of a new dawn, has indeed something to offer to the pleasure-loving taste of dilettantism. It has given us works of the greatest value, when judged by the aesthetic criteria of pure art; but of these very few conform to the original practical program. Let us look for the causes of this disappointment. The principle—so simple that one is almost embarrassed to write it down—that the structure of any object must be governed, first and foremost, by the rigorous law of specific function, seems altogether too simple to be grasped by the ever-complicated artistic mind, with its constant fixation on the Ideal. The need, in creating a utilitarian object, to determine the class to which it belongs and consider the methods of construction most appropriate to its practical use; the question whether the object, once made, can be reproduced by a rational process: such are the issues that must be resolved before one ever starts to think of outward embellishments or artistic originality. But minds accustomed to soar in more exalted regions cannot, it seems, be expected to pay serious attention to such prosaic matters without doing violence to the true artistic temperament.

The contrast between the two classes of qualities is all too obvious. How are we to expect privileged beings, endowed by Nature with the gift of finding ideal forms to convey the loftier sense, the deeper meaning that they infuse into material things—how are we to expect such dreamers to display a considered understanding of the precise conditions of practical living? In all that they do, their visionary nature, the ineradicable stamp of the tradition to which they are bred, will out—even against their will and without their knowledge. All such artists, who devote themselves to the rebirth of handicraft with valuable inventive gifts, but without strict obedience to the discipline of the métier, will find their clientele in a select circle of amateurs who seek only to possess unique and precious objects, and to whom it is a matter of total indifference whether or not the works in question are models of practical usefulness.

There are, of course, some gratifying exceptions: cases in which an artist becomes conscious that the nature of his own talent is propelling him in a new direction. To be successful, such an artist must put his former work out of his mind, and devote himself body and soul to his new vocation. Like every human activity that aspires to bear lasting fruit, this demands unstinting commitment and hard work—all the more so because the artist lacks the fundamental experience that only a long, practical apprenticeship can confer.

I do not want these remarks to be misunderstood. It is a delight to find an artist who has previously worked only with brush, pencil, or chisel, expanding his expressive range and gaining access to sources that have all too long been cut off from the higher regions of art. Such is the liberation that we owe to the precious contents of our showcases. If these new departures had brought us only such creations as the drinking glasses by Koepping—masterworks that are a delight to the eye, though they have no pretension to handicraft status—or the bronze lamp by Vallgren, which is intended for use but priced at 1,500 francs, then we should have cause enough to celebrate the revival of a specialized art form that was the pride of former ages: the art of the magnificent showpiece.[2] We must be thankful for every enrichment of the realm of beauty; for it can never be too rich. With objects of this sort, however, utility is an irrelevance; they offer no basis for the development of handicraft.

The moral of all this is that we must not shrink from upholding the old division of art into two clearly defined camps—except that a new factor has emerged, which somewhat alters the method of classification.

On one side is everything that owes its existence to the principle of *L'ART POUR L'ART:* the art that seeks only to gratify the eye or the mind. First of all—as in the former classification—this includes large-scale sculpture and easel painting, to which must be added all those objects that spring from the fantastic or poetic imagination, whatever the name under which they present themselves. On the other side is Useful Art [*Nützliche Kunst*] (whether we choose to call it by that name or by that of decorative or applied art): the art which must confine itself to exclusively ornamental or purely practical functions, and which ought, logically speaking, to include architecture.

With every object thus firmly assigned to its category, ideas will be clarified. Once every artist is quite clear in his own mind, before starting a piece of work, as to the category to which he intends it to belong, then we shall see an end of the multitude of errors that cast a cloud over the future and threaten the existence of the fine movement of which the late nineteenth century is so proud.

NOTES

1. The first part of Bing's article appeared in *Dekorative Kunst* 1 (1897–98): 1–3, 68–71.

2. Karl Koepping (1848–1914) was a German engraver and designer, known for his glassware designs in Art Nouveau style; Ville Vallgren (1855–1940) was a Finnish sculptor who made miniature bronze figurines and objets d'art, participating in the Berlin, Munich, and Vienna Secessionist exhibitions among others.

HERMANN MUTHESIUS

The Significance of Applied Art

Wherein lies the significance of modern applied art? How does this small and specialized field, of which until recently the wider public knew nothing, come to be a subject of academic teaching? The aim of my lectures during the present semester will be to discuss the importance and the wider relevance of this topic. An outline of the genesis and evolution of the applied art idea will serve as a logical framework for an account of the significance of applied art, both for the present and, no doubt in increased measure, for the future. However, in this introductory lecture, it may be worthwhile playing a spotlight, as it were, across the subject as it presently confronts us, in order to identify the most important points in advance and to understand their significance. Our detailed arguments will thus have a better-defined end in view, and our conclusions will emerge with greater clarity.

The significance of modern applied art is, at one and the same time, artistic, cultural, and economic. I mention its artistic significance first, both because it is more or less self-explanatory and because, until very recently, this exhausted the significance of the whole movement. The cultural significance of applied art is not yet so clearly visible; the forces involved are only now beginning to operate. As for its economic significance, this lies almost exclusively in the future. Even so, it may be possible to rest our hopes on historic parallels.

In Germany, the artistic significance of applied art became evident to all through a documentary event of the first importance that occurred last summer. The Third German Applied Art Exhibition, which recently closed its doors in Dresden, set out for all to see the present state of the applied arts in Germany.[1] It may therefore be in order to outline that present state in a few brief words.

Every visitor to the Dresden exhibition must first have been struck by the fact that all the work on show, from a small piece of embroidery to a fully decorated and furnished room, spoke a distinctive artistic language. This language has nothing in common with that of the old applied art, which was in its heyday in the 1880s and 1890s. A fundamental change of aim has taken place. The use of external decorations of historic styles is no longer on the agenda; there is an effort to speak a new, autonomous, artistic language. That is the most evident feature of the products of modern applied art. To have escaped from the rut in which the last century was stuck, with its constant filtering and refiltering of historic art, represents a major achievement. Only a youthful and enthusiastic age could have taken such a step.

Centuries had passed since there had last been a fresh start in the realm of style. When the Renaissance abandoned the principles of the Gothic, there was the same enthusiasm for innovation that we have seen in the modern applied art movement; at that time, however, the only aim in view was to appropriate the newly rediscovered forms of antiquity. People were not looking forward but backward. Of course, during the Renaissance and since, much that is new has evolved from those antique forms. Whether by exploring byways or by introducing elements from outside, Arab (German Renaissance ornament), Chinese (Rococo art), or other, every successive trend has created a formal language so specific to its own time that we can now date it almost within a decade. But everything still represented a variation on a theme that had been defined once and for all by the antique. The most autonomous of these variations was the Rococo, a sudden outburst of idiosyncrasy that remains the closest parallel to the revolutionary tendencies of modern applied art, with its abandonment of all that has gone before. Modern applied art does not, however, allow any admixture of material from historic or exotic sources: its leitmotiv is the principle of autonomous design.

Whatever one may think of the tangible results of this effort to eschew historical allusions, one thing is certain: the attempt to create works of convincing artistic effect on the basis of an absolutely autonomous design has been successful. Friend and foe alike must confess as much; and none of the movement's foes has ever dared deny that this is a major national achievement, and one that must not be underrated.

Evident though this outward aspect of the phenomenon may be, the motivating power behind the modern applied art movement does not consist exclusively, or even mainly, in the adoption of new forms unknown to historic art. It lies, rather, in an idea of applied art utterly different from that of the 1880s and 1890s. Then, designers worked in a state of infatuation with the art of the past. Such was their infatuation that they longed to produce works exactly like those of their historic forerunners. And yet their "exactly like" applied only to the outward form. They forgot that outward form could only be an expression of the inner influences that prevailed when the objects were first made; that objects from the past were perfect solely because they constituted a cogent formal expression of the intellectual, material, and social circumstances of their time. No one thought to reflect that the intellectual, material, and social circumstances of our time were totally different—and that to imitate the outward appearance of bygone artifacts was to put fakes into circulation. In itself, the rapid turnover of styles in the latter half of the nineteenth century only goes to show how little relation there was between the outward form of these brand-new objects and the spirit of the age in which they were made. They wore a stylistic garb that might be likened to those masquerade costumes that we wear for one evening and change at will.

The impulse to break free of fancy dress and face up to the circumstances of our own time is the prime motivating power of the new movement in applied art. The circumstances of the time are reflected, first of all, in the necessary demand for practicality. The practical demands for which old furnishings and utensils were made differ in many ways from those of modern use. The shape of a chair relates to domestic and social customs, as well as to fashions in dress. Table manners now are very different from those of the past; a far greater concern with cleanliness has led to the invention of new utensils; our sense of hygiene is not so much improved as entirely new. As a result, domestic arrangements have changed. The old stock of utensils has been augmented by a quantity of new ones; others have changed their basic shapes; and a fair number of old items have fallen out of use. Our habits of life are in the midst of a total transformation.

To respond to the conditions of the age in which we live, we must first do justice to the specific factors that govern the individual object. At the very outset, the sum and substance of modern applied art was this: first to clarify the function of the object, and then to evolve the form from that function. However, as soon as the designer's mind was diverted from the superficial imitation of older art—as soon as he faced reality—other necessary demands added themselves. Every material imposes conditions of its own. Stone and wood require different dimensions and forms; so do wood and metal; and, among metals, so do wrought iron and silver. Design based on function thus came together with design based on the character of the material; and with respect for material went respect for the form of construction appropriate to that material. Function, material, and construction are the only imperatives that the modern artist-craftsman observes.

In actuality, the form of the object is not always exclusively determined by these three fundamental principles of design. For human feeling intervenes between the mind and the hand. And it intervenes with particular force in those works that are designed to please. The engineer may be able to exclude emotion—though even this is doubtful; at all events, it would be totally absurd to expect an artist-designer to suppress emotion, and with it imagination, in order to develop forms through a mathematical and logical train of thought. There is an emotional element in modern applied art—perhaps more so than in the past. But an emotion that is channeled into the effort to achieve the outward appearance of historic art is very different from an emotion that is free of historical reminiscences. In any case, the strict principle of design by function, material, and construction provides a bulwark against any relapse into historical sentiment, and thus into irrationality.

Design based on historical reminiscences almost inevitably entailed a violation of these three principles. This is all too apparent from the applied art of the age of imitation (mainly the second half of the nineteenth century). It was an age of rapidly changing fashions in style; and it was also the age that witnessed the worst excesses of irrational ornament and counterfeit material. Substitutes and simulations were everywhere. Wood was simulated in fireproof pasteboard, stone in stucco or even in galvanized iron, bronze in pewter. Even the most basic sense of propriety had been lost. And why? Mostly because the prevalence of historical sentimentality had left people infatuated with outward form. The adherents of modern applied art have outgrown the attitudes of that period; but the general public and the common craft trades are still utterly mired in them. As witness the German painter and decorator, who regards it as the summit of his art to make papier-mâché look like walnut wood, or a galvanized bathtub like marble.

The new applied art despises all these simulations and substitutes. No simulation of any kind: let every object appear to be what it is; let every material appear in its own character. And so, one of the most significant principles of craft design emerges: that of inner truthfulness. With it comes its corollary, the principle of sound workmanship. For sound workmanship is none other than the outward and visible sign of an inward truth. As a matter of simple logic, there has thus emerged a principle that was almost entirely lost from view in the industrial production of the nineteenth century. True enough, other factors, economic and social, played their parts in its loss; but it was the emergence of a vigorous applied art movement that established the primacy of sound workmanship. Here may well lie the movement's most fruitful achievement, and its most far-reaching consequences.

However, it is also here that the struggle against the status quo is the most difficult. To apply the principles of truthfulness and sound workmanship to anything, even in the field of handicrafts, is to impugn the attitudes of a whole generation. No one looks for sound workmanship until his own character has undergone the necessary evolution. The applied arts in the nineteenth century lost touch with the idea of sound workmanship because the consumer classes attached no importance to it. Social pretensions were a direct result of the power struggle between classes. The emergent bourgeoisie had a need for ostentation and display, but no means of satisfying it, except superficial and inexpensive ones. On these it depended in its efforts to rival, if not outdo, those classes that had traditionally been its betters. This was an entirely unprecedented situation for any member of the middle class. The nineteenth-century bourgeois norm was the ambition—not to say the pathological craving—to seem more than one was.

We now take this so much for granted that we are barely aware of it. But we can illustrate its reality by mentally comparing a room in the house of a prosperous present-day bourgeois with one belonging to a person of equivalent status in Chodowiecki's day; or by comparing the décor favored by a stage celebrity of the present, as shown in *Die Woche,* with the rooms in Goethe's house in Weimar.[2] I need not describe the details: anyone can call them to mind. On one side ostentation, on the other unassuming modesty; here a room crammed with specious pomp, and there the utmost decency and restraint; here a second-hand, gimcrack version of aristocratic art, and there the unvarnished bourgeois spirit.

To this very day, alas, interior decoration in Germany is exclusively founded on social pretensions; and its needs are supplied by an art industry that works with simulations and substitutes. For the modern applied art movement, this is the sticking point. Here, mountains must be scaled and strongholds stormed. Will the war be won? It is still hard to say. But one thing is clear; applied art now faces a daunting educative task. And in this it has already progressed far beyond any popularly accepted definition of its role. It is becoming something more than applied art: it is becoming a means of cultural education. Applied art now has the goal of reeducating all classes of present-day society in the virtues of sound workmanship, truthfulness, and bourgeois simplicity. If it succeeds, it will profoundly alter our culture, and the consequences will be far-reaching. Not only will it transform the rooms and buildings in which people live: it will directly influence the character of a generation. To teach people how to arrange their rooms decently is to educate their character, by doing away with the parvenu pretentiousness that gives rise to current fashions in décor.

By observing the true principles of the new movement in applied art, we thus expand the importance of applied art to society. But, even in purely artistic terms, we can already see how the once-narrow limits of applied art are being overstepped. Starting from the basic idea of giving a tasteful form to craft products, applied art has already become a force that transforms the look of our homes themselves. As a consequence, before long we shall have a new culture of domesticity. Such is the goal toward which applied art now aspires.

It is only a step from the décor of a room to the design of a dwelling house. It can already be observed how architecture, beginning with that of small country houses, is coming under the influence of the applied arts. The new movement in domestic architecture may be broadly defined as follows: the ornate villa, with its load of historical paraphernalia, is replaced by a simple house that conforms to rural, vernacular patterns and is built in accordance with logical and practical principles. This revolution in architectural thinking is the same that has led from the old applied art, with its use of historical forms, to the new applied art, based on practical principles. The applied art influence here is evident, even if unconscious. And the simple logic of applied art is about to extend still further into the realm of architecture. The new trend in country-house building is only the beginning of a move toward simplicity in architecture as a whole. Given the enormous importance of architecture within the culture of any age, it may be said that the true mission of the applied art movement will be accomplished only when its principles are extended to the whole field of private and public architecture.

The movement that has made such a vigorous start in the applied arts has its parallels in the arts of painting and sculpture. I can do no more than allude to these here. In recent painting, there is an effort to compose in the rigorous spirit of the mural painting of the past. This marked characteristic of our own time is evident in poster design, in the graphic arts, and in illustration, as well as in some departments of painting. Sculpture, too, shows a welcome tendency toward a taut stylization, a lapidary quality, that leaves behind it the genre tendencies and theatrical affectations of recent times. Perhaps the most gratifying sign of this is the new Bismarck Memorial in Hamburg.

. . .

Since it first appeared within applied art, the new movement has spread through all the arts, so that it can already be described as a universal artistic movement. At the same time, it must be admitted that it has remained an almost exclusively intellectual movement, with little or no impact on the economic life of our time. Born and nurtured in intellectual circles, it has hitherto spread from mind to mind. In a field of activity that is a business as well as an art, the new movement has to find its feet in economic terms. Which is where the difficulties begin. These might well seem to have been exacerbated, just recently, when those with vested interests in applied art, the manufacturers and dealers, denounced the new movement and its exponents, the Applied Art Exhibition in Dresden, and the schools of arts and crafts. As is well known, a petition with hundreds of signatures was handed to the state governments of the Reich. This might appear to constitute a serious threat to the applied art movement: it might seem that an adversary has arisen, armed with sufficient economic power to destroy all the artistic initiatives that have taken place in the world of handicraft.

To put all such fears in their true perspective, we have only to reflect that the applied art movement is a spontaneous product of the intellectual life of the age. It springs from an inner necessity, whereas the objections to it are purely pecuniary in nature. The protests represent nothing more than the signatories' dismay at the constant advance of new ideas, year after year, which has disturbed—not to say overturned—customary ways of doing business in the applied art industry. Hence the protests. Fundamentally, these are no more than a welcome sign that a movement hitherto confined to a small group of intellectuals is now hammering on the gates of the art industry, and undermining its foundations where they are weakest. The protesters are those who stood to gain most from the status quo—in which the manufacturer professed to be guided by public taste, while in fact the public meekly accepted the stylistic idiocies foisted upon it by the manufacturer. Suddenly, the customers are starting to think for themselves; they are startled and excited by the things that artists are producing; they have seen exhibitions and glimpsed wondrous, harmonious interior designs created by artists. They are beginning to doubt the advice that they get from manufacturers and dealers. It is only natural and human for the manufacturer and the dealer to resist such inconvenient developments. It is equally clear that all their protests and attacks are destined to fall silent in the face of a massive groundswell within the culture of the age.

What is more, it is already becoming clear that it is by no means an act of commercial suicide to give one's allegiance to the modern movement. A number of producers of applied art who have logically and consistently followed this path have achieved a notable commercial success. I need only mention the Dresden Art Handicraft Workshops [Dresdner Werkstätten für Handwerkskunst], which in eight years have evolved from modest beginnings into a concern that employs cabinetmakers by the hundreds and measures its turnover in millions.[3] One thing is necessary: the manufacturer must be committed to the new movement, not only as a matter of financial self-interest but with his whole heart. Then, success is ensured. In fact, we may say that the future is not on the side of those who denounce the new movement but of those who join it. For they are swept forward by the intellectual tide of the age, against which the others vainly attempt to make headway.

At all events, the most urgent issue of the day is that of the economics of the new applied art. It is no solution to have the artisans and the factories simply make things in a so-called new style instead of in historical styles. This has already been tried, with the *Jugendstil* or Secession style, which industry presented as its latest stylistic offering, only to see it rapidly superseded in its turn by Empire and Biedermeier revivals.[4] The ideas behind the new applied art are too serious to be caught up in this frivolous game of stylistic fashion. The applied art movement is not about any such thing as a "modern style." To proclaim anything of the sort would be hasty and facile. A new style does not emerge overnight, and cannot be invented. It arises from the earnest aspirations of a whole age; it is the visible manifestation of the inner, spiritual impulses of the time. If those impulses are authentic, then an authentic—i.e., original and enduring—style will emerge; but if they are facile and superficial, then the result will be something like the rapid succession of stylistic imitations that we have seen over the past fifty years. It is impossible to predict, at present, what style will emerge from the serious efforts that are currently being made within modern applied art. The answer can only be guessed at. It is not for us to compel the age to furnish us with a style; our business is to be creative, with total commitment and sincerity, and in ways that we can answer for with a clear conscience. Style cannot be anticipated: it is the sum of the honest aspirations of an age. It will be for posterity to define the style of our time: that is, to determine what common features are to be discerned in the most substantial and most serious efforts of the best people now working.

Such is the aspiration that impels our present leaders in the applied art movement; we may therefore expect that, without any deliberate intention on their part, they will evolve the style of our time, simply by pressing forward and following their own inner impulse. As for industry, the best it can do is to espouse this aspiration. To do so, however, would require a fundamental reappraisal of its position. For the manufacturer has hitherto made a point of declining to mix ethics or morality with his business, which he professes to conduct strictly in accordance with the supposed wishes of the public. As a result, things have been made to look dear and sell cheap. The public, in every social class, has snapped them up in vast quantities. This way of doing business, and the acquiescence of the public, has ended by demoralizing producers and consumers alike. For what manufacturer can derive satisfaction from producing trash all his life? And what customer can take enduring pleasure in worthless articles? It is time for a complete change of heart, and this has to begin with the producer. He need only transfer to his business the decent and upright principles that govern his private life. As a private man, he does not act reprehensibly; and so, as a man of business, he must not produce reprehensibly. That is to say, he must not produce objects that are simulations and substitutes: things that pretend to be something more than they are.

It is perfectly possible, as anyone knows who is familiar with English life and attitudes, for such principles to become the common property of a whole nation. The English manufacturer, almost without exception, takes the line of following his own best conviction and producing none but workmanlike objects. However much advantage German craftsmanship may have derived of late from its celebrated adaptability, in areas connected with applied art and art manufactures this adaptability has in many cases proved to be a curse.

Fortunately, the taste for sound workmanship that is an accepted part of the English way of life has recently become more widespread in Germany also—a fact not unrelated to increased affluence. Here, once more, a wider historical tendency chimes with the basic principles of the applied art movement. No simulation of any kind: let every object appear to be what it is! It would be an enormous step forward, if manufacturing industry were to follow the example of applied art in this respect. For it stands to reason that when articles are not soundly made, however much labor is put into them, the best use is not made of the raw material. And so on the one hand a colossal sum of national wealth is squandered on that raw material; and on the other a futile piece of work is done. In the last resort, cheap things are dearer in every way than expensive ones.

. . .

The new applied art, which in Germany has already overstepped its own boundaries and become a universal art movement—and is indeed on the point of becoming a universal cultural movement—must, as it grows further, draw its economic consequences. And it is mainly from this viewpoint that it will be my task, in the lectures that follow, to give an account of its evolution to date.

NOTES

1. The Third German Applied Art Exhibition in Dresden was held in 1906–07.

2. Muthesius is here referring to the German-Polish painter and engraver Daniel Nikolaus Chodowiecki (1726–1801), known for recording the life and manners of the German middle class; the comparison is between the relative simplicity of Goethe's house in Weimar, where he died in 1832, and the overfilled interiors of turn of the century German houses.

3. The Dresden Workshops, founded in the spirit of craft revival, were associated with the *Jugendstil* (see note 4).

4. The *Jugendstil* was the German version of the French Art Nouveau style, based on sinuous organic forms, though more favorable to industrial design than the French version; the name comes from one of the earliest German art and crafts journals, *Jugend*, based in Munich. The German Biedermeier style is the name given to German architecture and decorative arts from c. 1820 to 1860; its name is derived from a fictional character, Gottlieb Biedermeier, in the journal, *Fliegende Blätter*, caricaturing middle-class vulgarity and philistinism.

WALTER GROPIUS

Manifesto of the Staatliche Bauhaus in Weimar

The ultimate aim of all visual arts is the complete building! To embellish buildings was once the noblest function of the fine arts; they were the indispensable components of great architecture. Today the arts exist in isolation, from which they can be rescued only through the conscious, cooperative effort of all craftsmen. Architects, painters, and sculptors must recognize anew and learn to grasp the composite character of building both as an entity and in its separate parts. Only then will their work be imbued with the architectonic spirit which it has lost as "salon art."

The old schools of art were unable to produce this unity; how could they, since art cannot be taught. They must be merged once more with the workshop. The mere drawing and painting world of the pattern designer and the applied artist must become a world that builds again. When young people who take a joy in artistic creation once more begin their life's work by learning a trade, then the unproductive "artists" will no longer be condemned to deficient artistry, for their skill will now be preserved for the crafts, in which they will be able to achieve excellence.

Architects, sculptors, painters, we all must return to the crafts! For art is not a "profession." There is no essential difference between the artist and the craftsman. The artist is an exalted craftsman. In rare moments of inspiration, transcending the consciousness of his will, the grace of heaven may cause his work to blossom into art. But proficiency in a craft is essential to every artist. Therein lies the prime source of creative imagination. Let us then create a new guild of craftsmen without the class distinctions that raise an arrogant barrier between craftsman and artist! Together let us desire, conceive, and create the new structure of the future, which will embrace architecture and sculpture and painting in one unity and which will one day rise toward heaven from the hands of a million workers like the crystal symbol of a new faith.

Type-Needs: Type-Furniture

Here we quit the anguished realms of fantasy and the incongruous, and resume a code with reassuring articles. The poet goes into decline, it's true; he chucks up cornices and baldacchinos and makes himself more useful as a cutter in a tailor's shop, with a man standing in front of him and he, metre in hand, taking measurements. Here we are back on *terra firma.* The uplifting calm of certainty!

When one factor in our technico-cerebro-emotional equation grows disproportionately, a crisis occurs, since the relationships are disturbed—the relationships between our cerebro-emotional being and the things we use that are around us: we continue to make them as before, or else we anticipate or react against recognized reality. The feeling for cause and effect falters. We are seized by disquiet because we no longer feel well adapted; we revolt against our enforced servitude to the *abnormal,* whether it is retrogressive or too far ahead of its time.

The compass will save us from this disturbance; the compass in this case is ourselves: a man, a constant, the fixed point that in truth is the only object of our concern. We must therefore always seek to rediscover the *human scale,* the human function.

Since the crisis has now come to a head, there is no more urgent task than to force ourselves to re-adjust to our functions, in all fields. To free our attention for a few moments from bondage to its habitual tasks and to think about *the why,* reflect, weigh up, decide. And to answer *the why* with innocence, simplicity, and candour. This is as much as to say, to set aside our acquired preconceptions, to deposit our fund of memories in the safe of our bank in the third basement, behind a steel door, and leaving alongside it the whole poetic of the past, to formulate our most fundamental desires.

To search for the human scale, for human function, is to define human needs.

They are not very numerous; they are very similar for all mankind, since man has been made out of the same mould from the earliest times known to us. Faced with the task of providing a definition of man, Larousse calls on just three images to portray his anatomy; the whole machine is there, the structure, the nervous system, the arterial system, and this applies to every single one of us exactly and without exception.[1]

These needs are type, that is to say they are the same for all of us; *we all need means of supplementing our natural capabilities,* since nature is indifferent, inhuman (extra-human), and inclement; we are born naked and with insufficient armour. Thus the cupped hands of Narcissus led us to invent the bottle; the barrel of Diogenes, already a notable improvement on our natural protective organs (our skin and scalp), gave us the primordial cell of the house; filing cabinets and copy-letters make good the inadequacies of our memory; wardrobes and sideboards are the containers in which we put away the auxiliary limbs that guarantee us against cold or heat, hunger or thirst, etc. These apparently paradoxical definitions take us far from Decorative Art; they are the very reason for this chapter.

In speaking of decorative art, we have the right to insist on the type-quality of our needs, since our concern is with the mechanical system that surrounds us, which is no more than an extension of our limbs; its elements, in fact, *artificial limbs.* Decorative art becomes orthopaedic, an activity that appeals to the imagination, to invention, to skill, but a craft analogous to the tailor: the client is a man, familiar to us all and precisely defined.

This view is shared by the designers of car bodywork, the furnishers of cinemas, the manufacturers of glassware and crockery, even by the architects who design apartments to let. Nevertheless, one of the big names in charge of the 1925 Exhibition recently disagreed violently; with his heart set on multifold poetry, he proclaimed the need of each individual for something different, claiming different circumstances in each case: the fat man, the thin man, the short, the long, the ruddy, the lymphatic, the violent, the mild, the utopian, and the neurasthenic; then the vocations: the dentist, and the man of letters, the architect and the merchant, the navigator and the astronomer, etc. He sees the character of an individual as dictating his every act, and by an elliptical process of reasoning, as shaping his tools—tools that will be particular, individual, and unique to him, and have nothing in common with those of his neighbour. *Life, that's life, I believe in nothing but life. You are killing the individual!* Thus a fabulous, uncountable field of activity for the orthopaedist, a field whose limitless immensity makes one dizzy.[2]

Would this then be, at last, miraculously, *the much sought after definition of the term:* DECORATIVE ART? To the *tool-object,* the *human-limb object,* is now opposed the *sentiment-object,* the *life-object.*

The argument would hold, since at the last count it is indisputable that only *poetry,* that is to say, happiness, carries authority. But first let us recognise the practical impossibility of this dream of an individual *sentiment-object,* in all its infinite multiplicity; let us observe that our interlocutor in fact has in mind an *objet d'art,* and we will reply to that later. And so, since happiness is our objective, let us propose an alternative definition of happiness: happiness lies in the creative faculty, in the most elevated possible activity. Life (and the cost of living!) subjects us to labour (labour that is generally imposed, and therefore scarcely creative) and for a great many people their hour of happiness is very far from the hours spent earning their bread. An elevated activity: to manage, by means of those stimulants which for us are the achievements of life—that is, music, books, the creations of the spirit—to lead a life that is truly one's own, truly oneself. That means a life that is *individual;* and thus *the individual is placed on the highest level, the only level,* but detached from the secondary level of his tools. These activities of the spirit, this introspection, which can delve only a little way, or very deeply, is life itself, that is, one's internal life, one's true life. So in no sense has life been killed, thank God! And neither has the individual!

Sentiment-objects or *objets d'art* are nothing but dross in comparison with this inner fire—slight charm and certain encumbrance, most likely trifles, clowns, jesters—intended merely for distraction (I am speaking here of decorative *objets d'art*). The legitimate *sentiment-object* lies far off and higher up, in a purified abode on a more elevated plane; then it is a *work of art,* and as such it is another matter altogether. For we may certainly believe in a hierarchy, and not put a piece of poker-work on the same level as the *Sistine Chapel* (nor glass beads, embroidery, or ornamental woodwork). But we will return to that later, and rest content for the time being with this initial classification.

For our comfort, to facilitate our work, to avoid exhaustion, to refresh ourselves, in one word to *free our spirit* and distance us from the clutter that encumbers our life and threatens to *kill it,* we have equipped ourselves through our ingenuity with *human-limb objects,* extensions of our limbs; and by making use of these tools, we avoid unpleasant tasks, accidents, the sterile drudgery which according to our interlocutor constitutes precisely the richness and multiplicity of life; we *organise our affairs* and, having won our freedom, we think about something—about art for example (for it is very comforting).

The *human-limb objects* are type-objects, responding to type-needs: chairs to sit on, tables to work at, devices to give light, machines to write with (yes indeed!), racks to file things in.

If our spirits vary, our skeletons are alike, our muscles are in the same places and perform the same functions: dimensions and mechanism are thus fixed. So the problem is posed and the question is: who will solve it ingeniously, reliably, and cheaply? Since we are sensitive to the harmony that brings repose, we recognise an object that is in harmony with our limbs. When *a* and *b* are equal to *c, a* and *b* are equal to each other. In this case, *a* = our *human-limb objects; b* = our sense of harmony; *c* = our body. Thus *human-limb objects* are in accord with our sense of harmony in that they are in accord with our bodies.* So we are satisfied . . . *until the next development in these tools.*

We have now identified decorative art as commensurate with the art of the engineer. The art of the engineer extends across a wide spectrum of human activity. If at one extreme it encompasses pure calculation and mechanical invention, at the other it leads towards *Architecture.*

Can one then speak of the architecture of decorative art, and consider it capable of permanent value?

The permanent value of decorative art? Let us say more exactly, of the *objects* that surround us. This is where we exercise our judgement: first of all the Sistine Chapel, afterwards chairs and filing cabinets; without doubt this is a question of the secondary level, just as the cut of a man's jacket is of secondary importance in his life. Hierarchy. First of all the Sistine Chapel, that is to say works truly etched with passion. Afterwards machines for sitting in, for filing, for lighting, type-machines, the problem of purification, of simplification, of precision, before the problem of poetry.[†]

*When the typewriter came into use, letter paper was standardised; this standardisation had considerable repercussions upon furniture as a result of the establishment of a module, that of the *commercial format.* Typewriters, file-copies, filing trays, files, filing drawers, filing cabinets, in a word the whole furnishing industry, was affected by the establishment of this standard; and even the most intransigent individualists were not able to resist it. An international convention was established. These questions are of such importance that international commissions meet regularly to establish the standards. The *commercial format* is not an arbitrary measure. Rather, let us appreciate the wisdom (the anthropocentric mean) that established it. In all things that are in universal use, individual fantasy bows before human fact. Here are some figures: the ratio of vertical to horizontal dimension in the commercial format is 1·3. That of a sheet of Ingres paper is 1·29. That of the sectors of the plans of Paris established by Napoleon I is 1·33; that of the Taride plans 1·33. That of most magazines 1·28. That of canvases for figure painting (time-honoured sizes) is 1·30. That of daily newspapers from 1·3 to 1·45. That of photographic plates 1·5; that of books 1·4 to 1·5, that of kitchen tables in the Bazaar de l'Hotel-de-Ville 1·5; etc., etc.

[†]Having established this hierarchy—that is, this channelling of our attention only to those things worthy of it—there remains all round us that group of tools which *we call furniture.* During the long and scrupulous process of development in the factory, the Thonet chair gradually takes on its final weight and thickness, and assumes a format that allows good connections; this process of perfecting by almost imperceptible steps is the same as that to which an engine is subjected, whose poetry is to run well—and cheaply. The Maples armchair, which is attuned to our movements and quick to respond to them, assumes an ever

Much has happened since the age of the Great Kings: the human spirit is more at home behind our foreheads than beneath gilt and carved baldacchinos. 'You have suppressed everything that money can provide'; significant words. Gold, lacquer, marble, brocade are caresses which we look for in the garden of caresses: the ballet, the dance-halls, the elegant restaurants where we dine. Caresses of our senses which are perfectly legitimate at the right time and which deserve to be given well.

Eventually we leave, take a few steps in the bracing air, and return home. We pick up a book or a pen. In this mechanical, discreet, silent, attentive comfort, there is a very fine painting on the wall. Or else: our movements take on a new assurance and precision among walls whose proportions make us happy, and whose colours stimulate us.

Decorative art is an inexact and wordy phrase by which we denote the totality of *human-limb objects*. These respond with some precision to certain clearly established needs. They are extensions of our limbs and are adapted to human functions that are type-functions. Type-needs, type-functions, therefore type-objects and type-furniture.

The human-limb object is a docile servant. A good servant is discreet and self-effacing, in order to leave his master free.

Certainly, works of decorative art are tools, beautiful tools.

And long live the good taste manifested by choice, suitability, proportion, and harmony!

NOTES

1. Le Corbusier is referring to the famous French publishing family of encyclopedias and dictionaries; his definition probably comes from the *Nouveau Larousse illustré* (7 vols., 1897–1904).

---

more distinctive profile. The stenographer's desk becomes daily more convenient in the battle of the market place. We have seen the 'American desk', which seemed to have achieved definitive form, make an about-turn because its development showed up a flaw in its conception. We have learnt that in the context of the rigorous order demanded by business, *it is necessary to have a file on the filing system itself.* The businessman appends to himself supporting limbs: his secretary, his accountant, etc. His documents need a precise place according to type; they are put away in a particular drawer, and the game of filing cards allows them to be retrieved immediately; this function has staff assigned to it, and they have their own furniture. The 'American desk' filed things in a disorderly fashion. So now we have the invaluable arrays of precisely detailed filing cabinets. This new system of filing which clarifies our needs, has an effect on the lay-out of rooms, and of buildings. We have only to introduce this method into our apartments and decorative art will meet its destiny: type-furniture and architecture.

2. Le Corbusier could here be referring to the French architect and writer Charles Plumet (1861–1928); with Louis Bonnier, Plumet was in charge of the general plan and architectural programs for the 1925 Exposition Internationale des Arts Décoratifs et Industriels in Paris.

THE THEORY OF FUNCTION

GOTTFRIED SEMPER

from *Concerning the Formal Principles of Ornament and Its Significance as Artistic Symbol*

The rich and precise language of the Hellenes employs a single word to denote both the ornament with which we decorate ourselves, or the objects of our affection, and the supreme natural law that is the order of the universe.

This profound dual meaning of the word κοσμος affords the key to the Hellenic view of the world and art. To the Hellene, ornament reflected cosmic law; it was a manifestation of the universal world order within the phenomenal world of sense. As a universally comprehensible, self-explanatory symbol of the presence of natural law in visual art, it was essential to all formal design—and essential, above all, to the cosmic art, par excellence, that of architecture. The aesthetic of the Hellenes, in so far as it pertains to the laws of formal beauty, is based on simple principles that are most evident and most readily grasped in the adornment of the body.

In taking ornament in this cosmic sense as the topic of today's lecture, I feel that I must first of all disown any intention of giving the distinguished ladies here present any hints or instructions concerning an art of which Nature has made them past mistresses from infancy on. On the contrary, as an architect, I am convinced that it is largely the subtler discriminations of the fair sex that have elevated the law that guides my own work, over the ages, from a rough and untutored formative impulse to the form of an art guided by principles. At the same time, ladies and gentlemen, I would remind you that it is an artist who addresses you: one who is well able to present things in his own manner, but to whom verbal presentation does not come easily.

When a human being adorns something, he is more or less consciously emphasizing a natural law applicable to the object that he decorates. It is true that the earliest attempts to enhance the natural form of the human body through artificial additions were intended to inspire fear rather than to enhance the attraction of the figure in question; but even this denial of normality reveals laws governing the figure. This early form of adornment combines in turn with the first stirrings of a rhetorical symbolism, one that has fundamentally nothing to do with cosmetic concerns. Finally, the impulse to demonstrate heroic resistance to bodily pain inspired people to disfigure and mutilate, rather than to adorn, the body or parts thereof.

So the prairie Indians, in their savage war dances, cover their heads with fearsome animal masks borrowed from the alligator, the bison, or the bear. Similar masks are found among the savages of the South Sea Islands. The Botocudo perforate their lower lips and insert great wooden plugs, bones, sea shells, and the like into the incisions, thus dragging the lip far down and stretching it alarmingly. The savages of New Holland [Australia] carve deep incisions into their skins and scarify their bodies, arms, and legs, with no regard for symmetry or any other rule. What is most remarkable is that vestiges of these raw and primitive manifestations of the decorative instinct survived and continued to evolve among the most civilized nations, at least in vestigial and symbolic form over the centuries.

Thus, the horrendous animal masks of the Indian braves reappear in refined form among the Egyptians, in the shape of the mystic, hieratic headdress worn by the priest who personifies a god. Very early on, the mask became a symbol of all that is occult, mysterious, and awe-inspiring. Often, in later artistic representations, nothing remains of the animal mask but its essential attribute: as with the bull's horns on the tiara worn by the Assyrian monarchs, or the ram's horns on the headdress of the Egyptian Pharaohs, which Alexander the Great in turn adopted in his capacity as son of Zeus Ammon.[1] The terrifying Gorgon that adorns the aegis of the remote and unapproachable Pallas Athene is also a mask.

The Gorgon mask, as an amulet to ward off magic, appears on many surviving ancient necklaces and other items of personal adornment. It is also used as an appropriate symbol of concealment, in order to finesse a transition—to mask a join, as it were—that would otherwise be hard for the artist to contrive in a satisfying way. The mask was a significant symbol in visual art, long before it was taken up by theatrical drama. In Naples, to this day, a pretty woman adorns her neck with this—or another, equally fierce—amulet against the evil eye.

Everywhere and in every age, such aids against magic have been worn on bracelets and rings. So ancient is the practice that it is doubtful whether the piece of jewelry was designed to attach the protective amulet to the body or whether, on the contrary, the setting and fastening of the talisman were the original source of the aesthetic ornament. The pierced lips and massive bone pendants of the Botocudo may be regarded as the first, rudimentary precursors of the graceful and aesthetically important ear pendants—the favorite jewels of antiquity—which were particularly favored by Hellenic beauties, and which have recently and undeservedly fallen out of fashion.

The piercing of the lips was still practiced, no doubt in a somewhat refined form, by the civilized Aztecs and Toltecs of Mexico and Peru at the time of the Spanish conquest. Additionally, it was common among them to pierce the nasal septum and ear lobes, and to insert rings bearing heavy crescent-shaped gold and silver pendants.

Travelers tell us that the Arab and Bedouin beauties, who are generally by no means indifferent to nobility of form, wear hanging nose ornaments of the same kind; the wearing of heavy ear pendants is universal among them. Among the Assyrians, Medes, and Persians, men wore heavy earrings richly set with precious stones, and a great variety of these can be seen on the bas-reliefs from Nineveh, now in London and Paris.

Similarly, the cannibal custom of painting and tattooing the body—the crudest beginnings of which we find in the skin painting and scarification practiced by the New Hollanders—has gradually assumed more civilized forms. Its offshoots are still to be found in the most recent times and among the most cultivated peoples.

Among the refined Egyptians, not only was it customary for women to apply antimony black to their eyebrows and lashes, and to lengthen them, but Egyptian beauties, like the Oriental ladies of the present day, also painted the palms of their hands, their nails, and the soles of their feet with elegant arabesques.

The Celts and Britons, by no means an uncultivated people when the Romans first encountered them, were highly adept at skin coloring. The principal pigment that they used was the blue dye, woad (*glastum*). On certain social occasions, as Pliny expressly says, the Celtic maidens and wives would appear in blackface, as it were, with their whole bodies painted with blue-black ink.[2] It is said that the celebrated bluestockings represent the last vestige and refinement of this ancient British fashion.[3] The Celts were also expert dyers, and—by way of a continuation of the art of pattern drawing originally practiced on their own skins—they were the inventors of the multicolored check patterns that form the national dress of Scotland to this day.

Tattooing may be regarded as a sign of progress in this genre. Among living peoples, it is the New Zealanders and South Sea Islanders who have carried this art the furthest, covering their bodies, more or less according to rank, wealth, and personal distinction, with elegant arabesques. The taste that they exhibit in this medium of epidermal encaustic, employing scrolls and other ornaments to trace and emphasize the contour and direction of the muscles, is said to be admirable. There is an evident kinship between these ornamental forms and those that appear on the artifacts and buildings of the Assyrians, Egyptians, Etruscans, and early Greeks: so that it would not be too great a paradox to ascribe the origin of certain traditional surface ornaments to the art of tattooing.

The custom of painting and tattooing the skin was not entirely unknown to the Hellenes and to related cultures—not to speak of the practice, which spread from the East to Greece and Rome, of anointing every part of the body with fragrant, balsamic essences; or the use of red, white, and black cosmetic paints and beauty spots among the Greek women (whose love of personal adornment incurred the biting sarcasm of the wittiest writers of their nation). Traces of the custom persisted, if only as a matter of priestly tradition, in the body painting traditionally practiced in religious festivities and processions. In accordance with an ancient Etruscan custom, a Roman general who had earned a Triumph would paint himself all over with red lead; he did so as the representative of Capitoline Jupiter, whose clay effigy was repainted in the same way every year.

The women of Thrace, who were kinsfolk of the Hellenes, went to even greater lengths in their respect for ancient tradition. Among them, tattooing was a mark of status. Their husbands scored and burned their skins with long stripes, and a woman without such scars was regarded as a social inferior.

This custom of body painting and tattooing undoubtedly bears a close relation not only to the principle of polychromy in the arts of antiquity but to the deepest origins of all art. The human delight in ornament emerges, very early on, in the decoration of domestic animals. Here too, it initially blends with rhetorical symbolism and superstitious notions. Only later does it take a pure form and observe laws of its own. I mention animal decoration only because the principles of a certain class of ornament, on which I shall enlarge in due course, are particularly well exemplified in the fluttering ribbons, plumes, and tassels that adorn our mettlesome steeds and our other draft animals and beasts of burden.

These preliminary hints are intended to show that the artistic feeling active in ornament, though it first appears at a very early stage, long remains uncertain of its own true nature; that it does not initially appear in its pure and disinterested form. It only more or less unconsciously obeys the universal cosmic law which the Greeks, as I believe, were the first and only nation to interpret and apply universally.

What is this cosmic law?

Perhaps we can trace it by dividing ornament into categories, based on the differences in character between the decorative elements concerned. In general terms, the following three classes of ornamental objects may be distinguished:

1. The pendant.

2. The ring.

3. The class of ornament for which, lacking an extant and self-explanatory term, I am compelled to coin a name: I shall call it *directional* ornament—subject to the explanation that I intend to give in due course.

Pendant ornament is primarily associated with those qualities of visual form that we call *symmetry*. It is itself symmetrical; it adorns the body by alluding to the relationship between that body and something universal, to which the perceived entity is tied, thus conveying that the entity is at rest and in a stable relationship with the ground on which it stands. Because of this allusion to the relation between the particular and the universal, this kind of ornament may also justifiably be given the name of *macrocosmic* ornament.

Examples of symmetrical ornament are the nose and ear pendants that I discussed a moment ago. As heavy bodies that hang free, they swing with the wearer's every movement and thereby prepare us for the moment of tranquillity and balance that will ensue. At rest, the contrast between the vertical line maintained by the ornament and the sinuous lines of the organic form enhances the lively attraction of the latter. And so an ear pendant, by conforming to a vertical line in obedience to gravity, sets off the delicate forward curve of the nape of the neck, which is not subject to gravity. The Bedouin, with his eye for beauty, achieves the same effect by adorning the proud neck of his favorite mare with a dangling crescent, or by garnishing his saddle with straps hung with brightly colored tassels and metal ornaments.

The aesthetic value of symmetrical ornament is markedly enhanced by its influence on the actions of the individual whom it adorns. At rest, posture must be corrected; in motion, a degree of dignified restraint must be observed, so that the ornament does not upset the finer susceptibilities by oscillating in too rapid or irregular or angular a fashion.

This ornament has the same effect even on the noble horse, which arches its muscular neck even more proudly when its ornamental harness is on. The nature and individuality of the customary motions of a lady's earrings allow us to draw conclusions with some degree of certainty as to her nature and character.

Perhaps nose ornaments are still more exacting in this respect—in that a less than noble bearing of the head, or an over-hasty, thoughtless movement, infallibly causes the absurdest oscillations, which, being thus placed in the very center of the face, are bound to do violence to the aesthetic sensibilities. For which reason this ornament is found only among those nations that keep their women in a state of extreme subjection and under strict tutelage.

A convincing example of the aesthetic effect of the principle under discussion is the artistic pleasure evoked by comely female figures bearing vessels of water on their heads. These were the source of the canephori and caryatids that are important motifs in architecture. Mention of these symmetrical, draped figures leads us to the use of drapery folds as a macrocosmic ornament—one whose aesthetic significance was clearly recognized by the ancients and is still acknowledged by the nations of the East. The looks, and indeed the customs, of many Oriental peoples are visibly influenced by the long, draped garments that they customarily wear.

We Europeans have never had a very developed feeling for this kind of ornament; I need only mention the bulky hooped skirts, the crinolines, and the flounced dresses that manifestly belong to annular rather than macrocosmic ornament. And how are we to classify our tailcoats? Are they directional ornaments, or misplaced pendants, or a cross between the two?

Among the Hellenes and the Romans, garments, both as macrocosmic ornament and otherwise, were configured and nuanced in the noblest and subtlest way, from the draped *chiton* of majestic Hera and the stiffly pleated *peplos* of Pallas Athene to the kilted skirts of Artemis Agrotera—

nuda genu nodoque sinus collecta fluentis.[4]

An element closely allied to draperies, and to the other ornaments in this class, is that of the hair and beard. The hair of the head, with the beard, is a natural ornament flexible enough to be adapted to any cosmetic purpose. At rest, it serves as macrocosmic or symmetrical ornament. Thus, the Assyrian hair and beard, which hangs in symmetrical, vertical ringlets, expresses the grave demeanor of the Oriental potentate. The rigorous discipline of the Egyptian state caused the hair and beard to appear as symbols of disorder and confusion; both were shorn off and replaced by a conventional headdress—or, in private life, by a highly conventional wig structure with vertical ringlets.

The Hellenes mitigated the Assyrian principle and derived from it the ambrosial locks of Olympian Zeus. On archaic reliefs, Rhea, the mother of Zeus and Hera, still appeared with tresses hanging straight down; and hieratic law decreed that none might enter the Heraeum, near Argos, but with braided hair. Demeter and Athena, too, are characterized—especially in earlier art—by hanging braids and symmetrical drapery folds. Apollo and Artemis, on the other hand, appear with flowing locks bound up in a knot at the front, entirely in keeping with the nature of those deities. Ares, ever ready for battle, has short, curly, bristling hair, as has the sprightly Hermes. Such was the Greeks' familiarity with the multiple significance of the natural ornament of head hair.

At the outset, I described the class of ornament under discussion as predominantly symmetrical—and so it is, though in draperies, as art progressed, this symmetry came to be more freely interpreted in terms of an equilibrium of masses. Part of the necessity for this was that drapery simultaneously belongs to another category of ornament, which I shall discuss later; in other words, it unites two qualities within itself.

Otherwise, every type of ornament that belongs to this class is to be regarded as strictly symmetrical. A single earring, or two earrings of different lengths and weights, would not be permissible—although a single bracelet or a number of bracelets on one arm, while the other remains unadorned, or a diagonally positioned head ornament, or a diagonal belt, does not necessarily offend our sense of beauty and may at times give pleasure.

Still less do we crave symmetry in what—for want of a better expression—I shall call directional ornament.

2. ANNULAR OR RING ORNAMENT

Annular ornament differs in principle from the category just discussed, in that it relates directly, without an intermediary, to the body or member that it adorns. This it does by setting off the form and color of the figure, or by emphasizing the visual relationships between its component parts.

Annular ornament is mainly proportional: it serves to emphasize the proportions of the body, to remedy deficiencies, and in some circumstances to maintain, by exaggeration—that is, by violating the laws of strict proportionality—certain effects that may be characteristic or may suit a specific purpose.

It is the nature of such ornaments to be peripheral or peripheral-radial configurations, with the object adorned as the nucleus or central focus to which they relate. Here again, it is mostly the head—the emblem, as it were, of the whole person—that serves as the object of this class of ornament. By contrast with the preceding class, which I called macrocosmic, I would call this microcosmic.

A simple garland of leaves reveals the law governing all such ornament: *a peripheral encircling of the head.* The sequential arrangement of the leaves, strung together on the cord, gives us the radial principle, which, in a natural and thus universally comprehensible way, indicates its own central point of focus. To make this unity of reference clear and comprehensible, it is necessary to establish a regular arrangement of the parts, a eurhythmic sequence.[5]

It is therefore clear from the outset that the law of eurhythmy is the active principle of microcosmic ornament. This is evident in the pleasure that a string of beads will give to the simplest child of Nature. The eurhythmic garland sequence is of greater antiquity than the purely peripheral ring, which the Greeks first elevated into a symbol of supreme power and majesty, either as a golden diadem, κορώυη, or as the cylindrical πόλος.

A dual significance attaches to the head-encircling garland when its component elements are erect and point upward. Whether they be leaves from trees, or feathers from birds, or other objects taken or imitated from Nature, they convey by their erect position that they are the culmination and conclusion of the design, and that the part of it to which they pertain is the head. Headdresses of this kind include the feather crowns of the Mexican caciques. The Assyrian tiara has a feather crown as its nucleus, and this remains visible above the diadem that surrounds it.

Almost every culture known to ethnology has been seduced into barbaric lapses of taste by the attempt to lend authority to the human head—and to its individual possessor—at the expense of good proportions, by loading it with superstructures and other top-heavy ornaments. Only the Hellenic and kindred cultures never did this; and this in itself justifies their claim to be the only nonbarbarians.

We ourselves still have our grenadier caps and our tubular felt hats: forms of unexampled barbarity. The necklace, too (πδεριδέσαια *monile*), takes a peripheral and simultaneously radial-eurhythmic form. The component units here may be feathers—as in the broad collar worn in ancient Egypt, which was the prototype of the aegis of Pallas Athene—or, more frequently, hard, inorganic, regular solids such as stones, teeth, bones, pearls, and artificial imitations thereof. Originally drilled through and strung on cords, these were later richly set in metal and linked in a eurhythmic sequence.

Here again, the radial configuration draws attention to what is contained within; and a regular, geometric sequence of inanimate objects, usually taken from the mineral kingdom, serves by contrast to set off the swelling forms of the living organism.

The colors of the jewelry, the metallic glitter, and the light refracted by the cut gems also serve to attract the eye to the object adorned. The color effects may be calculated to emphasize a good complexion, or to correct a poor one, by juxtaposition and assimilation.

Chevreul, in his little book on color harmony, gives useful hints as to this and other points of the art of the toilette.[6] The belt or girdle around the body—which, according to the Book of Genesis, is the oldest form of adornment known to the human race—is analogous to the necklace. Both serve to mark and bridge a transition: the transition between head and shoulders, or the transition between legs and trunk. Taken together, girdle and necklace reinforce and emphasize, as it were, the proportional triad of the human form.

At the same time, in its practical function, the girdle or belt is the emblem of power and of readiness for battle. And so, along with the tiara, the low-slung, gold-tasseled, purple ξωύη περσική was the attribute of the Great King, with which his conqueror and heir, Alexander, solemnly invested himself.

Aphrodite dons the girdle of the Graces to make sure of her power. The Hellenic poets constantly bestow on lovely women the epithet "beautifully girdled": a proof of the high regard in which this ornament was held among them. The girdle enjoyed an almost equal degree of reverence in the medieval age of chivalry and romance. It remains to this day the most important article of dress among the nations of the East.

Here we might also refer to the hem of the garment, which was an important adornment among the Hellenes. In a sense, this too is an annular ornament: it forms the lower termination of the figure, in opposition to the crowning glory of the head. The idea of a multiple array of flounces, shortening and distorting the proportions, was unknown among the ancients.

Next in importance among annular ornaments are those that serve to emphasize the graceful proportions and skin tones of the extremities of the figure: another very ancient form of decoration, which has survived among us only in the bracelet. In antiquity there was a custom, still prevalent in the East, of ringing not only the wrist but also the upper arms and the ankles.

Of all annular ornaments the least significant, aesthetically speaking, are finger rings, which the Greeks adopted only when Asiatic customs began to take hold. Previously, Greeks and Romans alike had regarded them almost exclusively as rhetorical ornaments: settings for amulets, emblems of rank, mementoes, signets, and so on.

The principle of annular ornament in general is that anything that is intended to appear stout, convex, voluminous, is to be encompassed with tight annular work, so that the tight hold exerted by the golden fetters on the ornamented member serves to reinforce these qualities. In its crudest manifestation, this law is to be seen in the bone bangles of the Kaffirs, which are placed on the upper arm in youth and dig deep into the muscles as these develop.

In a nobler interpretation of the same law, the aesthetically refined nations of antiquity loved to wrap the upper arm and the fleshy part of the forearm in serpentine coils: an emblem that achieves its purpose without physical duress and with enhanced effect. The converse applies to the adornment of those parts that are to appear delicate and small in bulk: not fleshy, but elastic and firm. Bonds on these must be loose and articulated, and must allow freedom of movement. Such is the law that we see obeyed by the Hellenic beauties—and indeed to this day by Hindu ladies, who love to wear loose anklets.

The principle enunciated here applies fully both to necklaces and to girdles. The forms of necks and shoulders vary a great deal, both in expression and in character, and for every neck there is a necklace that is suitable in form, in color, and especially in width and form of fastening. A slender, English swan neck, for example, may be set off by a narrow band, halfway up. A lady of a more Roman cast of beauty will not choose to wear the same ornament—unless, that is, fashion dictates.

In accordance with this law, the belt or girdle must always be so placed that it appears to sag, as it were, resting on the hips, and to be wide. This is what best emphasizes a slender figure: a rule that has constantly been breached by the fashions of our century—if, indeed, this ornament can be said to exist among us at all. In this, as in other respects, the East has preserved the ancient tradition, and with it the finer principles of costume.

The same law may be applied to the encirclement of the head. Not every chaplet suits every beautiful woman. The law holds good, above all, for the soft and manageable hair of the head itself. There are any number of ways in which this can be dressed in a peripheral pattern to form the most beautiful headdress of all—the adornment assigned by the Hellenic artists to the pure formal beauty of, for example, Aphrodite.

3. DIRECTIONAL ORNAMENT

It remains for me to discuss the class of ornament that is designed to emphasize the direction and motion of the body; this is undoubtedly more spiritual than those so far discussed, in that it more closely concerns the grace of movement, the character, and the expression of the figure.

This ornament differs in essential respects from the kinds already named. It is not necessarily symmetrical; nor is it a rhythmic encirclement of any part. It relates entirely to the antithesis between the front and back of a figure or object, and is intended primarily to be seen in profile. This is the universal characteristic of this class of ornament, which is further divided into two categories: static and flying.

The latter, flying form not only indicates direction but serves to emphasize the speed with which the figure is moving in that direction. The static form includes, for example, the φάλαρου τιάρας, the jewel on the front of the tiara of the Persian monarch; likewise the Uraeus serpent on the brow of an Egyptian god. Similar ornaments were revived in the fifteenth and sixteenth centuries and became a favorite theme of the master goldsmiths of the age: Caradosso, Benvenuto Cellini, and others.[7]

To the same class belongs the brooch, the clasp that holds the corners of a cloak together across the breast or on the shoulder: a symbol of the dignity of high priest among both the Aztecs and the Jews. The popes have also adopted it; they adorn the button that fastens the scapular with the largest and finest gems from the Vatican treasury, in settings by the most eminent artists. The so-called faveurs worn by ladies in the sixteenth and seventeenth centuries were a richly worked ornament of the same kind. Degenerate versions of both have survived among us, in the form of patriotic rosettes and pins (brooches).

Directional ornament is most effective in military headgear; and here a natural feeling seems to have guided all nations to the same forms. The New Zealander wears a helmet crest almost identical to that of the ancient Hellene. The comb of the cock, and of other combative birds, was the model here.

Among the Assyrians and Egyptians, the helmet crest (φάλος) was rigid and immobile, as were the *phalerae* on their horses' heads; though the Egyptians also acquired the habit of adorning both themselves and their horses with single feathers placed above the right ear. A rigid crest was also the mark of the heavily armed Roman legionary.

The Hellenes and Etruscans, by contrast, had long, flying, trailing crests, made from the manes of horses. This flying crest was also a prime mark of the medieval knight; it survives to this day, but its fluttering plume has degenerated into a wobbling, close-cropped, horsehair sausage. This entirely lacks the character of forward impetus and intrepid haste that is implicit in the crests of antiquity. Still less directional are our latter-day civilian hats, on which back and front are interchangeable.

Just as a garment at rest was correctly defined as a macrocosmic ornament, a garment flying in the breeze must obviously count as a directional ornament. An inexhaustible means of lending a pleasing emphasis to the direction and the motion of a figure is afforded by fluttering ribbons, strings, tassels, and the like. These, too, embody twin principles of ornament, except that here the mobile element outweighs the other, earthbound element—and that, because the materials chosen are so light, their motion is more or less independent of that of the wearer. They respond not to every haphazard twist or turn but only to the laws of motion and the general direction in which the body moves.

This twofold quality governs the practical use of the ornament in question. Light, fluttering ribbons and bows are appropriate for youthful and feminine forms; but, given the right mood, this variety of ornament also enhances the gravity of a figure. The requisite mood may be generated by wide, heavy, tasseled ribbons and the like. Such are the terminations of the diadem (the παραγνάθιδες), which hang down the back, and the *taeniae* that fasten the consecrated garland: the emblems of monarchy and of priestly consecration. The ornaments and embroideries on ribbon ornaments are to be chosen in keeping with its mobile character, so that they follow the motion. In this, as elsewhere, the nations of antiquity, and the half-barbarian Hindus and other Orientals, show a finer tact than we.

The head hair, in its infinite flexibility, can be included in this class of ornament also: either flying free, or put up in a chignon at the front (the attribute of Apollo, Artemis, or Eros), or tied at the back, a graceful directional ornament favored by Hellenic, Etruscan, and Roman ladies.

The pigtail or queue worn by the Chinese and by our own ancestors, and the bag or purse wig, are caricatures of directional ornament.

The three principles of ornament described here must combine purposefully in the figure ornamented: that is, as an overall impression they must enhance and reflect its nature and character. The primary rule is this: ornament must neither distract attention from the object, by overloading it, nor spoil the harmony of the figure by being ill chosen and ill arranged.

An easy means of promoting the purposeful combination of the three ornamental principles is to ensure that one of the three is predominant.

It is interesting to observe how differences in national character are reflected in the dominance of one or other ornamental principle. The earthbound, law-abiding regularity of Egyptian art is reflected in the dominance of symmetrical ornament; we find analogous tendencies in the style of Egyptian architecture. The Assyrians preferred the annular ornament and the cincture; here we detect the feudalistic, dynastic, yet centralizing culture of that nation, as expressed in their architecture, and also in that of the Chaldeans and Persians.

The forest Indian of North America, decked in the flight feathers of the eagle, has a special feeling for the asymmetrical principle, with its emphasis on motion and direction entirely in keeping with his nomadic life as a hunter. In the same way, the French as a nation love plume and ribbon ornament above all.

Among the Hellenes, sensitive as they were to beauty in all its forms, we find the freest combination of the three principles, each operating in the field appropriate to it. They alone achieved the glorious union of perfect equality and harmonious singleness of purpose. The same applies to Hellenic architecture in general, the principle of which is entirely identical with the creative principle of Nature: namely, to express through the form of every object the concept that underlies that object. Hellenic architecture assembles lifeless matter into an artfully contrived and articulated ideal organism, in which every member has its own distinct, ideal essence while finding expression as a functioning organ of the whole. It clothes the bare form in an elucidatory symbolism that fulfills precisely the same purpose as the adornment of the body: namely, to emphasize the regularity and character of the form on every side, while sharply distinguishing the individuality and functional relatedness of its parts.

This is why the Greek word for building therefore also means adorning, with a dual meaning very like that which we mentioned earlier in connection with the word κοσμος. The pendant, the garland, and the hitherto nameless ornament that marks direction are the principal symbols employed in Hellenic architecture to attain the effect I have mentioned. They have their analogies not in Nature as such but, almost exclusively, in the adornments of the human body. In most cases, they have been given names that indicate this.

Thus, for example, the guttae or drops on the Doric entablature are a pendant ornament that contrasts sharply with the inclined undersurface of the mutules. The corona or sima of a gabled roof has the name, the function, and even the ornamentation of a crowning garland or diadem. The same symbol appears as the termination of the individual members of the building and appears, when bearing a load and, as it were, elastically withstanding the pressure, as a symbol of conflict (*cyma*).

As the head of the temple is garlanded with the corona, the frieze with its metopes encircles it at the place where the dominant set of proportions terminates and unites with the supporting colonnade. This is, as it were, the broad, eurhythmically constructed necklace of gems, the monile, worn by the architectural organism.

Corresponding to this, a wide diazoma or passage separates the substructure from the main structure and mediates the transition from the supporting to the bearing base, analogous to the girdle on a human figure, and with belt-like ornamental characteristics.

As for the palmettes of the acroteria that adorn the pediment, and the comb-like ornaments on the ridge tiles, who does not recognize the directional ornament of the helmet crest?

What I have just said might serve as the foundation of a whole theory of beauty—something that would be extremely difficult to develop succinctly, let alone entertainingly. Nevertheless, ladies and gentlemen, I crave your indulgence for concluding this lecture with a few hints on the subject. . . .

NOTES

1. Alexander the Great (356–323 BCE), king of Macedon, conquered much of Asia, including Egypt; he went to the oasis of Amon and was acknowledged as the son of Amon-Ra; his divine status was reflected in his symbolic headdress combining attributes of Zeus and Amon.

2. Pliny, *Natural History,* Book 22: ii, "Simili plantagini—glastum in Gallia vocatur—Britannorum coniuges nurusque toto corpore oblitae quibusdam in sacris nudae incedunt, Aethiopum colorem imitantes."

3. Bluestocking was a pejorative term referring to women with literary or intellectual pretensions.

4. "Knees bare, her flowing dress tucked up in a knot." Venus disguised as a divine huntress, in Virgil, *Aeneid* 1.320.

5. This is Semper's own term to express the directional forces of energy as felt within the human body.

6. Michel-Eugène Chevreul, *De la Loi du contraste simultané, des couleurs*, 2 vols. (Paris, 1839); trans. by J. Spanton, *The Laws of Contrast of Colour and Their Applications to the Arts and Manufactures* (London, 1883).

7. Cristoforo Foppa, called Caradosso (1452–1526/7), was one of the most famous fifteenth-century goldsmiths, but none of his works seem to have survived in precious metals. Benvenuto Cellini (1500–1571) was a highly accomplished Mannerist sculptor and the most celebrated goldsmith of Renaissance Italy; he is known for his colorful *Autobiography*.

ALOIS RIEGL

Introduction to *A Historical Grammar of the Visual Arts*

It is now about a century and a half since art history first came into existence as a science: or, in other words, since work began on the edifice of a history of art. In the beginning, that edifice was in the charge of an architect, whose name was aesthetics.[1] Aesthetics laid the foundations and drew up the plans that were to govern the future completion of the whole. Three connected ranges of building were to occupy a single, shared foundation: architecture in the centre, flanked by side wings for sculpture and painting. It soon became apparent that some forms of art could not be accommodated within these three parts: for them, a fourth was built on at the rear, being architecture, and this was given the name of applied art [*Kunstgewerbe*]. The builders set to work with a will on all four structures.

But the higher the edifice rose, the more disagreeably evident it became that the builders' initial enthusiasm had led to excessive haste. The foundations proved too weak; and many of the materials, too, were ill chosen and inadequately prepared. Naturally, the architect—aesthetics, that is—took all the blame and was dismissed. It was concluded that solidity was the great priority: there was no need for the work to proceed under a single direction; what mattered was to take all necessary precautions for each of the four structures separately. This was the beginning of the second phase of art-historical scholarship, in which the foundations were reinforced and the materials reworked: the phase of detailed research. The work of construction was not neglected, but it continued unevenly, and without a plan, precisely because there was no longer a single architect in charge of the work. Those who worked on one wing of the building took no account of the others. As a consequence, the four parts grew taller but also increasingly lost touch with each other.

This could not long go unnoticed. Today, solid though the edifice may be internally, it lacks joins to tie it together; it has the air of a ruin. Some connection must be restored between its four parts, and the whole must be made to convey a unified impression. This cannot happen without a plan: what is needed is meticulous, unified, overall direction. Who is to provide this? Aesthetics has been sent packing, and is long since defunct, aside from a lingering presence in a few philosophy classrooms. But it has left behind it an heir. A youthful heir, unnamed as yet, but it is there, and can already point to a number of experiments that show at least some promise for the future because it has learned its art-historical lesson. The old aesthetics sought to give instruction to art history; its successor—modern aesthetics, if you will—is content to learn from art history. It is aware that only art history justifies its existence.

What have been the most notable attempts to restore some unity to the disintegrating edifice of art history? The earliest was Gottfried Semper's attempt to define the work of art as the resultant of the forces of function, material, and technique.[2] We shall return to this in due course; but Semper's idea could never have led to a unified approach to artistic creation as a whole; it proved significant only for the applied arts. Two other attempts were more successful in achieving a general relevance. Both sought to superimpose a higher duality on the original fourfold division; and, since the two aspects of that duality were mutually complementary, they naturally formed a higher unity.

The earlier of the two proposals was to categorize all artistic creation under two heads: idealistic and naturalistic.[3] There is some virtue in this, except that no one has ever yet succeeded in distinguishing the two with any degree of certainty. As a result, one party declares all art to be naturalistic, and the other retorts that all art has never been anything else but idealistic. It is clear that these two categories, although based on a real antithesis, are not conducive to a clear unity. No edifice can be built out of such shaky elements as these.

The other and later proposal is to divide all art into the categories of sculpture and painting.[4] This, again, does not in itself make matters clear, because there is as yet no agreed definition of what is sculptural and what is pictorial. What some call sculptural, others call pictorial.

Attempts have thus been made, unsuccessfully, it is true, but this is no reason to despair of the possibility of a solution. Let us look more closely at the nature of these attempts.

I shall take a concrete instance. The Attic art of the later fifth century B.C.E. furnishes us with examples of every artistic category: the architecture of the Parthenon, the sculptures of Phidias, and numerous vase paintings. I will assume that you can identify all these at sight as fifth-century Attic work. Is that recognition in itself science? No, since this would make the antique dealer into a scientist. It is a cognitive ability, acquired through practice; it is knowledge; it is lore; but it is not science. Science begins only when the following question is asked: Why are the works of fifth-century Attic art as they are and not otherwise? All modern science is based on the universality of cause and effect: that is, the impossibility of a miracle. Every phenomenon is the necessary effect of some cause. Science looks for that cause.

Throughout its existence, the history of art has honestly sought to fulfill this requirement. Not content with simply determining place and time, it has always inquired as to causes. Initially, it sought those causes in aesthetics: that is, in a priori laws equally applicable to the arts of architecture, sculpture, and painting. That was the position adopted by, say, Winckelmann.[5] In time, those a priori laws proved untenable—that is, as we put it earlier, aesthetics proved incompetent to manage the construction of the edifice. At that point, unity was abandoned, and the search for causes continued within the individual arts. Thus, the history of Greek temple architecture was traced back from the Parthenon, and a chain of causality or evolution was constructed from the temples of Egypt to the Parthenon. The same happened in sculpture. We now have an evolutionary history of sculpture that runs from the Old Kingdom in Egypt to Phidias. Similarly, in painting, we are able to trace a clear, causal relationship between the mural paintings of ancient Egypt and the Attic vases of the fifth century.

This has been the method pursued by art history as a science over the past half century. Not content with defining the origins of the individual work of art in terms of time and place, it has always looked for causality; but it has pursued that causality only within the individual arts. That is to say, the builders have worked on the wings in isolation, scrupulously avoiding sidelong glances at other parts of the edifice.

Today, we see the study of art history entering a new phase. People are starting to wonder: Does the Parthenon obey no evolutionary laws but those of architecture? Do the sculptures of Phidias obey none but those of sculpture, and the Attic vases none but those of painting? Is there no interconnection between those laws? Or are there some overriding laws that are obeyed by all works of visual art, uniformly and without exception? Laws of which the laws of architecture, sculpture, and painting are mere secondary derivatives?

We can see, today, that works of art—however different they may be in individual terms—share certain common elements. Must not the evolution of those shared elements be a shared and universal one? Must not the whole of visual art share a common evolution? As a concrete instance: the column, the statue, and the vase have in common (1) three-dimensional form, (2) the associated two dimensional plane. Form and plane are the elements of visual art. The relationship between them may vary; but close scrutiny will reveal that in the Parthenon, in the sculptures of Phidias, and in Attic vase painting this relationship is an identical one. The evolutionary law that governs these two elements must therefore be equally binding for all four categories of art.

So now we see what to do. We must concentrate, not on individual works of art as such, or even on individual classes of art as such, but on those elements that require to be clearly distinguished and apprehended in order to construct a true and unified culmination for the theoretical edifice of art history. Those elements are multiple; they are not yet a unity. But they conduce to unity, because they link the categories of art one with another; they are the transitional members that lead to the true culmination of the edifice: the ultimate, directing factor of all artistic creativity. Such, it seems to me, is the task that confronts the science of art history for the future.

This is not to detract in any way from the value of the older method of detailed factual research. In the future, as in the past, no edifice can ever be built without good building materials—that is to say, without a reliable definition of time and place. Researches within the individual classes of art will continue to be pursued with success and with profit. But the true culmination of the whole, the knowledge of the essence of art, will emerge only from an evolutionary history of the elements of art, as dictated by the supreme, leading factor of all human artistic creation.

Here perhaps I can clarify matters by pointing to a number of analogies between visual art and language. Language, too, has its elements; and the evolutionary history of those elements is what we call the historical grammar of the language in question. One who wants only to speak a language needs no grammar; nor does one who wants only to understand it. But one who wants to know why a language has evolved thus and not otherwise, or who wants to comprehend its position within the culture of humanity as a whole—one who wants to grasp the language scientifically—stands out in need of its historical grammar.

Much the same applies to the visual arts. We have long been accustomed to use the metaphor of a "language of art." We say that every work of art speaks its own specific language—though, naturally, the elements of visual art differ from those of language proper. Now, if there is a language of art, then there is also a historical grammar of that language. This is, of course, only a metaphor; but if we accept the one metaphor we may surely allow that the other also applies.

One who wants to create a work of art—the visual artist—has no need of the historical grammar of art. Nor does one who wants to enjoy the work of art objectively. But one who wants to comprehend a work scientifically will not henceforth be able to dispense with that grammar.

You will now understand what I mean, when I undertake to provide a historical grammar of visual art. It might also be called a theory of the elements of visual art.

To avoid misunderstandings, I must warn you in advance that this is not an introduction to art history. Far from it: if there are any beginners among you, I would urge them to unregister from this class without delay. Only advanced students, who already know something of all the periods of art, and have at least the most important landmarks present in their minds, will derive benefit from this course. I shall constantly have to cite examples, and to allude to others in passing. To show visual reproductions of all these works is impossible, although I shall do so as often as I can. But the available material is limited, and it is a physical impossibility to show everything. A detailed knowledge of the subject is therefore essential.

(Few classes; profitable; only stimulus intended; first attempt.)[6]

We have to deal with the following: (1) the elements, (2) their evolutionary history, (3) factor governing evolution.

Elements

What these constitute is best shown by a catalogue entry, e.g.:

1	2	3		4

Cup in terra-cotta, tall stem, on the bowl battle of centaurs in black-figure painting.

1. What is it for? Function comes first and counts as the most important element. One thinks of its practical use, and of its specific class of vessel.

2. and 3. Terra-cotta hides in fact two points: material and technique, what is it made of and how?

These three elements seem outwardly the most important, and are always given priority over the fourth. They are also the most physical and the most obvious ones. The aesthetics of the 1860s based its whole theory of art on them: Gottfried Semper, in his *Style,* uses empirical aesthetics. According to him, every work of art is a resultant of function, material, and technique. Let us see whether there are other elements. There is one on the catalogue entry itself, which in its detailed description gives (a) details of form, (b) surface ornament.

Every work of art as a whole is three-dimensional—shaped, but also enclosed by planes. Form and plan maintain a specific relationship (plane, for instance, may well far outweigh form; but disembodied works of art, pure planes, do not exist). We thus gain a further element: the relationship between form and plane that is present in every work of art. Semper's aesthetics assumed that this could safely be ignored. The most recent aesthetics has taken it into account and erected on it the distinction between sculptural and pictorial qualities.

But yet another element lies within this, in the word "cup," whose meaning remains obscured by the dominant functional description. Let us take another catalogue entry.

Statue of Artemis, bronze.

Statue? Is that a function? Apparently not. No practical use involved (if it were, say, a caryatid, the function would come first: e.g., table leg in the form of the goddess Artemis). So is this statue without a function? Not at all. Just no practical function. We shall go into this in detail later. But it is directly followed by the words "of Artemis": i.e., this is the statue of a goddess in human shape, and thus the reproduction of a human figure. This immediately gives us the answer to the question "what?"—the motif of the work. That is another factor.

What about "cup"? Here the motif conceals itself behind the word that indicates function. We know at once, when we hear the word "cup," what the motif looks like. But there is a motif all the same: a motif taken from Nature, just as with the statue. In the case of the statue, it is taken from organic Nature and can therefore be specified in words. With the cup, the motif is drawn from inorganic, crystalline Nature and requires closer description—which is generally provided later in the entry. Another specimen of applied art, is, e.g., "Table leg in the form of Artemis." Here there is a prototype taken from organic Nature, which is therefore mentioned at once. Recent aesthetics has sought to define the motif, too, as a primary principle: naturalistic versus idealistic forms.

We thus have five elements:

1. Function: what for? This is mostly interpreted rather too narrowly, in terms of a practical, utilitarian function related to the needs of one of our five senses.
2. Raw material: made of what?
3. Technique: made with what?
4. The motif: what?
5. Form and plane: how?

The attempt has already been made to use all of these five elements as the basis of a new and comprehensive theory of art, and to declare their past evolution to be identical with the past evolution of visual art as such.

Semper's empirical aesthetics:

This aesthetics comes closest to materialism. Semper applied it only to the history of applied art [*Kunstgewerbe*]. Why? Take a "Statue of Artemis," for instance. How can the style there be deduced from the function, material, and technique? And without a clear indication of practical function? Even with architecture, there would have been difficulties. Semper did intend to deal with architecture, but never got around to it—certainly not by chance.

Let us take a third catalogue entry:

Oil painting, landscape, on copper.

As with the statue, no practical function is apparent, and the defining influence of material and technique is even less evident. This explains why classical archeologists and art historians eagerly took up Semper's arguments for applied art, but never dreamed of applying them to what they called high art.

Then, however, historians wanted to create a connection within high art, notably between sculpture and painting, but also with architecture. Two elements remained: 1. the motif, 2. and form and plane. I have already mentioned that both were promoted to the status of determining principles, but it proved impossible even to agree on the distinction between the two. Why was this? Because the situation with these two was the same as with the three other, more materialistic, elements which Semper had singled out as guiding principles of the evolutionary process. None of the five could be regarded as a guiding principle in and of itself. All are vehicles of evolution; but evolution is guided by another element, distinct from these five and superior to them. What is, then, the supreme principle of evolution in all visual art? If these five elements of art offer a multiplicity, then there must be some higher unity above them, to which they are subject.

What is this higher unity?

Why does man create works of art? What is the function of works of art? This seems to bring us back to the question (and element) of function, which we have already discussed and which is so crucial to Semper's empirical aesthetics. Semper, however, speaks of function purely in an external, literal sense. Let us consider what external function a work of art may serve. There can be no artwork without an external function, nor an external function without any art. Whatever is created by the human hand must in some way acquire the label of art.

1. Utilitarian function: Supplying the needs of one of our five senses. Cup, drinking vessel (gratification of the sense of taste). Is this an artistic function? No. So practical, utilitarian function is not identical with artistic function. This covers applied art and architecture (but where this constitutes a monument—e.g., obelisk—it begins to turn into sculpture).

2. Ornamental function: Filling up a void, the *horror vacui*, the tattooed islander. Tattooing has no utilitarian function; it satisfies none of the five senses. (The eye does not come into this; here the eye is the intermediary organ that conveys impressions to the mind; nowadays we absorb all works of art through the eye. A utilitarian need, where the sense of sight is concerned, would be a need satisfied by, e.g., a pair of spectacles.) Thus, the ornamental function corresponds to a need of the mind. This brings us closer to the artistic function, which also clearly corresponds to an inner human need. But ornamental function is not the same as artistic function. There are works of art that make no attempt to fill a void: e.g., the statue of Artemis is a work of art, but it was not conceived in order to fill up a vacant corner of the temple; the cup is a work of art, but it was not conceived in order to adorn a table. There is art in both, but neither was made to fill a gap. Works of art with an ornamental function are called "decorative." They mark the transition from applied to so-called high art: e.g., a costly statue can be used to perform an ornamental function.

3. Imaginative function: Statue of Artemis. Made in order to arouse in the

viewer a specific imaginative idea, that of a specific divine power beneath whose protection the viewer can feel secure. This function, too, clearly arises from an inner human need rather than from those of the five outward senses. There is thus an obvious temptation to regard this imaginative function as identical to the artistic one. Works of art rooted in this imaginative function are defined as "higher art," as distinct from both applied and decorative art (the latter partly coincides with "higher" art: the Campo Santo frescoes in Pisa, or the Parthenon frieze, are just as much decorative as "higher" art).[7] There are, in fact, cases where the two more or less coincide: the statue of a Greek deity, the Christian crucifix. But this is where they coincide, not where they become identical.

In identifying the three outward functions of the work of art, we have not yet, however, found *the* function of art itself.

Human artistic creation represents a creative competition with Nature.

By this I mean two things:

1. Dependence on Nature, in the widest sense of the word: the Nature that surrounds us and the Nature within us; in a word, "the World." Man is an integral part of this Nature and this World, and cannot go beyond it. In his art, he is inescapably bound to prototypes from Nature: whether organic Nature or inorganic Nature. However monstrous the form he creates, every one of its individual components will derive from some natural prototype. To this extent it is correct to say, as some do, that human artistic activity can never be anything else but naturalistic.

2. This therefore entails a creative contest with Nature; above all it is not an imitation of Nature, nor a reproduction of Nature, nor does it spring from a desire to give the illusion of natural phenomena. That would mean that the artist had failed in his purpose. Strictly speaking, a successful, illusory representation of Nature is in any case unimaginable. Man can never bestow life and motion onto his organic works; not even an inorganic thing, a crystal, can be faithfully reproduced. Even if the external form were the same, the internal structure, the stratification of the molecules, would be utterly different.

Artistic creation therefore never can be—and indeed never sets out to be—a replication of Nature, but rather a creative contest with Nature: i.e., it is based on an imaginative idea of Nature. In art, man re-creates Nature as he would like it to be, or indeed as it already is in his imagination. (How this was elicited, we shall see presently. But for now let us turn to the issue of principles.)

The truth of this statement will become apparent if one looks at ancient Greek art, but, as we shall see, it also applies to the Christian medieval period and to the rational modern age, with its faith in causality. Now we can see why it is said that all human artistic creation is, and always has been, idealistic. For, while man in his artistic activity has always kept Nature and Nature alone in his sights, it has never occurred to him to depict that Nature, as it is, for its own sake. This, in turn, leads us back one step further—which is as far as the present state of human knowledge permits—to ask: why does man feel impelled to improve on Nature by means of art?

This compulsion, which is identical with the creative artistic impulse [*Kunstschaffenstrieb*], springs directly from human aspiration for happiness: the same aspiration that ultimately accounts for all of human culture.

Man constantly yearns for harmony. He sees this harmony constantly imperiled and endangered by natural objects and phenomena, which exist in a state of constant conflict both among themselves and with humanity. Were Nature truly as it appears to man's senses, in all its detail, he would never be able to achieve this desired harmony. And so, in works of art, man fashions for himself a view of Nature that enables him to escape from constant unrest, convincing him that Nature is better than it seems. He seeks to bring order to apparent chaos, to eliminate raw chance, against which he would otherwise have no defense. At any moment, a bolt of lightning from the sky can strike him down, and kill him as easily as it would an animal or a tree; this makes him uneasy. He therefore fashions a view of Nature in which he is protected from lightning. This view may take various forms: man might present lightning as the action of Jupiter Tonans or of a Christian God; he might also see it as a natural law of causality against which one installs a lightning rod. In all cases, however, the chosen view of Nature lulls man into a belief in harmony.

Such a reassuring view of Nature is something that man creates for himself in his imagination. And it affects his relation to everything in the world, without exception. Not just the relationship between man and Nature outside man—which we call his view of Nature in the narrower sense—but also the relationship between man and man, which we call his view of morality. All of this may be summed up as human *Weltanschauung,* or world-view. Now, when Nature presents itself to the human imagination in its true essence, rather than in its fragmentary, sensory manifestations, man is eager to behold that essence in tangible form. That is the ultimate source of all artistic creation.

We can therefore expand our definition as follows: Artistic creation is the creative competition with Nature that expresses a harmonious world-view.

Herein lies the true function of art. All the external functions which we have so far encountered are simply welcome opportunities for man to activate this supreme function of art. The creative artistic impulse, i.e., the human need for harmony, never lets such an opportunity slip by without springing into action. Thus, every object made with an external function is, to a greater or lesser degree, also a work of art. A strict distinction must nevertheless be drawn between an external and an artistic function. The artistic function coincides with the imaginative function when the imagination directly addresses the harmonious world-view: e.g., in a statue of a Greek deity (Jupiter Tonans, say) or in a crucifix. And such an observation, in turn, reveals the fundamental flaw in Semper's claim that artistic creation begins with practical, utilitarian function.

According to Semper, applied art was originally the only art, from which the human artistic sense gradually developed. But practical function and artistic function have always been two totally distinct human needs. Nor is it even certain that the practical, utilitarian function appeared first, and that the artistic function then pressed it into service. Perhaps it all began with the ornamental function—tattooing—or even with the imaginative function. The earliest monumental art, at least in Egypt, presents us so overwhelmingly with higher art—i.e., art serving an imaginative function—and the utilitarian is so subordinated to the imaginative (as in the use of the lotus as an ornamental motif), that we are tempted to look on the imaginative as the older and more basic of the two. Another element that suggests the primacy of imaginative function in human artistic creativity (the fetish) will shortly be discussed in another context.

Visual art is thus a cultural phenomenon like any other, and ultimately its evolution depends upon the same factor that governs all human cultural evolution: the world-view [*Weltanschauung*] as an expression of the human need for happiness. This world-view has differed at different times and in different places; but one must always learn what it is in order to become acquainted with the inmost essence of the art of the peoples and ages in question. If visual art is nothing other than a mental view of Nature, then we need to know in each culture, whether and to what extent Nature was regarded as in need of, and capable of, improvement, and where that improvement was sought. The answer, in every case, is to be found in the world-view of the culture concerned.

NOTES

There are two unfinished drafts for this book, both published as *Historische Grammatik der bildenden Künste, 1897–99*. The second draft is based on lecture notes, and is the one presented here. The first draft is written separately as a manuscript and has been translated into French as *Grammaire Historique des Arts Plastiques*, ed. by O. Pächt, trans. by E. Kaufholz (Paris, 1978), and forthcoming by Zone Books in an English translation. There are important differences between the two drafts, especially in the introductions: only in the second does Riegl offer an overview of the history of art.

1. Riegl explains below that Johann Winckelmann represents this approach.

2. See Semper's Introduction to his *Style in the Technical and Tectonic Arts* in this anthology.

3. It is not clear to whom Riegl is referring.

4. This seems to refer to the art historian, Heinrich Wölfflin.

5. J. Winckelmann's most influential work was *History of the Art of Antiquity* (*Geschichte der Kunst des Altertums*) (Dresden, 1764).

6. This next section is written in abbreviated form, as notes for a lecture.

7. Here Riegl makes an interesting distinction between his notions of *applied* art [*Kunstgewerbe*] and *decorative* art [dekorative *Kunst*] where the former is purely practical and the latter includes frescoes or friezes, and thus overlaps with high art.

GEORG SIMMEL
Adornment

§5. Adornment.[1] Man's desire to please his social environment contains two contradictory tendencies, in whose play and counterplay in general, the relations among individuals take their course. On the one hand, it contains kindness, a desire of the individual to give the other joy; but on the other hand, there is the wish for this joy and these "favors" to flow back to him, in the form of recognition and esteem, so that they be attributed to his personality as values. Indeed, this second need is so intensified that it militates against the altruism of wishing to please: by means of this pleasing, the individual desires to *distinguish* himself before others, and to be the object of an attention that others do not receive. This may even lead him to the point of wanting to be envied. Pleasing may thus become a means of the will to power: some individuals exhibit the strange contradiction that they need those above whom they elevate themselves by life and deed, for they build their own self-feeling upon the subordinates' realization that they *are* subordinate.

The meaning of adornment finds expression in peculiar elaborations of these motives, in which the external and internal aspects of their forms are interwoven. This meaning is to single the personality out, to emphasize it as outstanding in some sense—but not by means of power manifestations, not by anything that externally compels the other, but only through the pleasure which is engendered in him and which, therefore, still has some voluntary element in it. One adorns oneself for oneself, but can do so only by adornment for others. It is one of the strangest sociological combinations that an act, which exclusively serves the emphasis and increased significance of the actor, nevertheless attains this goal just as exclusively in the pleasure, in the visual delight it offers to others, and in their gratitude. For, even the envy of adornment only indicates the desire of the envious person to win like recognition and admiration for himself; his envy proves how much he believes these values to be connected with the adornment. Adornment is the egoistic element as such: it singles out its wearer, whose self-feeling it embodies and increases at the cost of others (for, the same adornment of all would no longer adorn the individual). But, at the same time, adornment is altruistic: its pleasure is designed for the others, since its owner can enjoy it only insofar as he mirrors himself in them;

he renders the adornment valuable only through the reflection of this gift of his. Everywhere, aesthetic formation reveals that life orientations, which reality juxtaposes as mutually alien, or even pits against one another as hostile, are, in fact, intimately interrelated. In the same way, the aesthetic phenomenon of adornment indicates a point within sociological interaction—the arena of man's being-for-himself and being-for-the-other—where these two opposite directions are mutually dependent as ends and means.

Adornment intensifies or enlarges the impression of the personality by operating as a sort of radiation emanating from it. For this reason, its materials have always been shining metals and precious stones. They are "adornment" in a narrower sense than dress and coiffure, although these, too, "adorn." One may speak of human radioactivity in the sense that every individual is surrounded by a larger or smaller sphere of significance radiating from him; and everybody else, who deals with him, is immersed in this sphere. It is an inextricable mixture of physiological and psychic elements: the sensuously observable influences which issue from an individual in the direction of his environment also are, in some fashion, the vehicles of a spiritual fulguration. They operate as the symbols of such a fulguration even where, in actuality, they are only external, where no suggestive power or significance of the personality flows through them. The radiations of adornment, the sensuous attention it provokes, supply the personality with such an enlargement or intensification of its sphere: the personality, so to speak, *is* more when it is adorned.

Inasmuch as adornment usually is also an object of considerable value, it is a synthesis of the individual's having and being; it thus transforms mere possession into the sensuous and emphatic perceivability of the individual himself. This is not true of ordinary dress which, neither in respect of having nor of being, strikes one as an individual particularity; only the fancy dress, and above all, jewels, which gather the personality's value and significance of radiation as if in a focal point, allow the mere *having* of the person to become a visible quality of its *being*. And this is so, not *although* adornment is something "superfluous," but precisely *because* it is. The necessary is much more closely connected with the individual; it surrounds his existence with a narrower periphery. The superfluous "flows over," that is, it flows to points which are far removed from its origin but to which it still remains tied: around the precinct of mere necessity, it lays a vaster precinct which, in principle, is limitless. According to its very idea, the superfluous contains no measure. The free and princely character of our being increases in the measure in which we add superfluousness to our having, since no extant structure, such as is laid down by necessity, imposes any limiting norm upon it.

This very accentuation of the personality, however, is achieved by means of an impersonal trait. Everything that "adorns" man can be ordered along a scale in terms of its closeness to the physical body. The "closest" adornment is typical of nature peoples: tattooing. The opposite extreme is represented by metal and stone adornments, which are entirely unindividual and can be put on by everybody. Between these two stands dress, which is not so inexchangeable and personal as tattooing, but neither so unindividual and separable as jewelry, whose very elegance lies in its impersonality. That this nature of stone and metal—solidly closed within itself, in no way alluding to any individuality; hard, unmodifiable—is yet forced to serve the person, this is its subtlest fascination. What is really elegant avoids pointing to the specifically individual; it always lays a more general, stylized, almost abstract sphere around man—which, of course, prevents no finesse from connecting the general with the personality. That new clothes are particularly elegant is due to their being still "stiff"; they have not yet adjusted to the modifications of the individual body as fully as older clothes have, which have been worn, and are pulled and pinched by the peculiar movements of their wearer—thus completely revealing his particularity. This "newness," this lack of modification by individuality, is typical in the highest measure of metal jewelry: it is always new; in untouchable coolness, it stands above the singularity and destiny of its wearer. This is not true of dress. A long-worn piece of clothing almost grows to the body; it has an intimacy that militates against the very nature of elegance, which is something for the "others," a social notion deriving its value from general respect.

If jewelry thus is designed to enlarge the individual by adding something super-individual which goes out to all and is noted and appreciated by all, it must, beyond any effect that its material itself may have, possess *style*. Style is always something general. It brings the contents of personal life and activity into a form shared by many and accessible to many. In the case of a work of art, we are the less interested in its style, the greater the personal uniqueness and the subjective life expressed in it. For, it is with these that it appeals to the spectator's personal core, too—of the spectator who, so to speak, is alone in the whole world with this work of art. But of what we call handicraft—which because of its utilitarian purpose appeals to a diversity of men—we request a more general and typical articulation. We expect not only that an individuality with its uniqueness be voiced in it, but a broad, historical or social orientation and temper, which make it possible for handicraft to be incorporated into the life-systems of a great many different individuals. It is the greatest mistake to think that, because it always functions as the adornment of an individual, adornment must be an individual work of art. Quite the contrary: *because* it is to serve the individual, it may not itself be of an individual nature—as little as the piece of furniture on which we sit, or the eating utensil which we manipulate, may be individual works of art. The work of art cannot, in principle, be incorporated into another life—it is a self-sufficient world. By contrast, all that occupies the larger sphere around the life of the individual, must surround it as if in ever wider concentric spheres that lead back to the individual or originate from him. The essence of stylization is precisely this dilution of individual poignancy, this generalization beyond the uniqueness of the personality—which, nevertheless, in its capacity of base or circle of radiation, carries or absorbs the individuality as if in a broadly flowing river. For this reason, adornment has always instinctively been shaped in a relatively severe style.

Besides its formal stylization, the *material* means of its social purpose is its *brilliance*. By virtue of this brilliance, its wearer appears as the center of a circle of radiation in which every close-by person, every seeing eye, is caught. As the flash of the precious stone seems to be directed at the other—like the lightning of the glance the eye addresses to him—it carries the social meaning of jewels, the being-for-the-other, which returns to the subject as the enlargement of his own sphere of significance. The radii of this sphere mark the distance which jewelry creates between men—"I have something which you do not have." But, on the other hand, these radii not only let the other participate: they shine in *his* direction; in fact, they exist only for his sake. By virtue of their material, jewels signify, in one and the same act, an increase in distance and a favor.

For this reason, they are of such particular service to vanity—which needs others in order to despise them. This suggests the profound difference which exists between vanity and haughty pride: pride, whose self-consciousness really rests only upon itself, ordinarily disdains "adornment" in every sense of the word. A word must also be added here, to the same effect, on the significance of "genuine" material. The attraction of the "genuine," in all contexts, consists in its being more than its immediate appearance, which it shares with its imitation. Unlike its falsification, it is not something isolated; it has its roots in a soil that lies beyond its mere appearance, while the unauthentic is only what it can be taken for at the moment. The "genuine" individual, thus, is the person on whom one can rely even when he is out of one's sight. In the case of jewelry, this more-than-appearance is its *value,* which cannot be guessed by being looked at, but is something that, in contrast to skilled forgery, is *added* to the appearance. By virtue of the fact that this value can always be realized, that it is recognized by all, that it possesses a relative timelessness, jewelry becomes part of a super-contingent, super-personal value structure. Talmi-gold and similar trinkets are identical with what they momentarily *do* for their wearer; genuine jewels are a value that goes beyond this; they have their roots in the value ideas of the whole social circle and are ramified through all of it. Thus, the charm and the accent they give the individual who wears them, feed on this super-individual soil. Their genuineness makes their aesthetic value—which, too, is here a value "for the others"—a symbol of general esteem, and of membership in the total social value system.

There once existed a decree in medieval France which prohibited all persons below a certain rank to wear gold ornaments. The combination which characterizes the whole nature of adornment unmistakably lives in this decree: in adornment, the sociological and aesthetic emphasis upon the personality fuses as if in a focus; being-for-oneself and being-for-others become reciprocal cause and effect in it. Aesthetic excellence and the right to charm and please, are allowed, in this decree, to go only to a point fixed by the individual's social sphere of significance. It is precisely in this fashion that one adds, to the charm which adornment gives one's whole appearance, the *sociological* charm of being, by virtue of adornment, a representative of one's group, with whose whole significance one is "adorned." It is as if the significance of his status, symbolized by jewels, returned to the individual on the very beams which originate in him and enlarge his sphere of impact. Adornment, thus, appears as the means by which his social power or dignity is transformed into visible, personal excellence.

Centripetal and centrifugal tendencies, finally, appear to be fused in adornment in a specific form, in the following information. Among nature peoples, it is reported, women's private property generally develops later than that of men and, originally, and often exclusively, refers to adornment. By contrast, the personal property of the male usually begins with weapons. This reveals his active and more aggressive nature: the male enlarges his personality sphere without waiting for the will of others. In the case of the more passive female nature, this result—although formally the same in spite of all external differences—depends more on the others' good will. Every property is an extension of personality; property is that which obeys our wills, that in which our egos express, and externally realize, themselves. This expression occurs, earliest and most completely, in regard to our body, which thus is our first and most unconditional possession. In the *adorned* body, we possess *more;* if we have the adorned body at our disposal, we are masters over more and nobler things, so to speak. It is, therefore, deeply significant that bodily adornment becomes private property above all: it expands the ego and enlarges the sphere around us which is filled with our personality and which consists in the pleasure and the attention of our environment. This environment looks with much less attention at the unadorned (and thus as if less "expanded") individual, and passes by without including him. The fundamental principle of adornment is once more revealed in the fact that, under primitive conditions, the most outstanding possession of women became that which, according to its very idea, exists only for others, and which can intensify the value and significance of its wearer only through the recognition that flows back to her from these others. In an aesthetic form, adornment creates a highly specific synthesis of the great convergent and divergent forces of the individual and society, namely, the elevation of the ego through existing for others, and the elevation of existing for others through the emphasis and extension of the ego. This aesthetic form itself stands above the contrasts between individual human strivings. They find, in adornment, not only the possibility of undisturbed simultaneous existence, but the possibility of a reciprocal organization that, as anticipation and pledge of their deeper metaphysical unity, transcends the disharmony of their appearance.

NOTE

1. In the original, this section, printed in smaller type, is called "*Exkurs über den Schmuck*" (Note on Adornment).—According to the context, "*Schmuck*" is translated as "adornment," "jewels," or "jewelry." [Tr. K. H. Wolff]

NORBERT ELIAS

"On the Use of the Knife at Table" and
"On the Use of the Fork at Table"

USE OF THE KNIFE AT TABLE

4. The knife, too, by the nature of its social use, reflects changes in the human personality with its changing drives and wishes. It is an embodiment of historical situations and structural regularities of society.

One thing above all is characteristic of its use as an eating implement in present-day Western society: the innumerable prohibitions and taboos surrounding it.

Certainly the knife is a dangerous instrument in what may be called a rational sense. It is a weapon of attack. It inflicts wounds and cuts up animals that have been killed.

But this obviously dangerous quality is beset with emotions. The knife becomes a symbol of the most diverse feelings, which are connected to its function and shape but are not deduced "logically" from its purpose. The fear it awakens goes beyond what is rational and is greater than the "calculable," probable danger. And the same is true of the pleasure its use and appearance arouse, even if this aspect is less evident today. In keeping with the structure of our society, the everyday ritual of its use is today determined more by the displeasure and fear than by the pleasure surrounding it. Therefore its use even while eating is restricted by a multitude of prohibitions. These, we have said, extend far beyond the "purely functional"; but for every one of them a rational explanation, usually vague and not easily proved, is in everyone's mouth. Only when these taboos are considered together does the supposition arise that the social attitude toward the knife and the rules governing its use while eating—and, above all, the taboos surrounding it—are primarily emotional in nature. Fear, distaste, guilt, associations and emotions of the most disparate kinds exaggerate the real danger. It is precisely this which anchors such prohibitions so firmly and deeply in the personality and which gives them their taboo character.

5. In the Middle Ages, with their upper class of warriors and the constant readiness of people to fight, and in keeping with the stage of affect control and

the relatively lenient regulations imposed on drives, the prohibitions concerning knives are quite few. "Do not clean your teeth with your knife" is a frequent demand. This is the chief prohibition, but it does indicate the direction of future restrictions on the implement. Moreover, the knife is by far the most important eating utensil. That it is lifted to the mouth is taken for granted.

But there are indications in the late Middle Ages, even more direct ones than in any later period, that the caution required in using a knife results not only from the rational consideration that one might cut or harm oneself, but above all from the emotion aroused by the sight or the idea of a knife pointed at one's own face.

> Bere not your knyf to warde your visage
> For therein is parelle and mykyl drede

we read in Caxton's *Book of Curtesye* (v. 28).[1] Here, as everywhere later, an element of rationally calculable danger is indeed present, and the warning refers to this. But it is the general memory of and association with death and danger, it is the *symbolic* meaning of the instrument that leads, with the advancing internal pacification of society, to the preponderance of feelings of displeasure at the sight of it, and to the limitation and final exclusion of its use in society. The mere sight of a knife pointed at the face arouses fear: "Bear not your knife toward your face, for therein lies much dread." This is the emotional basis of the powerful taboo of a later phase, which forbids the lifting of the knife to the mouth.

The case is similar with the prohibition which in our series of examples was mentioned first by Calviac in 1560: "If you pass someone a knife, take the point in your hand and offer him the handle, 'for it would not be polite to do otherwise."[2]

Here, as so often until the later stage when the child is given a "rational" explanation for every prohibition, no reason is given for the social ritual except that "it would not be polite to do otherwise." But it is not difficult to see the emotional meaning of this command: one should not move the point of the knife toward someone as in an attack. The mere symbolic meaning of this act, the memory of the warlike threat, is unpleasant. Here, too, the knife ritual contains a rational element. Someone might use the passing of the knife in order suddenly to stab someone. But a social ritual is formed from this danger because the dangerous gesture establishes itself on an emotional level as a general source of displeasure, a symbol of death and danger. Society, which is beginning at this time more and more to limit the real dangers threatening men, and consequently to remodel the affective life of the individual, increasingly places a barrier around the symbols as well, the gestures and instruments of danger.

Thus the restrictions and prohibitions on the use of the knife increase, along with the restraints imposed on the individual.

6. If we leave aside the details of this development and only consider the result, the present form of the knife ritual, we find an astonishing abundance of taboos of varying severity. The imperative never to put a knife to one's mouth is one of the gravest and best known. That it greatly exaggerates the actual, probable danger scarcely needs to be said; for social groups accustomed to using knives and eating with them hardly ever injure their mouths with them. The prohibition has become a means of social distinction. In the uneasy feeling that comes over us at the mere sight of someone putting his knife into his mouth, all this is present at once: the general fear that the dangerous symbol arouses, and the more specific fear of social degradation which parents and educators have from early on linked to this practice with their admonitions that "it is not done."

But there are other prohibitions surrounding the knife that have little or nothing to do with a direct danger to the body, and which seem to point to symbolic meanings of the knife other than the association with war. The fairly strict prohibition on eating fish with a knife—circumvented and modified today by the introduction of a special fish knife—seems at first sight rather obscure in its emotional meaning, though psychoanalytical theory points at least in the direction of an explanation. There is a well-known prohibition on holding cutlery, particularly knives, with the whole hand, "like a stick," as La Salle put it, though he was only at that time referring to fork and spoon.[3] Then there is obviously a general tendency to eliminate or at least restrict the contact of the knife with round or egg-shaped objects. The best-known and one of the gravest of such prohibitions is on cutting potatoes with a knife. But the rather less strict prohibition on cutting dumplings with a knife or opening boiled eggs with one also point in the same direction, and occasionally, in especially sensitive circles, one finds a tendency to avoid cutting apples or even oranges with a knife. "I may hint that no epicure ever yet put knife to apple, and that an orange should be peeled with a spoon," says *The Habits of Good Society* of 1859 and 1889.[4]

7. But these more or less strict particular prohibitions, the list of which could certainly be extended, are in a sense only examples of a general line of development in the use of the knife that is fairly distinct. There is a tendency that slowly permeates civilized society, from the top to the bottom, to restrict the use of the knife (within the framework of existing eating techniques) and wherever possible not to use the instrument at all.

This tendency makes its first appearance in a precept as apparently trivial and obvious as: "Do not keep your knife always in your hand, as village people do, but take it only when you need it."[5] It is clearly very strong in the middle of the last century, when the English book on manners just quoted, *The Habits of Good Society*, says: "Let me give you a rule—everything that can be cut without a knife, should be cut with fork alone." And one need only observe present-day usage to find this tendency confirmed. This is one of the few distinct cases of a development which is beginning to go beyond the standard of eating technique and ritual attained by court society. But this is not, of course, to say that the "civilization" of the West will actually continue in this direction. It is a beginning, a possibility like many others that exist in any society. All the same, it is not inconceivable that the preparation of food in the kitchen will develop in a direction that restricts the use of the knife at table still further, displacing it even more than hitherto to specialized enclaves behind the scenes.

Strong retroactive movements are certainly not inconceivable. It is sufficiently known that the conditions of life in the World War I automatically enforced a breakdown of some of the taboos of peacetime civilization. In the trenches, officers and soldiers again ate when necessary with knives and hands. The threshold of delicacy shrank rather rapidly under the pressure of the inescapable situation.

Apart from such breaches, which are always possible and can also lead to new consolidations, the line of development in the use of the knife is quite clear.* The regulation and control of emotions intensifies. The commands and prohibitions surround the menacing instrument become ever more numerous and differentiated. Finally, the use of the threatening symbol is limited as far as possible.

One cannot avoid comparing the direction of this civilization-curve with the custom long practiced in China. There, as has been said, the knife disappeared many centuries ago from use at table. To many Chinese the manner in which Europeans eat is quite uncivilized. "The Europeans are barbarians," people say there, "they eat with swords." One may surmise that this custom is connected with the fact that for a long time in China the model-making upper class has not been a warrior class but a class pacified to a particularly high degree, a society of scholarly officials.

---

*See Andresen and Stephan, *Beiträge,* vol. 1, p. 10, which also contains the information that the use of the fork only began to penetrate the upper strata of society in the north at the beginning of the seventeenth century. [L. Andresen and W. Stephan, *Beiträge zur Geschichte der Gottorfer Hof-und Staatsverwaltung von 1544–1659,* 2 vols. (Kiel, 1928)]

8. What is the real use of the fork? It serves to lift food that has been cut up to the mouth. Why do we need a fork for this? Why do we not use our fingers? Because it is "cannibal," as the "Man in the Club-Window," the anonymous author of *The Habits of Good Society* said in 1859. Why is it "cannibal" to eat with one's fingers? That is not a question; it is self-evidently cannibal, barbaric, uncivilized, or whatever else it is called.

But that is precisely the question. Why is it more civilized to eat with a fork?

"Because it is unhygienic to eat with one's fingers." That sounds convincing. To our sensibility it is unhygienic if different people put their fingers into the same dish, because there is a danger of contracting disease through contact with others. Each of us seems to fear that the others are diseased.

But this explanation is not entirely satisfactory. Nowadays we do not eat from common dishes. Everyone puts food into his mouth from his own plate. To pick it up from one's own plate with one's fingers cannot be more "unhygienic" than to put cake, bread, chocolate, or anything else into one's mouth with one's own fingers.

So why does one really need a fork? Why is it "barbaric" and "uncivilized" to put food into one's mouth by hand from one's own plate? Because it is distasteful to dirty one's fingers, or at least to be seen in society with dirty fingers. The suppression of eating by hand from one's own plate has very little to do with the danger of illness, the so-called "rational" explanation. In observing our feelings toward the fork ritual, we can see with particular clarity that the first authority in our decision between "civilized" and "uncivilized" behavior at table is our feeling of distaste. The fork is nothing other than the embodiment of a specific standard of emotions and a specific level of revulsion. Behind the change in eating techniques between the Middle Ages and modern times appears the same process that emerged in the analysis of other incarnations of this kind: a change in the structure of drives and emotions.

Modes of behavior which in the Middle Ages were not felt to be in the least distasteful are increasingly surrounded by unpleasurable feelings. The standard of delicacy finds expression in corresponding social prohibitions. These taboos, so far as one can be ascertained, are nothing other than ritualized or institutionalized feelings of displeasure, distaste, disgust, fear, or shame, feelings which have been socially nurtured under quite specific conditions and which are constantly reproduced, not solely but mainly because they have become institutionally embedded in a particular ritual, in particular forms of conduct.

The examples show—certainly only in a narrow cross-section and in the relatively randomly selected statements of individuals—how, in a phase of development in which the use of the fork was not yet taken for granted, the feeling of distaste that first formed within a narrow circle is slowly extended. "It is very impolite," says Courtin in 1672, "to touch anything greasy, a sauce or syrup, etc., with your fingers, apart from the fact that it obliges you to commit two or three more improper acts. One is to wipe your hand frequently on your serviette and to soil it like a kitchen cloth, so that those who see you wipe your mouth with it feel nauseated. Another is to wipe your fingers on your bread, which again is very improper. [N.B. The French terms *propre* and *malpropre* used by Courtin and explained in one of his chapters coincide less with the German terms for clean and unclean (*sauber* and *unsauber*) than with the word frequently used earlier, *proper*.] The third is to lick them, which is the height of impropriety."[6]

The *Civilité* of 1729 by La Salle, which transmits the behavior of the upper class to broader circles, says on one page: "When the fingers are very greasy, wipe them first on a piece of bread." This shows how far from general acceptance, even at this time, was the standard of delicacy that Courtin had already represented decades earlier. On the other hand, La Salle takes over fairly literally Courtin's precept that "*Bienséance* does not permit anything greasy, a sauce or a syrup, to be touched with the fingers." And, exactly like Courtin, he mentions among the ensuing *incivilités* wiping the hands on bread and licking the fingers, as well as soiling the napkin.[7]

It can be seen that manners are here still in the process of formation. The new standard does not appear suddenly. Certain forms of behavior are placed under prohibition, not because they are unhealthy but because they lead to an offensive sight and disagreeable associations; shame at offering such a spectacle, originally absent, and fear of arousing such associations are gradually spread from the standard setting circles to larger circles by numerous authorities and institutions. However, once such feelings are aroused and firmly established in society by means of certain rituals like that involving the fork, they are constantly reproduced so long as the structure of human relations is not fundamentally altered. The older generation, for whom such a standard of conduct is accepted as a matter of course, urges the children, who do not come into the world already equipped with these feelings and this standard, to control themselves more or less rigorously in accordance with it, and to restrain their drives and inclinations. If a child tries to touch something sticky, wet, or greasy with his fingers he is told, "You must not do that, people do not do things like that." And the displeasure toward such conduct which is thus aroused by the adult finally arises through habit, without being induced by another person.

To a large extent, however, the conduct and instinctual life of the child are forced even without words into the same mold and in the same direction by the fact that a particular use of knife and fork, for example, is completely established in the adult world—that is, by the example of the environment. Since the pressure or coercion of individual adults is allied to the pressure and example of the whole surrounding world, most children, as they grow up, forget or repress relatively early the fact that their feelings of shame and embarrassment, of pleasure and displeasure, are molded into conformity with a certain standard by external pressure and compulsion. All this appears to them as highly personal, something "inward," implanted in them by nature. While it is still directly visible in the writings of Courtin and La Salle that adults, too, were at first dissuaded from eating with their fingers by consideration for each other, by "politeness," to spare others a distasteful spectacle and themselves the shame of being seen with soiled hands, later it becomes more and more an inner automatism, the imprint of society on the inner self, the superego, that forbids the individual to eat in any other way than with a fork. The social standard to which the individual was first made to conform by external restraint is finally reproduced more or less smoothly within him, through a self-restraint which may operate even against his conscious wishes.

Thus the sociohistorical process of centuries, in the course of which the standard of what is felt to be shameful and offensive is slowly raised, is re-enacted in abbreviated form in the life of the individual human being. If one wished to express recurrent processes of this kind in the form of laws, one could speak, as a parallel to the laws of biogenesis, of a fundamental law of sociogenesis and psychogenesis.

NOTES

1. W. Caxton, *Book of Curtesye* (Westminster, 1477).

2. C. Calviac, *Civilité* (1560).

3. Jean Baptiste de Saint La Salle, *Les Règles de la bienséance et de la civilité chrétienne* (Rouen, 1729).

4. Anonymous, *The Habits of Good Society: A Handbook of Etiquette for Ladies and Gentlemen* (London, 1859, 2nd ed. 1889).

5. Anonymous, *Civilité française* (Lièges, 1714?).

6. Antoine de Courtin, *Nouveau traité de la civilité qui se pratique en France*, ed. by M.-C. Grassi (Saint-Etienne, 1998).

7. See note 3 above.

II

*MATERIALS
AND
TECHNIQUES
OF THE
DECORATIVE
ARTS*

INTRODUCTION

THE ARTIST-DESIGNER AND THE MACHINE

The second group of writings focuses on mechanized art production, a theme that dominated a large portion of the debate about decorative art as a whole. The texts reveal how certain theoretical positions reappeared throughout this two-century period, even while undergoing transformation at the hands of different writers. As we saw in the previous section, eighteenth-century writers like d'Alembert assumed that the functional character of decorative art was its defining trait, responsible for constituting it as a distinct artistic category. But while these earlier writers focused on the potential benefits of its functional properties, later nineteenth-century authors were skeptical of the artistic quality of industrially produced objects. Among these, British designers and architects stood out as the best known, if not the earliest, reformers of design; their theoretical discussions of decorative art not only dramatically transformed the making of interior furnishings but also introduced new ways of thinking about the relation of material and technique to function and beauty.

These nineteenth-century writings are now mostly read as precursors of later, twentieth-century theories of Modernism. Such readings, as Pevsner's *Pioneers of Modern Design,* are useful for constructing narratives of artistic and architectural reform but overlook the larger contribution of nineteenth-century British reformers to the development of decorative art theory as a whole—not just that of Modernism. When placed in the company of similar contemporary writings on industrial art, these familiar texts emerge as the major carriers of two conflicting reactions toward mechanical production: admiration for their financial and economic benefits on the one hand, and artistic contempt for machine production on the other. Only at the turn of the nineteenth century did designers and industrialists attempt to reconcile these two responses in a machine aesthetic.

As early as the eighteenth century, Diderot and Goethe voiced arguments respectively for and against the emerging industrial arts. Diderot praises the conceptual ability of inventors in the *Encyclopedia* (1751), advocating the intellectual and financial merits of the mechanical arts; as he succinctly puts it, technical development is vital both to the country's and the people's continued prosperity and well-being. On the other hand, Goethe vehemently rejects the aesthetic claims of industrial objects, in a fragmentary text of 1797, on the grounds that they lack the human touch—the only quality capable of endowing an object with beauty and a soul. To strengthen his case, Goethe concedes that a decorated hand-made object can be imbued with eternal beauty (such as Herakles's belt in *The Odyssey*) as long as the craftsman fashions it with sufficient passion and skill. Thus, while prepared to collapse the traditional distinction between the fine arts and hand-made crafts, Goethe draws the line at the machine-made object.

Goethe's evocative fragment expresses *in nuce* the position more cogently articulated by nineteenth-century British reformers. The poet's idealized evocation of the master craftsman becomes a tale of the skilled maker sacrificed on the altar of capitalism and mechanized production. The notion of craftsman and of craftsmanship certainly lent itself to romanticized interpretations: human traces on hand-made works became not only the visible imprints of a creative human soul but even carriers of spiritual, moral, and political values. Pugin's *True Principles of Pointed or Christian Architecture* (1841) reveals to what extent manual production, and the human imprint, could be invested with religious (for him Catholic) virtues. In a similar vein, Ruskin celebrates fine craftsmanship in his *Seven Lamps of Architecture* (1849), assuming it to be the external, visible evidence of internal moral and religious virtues. Most expressive of this period's veneration of craft is Ruskin's remark that the only question to ask of decoration is whether its maker was happy while working—a happiness, he assumes, that would be empathetically conveyed to the viewer.

Ruskin's romantic defense of manual production was even reinforced by supporting technical arguments. Semper, for instance, writing about contemporary decorative arts displayed in the Great Exhibition of 1851, attributes their poor quality to a lack of relation between the material used and the maker's tool. As he explains, in the past, new materials and tools automatically engendered new decorative patterns; but with the loss of any natural relation between materials and tools—when granite can be cut like butter—mankind has dried up the source from which new artistic forms emerge. For Semper the primary culprit is the contemporary abundance of technical means, but he joins Pugin, Ruskin, and Morris in seeing capitalism as the secondary culprit. Commerce and science, according to Semper, are together responsible for having bred the pernicious innovations that have, in turn, corrupted the modern soul.

The condemnation of industrial production remained quite forceful in British artistic and intellectual circles throughout the nineteenth century. At the same time, however, these critics had to contend not only with industrial art's commercial success but also with emerging discord among their own ranks. Owen Jones, for instance, was quite willing to reform the industrial arts by providing designers with distilled rules of design, applicable to all surfaces and modes of production. Indeed, his famous *Grammar of Ornament* (1856) was a godsend to industrial manufacturers, although its aim was not to encourage but rather to improve current production. Even Morris, in the 1888 article presented here, recognizes both sides of the argument about machine production. Like Diderot, he sees the potential benefits of mechanized labor for the workers, but like Goethe, Pugin, and Ruskin, he also despises its cheap, inhuman products. Morris's position effectively summarizes the inner conflict of socialist reformers for whom the machine is both a labor-saving device and a degrading influence on art and the work force.

The importance of this nineteenth-century debate in Europe and Britain can be gauged by the number and variety of writers who felt the need to pronounce on the subject. Most of them were outside the world of industrial art, and naturally rose to the defense of the hand-made. One interesting example is provided by the sculptor and art theorist Adolf von Hildebrand. In a fragmentary piece of the 1890s, he presents an undeveloped version of his extremely influential theory of visual perception (published as *The Problem of Form in Painting and Sculpture* [1893]. Here Hildebrand dismisses machine-made art on the grounds that true art must somehow coerce the viewer's own gaze into participating in a visual exchange. Machine art, though perfect in its reproduction of true art, can offer only a lifeless mask, a simulation of the outward appearance of artistic productions that cannot fool and engage human perception.

Among designers, however, there was a growing reaction to criticism of industrial production. British designer Walter Crane is representative of the position of the younger generation of the Arts and Crafts movement. Building on notions received from both Semper and Ruskin, Crane argues, in his *Claims of Decorative Art* (1892), that although there exist different types and classes of art—industrial, decorative, applied, and fine—the highest is no longer the fine arts but those in the service of useful and important objects. In the past the craftsman had been an artist and, Crane now suggests, the designer has inherited his role; in the crass world of commercial production, only the designer appreciates the artistic idiom of each material. Without either fully rejecting or accepting industrial design, Crane here implies that machine-made art is possible if developed under the careful eye of an artistic designer such as himself.

Continental practitioners and designers were willing to put forth an even more radical defense of a machine aesthetic than their British counterparts. Writing in 1895, French critic Rioux de Maillou unabashedly calls out for a machine aesthetic—a call answered by Le Corbusier a few decades later. Maillou transforms the weaknesses of decorative art into its strengths, arguing that ornament and decoration are a democratic art, capable of meeting the common people's aspiration for beauty. Influenced by the French socialist, J.-P. Proudhon, Maillou recognizes that the machine makes the worker into its slave even though it provides new goods to the lower classes. His clever solution is to see the machine as a source of social progress and mobility: the machine liberates the worker's mind, allowing ambitious ones to become designers themselves and to fashion a new beauty suited to the machine. On almost purely political grounds, Maillou condemns the beauty of aristocratic handcrafted art, envisioning in its stead a democratic, abstract beauty, stamped by the designer's will upon industrial form.

By the turn of the century, the politicization, as well as polarization, of the debate over mechanized art had pushed even Arts and Crafts craftsmen toward machine-made art. The Belgian designer Henry van de Velde is an example of a late convert to mechanical production. In a pamphlet of 1895, van de Velde rejects the political and religious ideologies used in the debate over industrial art. In contrast to Maillou and others, he emphatically dismisses any connection between industrial art and socialism, reminding one to what extent the two were linked in the minds of most theorists of decorative art. Van de Velde, however, is prepared to relinquish craftsmanship on other grounds. As he puts it, the true spirit of art survives today in a desire for adornment—a desire only the industrial arts can satisfactorily fulfill. And though the fine arts have retained the external form of craft, they have lost all spiritual content by remaining wedded to useless, dead forms of art. In contrast, makers of machine-made decorative arts have given up hand-made craftsmanship in order to pursue the embellishment of life—the true goal of art.

Van de Velde's theoretical position represents a last attempt to reconcile the tenets of the Arts and Crafts movement with those of industrial production. Many practicing architects in both Europe and the United States had in the meantime abandoned such a project. The American architect Frank Lloyd Wright, for instance, dramatically supports the idea of a machine aesthetic in "The Art and Craft of the Machine" (1901). Though influenced by the Arts and Crafts movement, Wright nonetheless defends mechanical beauty and fabrication, offering his own interpretation of Morris's writings. According to Wright, the machine can and will fulfill the highest ideals of art. Critics of machine art, he insightfully comments, have succeeded not in diminishing the power of the machine, but in eliminating ornament, that which the machine cannot make.

For Wright, the triumph of the machine was inevitable, as was the consequent disappearance of ornament and detailed decoration. Le Corbusier, publishing *The Decorative Art of Today* in 1925, lived to see the artistic category of decorative art become a misnomer, one whose label bore no relation to its content. What Le Corbusier offers here is a celebration of undecorated art rather than a celebration of the machine, for he believes that modern life requires a new vocabulary of functional forms. But, this does not mean that machine-made art is beautiful. On the contrary, Le Corbusier is simply willing to institute a complete separation of the arts. The fine arts are still superior to the others in that they alone can provoke "elevated sensations," invested with "the passion of a man," and below them are objects meant for work and utility. Not only must decorative arts be practical and industrially made, but in so doing they lose all claim to being sensual, pleasing objects. They are neither decorative nor are they art.

Le Corbusier's rejection of the "artistic" appeal of all objects that are not architecture, painting, or sculpture brings us back to where we began, with a simple recognition of the social advantages of mechanical arts. The most ardent exponent of pure design is at the same time the harshest critic of industrial design's claims to beauty. The machine triumphs by providing man with what he needs for work, in the most efficient and effective way possible. The machine aesthetic first propounded by Bing and Wright becomes for Le Corbusier a defense of functional mechanical labor, devoid of aesthetic qualities.

THE THEORY OF TECHNIQUE

While designers and architects worried about the impact of the machine on human creativity, historically minded writers, like Semper and Riegl, explored technical forms of artistic production in earlier preindustrial cultures. The earliest and most ambitious of these studies is Semper's unfinished *Style in the Technical and Tectonic Arts* (Der Stil in den technischen und tektonischen Künsten [1860]). Inspired by contemporary philological studies of etymological roots, Semper attempts to reveal the eternal symbols of artistic language through an analysis of their technical origins. For Semper the four basic "technical" arts developed out of four types of raw materials, each of whose specific physical properties affected the art itself: thus from flexible and tough material comes textile art, from soft and plastic one comes ceramic art, from elastic and rod-shaped material comes tectonics (carpentry, etc.) and, finally, from firm and resistant material comes stereotomy (masonry, etc.). The interaction of these four basic arts, and their influence on architectural forms, should explain the evolution of all plastic arts as variations on a discrete set of primary artistic forms. In thus excluding the role of human expression and creativity, Semper attempts to treat art as a technical product and to elevate its study to that of a science, eliminating its aesthetic, subjective character.

Riegl, as already noted, wrote strongly against Semper and his technical theories. In fact, his *Problems of Style* (1893) can hardly be understood if one does not know what he was reacting to. Riegl there offers the first continuous history of ornament, a domain until then completely colored by Semperian theories of artistic development. In response to Semper, Riegl unveils an ambitious vision of artistic drive, seeing it as the hidden force behind all artistic creation and development. But to do so, he must painstakingly prove the existence of a universal instinct to adorn and of ornament's ability to travel from one culture to another. Although Riegl's book had little immediate impact his notion of *Kunstwollen*, of artistic volition or impulse, later served as an extremely effective antidote to the Semperian, technical interpretations of the history of ornament.

The two introductions by Riegl and Semper demonstrate in what terms the debate about contemporary industrial art was carried over from the world of artistic practice into that of art history. To a large extent, this scholarly debate focused on one element, as had Semper and Riegl, namely ornament—the material expression of artistic ambition and industrial production (presented in Part III of this anthology). The debate over machine-made art itself continued throughout the first half of the twentieth century, but as I have argued in the Introduction, it no longer focused on decorative art. Rather, it led to the abandonment of the idea of decoration and ornament, for which were substituted that of design, material culture, industrial art, folk art, craft, even kitsch.

Writing in 1938, British philosopher R. G. Collingwood contributes a final sally to the moribund debate, revealing to what extent the notion of "art" itself had become divisive and controversial. In his *Principles of Art*, Collingwood tries to reestablish the crucial distinction between, on the one hand, high art and artistic creation and, on the other, craft or skilled execution. Like Riegl, Collingwood blames the technical interpretations of art for having eliminated artistic vision and imagination; and like Semper he is skeptical of contemporary techniques that distort the relation between the material and the tool. But Collingwood's purpose in writing his book is more ambitious than that of either Riegl or Semper. He rescues poetry and all the fine arts from the now sullied category of art by redefining art itself. To do so, Collingwood breaks with the Kantian aesthetic tradition, reviving in its stead the Greek concept of a beauty grounded in eros—that which draws one toward the good (in a passage not contained in the excerpt). Thus in salvaging the artistic creativity of the fine arts from the impinging domain of craft, Collingwood detaches it completely from the visual, sensual pleasure that had defined the philosophical domain of aesthetics over the past two centuries.

Collingwood's violent reaction to craft, and to its inclusion within the concept of art, is perhaps an extreme response to a debate that was almost exhausted. But his contribution also functions as an effective summary of some of the dominant themes defining the debate about machine-made art: for one, his text shows the acceptance and success of ideas first articulated by the leaders of the Arts and Crafts movement; second, the tension between skill and imagination in his writing demonstrates that the argument between Semper and Riegl remains unresolved; and, finally, his attempt to redefine beauty not only reveals an unexpected affinity with Le Corbusier's exclusion of sensual beauty from the domain of craft but is also a radical, almost prophetic, vision of artists' future rejection of sensual beauty as the basis of fine art.

DENIS DIDEROT

Art

Art S.M. (Encyclopædic Order. Understanding. Memory. Natural Science. Applied Science. Art) Abstract metaphysical term. Originally observations were made of the nature, purpose, uses, and qualities of beings and their symbols; later the term art or science was applied to the centre or point of junction to which observations are related in order to form a system of principles, methods, and rules tending towards coordination. That, in general terms, is what an art is. *Example:* People pondered the use of words and then invented the word *grammar*. Grammar is the name given to the system of principles and methods applied to a certain subject; the subject in this case is articulate sound. The same applies to other arts and sciences.

ORIGIN OF ARTS AND SCIENCES: Arts and sciences derive from man's industry being applied to natural phenomena, whether for his needs, his comfort, his amusement, or just his curiosity. Our specialized observations and reflections on any subject are called either an art or a science according to the nature of what logicians would call their formal object. If it involves doing, the body of principles and observations relating to it constitutes an art: if, on the contrary, the object is one which involves examination and thought about its various aspects, the body of principles and observations is called a science. Metaphysics is thus a science while ethics is an art. The same distinction applies to theology and pyrotechnology.

THEORY AND PRACTICE OF ARTS: It follows from the foregoing that all arts must have both a theoretical and a practical side. The theory of an art consists merely of unapplied knowledge whereas the practice of it involves the habitual and instinctive application of the same knowledge. It is difficult, almost impossible, to progress very far in the practice of an art without any theory, and conversely it is hard to have a real grasp of the theory without some practical experience. In every art there are a great many things connected with material, instruments, and technique which are only learnt by use. Practice provides the physical phenomena and shows up the practical difficulties and it is the task of theory to explain the phenomena and solve the difficulties. It follows from this that in order to speak intelligently about his art, an artist must be able to bring his reason to bear on it.

DISTINCTION BETWEEN MECHANICAL AND LIBERAL ARTS: If one examines the products of various forms of art it is clear that some of them owe more to the mind of the artist than to his manual efforts while with others it is the opposite. This difference gives rise to two things: the fact that some arts are conceded a higher place in the scale of values than others, and the division into liberal arts and mechanical arts. Although this division is basically sound it has had the unfortunate effect of causing certain highly estimable and very useful people to be despised and of encouraging in us a very natural laziness which has already led us too easily to believe that a close application in studies of material things, particular experiments and the like is in some way a derogation of human dignity and further that to practise, or even to study, the *mechanical* arts is to lower oneself to subjects in which research is laborious, thought undignified, and exposition difficult. Occupation with them is considered to impart a slur and is moreover wearisome for their number is incalculable, and their value infinitesimal. *Minui majestatem mentis humanæ, si in experimentis et rebus particularibus. . . .* (Bacon—*Novum Organum*).[1] This prejudice has tended to fill cities with intellectual snobs and useless contemplatives and the countryside with petty tyrants who are ignorant, idle, and haughty. It was not subscribed to by Bacon, one of the first geniuses of England, nor by Colbert,[2] one of France's greatest ministers, nor by men of intelligence and wisdom in any age. Bacon regarded the history of the *mechanical arts* as the most important branch of true philosophy and was therefore not the man to disdain the practice of them. Colbert regarded the establishment of industries and factories as the surest source of wealth for a country. In the opinion of modern thinkers with sound ideas on the values of things, the man who gave France all her engravers, painters, sculptors, and artists of all sorts, who beat the English at the knitting-machine, the Genoese at making velvet, and the Venetians at glassblowing, certainly did no less for the State than those who fought and vanquished her enemies. In the eyes of the philosopher there is perhaps more merit in having produced the Le Bruns, the Le Sueurs, and the Audrans, in having painted and engraved the battle of Alexandria and woven the victories of our generals into tapestries than in having actually won the victories.[3] If we put the real benefits derived from the highest science and most widely honoured arts on the one side of the scales, and on the other side those derived from the mechanical arts, we shall find that the relative esteem in which the two sides are held will in no way correspond with their true usefulness, and that far more praise is given to those who spend their time in making us think that we are happy than to those who exert themselves in seeing that we are so in fact. A strange set of standards which requires men to be usefully employed yet disdains one who is useful!

OBJECTS OF ART IN GENERAL: Man is only the minister or interpreter of nature: he is limited to what he knows, either from experience or as a result of reflection, about his surroundings. His arm, however strong and supple it may be, can achieve but little unaided: to achieve greater things man requires tools and knowledge. Tools are additional muscles to his arm, and knowledge is new energy for his mind. The object of all *art* in general, or of any system of laws tending towards a special end, is to superimpose on a basis provided by nature certain determinate forms. This natural basis can be either matter or thought, some emanation of the human brain or some manifestation of nature itself. In the *mechanical arts,* which I emphasize all the more here because others have neglected them, *men's capabilities are limited to bringing together or separating natural objects. Whether he can achieve all things or nothing, depending upon whether the bringing together or separating is or is not possible.* (See Bacon's *Novum Organum.*)

NOTES FOR A GENERAL TREATISE ON THE MECHANICAL ARTS: Very often little is known of the origin of mechanical arts and not much more of their history. This is the natural outcome of the contempt felt in all ages and by all nations, whether scholarly or warlike, for those who engage in them. Accordingly, one has to fall back on philosophic speculation and, starting from some likely hypothesis or some fortuitous event, work one's way up to the present time. I will explain this by an example which I prefer to take from the *mechanical arts,* which are less known than from the *liberal arts* which have received much wider fame under a variety of forms. Supposing nothing were known of the origin of glass-making or paper-making, what would a philosopher do if he proposed to write a history of these arts? He might imagine a scrap of linen fallen by chance into a vessel of water and remaining there until it was dissolved, so that instead of a piece of cloth in the bottom of the vessel when it was emptied there was nothing to be seen but a sort of sediment and perhaps a few threads to indicate that the raw material of the sediment had once been in the form of linen. As for glass-making, he might imagine that man's earliest habitations were made of baked earth or brick: now it is impossible to bake bricks at any great heat without some of the material becoming vitrified; that, therefore, might be the form in which glass first became known. But what a difference between that dirty, greenish scale and the clear transparency of plate-glass! Nevertheless, that is the sort of chance circumstance from which the philosopher will start in order to arrive at the point reached today in the art of glass-making.

ADVANTAGES OF THIS METHOD: Starting off like this, the progress of an art would be presented more clearly and more instructively than it would be by the actual history if it were known. The obstacles which had to be surmounted in order to perfect the art would appear in an entirely natural order, and the synthetic explanation of the successive steps in its development would make the process intelligible to even the most ordinary brains and would set artists on the right road in their search for perfection.

ORDER TO BE FOLLOWED IN SUCH A TREATISE: With regard to the order in which such a treatise should be presented, I think the best thing would be to relate the arts to natural phenomena. A comprehensive list of the latter would give rise to many unknown *arts*. Many more would arise from a circumstantial examination of the different aspects of the same phenomena. The first of these requires an extensive knowledge of natural history, and the second demands a considerable ability in dialectic. A treatise on the *arts*, therefore, is not, as I see it, the task for an ordinary man. Don't let it be imagined that the ideas I have put forward are profitless and that I am promising mankind merely imaginary discoveries. After remarking in company with a philosopher whom I never tire of praising, what I am never tired of saying, that natural science is incomplete without the arts, after having called upon the naturalists to crown their work in the animal, vegetable, and mineral kingdoms with some experience of the mechanical arts, I make bold to follow his example and add: *Ergo rem quam ago, non opinionem, sed opus esse; camque non sectae alicujus, aut placiti, sed utilitatis esse et amplitudinis immensae fundamenta.* This is no mere system; these are no mere human fancies: they are the finding of experience and the foundations of a vast edifice.[4] Anyone who thinks differently is only trying to narrow the scope of our studies and inhibit the human brain. Many of our fields of study we owe to chance: chance has opened up some of the most important ones without our ever having sought them; can we therefore assume that we shall find nothing new when we add our efforts to its caprice and bring some order and method into our researches. If we now possess secrets hitherto undreamed-of, and if history may serve as a guide, why should the future not hold for us secrets of which at present we have no inkling? If one had said a few centuries ago to the sort of people who measure possibilities by the restricted standards of their own genius and who cannot imagine anything they do not know, that there existed a powder which could split rocks and knock down even the thickest walls at fantastic distances, of which a small quantity buried in the earth could shake the ground, forcing its way to the surface and leaving a crater large enough to swallow a town, all they would have done would have been to compare these effects with those obtainable by wheels, pulleys, levers, counterweights and the other mechanical devices they knew, and pronounce the powder a myth or else say that only lightning or the force which produces earthquakes, and which cannot be imitated by man, would be capable of performing such terrifying prodigies. That is how the great philosopher put it to his own age and to all ages that followed. Still following his example, let us go on to ask how much false reasoning would have been caused by the projected machine to raise water by the use of fire, as it was first attempted in London, particularly if the inventor had had the modesty to admit to being ignorant of mechanics? If such were the only judges of inventions in the world, nothing great or small would ever be achieved. Let those then who hasten to pronounce upon new inventions which have no implicit contradiction, and which are very often no more than slight modifications of existing machines bespeaking no more ability than that of a skilled worker; let those, I say, who are so limited as to classify such inventions as impossibilities, understand that they themselves do not know enough to be able to guess at the truth—As Lord Chancellor Bacon would say to them: *Qui sumpta,* or less pardonable still, *qui neglecta ex his quae praesto sunt conjectura, ea aut impossibilia, aut minus verisimilia, putet; eum scire debere se non satis doctum, ne ad optandum quidem commode et apposite esse.*[5]

ANOTHER REASON FOR RESEARCH: A thought which should encourage us even more in our researches and determine us to study our surroundings closely is that centuries have passed by without men's having seen things which were, so to speak, under their noses. Printing and engraving are examples. How strange a thing is the human mind! When it is a question of research, it mistrusts its own powers and surrounds itself with difficulties of its own creation so that its quest appears impossible, but when things come to light by chance, it cannot understand why for so long it has not even been looking for them, and then it is sorry.

REMARKABLE DIFFERENCE BETWEEN MACHINES: Having put forward my ideas about a philosophical treatise on art in general, I shall pass on to some particular observations on the method of dealing with certain mechanical arts. One sometimes uses an extremely complicated machine in order to produce an apparently simple result; in other cases a really very simple machine is used for quite complicated performances. In the first case, the effect it is required to produce being easily understood and the knowledge of it not cluttering the brain or overtaxing the memory, we will start by naming the result and then proceed to describe the machine which achieves it. In the second case, on the other hand, it will be more to the point to start with the machine and then study the effect. The effect of a clock is to divide time into equal portions by the use of a hand which travels slowly and at a uniform speed in accordance with a fixed plan. If therefore I were showing a clock to someone who had not seen one before I should first of all teach him what it did and only after that come to the mechanism. I should be very careful not to follow the same course with someone who asked me what knitting was, or cloth, drugget, velvet, or satin. I should start here with the process involved in these manufactures. Once that is understood, the product of the machine becomes discernible in a flash, which would not be the case without the preliminary explanations. To convince one-self of the soundness of these observations one has only to try to give an exact definition of *gauze*, assuming one has no notion of gauze-making machinery.

GEOMETRY OF THE ARTS: It will be freely admitted that there are but few artists who do not need to know the elements of mathematics, but a paradox not so readily seen is that in many cases such knowledge would be harmful to them if their wide practical familiarity with physical things were not there as a corrective to theory—knowledge of places, positions, irregular figures, substances, and their characteristics, elasticity, rigidity, friction, consistency, durability, effects of air, water, cold, heat, dryness, etc. It is clear that academical mathematics consist only of the simpler and less involved elements of the mathematics of workshops. There is no such lever in real life as Varignon[6] imagines in his propositions; there is no natural lever of which all the conditions can be brought to calculation. Among these conditions there are many of great practical importance which, though they are appreciable, cannot be measured by even the most precise mathematical computation. From this it follows that one whose knowledge of science is purely theoretical is usually a pretty clumsy fellow, while an artist whose knowledge of science is only practical is but a very limited craftsman. But, it seems to me, experience shows that an artist can more easily dispense with theory than any man, no matter what he be, can do without a certain measure of practical knowledge. The whole question of friction, for example, has remained, in spite of calculations, a matter of experience and experiment. How far would theory take us on its own? How many bad machines are designed every day by people who imagine that levers and wheels and pulleys and ropes work in a machine as they do on paper and who, having no practical experience, know nothing of the difference between an actual machine and its sectional drawing. Another observation which we shall make here, since it fits the occasion, is that there are machines which work perfectly well on a small scale but will not work on a large scale and, conversely, some which work all right on a large scale but will not function on a small scale. Among the latter must be classified, I think, all those of which the effect is mainly dependent on a considerable weight in the component parts, or on the force of reaction of a fluid, or on some considerable quantity of elastic material to which the machines are to be applied: in miniature the weight of the parts is reduced, the reaction of the fluid becomes hardly noticeable, the forces counted upon disappear, and the machine is ineffective. But as in the size of a machine there is a point, if one may so express it, beyond which it will be without effect, so there is another point beyond which, or short of which, it will not produce the greatest effect of which its mechanism is capable. Every machine has, in mathematical parlance, a dimension of maximum efficiency just as, in the construction of it, each part considered in relation to its most nearly perfect functioning is of a size determined by the other parts; all things are of a size determined, with a view to their most nearly perfect functioning, by the machine of which they are part, by the use to which they are to be put, and by a host of other factors. But, it will be asked, what is this point in the size of a machine above or below which it is either too large or too small? What is the true and absolute size of a really good watch, or a perfect mill, or the best possible ship? It is for the experimental science of centuries, assisted by the most accurate theoretical work, to provide an approximate answer to these questions, and I am convinced that a satisfactory answer is impossible to obtain from either of the branches of science working separately and very difficult when they are united.

THE LANGUAGE OF ART: I find the language of art very imperfect in two respects, the lack of accurate terms and the multiplicity of synonyms. There are some tools which have a number of names, while others have nothing but the generic term, *engine, machine,* etc., with no specific qualification; sometimes the smallest difference is enough to make the artist abandon the generic term and invent a special name, at others some instrument, peculiar both in form and in use, has no name or else shares a name with some other instrument with which it has nothing in common. It is desirable that more attention should be paid to the analogy between shapes and uses. Geometricians use more figures than names, but in the language of the arts, hammers, pliers, buckets, spades, etc., have almost as many names as there are crafts. The language changes very largely from one to another. I am convinced, however, that the most obscure processes and the most complicated machines could be explained in a few ordinary, familiar words, if one made up one's mind not to employ technical terms except where they represent particular ideas. One ought surely to be convinced of the truth of my contention when one considers that complicated machines are no more than a combination of simple machines, that the number of simple machines is limited, and that, in the explanation of any process, every movement of it can be reduced, without any great inaccuracy, to either a linear movement or a rotary movement. What is needed, then, is that a sound logician, familiar with the arts, should take their grammar in hand. The first thing he would have to do would be to fix the relative values of big, large, medium, narrow, thick, thin, small, light, etc. In order to do that he would have to try to find a constant in nature, or fix the mean values of height, size, and strength of man and relate to them all the existing vague expressions of quantity, or at least prepare a comparative table and invite artists to make their various languages conform to it. The second step would be to consider the differences and resemblances between one instrument and another, or between one process and another, and decide whether they should retain a common name or be given different ones. I have no doubt that whoever undertakes this task will find fewer new words to be introduced than synonyms to be got rid of, and more difficulty in defining common terms, such as *grace* in painting, a *knot* in lacemaking, or a *groove* in a number of arts, than in explaining the most complicated machinery. It is the lack of exact definitions and their multiplicity rather than the variety of motions in the processes that makes clear speaking about the arts so difficult. The second difficulty can be remedied only by familiarizing oneself with the subjects; they are well worth it both from the practical advantage gained and on account of the honour they do to the human mind. In what physical or metaphysical system will one find more intelligence, more wisdom, more system than in a machine for spinning gold thread, or making stockings, or lace, or gauze, or in clothworking or the manufacture of silk. What mathematical exposition is more complicated than the mechanism of some clocks or the processes through which hemp passes or the silkworm's cocoon before either gives a workable thread. What more beautiful, more delicate, more singular projection is there than that of a pattern held by the cords of a simple and passing from them on to the threads of the warp. What has anyone ever conceived in any field whatsoever more subtle than the shading of velvet. I should never be done if I undertook the task of citing all the marvels that manufacturing processes have to show to those whose eyes are neither too familiar nor too dull to see.

With the English philosopher I will stop at the three inventions, unknown to the ancients, whose inventors, to the shame of modern history and poetry are scarcely known: I mean the art of printing, the discovery of gunpowder, and of the properties of a magnetized needle. What a complete revolution these three discoveries made in the field of letters, in the art of war and in that of navigation! The magnetized needle guided our vessels into hitherto unknown parts of the globe; printing made possible the exchange of ideas between scientists all over the world and for all time to come; gunpowder has given birth to all those masterpieces of architecture which guard our frontiers and those of our enemies; these three arts have, one might almost say, changed the face of the earth.

Let us at last give the artists their due. The liberal arts have adequately sung their own praises; they might now use what voice they have left to celebrate the mechanical arts. It is for the liberal arts to lift the mechanical arts from the contempt in which prejudice has kept them so long, and it is for the patronage of kings to protect them from the poverty in which they still languish. Artisans have believed themselves contemptible because people have looked down on them; let us teach them to have a better opinion of themselves; that is the only way to obtain more nearly perfect results from them. We need a man to rise up in the academies and go down to the workshops and gather material about the arts to be set out in a book which will persuade artists to read, philosophers to think on useful lines, and the great to make at last some worthwhile use of their authority and their wealth.

A suggestion which we make bold to advance to scientists is to practise what they themselves preach to us and not to judge things too hurriedly nor to condemn an invention as useless because it has not in its early stages all the advantages one might ask of it. Would not Montaigne, an extremely philosophic man be it said, blush if he were amongst us now at having written that firearms were of so little effect, apart from the shock to the ears, which people already scarcely noticed, that he hoped the use of them would soon be abandoned?[7] Would he not have shown greater wisdom had he encouraged men of his day to find as a substitute for the slow-match and the wheel-lock some device which more nearly corresponded with the swift action of powder, or if he had predicted that such a device would one day be invented? Put Bacon in the place of Montaigne and you will see him examine the material philosophically and prophesy, I make bold to say, grenades, mines, guns, bombs, and the whole gamut of military explosives. But Montaigne is by no means the only philosopher to have pronounced hasty judgments on the possibility or impossibility of machines. Did not Descartes, that extraordinary genius whose fate it was to mislead as well as to lead, and others as worthy as the author of the *Essais,* pronounce the mirror of Archimedes to be a mere fable?[8] Yet that very mirror is on view to all scientists in the *Jardin du Roi,* and the effects it produces in the hands of M. de Buffon, who discovered it, leave one in no doubt about its effects on the walls of Syracuse when it was in the hands of Archimedes.[9] Such notable examples are surely enough to make us wary.

We invite artists for their part to consult with scientists and not to allow their discoveries to die with them. They must realize that it is a theft from society to keep useful knowledge secret and that to put individual before public interests in such cases is no less blameworthy than in a thousand others where they would not hesitate to speak out. If they are forthcoming they will rid themselves of a number of delusions, particularly the one under which they almost all labour, that their art has reached the highest peak of perfection. Their lack of knowledge often leads them to blame their material for what is in fact a limitation in themselves. Obstacles appear insurmountable to them as soon as they experience difficulty in seeing a way over them. Let us experiment: let every one join in the experiments, the artist offering his manual skill, the academician his knowledge and advice, and the rich man the cost of time and materials. Then, very shortly, our arts and manufactures will have all the superiority we wish over those of other countries.

THE SUPERIORITY OF ONE INDUSTRY OVER ANOTHER: What will give, however, one industry superiority over another is first and foremost the quality of the materials used. To this must be added speed and perfection in execution. The quality of the materials is a matter of careful choice. Speed and perfection in execution depend entirely on the number of workers employed. Where they are numerous, each process is the job of a different man. One man performs and always will perform one operation and one only; another will always perform some other operation; this results in each operation being done well and swiftly and in the best article still being the cheapest. Besides, taste and workmanship will necessarily improve where there is a large number of workers, because it is unlikely that among them there will be none capable of thinking and arranging things and finally discovering the one way by which they can surpass their fellows, be it a way to save material or time or to improve the industry by means of a new machine or a more convenient movement. If foreign manufacturers cannot beat those of Lyons it is not because they do not know how we work: everyone has the same methods, the same silks, and much the same way of doing things, but it is only at Lyons that you will find thirty thousand workers all engaged in the same manufacture.

We could carry this article even further, but what we have just said will be enough for those who are capable of thinking, while for the others we should never be able to say enough. Some rather heavy metaphysical passages will be found in it, but that could not be avoided. We had to speak about art in general and our propositions therefore had to be general. It is only common sense that the more general a proposition is the more abstract it must be, abstraction being the extension of a truth by removing from it the details which limit it to the particular. If we had been able to spare the reader these thorny passages we should also have saved ourselves a great deal of work.

NOTES

1. Francis Bacon, *Novum Organum* (1620) 1:82, "The dignity of the human mind is impaired by long and close intercourse with experiments and particulars." In *The Works of Francis Bacon,* ed. by J. Spedding, R. L. Elis, and D. D. Heath (New York, 1968; reprint of London, 1870), 4:81.

2. Jean-Baptiste Colbert (1619–1683) served under King Louis XIV as Conseiller du Roi, Contrôleur Général des finances, and Surintendant et Ordonnateur Général des Bâtiments, Arts et Manufactures. In this last capacity he founded the Gobelins as the Manufacture Royale des Meubles de la couronne, bringing together tapestry-makers, engravers, sculptors, goldsmiths, founders, lapidaries, and cabinetmakers.

3. Diderot is praising Colbert's patronage of the most important French painters of the seventeenth century: Charles Le Brun (1619–1690), Eustache Le Sueur (1616–1655), and Claude Audran II (1639–1684), all of whom helped decorate royal residences, such as the Louvre and Versailles.

4. Bacon, *Cogitata et visa,* in *Works of Francis Bacon* (as in note 1 above), 3:618.

5. Bacon, *Cogitata et visa,* in *Works of Francis Bacon* (as in note 1 above), 3:615.

6. The French mathematician Pierre Varignon (1654–1722) was an intimate friend of Newton and Leibnitz and the most powerful advocate of differential calculus.

7. Michel de Montaigne (1533–1592) is best known as the author of *Essais,* which established a new literary form, reflecting the spirit of skepticism inspired by classical authors, especially Plutarch.

8. René Descartes (1596–1650) was a French mathematician and philosopher, whose fame rests on his *Discours de la méthode* (1637) in which he attempted to unify all knowledge as the product of clear reasoning from self-evident premises.

9. Georges Louis Leclerc de Buffon (1707–1788) was a French naturalist, and author of a forty-four-volume *Histoire naturelle* (1749–1804). He was also Keeper of the Jardin du Roi, where he was able to recreate the "*miroir ardent,*" whose workings he explained in the article "Invention des miroirs ardents pour brûler à une grande distance," in *l'Histoire de l'Académie Royale des Sciences,* 1747, pp. 82–101.

JOHANN WOLFGANG VON GOETHE
Art and Handicraft

All arts begin with the necessary. There is hardly a thing, among all those that we own or use, that we cannot fashion into a pleasant shape, position in a suitable place, and bring into a certain relationship with other things. This natural sense of rightness and propriety, which leads to the first attempts at art, must never desert the artist who seeks to climb the last and loftiest peak, so closely is it linked with the sense of the possible and feasible. These, taken together, are the true basis of every art. And yet, alas, since the very earliest times, human beings have never made any *natural* progress in the arts, any more than in their civil, moral, and religious institutions. On the contrary, generations have succumbed to mindless imitation, false application of true experience, blind tradition, and complacent inheritance from one generation to the next. All of the arts have suffered to a greater or lesser degree from such influences—as they still do to this day: for our own century, enlightened though it has been in many intellectual matters, has proved less adept, perhaps, than any other in compounding pure sensuality with intellect. And this alone is the way to generate a true work of art.

We are richer in all those things that can be inherited: all the advantages of manual dexterity, the whole mass of mechanical skills. But what seems to have become more of a rarity in our age is that which needs to be inborn: the spontaneous talent that reveals the true artist. I hold nevertheless that it still exists as much as ever it did; but that, being a highly delicate plant, it has found neither the soil, nor the weather, nor the husbandry that it requires.

If we look at those works of art that survive from antiquity, or if we reflect on the descriptions that have come down to us, it becomes evident that, for those nations among whom art flourished, everything they possessed, even the merest utensil, was a work of art and was decorated accordingly.

The work of a true artist bestows on his material an inward and eternal value; whereas the form that a mechanical worker confers on even the most precious metal—excellent though the workmanship may be—always retains a trivial and indifferent quality that can give pleasure only so long as it remains new. This, to me, seems to mark the true distinction between luxury, on one hand, and the enjoyment of true wealth, on the other. What constitutes luxury, as I see it, is not that a rich man possesses many precious things but that he possesses things whose form he must change in order to acquire a momentary pleasure for himself and a certain standing in the eyes of others. True wealth, on the other hand, consists in the possession of things that one can keep for a lifetime, enjoy for a lifetime, and enjoy all the more as one's knowledge increases. According to Homer, a certain belt was so excellent that the artist who made it was entitled to take his ease for the rest of his life.[1] In the same way, we might say of the owner of that belt that he was entitled to enjoy it for the rest of his life.

Similarly, the Villa Borghese is more opulent, more magnificent, more dignified as a palace than some vast royal dwelling in which there is little or nothing that an artisan or a manufacturer could not have produced.[2] Prince Borghese possesses what no one but he can possess, and what no one can procure at any price. Over the generations, he and his family will value and enjoy those possessions more, the purer their intellects, the more sensitive their feelings, the truer their taste becomes. And with them, over the centuries, many thousands of good, educated, and enlightened persons of every nation will join them in admiring and enjoying those same objects.

By contrast, the productions of the purely mechanical artist can never hold such interest, whether for him or for anyone else. For his thousandth work is like his first; and ultimately it exists a thousand times over. What is more, machinery and manufactures have lately been carried to the highest degree, and commerce has flooded the whole world with pretty, elegant, pleasing, ephemeral objects.

From this it will be seen that the only antidote to luxury—given the possibility and the will—lies in true art and a true artistic response. By the same token, the perfecting of machinery, the refinement of handicraft and factory production, bids fair to be the utter downfall of art.

Over the past twenty years, we have witnessed an increased public interest in the visual arts; and we have seen the effects of that interest on the ways in which art is talked about, written about, and purchased. Astute manufacturers and entrepreneurs have taken artists into their pay, and with their ingenious mechanical imitations they have battened on the lovers of art, who are gratified before they are educated. In seeming to gratify the nascent public interest, they have deflected and destroyed it.

The English, for instance, with their modern-antique ceramics, their red, black, and polychrome art, are making vast profits on every side; and yet, properly considered, all this gives no more satisfaction than a plain china vase, a pretty wallpaper, or a pair of fine buckles.

There is now to be a great painting factory, in which, they tell us, they intend

Johann Wolfgang von Goethe {151}

to copy any painting, rapidly, cheaply, and indistinguishably from the original, by means of totally mechanical operations such as any child can be employed to perform. If this comes to pass, then of course only the eyes of the common herd will be deceived. In the process, however, artists will be deprived of many sources of support and many opportunities to better themselves.

I close this observation with the wish that it may be of use to some individual, here or there: for the whole is rushing onward with irresistible force.

NOTES

1. Homer describes Herakles's belt in *The Odyssey* Book 11, lines 615–29, trans. by R. Fitzgerald (Garden City, 1961), p. 194.

2. The Villa Borghese was open to select visitors, such as Goethe, see his *Italian Journey*, ed. by T. P. Saine and J. L. Sammons, trans. by R. R. Heitner (New York, 1989).

A. WELBY PUGIN

On Metal-work

But to return to metal-work. We have in the next place to consider the use of cast-iron. When viewed with reference to mechanical purposes, it must be considered as a most valuable invention, but it can but rarely be applied to ornamental purposes.

Iron is so much stronger a material than stone that it requires, of course, a much smaller substance to attain equal strength; hence, to be consistent, the mullions of cast-iron tracery must be so reduced as to look painfully thin, devoid of shadow, and out of all proportion to the openings in which they are fixed. If, to overcome these objections, the castings are made of the same dimensions as stone, a great inconsistency with respect to the material is incurred; and, what will be a much more powerful argument with most people, treble the cost of the usual material. [Plates 7a, b]

Moreover, all castings must be deficient of that play of light and shade consequent on bold relief and deep sinkings, so essential to produce a good effect.

Cast-iron is likewise a source of continual repetition, subversive of the variety and imagination exhibited in pointed design. A mould for casting is an expensive thing; once got, it must be worked out. Hence we see the same window in green-house, gate-house, church, and room; the same strawberry-leaf,

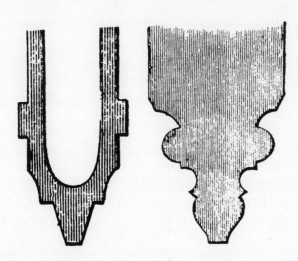

Plate 7a (left).
Cast-Iron Mullion
Plate 7b (right).
Stone Mullion

sometimes perpendicular, sometimes horizontal, sometimes suspended, sometimes on end; although by the principles of pure design these various positions require to be differently treated.

Cast-iron is a deception; it is seldom or never left as iron. It is disguised by paint, either as stone, wood, or marble. This is a mere trick, and the severity of Christian or Pointed Architecture is utterly opposed to all deception: better is it to do a little substantially and consistently with truth than to produce a great but false show. Cheap deceptions of magnificence encourage persons to assume a semblance of decoration far beyond either their means or their station, and it is to this cause we may assign all that mockery of splendour which pervades even the dwellings of the lower classes of society. Glaring, showy, and meretricious ornament was never so much in vogue as at present; it disgraces every branch of our art and manufactures, and the correction of it should be an earnest consideration with every person who desires to see the real principles of art restored.

. . .

Silversmiths are no longer artists; they manufacture fiddle-headed spoons, punchy racing cups, cumbersome tureens and wine-coolers; their vulgar salvers are covered with sprawling rococo, edged with a confused pattern of such universal use that it may be called with propriety the *Sheffield eternal.* Cruet-stand, tea-pot, candlestick, butter-boat, tray, waiter, tea-urn, are all bordered with this in and out shell-and-leaf pattern, which, being struck in a die, does not even possess the merit of relief. Like every thing else, silver-work has sunk to a mere trade, and art is rigidly excluded from its arrangements.

Iron-smiths were artists formerly, and great artists too; Quentin Matsys for instance, whose beautiful well-top stands in front of Antwerp Cathedral, and whose splendid picture of the entombment of our Lord is the greatest ornament of the Musée of that city.[1] Quentin Matsys are not, however, of our generation; if you want some objects executed in iron rather different from what are in ordinary use, and go to a smith to whom you explain your wishes and intentions, the vacant stare of the miserable mechanic soon convinces you that the turning up of a horse-shoe is the extent of his knowledge in the mysteries of the smithy: you then address yourself to another, and one who is called a *capital hand;* and if he be sufficiently sober to comprehend your meaning, he will tell you that what you want is quite out of his line, that he only makes a particular sort of lock, and that he does not think there is a man in the trade who could undertake the job, which, after all, is perhaps a mere copy of a very ordinary piece of old iron-work; and this is a true picture of the majority of our artizans in the nineteenth century, the enlightened age of mechanics' institutes and scientific societies.

Mechanics' institutes are a mere device of the day; the Church is the true mechanics' institute, the oldest and the best. *She was the great and never failing school in which all the great artists of the days of faith were formed.* Under her guidance they directed the most wonderful efforts of her skill to the glory of God; and let our fervent prayer ever be, that the Church may again, as in days of old, cultivate the talents of her children to the advancement of religion and the welfare of their own souls;—for without such results talents are vain, and the greatest efforts of art sink to the level of an abomination.

NOTE

1. Quentin Massys (Matsys or Metsys) (c. 1466–1530) was a Flemish painter, influenced by Jan van Eyck as well as by contemporary Italian painters.

"The Lamp of Truth" and "The Lamp of Life"

THE LAMP OF TRUTH

XIX. The last form of fallacy which it will be remembered we had to deprecate, was the substitution of cast or machine work for that of the hand, generally expressible as Operative Deceit.

There are two reasons, both weighty, against this practice: one, that all cast and machine work is bad, as work; the other, that it is dishonest. Of its badness I shall speak in another place, that being evidently no efficient reason against its use when other cannot be had. Its dishonesty, however, which, to my mind, is of the grossest kind, is, I think, a sufficient reason to determine absolute and unconditional rejection of it.

Ornament, as I have often before observed, has two entirely distinct sources of agreeableness: one, that of the abstract beauty of its forms, which, for the present, we will suppose to be the same whether they come from the hand or the machine; the other, the sense of human labour and care spent upon it. How great this latter influence we may perhaps judge, by considering that there is not a cluster of weeds growing in any cranny of ruin which has not a beauty in all respects *nearly* equal, and, in some, immeasurably superior, to that of the most elaborate sculpture of its stones: and that all our interest in the carved work, our sense of its richness, though it is tenfold less rich than the knots of grass beside it; of its delicacy, though it is a thousandfold less delicate; of its admirableness, though a millionfold less admirable; results from our consciousness of its being the work of poor, clumsy, toilsome man. Its true delightfulness depends on our discovering in it the record of thoughts, and intents, and trials, and heart-breakings—of recoveries and joyfulnesses of success: all this *can* be traced by a practised eye; but, granting it even obscure, it is presumed or understood; and in that is the worth of the thing, just as much as the worth of anything else we call precious. The worth of a diamond is simply the understanding of the time it must take to look for it before it is found; and the worth of an ornament is the time it must take before it can be cut. It has an intrinsic value besides, which the diamond has not; (for a diamond has no more real beauty than a piece of glass;) but I do not speak of that at present; I place the two on the same ground; and I suppose that hand-wrought ornament can no more be generally known from machine work, than a diamond can be known from paste; nay, that the latter may deceive, for a moment, the mason's, as the other the jeweller's, eye; and that it can be detected only by the closest examination. Yet exactly as a woman of feeling would not wear false jewels, so would a builder of honour disdain false ornaments. The using of them is just as downright and inexcusable a lie. You use that which pretends to a worth which it has not; which pretends to have cost, and to be, what it did not, and is not; it is an imposition, a vulgarity, an impertinence, and a sin. Down with it to the ground, grind it to powder, leave its ragged place upon the wall, rather; you have not paid for it, you have no business with it, you do not want it. Nobody wants ornaments in this world, but everybody wants integrity. All the fair devices that ever were fancied, are not worth a lie. Leave your walls as bare as a planed board, or build them of baked mud and chopped straw, if need be; but do not rough-cast them with falsehood.

This, then, being our general law, and I hold it for a more imperative one than any other I have asserted; and this kind of dishonesty the meanest, as the least necessary; for ornament is an extravagant and inessential thing; and therefore, if fallacious, utterly base—this, I say, being our general law, there are, nevertheless, certain exceptions respecting particular substances and their uses.

xx. Thus in the use of brick: since that is known to be originally moulded, there is no reason why it should not be moulded into diverse forms. It will never be supposed to have been cut, and therefore, will cause no deception; it will have only the credit it deserves. In flat countries, far from any quarry of stone, cast brick may be legitimately, and most successfully, used in decoration, and that elaborate, and even refined. The brick mouldings of the Palazzo Pepoli at Bologna, and those which run round the market-place of Vercelli, are among the richest in Italy. So also, tile and porcelain work, of which the former is grotesquely, but successfully, employed in the domestic architecture of France, coloured tiles being inserted in the diamond spaces between the crossing timbers; and the latter admirably in Tuscany, in external bas-reliefs, by the Robbia family, in which works, while we cannot but sometimes regret the useless and ill-arranged colours, we would by no means blame the employment of a material which, whatever its defects, excels every other in permanence, and, perhaps, requires even greater skill in its management than marble.[1] For it is not the material, but the absence of the human labour, which makes the thing worthless; and a piece of terra cotta, or of plaster of Paris, which has been wrought by the human hand, is worth all the stone in Carrara, cut by machinery. It is, indeed, possible, and even usual, for men to sink into machines themselves, so that even hand-work has all the characters of mechanism; of the difference between living and dead hand-work I shall speak presently; all that I ask at present is, what it is always in our power to secure—the confession of what we have done, and what we have given; so that when we use stone at all, since all stone is naturally supposed to be carved by hand, we must not carve it by machinery; neither must we use any artificial stone cast into shape, nor any stucco ornaments of the colour of stone, or which might in any wise be mistaken for it, as the stucco mouldings in the cortile of the Palazzo Vecchio at Florence, which cast a shame and suspicion over every part of the building. But for ductile and fusible materials, as clay, iron, and bronze, since these will usually be supposed to have been cast or stamped, it is at our pleasure to employ them as we will; remembering that they become precious, or otherwise, just in proportion to the hand-work upon them, or to the clearness of their reception of the hand-work of their mould. But I believe no cause to have been more active in the degradation of our natural feeling for beauty than the constant use of cast-iron ornaments. The common iron work of the middle ages was as simple as it was effective, composed of leafage cut flat out of sheet iron, and twisted at the workman's will. No ornaments, on the contrary, are so cold, clumsy, and vulgar, so essentially incapable of a fine line or shadow, as those of cast iron; and while, on the score of truth, we can hardly allege anything against them, since they are always distinguishable, at a glance, from wrought and hammered work, and stand only for what they are, yet I feel very strongly that there is no hope of the progress of the arts of any nation which indulges in these vulgar and cheap substitutes for real decoration. Their inefficiency and paltriness I shall endeavour to show more conclusively in another place, enforcing only, at present, the general conclusion that, if even honest or allowable, they are things in which we can never take just pride or pleasure, and must never be employed in any place wherein they might either themselves obtain the credit of being other and better than they are, or be associated with the downright work to which it would be a disgrace to be found in their company.

· · ·

THE LAMP OF LIFE

XXI. I have dwelt, however, perhaps, too long upon that form of vitality which is known almost as much by its errors as by its atonements for them. We must briefly note the operation of it, which is always right, and always necessary, upon those lesser details, where it can neither be superseded by precedents, nor repressed by proprieties.

I said, early in this essay, that hand-work might always be known from machine-work; observing, however, at the same time, that it was possible for men to turn themselves into machines, and to reduce their labour to the machine level; but so long as men work *as* men, putting their heart into what they do, and doing their best, it matters not how bad workmen they may be, there will be that in the handling which is above all price; it will be plainly seen that some places have been delighted in more than others—that there have been a pause, and a care about them; and then there will come careless bits, and fast bits; and here the chisel will have struck hard, and there lightly, and anon timidly; and if the man's mind as well as his heart went with his work, all this will be in the right places, and each part will set off the other; and the effect of the whole, as compared with the same design cut by a machine or a lifeless hand, will be like that of poetry well read and deeply felt to that of the same verses jangled by rote. There are many to whom the difference is imperceptible; but to those who love poetry it is everything—they had rather not hear it at all, than hear it ill read; and to those who love Architecture, the life and accent of the hand are everything. They had rather not have ornament at all, than see it ill cut—deadly cut, that is. I cannot too often repeat, it is not coarse cutting, it is not blunt cutting, that is necessarily bad; but it is cold cutting—the look of equal trouble everywhere—the smooth, diffused tranquillity of heartless pains —the regularity of a plough in a level field. The chill is more likely, indeed, to show itself in finished work than in any other—men cool and tire as they complete: and if completeness is thought to be vested in polish, and to be attainable by help of sand paper, we may as well give the work to the engine-lathe at once. But *right* finish is simply the full rendering of the intended impression; and *high* finish is the rendering of a well-intended and vivid impression; and it is oftener got by rough than fine handling. I am not sure whether it is frequently enough observed that sculpture is not the mere cutting of the *form* of anything in stone; it is the cutting of the *effect* of it. Very often the true form, in the marble, would not be in the least like itself. The sculptor must paint with his chisel: half his touches are not to realise, but to put power into, the form: they are touches of light and shadow; and raise a ridge, or sink a hollow, not to represent an actual ridge or hollow, but to get a line of light, or a spot of darkness. In a coarse way, this kind of execution is very marked in old French woodwork; the irises of the eyes of its chimeric monsters being cut boldly into holes, which, variously placed, and always dark, give all kinds of strange and startling expressions, averted and askance, to the fantastic countenances. Perhaps the highest examples of this kind of sculpture-painting are the works of Mino da Fiesole; their best effects being reached by strange angular, and seemingly rude, touches of the chisel. The lips of one of the children on the tombs in the church of the Badia, appear only half finished when they are seen close; yet the expression is farther carried, and more ineffable, than in any piece of marble I have ever seen, especially considering its delicacy, and the softness of the child-features. In a sterner kind, that of the statues in the sacristy of St. Lorenzo equals it, and there again by incompletion.[2] I know no example of work in which the forms are absolutely true and complete where such a result is attained; in Greek sculptures it is not even attempted.

·   ·   ·

xxiv. I believe the right question to ask, respecting all ornament, is simply this: Was it done with enjoyment—was the carver happy while he was about it? It may be the hardest work possible, and the harder because so much pleasure was taken in it; but it must have been happy too, or it will not be living. How much of the stone mason's toil this condition would exclude I hardly venture to consider, but the condition is absolute. There is a Gothic church lately built near Rouen, vile enough, indeed, in its general composition, but excessively rich in detail; many of the details are designated with taste, and all evidently by a man who has studied old work closely. But it is all as dead as leaves in December: there is not one tender touch, not one warm stroke, on the whole façade. The men who did it hated it, and were thankful when it was done. And so long as they do so they are merely loading your walls with shapes of clay: the garlands of everlastings in Père la Chaise are more cheerful ornaments.[3] You cannot get the feeling by paying for it—money will not buy life. I am not sure even that you can get it by watching or waiting for it. It is true that here and there a workman may be found who has it in him, but he does not rest contented in the inferior work—he struggles forward into an Academician; and from the mass of available handicraftsmen the power is gone—how recoverable I know not: this only I know, that all expense devoted to sculptural ornament, in the present condition of that power, comes literally under the head of Sacrifice for the sacrifice's sake, or worse. I believe the only manner of rich ornament that is open to us is the geometrical colour-mosaic, and that much might result from our strenuously taking up this mode of design. But, at all events, one thing we have in our power—the doing without machine ornament and cast-iron work. All the stamped metals, and artificial stones, and imitation woods and bronzes, over the invention of which we hear daily exultation—all the short, and cheap, and easy ways of doing that whose difficulty is its honour—are just so many new obstacles in our already encumbered road. They will not make one of us happier or wiser—they will extend neither the pride of judgment nor the privilege of enjoyment. They will only make us shallower in our understandings, colder in our hearts, and feebler in our wits. And most justly. For we are not sent into this world to do anything into which we cannot put our hearts. We have certain work to do for our bread, and that is to be done strenuously; other work to do for our delight, and that is to be done heartily: neither is to be done by halves and shifts, but with a will; and what is not worth this effort is not to be done at all. Perhaps all that we have to do is meant for nothing more than an exercise of the heart and of the will, and is useless in itself; but, at all events, the little use it has may well be spared if it is not worth putting our hands and our strength to. It does not become our immortality to take an ease inconsistent with its authority, nor to suffer any instruments with which it can dispense, to come between it and the things it rules: and he who would form the creations of his own mind by any other instrument than his own hand, would also, if he might, give grinding organs to Heaven's angels, to make their music easier. There is dreaming enough, and earthiness enough, and sensuality enough in human existence, without our turning the few glowing moments of it into mechanism; and since our life must at the best be but a vapour that appears for a little time and then vanishes away, let it at least appear as a cloud in the height of Heaven, not as the thick darkness that broods over the blast of the Furnace, and rolling of the Wheel.

NOTES

1. The Della Robbias were an Italian family of sculptors and cermacists, active in Florence from the early-fifteenth century well into the sixteenth. Luca della Robbia (1399–1482) founded the family workshop, and is the best-known member of the family, contributing to the development of the early Renaissance in Florence.

2. Mino da Fiesole (1429–1484) was an Italian sculptor who produced many important tombs, altars, and tabernacles in Fiesole, Florence, and Rome.

3. Père-la Chaise, a famous Parisian cemetery established in 1804, is a remarkable museum of funerary sculpture and holds the remains of numerous French and foreign celebrities.

GOTTFRIED SEMPER

Science, Art, and Industry

How long did the inventor of oil painting toil with an old process that
no longer satisfied certain purposes before he discovered his new process? Bernard Palissy searched half his life for an opaque enamel for his faience before he
finally found what he sought.[1] These men knew how to use the invention because
they needed it, and because they needed it they searched and found it. In this
way, gradual progress in science went hand in hand with the mastery and the
awareness of how and to what end the invention could be applied.

Necessity was the mother of science. Developing empirically and with
youthful spontaneity, science soon drew confident deductions on the unknown
from the narrow field of acquired knowledge, doubting nothing and creating
its world from hypotheses. Later it felt confined by its dependence on application and became an object in itself. It entered the field of doubt and analysis. A
craze for classification and nomenclature superceded the ingenious or fanciful
systems.

In the end genius reconquered the vast amount of material collected by research and purely objective investigation was forced to submit to hypothetical
inference and to become the latter's servant in the procurement of further factual evidence derived from analogies.

Philosophy, history, politics, and a few higher branches of the natural sciences were raised to this comparative viewpoint by the great men of the past
two centuries, while in the other sciences, because of the abundance and complexity of their material, inferences only timidly begin to join with research.
Searching every day more judiciously, research makes astonishing discoveries.
Chemistry, in joining with physics and calculus, dares to defend the boldest hypotheses of the Greeks and the long-pitied broodings of the alchemists. Science
at the same time inclines decidedly toward the practical and at present stands
exalted as its guardian. Every day it enriches our life with newly discovered materials and miraculous natural forces, with new methods of technology, with
new tools and machines.

It is already evident that inventions are no longer, as before, a means for
averting privation and for enjoyment. On the contrary, privation and enjoyment
create the market for the inventions. The order of things has been reversed.

What is the inevitable result of this? The present has no time to become familiar with the half-imposed benefits and to master them. The situation resembles that of the Chinese, who should eat with a knife and fork. Speculation interposes itself there and lays out the benefits attractively before us; where there is none, speculation creates a thousand small and large advantages. Old, outdated comforts are called back into use when speculation cannot think of anything new. It effortlessly accomplishes the most difficult and troublesome things with means borrowed from science. The hardest porphyry and granite are cut like chalk and polished like wax. Ivory is softened and pressed into forms. Rubber and gutta-percha[2] are vulcanized and utilized in a thousand imitations of wood, metal, and stone carvings, exceeding by far the natural limitations of the material they purport to represent. Metal is no longer cast or wrought, but treated with the newest unknown forces of nature in a galvanoplastic way. The talbotype succeeds the daguerreotype and makes the latter already a thing forgotten. Machines sew, knit, embroider, paint, carve, and encroach deeply into the field of human art, putting to shame every human skill.

Are these not great and glorious achievements? By no means do I deplore the general conditions of which these are only the less important symptoms. On the contrary, I am confident that sooner or later everything will develop favorably for the well-being and honor of society. For now I refrain from proceeding to those larger and more difficult questions suggested by them. In the following pages I only wish to point out the confusion they now cause in those fields in which the talents of man take an active part in the recognition and presentation of beauty.

II

If single incidents carried the force of conviction, then the recognized triumphs at the Exhibition[3] of the half-barbaric nations, especially the Indians with their magnificent industries of art, would be sufficient to show us that we with our science have until now accomplished very little in these areas.

The same, shameful truth confronts us when we compare our products with those of our ancestors. Notwithstanding our many technical advances, we remain far behind them in formal beauty, and even in a feeling for the suitable and the appropriate. Our best things are more or less faithful reminiscences. Others show a praiseworthy effort to borrow forms directly from nature, yet how seldom we have been successful in this! Most of our attempts are a confused muddle of forms or childish triflings. At best, objects whose seriousness of purpose does not permit the superfluous, such as wagons, weapons, musical instruments, and similar things, we sometimes make appear healthier by the refined presentation of their strictly prescribed forms.

Although facts, as we said, are no argument and can even be disputed, it is easy to prove that present conditions are dangerous for the industrial arts, decidedly fatal for the traditional higher arts.

The *abundance of means* is the first great danger with which art has to struggle. This expression is illogical, I admit (there is no abundance of means but only an inability to master them); however, it is justified in that it correctly describes the inverted state of our conditions.

Practice wearies itself in vain in trying to master its material, especially intellectually. It receives it from science ready to process as it chooses, but before its style could have evolved through many centuries of popular usage. The founders of a flourishing art once had their material kneaded beforehand, as it were, by the beelike instinct of the people; they invested the indigenous motive with a higher meaning and treated it artistically, stamping their creations with a rigorous necessity and spiritual freedom. These works became universally understood expressions of a true idea that will survive historically as long as any trace or knowledge of them remains.

What a glorious discovery is the gaslight! How its brilliance enhances our festivities, not to mention its enormous importance to everyday life! Yet in imitating candles or oil lamps in our salons, we hide the apertures of the gas pipes; in illumination, on the other hand, we pierce the pipes with innumerable small openings, so that all sorts of stars, firewheels, pyramids, escutcheons, inscriptions, and so on seem to float before the walls of our houses, as if supported by invisible hands.

This floating stillness of the most lively of all elements is effective to be sure (the sun, moon, and stars provide the most dazzling examples of it), but who can deny that this innovation has detracted from the popular custom of *illuminating* houses as a sign the occupants participate in the public joy? Formerly, oil lamps were placed on the cornice ledges and window sills, thereby lending a radiant prominence to the familiar masses and individual parts of the houses. Now our eyes are blinded by the blaze of those apparitions of fire and the facades behind are rendered invisible.

Whoever has witnessed the illuminations in London and remembers similar festivities in the old style in Rome will admit that the art of lighting has suffered a rude setback by these improvements.

This example demonstrates the two main dangers, the Scylla and Charybdis, between which we must steer to gain innovations for art.

The invention was excellent but it was sacrificed in the first case to traditional form, and in the second case its basic motive was completely obscured by its false application. Yet every means was available to make it more lustrous and to enrich it at the same time with a new idea (that of a fixed display of fireworks).

A clever helmsman, therefore, must be he who avoids these dangers, and his course is even more difficult because he finds himself in unknown waters without a chart or compass. For among the multitude of artistic and technical writings, there is sorely needed a practical guide to invention that maps out the cliffs and sandbars to be avoided and points out the right course to be taken. Were the theory of taste (aesthetics) a complete science, were its incompleteness not compounded by vague and often erroneous ideas in need of a clearer formulation especially in its application to architecture and tectonics in general, then it would fill just this void. Yet in its present state it is with justification scarcely considered by gifted professionals. Its tottering precepts and basic principles find approval only with so-called experts of art, who measure the value of a work thereby because they have no inner, subjective standards for art. They believe they have grasped beauty's secret with a dozen precepts, while the infinite variation in the world of form assumes characteristic meaning and individual beauty just by the denial of any scheme.

Among the notions that the theory of taste has taken pains to formulate, one of the most important is the idea of style in art. This term, as everyone knows, is one for which many interpretations have been offered, so many that skeptics have wanted to deny it any clear conceptual basis. Yet every artist and true connoisseur feels its whole meaning, however difficult it may be to express in words. Perhaps we can say:

> Style means giving emphasis and artistic significance to the basic idea and to all intrinsic and extrinsic coefficients that modify the embodiment of the theme in a work of art.

According to this definition, absence of style signifies the shortcomings of a work caused by the artist's disregard of the underlying theme, and his ineptitude in exploiting aesthetically the means available for perfecting the work.

Just as nature in her variety is yet simple and sparse in her motives, renewing continually the same forms by modifying them a thousandfold according to the graduated scale of development and the different conditions of existence, developing parts in different ways, shortening some and lengthening others—in the same way the technical arts are also based on certain prototypical forms (*Urformen*) conditioned by a primordial idea, which always reappear and yet allow infinite variations conditioned by more closely determining circumstances.

Thus it happens that parts that appear essential in one combination are only alluded to in others; parts whose mark and germ are barely recognizable in the first combination perhaps step forth striking and predominant in the second.

The basic form, as the simplest expression of the idea, is modified in particular by the *materials* that are used in developing the form as well as by the *tools* that fashion it. Finally, there are a number of influences extrinsic to the work: important factors that are effective in determining form, such as place, climate, time, customs, particular characteristics, rank, position, and many others. Without being arbitrary and in conformance with our definition, we can divide the doctrine of style into three parts.

The theory of the primordial motives (*Urmotiven*) and the primary forms derived from them constitute the first, art-historical part of the theory of style.

It is without doubt gratifying when the primordial motive in a work of art, however removed it may be from its point of origin, pervades the composition like a musical theme. Certainly a clear and fresh conception is very desirable in an artistic work, because we gain thereby a foothold against the arbitrary and the insignificant and even positive guidance in invention. The new becomes engrafted onto the old without being a copy and is freed from a dependence on the inane influence of fashion. To illustrate this, let me be allowed to give one example of the far-reaching influence a primitive form may have on the development of the arts.

The mat and the woven carpet derived from it, later the embroidered carpet, were the earliest spatial dividers and thus became the basic motive for all later wall decorations and for many other related branches of industry and architecture. The technique that came into use with them might have taken a great many different directions, yet they always displayed their common origin in their style. We can actually see that in ancient times, from the Assyrians to the Romans and later in the Middle Ages, the divisioning and ornamentation of the wall, the principles of its coloring, even the historical paintings and sculpture used on it, as well as glass painting and floor decorations—in short, all related arts—remained dependent on the primordial motive, either consciously or unconsciously in a traditional way.

Fortunately, this *historical* aspect of the theory of style can be developed even amid our confused artistic conditions. What rich material for its understanding, comparison, and reflection was offered in the London Exhibition by the works already noted by people still living in the earlier stages of cultural development.

The second part of the doctrine of style should teach us how the forms evolving from the motives should take different shapes depending on our means, and how the material is treated stylistically within our advancing technology. Unfortunately, this aspect of style is more elusive. One example may show the difficulties in carrying out the basic principles of the *technical* theory of style.

The granite and porphyry monuments of Egypt exert an incredible sway over our feelings. In what resides this magic? Certainly in part because they are the neutral ground where the hard, resisting material engages the soft hand of man with his simple tools (the hammer and the chisel), and they enter into a pact: "So far and no further, in this manner and no other!" This has been the silent message for millennia. Their majestic repose and massiveness, the somewhat angular and flat elegance of their lines, the restraint shown in the treatment of the difficult material—their whole demeanor indicates a beauty of style that to us, who now can cut the hardest stone like cheese and bread, lacks necessity.

How should we treat granite now? It is difficult to give a satisfactory answer! The first thing might well be to use it only where its durability is demanded, and draw from this last condition the rules for its stylistic treatment. How little attention is paid to this in our time is shown by certain extravagances of the large granite and porphyry manufactures in Sweden and Russia.

This example leads to a more general question that by itself would provide sufficient material for a large chapter, if I were allowed to expand this essay into a book. Where does the depreciation of materials brought about by the machine, by their surrogates, and by so many new inventions lead us? What effect will the depreciation of labor, a result of the same causes, have on the painted, sculptured, and other kinds of decorative work? Naturally, I am not referring to the depreciation in fees, but in meaning, in the idea. Have not the new Houses of Parliament in London been made unbearable by the machine? How will time or science bring law and order to these thoroughly confused conditions? How do we prevent the general depreciation from also extending to all works executed in the old way by hand, how do we prevent them from being seen as antique, striking, or eccentric affectations?

While the technical theory of style presents such difficulties in the determination and application of its principles, the important third part of our theory can scarcely in our day be discussed at all. I mean the part that deals with the local, temporal, and personal influences on form extrinsic to the work of art and their accord with other factors, such as character and expression. These problems will be demonstrated in the course of this essay.

We pointed out earlier the dangers that threaten our industrial arts and art in general through the abundance of means—to use the expression just adopted. Now I pose the question, what influences are exerted on the art industries by speculation supported by large capital and directed by science? What will be the final result of this ever-expanding patronage?

"Speculation, when it recognizes its true advantages, will seek out the best forces and acquire them for itself; thus it will show more zeal in protecting and nurturing the arts and the artist than ever was done by a Maecenas or a Medici."

Indeed! But there is a difference in working for speculation and in executing one's own work as a free man. In working for speculation man is doubly dependent: a slave to his employer and to the latest fashion that provides the employer with a market for his wares. Man sacrifices his individuality, his "birthright," for a pottage of lentils. In former times the artist also practiced self-denial, but he sacrificed his ego only for the glory of God.

However, we will not follow this line of reasoning any further, for speculation leads directly to a specific goal that now seems more important to discuss in detail.

NOTES

1. Bernard Palissy (1510-1590) was a French glass painter and potter, who succeeded in developing different formulas for ceramic glazes, especially ones resembling stone, called *terres jaspées.*

2. Gutta Perch is a resin from the Isonandra Gutta tree used to make a natural type of plastic. It functioned as a suitable isolating material for telegraph wires as well as for making experimental jewelry and furniture, some of which were shown at the Crystal Palace Exhibition in 1851.

3. This is the Great Exhibition of 1851.

WILLIAM MORRIS

The Revival of Handicraft

THE REVIVAL OF HANDICRAFT. AN ARTICLE IN THE
"FORTNIGHTLY REVIEW," NOVEMBER 1888.

For some time past there has been a good deal of interest shown in
what is called in our modern slang Art Workmanship, and quite recently there
has been a growing feeling that this art workmanship to be of any value must
have some of the workman's individuality imparted to it beside whatever of art
it may have got from the design of the artist who has planned, but not executed
the work. This feeling has gone so far that there is growing up a fashion for de-
manding handmade goods even when they are not ornamented in any way, as,
for instance, woollen and linen cloth spun by hand and woven without power,
hand-knitted hosiery, and the like. Nay, it is not uncommon to hear regrets
for the hand-labour in the fields, now fast disappearing from even backward
districts of civilized countries. The scythe, the sickle, and even the flail are
lamented over, and many are looking forward with drooping spirits to the time
when the hand-plough will be as completely extinct as the quern, and the rattle
of the steam-engine will take the place of the whistle of the curly-headed
ploughboy through all the length and breadth of the land. People interested, or
who suppose that they are interested, in the details of the arts of life feel a desire
to revert to methods of handicraft for production in general; and it may therefore
be worth considering how far this is a mere reactionary sentiment incapable of
realization, and how far it may foreshadow a real coming change in our habits of
life as irresistible as the former change which has produced the system of machine-production, the system against which revolt is now attempted.

In this paper I propose to confine the aforesaid consideration as much as I
can to the effect of machinery *versus* handicraft upon the arts; using that latter
word as widely as possible, so as to include all products of labour which have
any claims to be considered beautiful. I say as far as possible: for as all roads
lead to Rome, so the life, habits, and aspirations of all groups and classes of the
community are founded on the economical conditions under which the mass
of the people live, and it is impossible to exclude socio-political questions from
the consideration of æsthetics. Also, although I must avow myself a sharer in

the above-mentioned reactionary regrets, I must at the outset disclaim the mere æsthetic point of view which looks upon the ploughman and his bullocks and his plough, the reaper, his work, his wife, and his dinner, as so many elements which compose a pretty tapestry hanging, fit to adorn the study of a contemplative person of cultivation, but which it is not worth while differentiating from each other except in so far as they are related to the beauty and interest of the picture. On the contrary, what I wish for is that the reaper and his wife should have themselves a due share in all the fulness of life; and I can, without any great effort, perceive the justice of their forcing me to bear part of the burden of its deficiencies, so that we may together be forced to attempt to remedy them, and have no very heavy burden to carry between us.

To return to our æsthetics: though a certain part of the cultivated classes of to-day regret the disappearance of handicraft from production, they are quite vague as to how and why it is disappearing, and as to how and why it should or may reappear. For to begin with the general public is grossly ignorant of all the methods and processes of manufacture. This is of course one result of the machine-system we are considering. Almost all goods are made apart from the life of those who use them; we are not responsible for them, our will has had no part in their production, except so far as we form a part of the market on which they can be forced for the profit of the capitalist whose money is employed in producing them. The market assumes that certain wares are wanted; it produces such wares, indeed, but their kind and quality are only adapted to the needs of the public in a very rough fashion, because the public needs are subordinated to the interest of the capitalist masters of the market, and they can force the public to put up with the less desirable article if they choose, as they generally do. The result is that in this direction our boasted individuality is a sham; and persons who wish for anything that deviates ever so little from the beaten path have either to wear away their lives in a wearisome and mostly futile contest with a stupendous organization which disregards their wishes, or to allow those wishes to be crushed out for the sake of a quiet life.

Let us take a few trivial but undeniable examples. You want a hat, say, like that you wore last year; you go to the hatter's, and find you cannot get it there, and you have no resource but in submission. Money by itself won't buy you the hat you want; it will cost you three months' hard labour and twenty pounds to have an inch added to the brim of your wideawake; for you will have to get hold of a small capitalist (of whom but few are left), and by a series of intrigues and resolute actions which would make material for a three-volume novel, get him to allow you to turn one of his hands into a handicraftsman for the occasion; and a very poor handicraftsman he will be, when all is said. Again, I carry a walking-stick, and like all sensible persons like it to have a good heavy end that will swing out well before me. A year or two ago it became the fashion to pare away all walking-sticks to the shape of attenuated carrots, and I really believe I shortened my life in my attempts at getting a reasonable staff of the kind I was used to, so difficult it was. Again, you want a piece of furniture, which the trade (mark the word, Trade, not Craft!) turns out blotched over with idiotic sham ornament; you wish to dispense with this degradation, and propose it to your upholsterer, who grudgingly assents to it; and you find that you have to pay the price of two pieces of furniture for the privilege of indulging your whim of leaving out the trade finish (I decline to call it ornament) on the one you have got made for you. And this is because it has been made by handicraft instead of machinery. For most people, therefore, there is a prohibitive price put upon the acquirement of the knowledge of methods and processes. We do not know how a piece of goods is made, what the difficulties are that beset its manufacture, what it ought to look like, feel like, smell like, or what it ought to cost apart from the profit of the middleman. We have lost the art of marketing, and with it the due sympathy with the life of the workshop, which would, if it existed, be such a wholesome check on the humbug of party politics.

It is a natural consequence of this ignorance of the methods of making wares, that even those who are in revolt against the tyranny of the excess of division of labour in the occupations of life, and who wish to recur more or less to handicraft, should also be ignorant of what that life of handicraft was when all wares were made by handicraft. If their revolt is to carry any hope with it, it is necessary that they should know something of this. I must assume that many or perhaps most of my readers are not acquainted with Socialist literature, and that few of them have read the admirable account of the different epochs of production given in Karl Marx' great work entitled "Capital." I must ask to be excused, therefore, for stating very briefly what, chiefly owing to Marx, has become a commonplace of Socialism, but is not generally known outside it. There have been three great epochs of production since the beginning of the Middle Ages. During the first or mediæval period all production was individualistic in method; for though the workmen were combined into great associations for protection and the organization of labour, they were so associated as citizens, not as mere workmen. There was little or no division of labour, and what machinery was used was simply of the nature of a multiplied tool, a help to the workman's hand-labour and not a supplanter of it. The workman worked for himself and not for any capitalistic employer, and he was accordingly master of his work and his time; this was the period of pure handicraft. When in the latter half of the sixteenth century the capitalist employer and the so-called free workman began to appear, the workmen were collected into workshops, the old tool-machines were improved, and at last a new invention, the division of labour, found its way into the workshops. The division of labour went on growing throughout the seventeenth century, and was perfected in the eighteenth, when the unit of labour became a group and not a single man; or in other words the workman became a mere part of a machine composed sometimes wholly of human beings and sometimes of human beings plus labour-saving machines, which towards the end of this period were being copiously invented; the fly-shuttle may be taken for an example of these. The latter half of the eighteenth century saw the beginning of the last epoch of production that the world has known, that of the automatic machine which supersedes hand-labour, and turns the workman who was once a handicraftsman helped by tools, and next a part of a machine, into a tender of machines. And as far as we can see, the revolution in this direction as to kind is complete, though as to degree, as pointed out by Mr. David A. Wells last year (1887), the tendency is towards the displacement of ever more and more "muscular" labour, as Mr. Wells calls it.[1]

This is very briefly the history of the evolution of industry during the last five hundred years; and the question now comes: Are we justified in wishing that handicraft may in its turn supplant machinery? Or it would perhaps be better to put the question in another way: Will the period of machinery evolve itself into a fresh period of machinery more independent of human labour than anything we can conceive of now, or will it develop its contradictory in the shape of a new and improved period of production by handicraft? The second form of the question is the preferable one, because it helps us to give a reasonable answer to what people who have any interest in external beauty will certainly ask: Is the change from handicraft to machinery good or bad? And the answer to that question is to my mind that, as my friend Belfort Bax has put it, statically it is bad, dynamically it is good.[2] As a condition of life, production by machinery is altogether an evil; as an instrument for forcing on us better conditions of life it has been, and for some time yet will be, indispensable.

Having thus tried to clear myself of mere reactionary pessimism, let me attempt to show why statically handicraft is to my mind desirable, and its destruction a degradation of life. Well, first I shall not shrink from saying bluntly that production by machinery necessarily results in utilitarian ugliness in everything which the labour of man deals with, and that this is a serious evil and a degradation of human life. So clearly is this the fact that though few people will venture to deny the latter part of the proposition, yet in their hearts the greater part of cultivated civilized persons do not regard it as an evil, because their degradation has already gone so far that they cannot, in what concerns the sense of seeing, discriminate between beauty and ugliness: their languid assent to the desirableness of beauty is with them only a convention, a superstitious survival from the times when beauty was a necessity to all men. The first part of the proposition (that machine-industry produces ugliness) I cannot argue with these persons, because they neither know, nor care for, the difference between beauty and ugliness; and with those who do not understand what beauty means I need not argue it, as they are but too familiar with the fact that the produce of all modern industrialism is ugly, and that whenever anything which is old disappears, its place is taken by something inferior to it in beauty; and that even out in the very fields and open country. The art of making beautifully all kinds of ordinary things, carts, gates, fences, boats, bowls, and so forth, let alone houses and public buildings, unconsciously and without effort, has gone; when anything has to be renewed among these simple things the only question asked is how little it can be done for, so as to tide us over our responsibility and shift its mending on to the next generation.

It may be said, and indeed I have heard it said, that since there is some beauty still left in the world and some people who admire it, there is a certain gain in the acknowledged eclecticism of the present day, since the ugliness which is so common affords a contrast whereby the beauty, which is so rare, may be appreciated. This I suspect to be only another form of the maxim which is the sheet-anchor of the laziest and most cowardly group of our cultivated classes, that it is good for the many to suffer for the few; but if any one puts forward in good faith the fear that we may be too happy in the possession of pleasant surroundings, so that we shall not be able to enjoy them, I must answer that this seems to me a very remote terror. Even when the tide at last turns in the direction of sweeping away modern squalor and vulgarity, we shall have, I doubt, many generations of effort in perfecting the transformation, and when it is at last complete, there will be first the triumph of our success to exalt us, and next the history of the long wade through the putrid sea of ugliness which we shall have at last escaped from. But furthermore, the proper answer to this objection lies deeper than this. It is to my mind that very consciousness of the production of beauty for beauty's sake which we want to avoid; it is just what is apt to produce affectation and effeminacy amongst the artists and their following. In the great times of art conscious effort was used to produce great works for the glory of the City, the triumph of the Church, the exaltation of the citizens, the quickening of the devotion of the faithful; even in the higher art, the record of history, the instruction of men alive and to live hereafter, was the aim rather than beauty; and the lesser art was unconscious and spontaneous, and did not in any way interfere with the rougher business of life, while it enabled men in general to understand and sympathize with the nobler forms of art. But unconscious as these producers of ordinary beauty may be, they will not and cannot fail to receive pleasure from the exercise of their work under these conditions, and this above all things is that which influences me most in my hope for the recovery of handicraft. I have said it often enough, but I must say it once again, since it is so much a part of my case for handicraft, that so long as man allows his daily work to be mere unrelieved drudgery he will seek happiness in vain. I say further that the worst tyrants of the days of violence were but feeble tormentors compared with those Captains of Industry who have taken the pleasure of work away from the workmen. Furthermore I feel absolutely certain that handicraft joined to certain other conditions, of which more presently, would produce the beauty and the pleasure in work above mentioned; and if that be so, and this double pleasure of lovely surroundings and happy work could take the place of the double torment of squalid surroundings and wretched drudgery, have we not good reason for wishing, if it might be, that handicraft should once more step into the place of machine-production?

I am not blind to the tremendous change which this revolution would mean. The maxim of modern civilization to a well-to-do man is, Avoid taking trouble! Get as many of the functions of your life as you can performed by others for you! Vicarious life is the watchword of our civilization, and we well-to-do and cultivated people live smoothly enough while it lasts. But, in the first place, how about the vicars, who do more for us than the singing of mass for our behoof for a scanty stipend? Will they go on with it for ever? For indeed the shuffling off of responsibilities from one to the other has to stop at last, and somebody has to bear the burden in the end. But let that pass, since I am not writing politics, and let us consider another aspect of the matter. What wretched lop-sided creatures we are being made by the excess of the division of labour in the occupations of life! What on earth are we going to do with our time when we have brought the art of vicarious life to perfection, having first complicated the question by the ceaseless creation of artificial wants which we refuse to supply for ourselves? Are all of us (we of the great middle class I mean) going to turn philosophers, poets, essayists—men of genius, in a word, when we have come to look down on the ordinary functions of life with the same kind of contempt wherewith persons of good breeding look down upon a good dinner, eating it sedulously however? I shudder when I think of how we shall bore each other when we have reached that perfection. Nay, I think we have already got in all branches of culture rather more geniuses than we can comfortably bear, and that we lack, so to say, audiences rather than preachers. I must ask pardon of my readers; but our case is at once so grievous and so absurd that one can scarcely help laughing out of bitterness of soul. In the very midst of our pessimism we are boastful of our wisdom, yet we are helpless in the face of the necessities we have created, and which, in spite of our anxiety about art, are at present driving us into luxury unredeemed by beauty on the one hand, and squalor unrelieved by incident or romance on the other, and will one day drive us into mere ruin.

Yes, we do sorely need a system of production which will give us beautiful surroundings and pleasant occupation, and which will tend to make us good human animals, able to do something for ourselves, so that we may be generally intelligent instead of dividing ourselves into dull drudges or duller pleasure-seekers according to our class, on the one hand, or hapless pessimistic intellectual personages, and pretenders to that dignity, on the other. We do most certainly need happiness in our daily work, content in our daily rest; and all this cannot be if we hand over the whole responsibility of the details of our daily life to machines and their drivers. We are right to long for intelligent handicraft to come back to the world which it once made tolerable amidst war and turmoil and uncertainty of life, and which it should, one would think, make happy now we have grown so peaceful, so considerate of each other's temporal welfare.

Then comes the question, How can the change be made? And here at once we are met by the difficulty that the sickness and death of handicraft is, it seems, a natural expression of the tendency of the age. We willed the end, and therefore the means also. Since the last days of the Middle Ages the creation of an intellectual aristocracy has been, so to say, the spiritual purpose of civilization side by side with its material purpose of supplanting the aristocracy of status by the aristocracy of wealth. Part of the price it has had to pay for its success in that purpose (and some would say it is comparatively an insignificant part) is that this new aristocracy of intellect has been compelled to forgo the lively interest in the beauty and romance of life, which was once the portion of every artificer at least, if not of every workman, and to live surrounded by an ugly vulgarity which the world amidst all its changes has not known till modern times. It is not strange that until recently it has not been conscious of this degradation; but it may seem strange to many that it has now grown partially conscious of it. It is common now to hear people say of such and such a piece of country or suburb: "Ah! it was so beautiful a year or so ago, but it has been quite spoilt by the building." Forty years back the building would have been looked on as a vast improvement; now we have grown conscious of the hideousness we are creating, and we go on creating it. We see the price we have paid for our aristocracy of intellect, and even that aristocracy itself is more than half regretful of the bargain, and would be glad if it could keep the gain and not pay the full price for it. Hence not only the empty grumbling about the continuous march of machinery over dying handicraft, but also various elegant little schemes for trying to withdraw ourselves, some of us, from the consequences (in this direction) of our being superior persons; none of which can have more than a temporary and very limited success. The great wave of commercial necessity will sweep away all these well-meant attempts to stem it, and think little of what it has done, or whither it is going.

Yet after all even these feeble manifestations of discontent with the tyranny of commerce are tokens of a revolutionary epoch, and to me it is inconceivable that machine-production will develop into mere infinity of machinery, or life wholly lapse into a disregard of life as it passes. It is true indeed that powerful as the cultivated middle class is, it has not the power of re-creating the beauty and romance of life; but that will be the work of the new society which the blind progress of commercialism will create, nay, is creating. The cultivated middle class is a class of slaveholders, and its power of living according to its choice is limited by the necessity of finding constant livelihood and employment for the slaves who keep it alive. It is only a society of equals which can choose the life it will live, which can choose to forgo gross luxury and base utilitarianism in return for the unwearying pleasure of tasting the fulness of life. It is my firm belief that we shall in the end realize this society of equals, and also that when it is realized it will not endure a vicarious life by means of machinery; that it will in short be the master of its machinery and not the servant, as our age is.

Meantime, since we shall have to go through a long series of social and political events before we shall be free to choose how we shall live, we should welcome even the feeble protest which is now being made against the vulgarization of all life: first because it is one token amongst others of the sickness of modern civilization; and next, because it may help to keep alive memories of the past which are necessary elements of the life of the future, and methods of work which no society could afford to lose. In short, it may be said that though the movement towards the revival of handicraft is contemptible on the surface in face of the gigantic fabric of commercialism; yet, taken in conjunction with the general movement towards freedom of life for all, on which we are now surely embarked, as a protest against intellectual tyranny, and a token of the change which is transforming civilization into socialism, it is both noteworthy and encouraging.

NOTES

1. David Ames Wells (1828–1898) was an American economist.

2. Ernest Belfort Bax (1854–1926) was an English writer who helped Morris found the Socialist League in 1885.

ADOLF VON HILDEBRAND
Hand Work—Machine Work

What makes an artist is not the extent of his creative work, nor the result, but rather the type of creativity itself, the natural generative process. If other ages have attained great refinement and perfection in their artistic products, this does not oblige us to achieve a superficially similar result by whatever means. That is the difference between hand work and machine work; and it may well be that the achievements of machinery—in producing results equal in practical usefulness to those hitherto produced by hand—have impaired our ability to perceive value in the process by which it is done, as distinct from the result as such. After all, where application and production are purely practical matters, it is quite natural not to inquire as to the origins of the fuel we burn. But where production is a mental thing, the use and application of the product consists in its re-production: in tracing the footsteps of the artist's imagination. A fragment of such true, productive human work is often more valuable than the greatest work of the machine, however deceptive its similarity to the true work of man: for the illusion is short-lived.

The true enjoyment of art resides in the contagious power that passes from what the human organ has imprinted in the work to the visual organs of the viewer, making him an active participant. It has nothing to do with a look of blank astonishment—the natural response to an artifact that is a mere mask, not the true face, of the artist's creation. Our age is an inartistic one, not because its works of art fall short of those of other ages, but because for the most part they are not the products of artistic, visual organs at all.

WALTER CRANE

The Importance of the Applied Arts, and Their Relation to Common Life

Man in a natural and primitive condition does not begin to think of art until his physical wants are satisfied, since art is, in its true sense, after all only a spontaneous manifestation of mental life in form, colour, or line,—the outcome of surplus human energy. It is only under what is called modern civilisation that this natural order is artificially reversed, and men are forced, to attempt at least, to produce forms of art in order to satisfy their physical wants. Our troubles and failures in art may mostly be traced, directly or indirectly, to this condition of things—all the horrors and abominations perpetrated in the name of art, from the productions of the poor man whom necessity compels to chalk on the pavement, through the countless vanities and inanities of the fashionable store, to the refined cruelty of what is known as the "pot-boiler" in the "fine art" exhibition.

The primitive hunter in his cave, when his earliest efforts in applied art, in the form of flint weapons, had secured to him a sufficiency of fish and game and furred overcoats, began to record his impressions of the chase, and to scratch the forms of his favourite animals on their bones. If these representations of reindeer, mammoth, and bison be indeed the earliest examples of art, it would seem that the first impulse in art is imitative rather than what I should term expressive or decorative—the spirit of the picturesque sketcher recording his impressions of natural forms rather than the ordered, systematic, applied art of the inventive designer, who uses natural forms or colours much as a musician his notes to produce a rhythmical arrangement—a tune, a pattern. If this inference is correct, we may perhaps take comfort in the thought that out of our present pictorial zeal and cultivation of the picturesque sketcher we may be led to the study of the more ideal and intellectual side of art.

However the conscious invention of line, and its variation in pattern came about, whether by the burnt stick of the idler (according to Mr. Whistler),[1] or on the soft clay of the primitive potter, it is tolerably obvious that certain primitive patterns are derived from certain necessities of construction, such as the chequer from the square plait of a rush matting, where not taken straight from Nature's pattern book as in fish or serpent scale, and fan from leaf and shell.

One of the most natural impulses in man is to make a mark or a cut upon something directly he has time on his hands. We can watch the development of this impulse in children. One line or mark suggests another, and strokes following one another in a certain order are found to have a pleasant and interesting effect. Strings of them round clay vessels were found to make them more exciting to the eye than the plain surface. The handles of dishes and hunting knives and horns, bows, hatchets, nay, even man's own skin, all offered opportunities for the early ornamental impulse in carving and painting patterns. The implements in constant use, on which, indeed, rude as they were, life itself depended; the things most familiar, most valuable, constantly before the eyes or in the hands,—these were the first things to receive the touch of art, which was then "applied," indeed, and applied only.

If we follow the manifestations of the artistic sense through the great historic periods we shall always find life and art, beauty and use, hand in hand,—the utmost artistic skill of invention and craftsmanship lavished upon cups and bowls, upon lamps and pitchers, upon dress and jewellery, upon arms and armour. We shall find the highest imagination, the most graceful fancy, and even wit, humour, and satire in the service of architecture, recording and reflecting the sentiment of the people: built into cathedral aisles and vaults, or glowing from the windows, frescoed upon the walls, or gleaming in the splendour of mosaic, or carved in endless fertility of resource on the stalls and misereres.

Under economic conditions of the production of all things for the service or delight of man for *use* instead of, as now, for *profit*, the craftsman was an artist, and all objects under his hand naturally developed a characteristic beauty. Ornament was organic, completely adapted to its material, and expressive of its object; but with all our industrial organisation, subdivision of labour, and machine production, we have destroyed the art of the people, the art of common things and common life, and are even now awakening to the fact.

Under a commercial system of production and exchange all art has been rigidly divided into classes, like the society it reflects. Since we have to sell it across the counter, as it were, we must take the weights and scales to it—we must apply to an article of commerce the tests and standards of commerce. Thus we have divided beauty and use, and made them up in separate parcels; or, perhaps, having reduced both to powder, we try a conscious blend of the two to suit average tastes. We have the arts all ticketed and pigeon-holed on the shelves behind us. We have "industrial," "decorative," or "applied" art, as we now call it, and "fine" art—fine art and "the arts not fine," as my friend Mr. Lewis Day has it.[2] Thus by degrees the vast general public, who must get their ideas of art, like other things, readymade, have been taught to understand by the word "art" chiefly that form of portable and often speculative property—

cabinet pictures in oil. Nor is this altogether wonderful, considering how, under our system of wholesale machine production, the appliances of common life have lost their individuality, interest, and meaning, together with their beauty. We are not sensible of any particular individual effort of thought or invention in an object which is only one of thousands turned out exactly like it. Plates, cups and bowls, chairs and tables; the moulding and panelling of our wood-work, and the metal-work of our sacred hearth itself, are taken as matters of course, like other productions of commerce. They were not specially made for you and me; they must be made to suit Smith and Jones equally well, or equally ill; and we shall probably be charmed to see them in each other's houses. We know that furniture and fittings are only made to sell at a profit while the fashion lasts. Trade demands its "novelties" every season, and it would never pay to let a man sit contentedly in the chair that was solidly built for his grandfather. Much better let him fall between two stools (as it were), in his uncertainty of choice in regard to which of the confidently named upholsterers' styles he will seat himself in.

Then as to the application of art to the walls of his dwelling itself is the average man in a much better case? You cannot expect him to put up costly and permanent decorations for the benefit of his landlord, either outside or inside. He is a wandering hermit-crab, only too glad to find an empty shell that will reasonably fit him, at a not too exorbitant rent; and as for decoration—well, at least there are paint and paperhangings.

Of course they that are rich can hire a great architect and dwell in a perfect grammar of ornament. They can import the linings of Italian temples and tombs, and the spoils of Eastern mosques, to breakfast, dine, or play billiards in. The only fear is that Tottenham Court Road will soon bethink itself of cheap imitations of such antique wreckage; that Westbourne Park and Camden Town may be even with Mayfair and South Kensington! Cannot the moderate citizen already command his household gods in any style at the shortest notice? Great is commercial enterprise! Nothing is too high or too low for it. Where your fancy is, there will the man of profits be also.

The distinct awakening of interest and practice in the applied arts, which is a mark of our time, I should be the last to belittle or attempt to ignore; but at the same time, with all it has done and is doing for our education, with all the remarkable skill and reproductive antiquarian energy it has called forth, I feel that we are landed in a strange predicament. For while on the one hand new sensibility to beauty in common things, and new desire for them, are awakened, on the other they are in danger of being choked by that very facility of industrial production which floods the market with counterfeit, set in motion by all the machinery of that commercial enterprise which is the boast of the age, but which all the time, by the very necessity of its progress, is fast obliterating the remains of ancient art and beauty from the face of the earth. So that it will be written of us that we were a people who gathered with one hand while we scattered with the other.

Economic conditions prevent our artisans from being artists. They have become practically, and speaking generally, slaves of machines. The designer is another being from the craftsman. It is only by a study of the conditions of the material in which a design is to be carried out that we can get even workable designs; and even at the best the designer who has no practical acquaintance with any of the handicrafts necessarily loses that stimulus to invention—that suggestive adaptability which the actual manipulation of the material and first-hand acquaintance with its own peculiar limitations and advantages always give.

One who develops a faculty for design has rarely a chance of being other than a designer. He has no time to make experiments, to strike out new paths. He must stick to the line by which he has become known in order to get a living. Nothing narrows a man so much as working continually in the same groove. The utmost that can be said for specialising a single capacity is that you get an extraordinary mechanical or technical facility at the cost of all other qualities. It may not be possible to be supreme in more than one art, but the arts illustrate each other, and a knowledge of other arts and their capacities and limitations is sure to react upon an artist's practice in the one which most absorbs him.

It is true we hear of artists here and there who, though in the eye of the world inseparably associated with some particular form of, say, pictorial ability, nevertheless cultivate some secret amour in the form of a handicraft.

. . .

I daresay furniture may be found to serve our turn, good enough for our shifting life of hurry, and strong enough to last out its own fashion. I only say that if we care for genuine art in these things, we cannot get them under the ordinary conditions of trade.

Yet there is not a thing we use, not the commonest appliance in our houses, that does not show some effort at least to have been spent upon it to make itself presentable to humanity. Unfortunately, nowadays, when native instinct and individual feeling have been so much swamped by forced mechanical industrial production, and the search for mere mechanical smoothness and superficial polish, instead of the finish which only comes of thought and loving care; these efforts to be ornamental are too consciously afterthoughts, while the eye is on the market and its blind chances and uninspiring averages. The added ornament to a thing of utility, instead of being a manifestation of the craftsman's feeling who made it, and his sense of pleasure in his work, is too often some miserable shred torn from the reminiscences of some dead language of decoration; all its grace and spirit gone, and even if moderately adapted in type and form to its purpose, is not calculated to bring a light to any eye, or joy to any heart, since it is but the product of joyless toil and competitive production—the mechanical smirk on the face of the thing of commerce that it is, intended to beguile the simple-minded and unwary into the momentary belief that it is a desirable and beautiful thing, when, in another sense than the poet's, it

——stands ready to smite once, and smites no more.[3]

This unhappy cheapening and vulgarising of ornament, so far from fostering a taste for art, only degrades and distorts the natural feeling for beauty, which with reasonable scope and pleasant surroundings would develop itself as it has always done. Let not commerce pride itself in cant phrase on its claim that it places "art within the reach of all," for how could that have become necessary until art had first been put out of reach? What could compensate for whole tracts of country desolated, and for the crowding of the people in our cities under conditions which put ideas of human dignity and beauty practically out of the question for the million?

Among secondary reasons for the decay of inventive and spontaneous design in the applied arts, I believe the hard-and-fast line which has been drawn between the artist and the craftsman is answerable, and the separation of the designer and the workman.

The designer is perhaps kept chained to some enterprising firm. Novelties are demanded of him—something "entirely new and original" every season, but not too much so. It is not surprising that the best talents should get jaded under such influences; that fancy should become forced or fantastic, and motive weak and tame, or perhaps lost altogether in a search after superficial naturalism, in defiance of fitness to material or use. Such a nemesis is too apt to overtake the specialised designer, who designs on paper only, without the stimulus of close acquaintance with, and practice in, some handicraft. The mere change of occupation is refreshing and invigorating, and stimulates the invention.

In so far as I have been successful as a designer, it has been, I believe, largely owing to my making myself acquainted with the conditions of the material in which a design was to be carried out; by striving to realise in thought, at least, the particular limitations and conditions under which it was intended to be worked; and I have always found that those very limitations, those very conditions, are sources of strength and suggestion to the invention. For I am old-fashioned enough to believe that every material has its own proper language—

regarded as a medium for expression in design—and it is the business of the designer to find this out.

The naturalistic or imitative impulse in art which is characteristic of our time, with the enormous and surprising development of the photograph, has had very visible effects upon art of all kinds. It is quite distinct from the expressive or inventive impulse, and though they may be a ground of reconciliation, the former is of far less consequence to art in its applied or related form than the latter.

· · ·

On the whole, however, the applied arts have shown a laudable independence and defiance of the pictorial mood. The dog no longer appears (after Landseer) on the hearthrug, but is often, in metal, relegated to his proper place on the hearth itself.[4] So far so good. Albeit the desire for some of the happy results in art which belong to ages of greater simplicity of life has produced in some cases strange results, and some combinations of ancient kitchen and modern drawing-room one has seen are not altogether happy. We get an impression of the affectation of primitive simplicity and homeliness with modern luxury and artificiality, from which, at any rate, we can draw a moral on the connection between art and life.

The movement, initiated by Mr. William Morris and the gifted artists associated with him, to which we owe so much, began in a genuine return to honesty of purpose, and to sincere design and sound workmanship, founded upon a study of good models in the past; but it was the outward and visible sign of an intellectual movement which has its eyes upon the future, and, like all revivifying and stimulating impulses in art, it is the offspring of hope and enthusiasm.

Let us look to it that this English Renaissance of ours is not extinguished,— that it does not fall utterly into the iron grasp of commercialism. We may figure art as the fair Andromeda chained to the rock of modern economic conditions, in danger from the all-devouring, desolating monster of gain, until the deliverer shall come.

NOTES

1. James Whistler (1834–1903) was a famous American painter, printmaker, and designer active in England and France and the leader of the Aesthetic movement.

2. Lewis Foreman Day (1848–1910) was an influential member of the Arts and Crafts movement, active in design as well as in design education.

3. From John Milton's *Lycidas* (1638) Book 66, line 131.

4. Sir Edwin (Henry) Landseer (1802–1873) was one of the most popular British painters of the nineteenth century, specializing in drawings of animals.

P. RIOUX DE MAILLOU

The Decorative Arts and the Machine

I

Art is both an individual and a social flowering, the ideal expression of a particularly gifted *ego,* capable of attuning to its own emotion the collective soul—whether it be a chosen few or an ecstatic multitude—to which it must speak, for it is after all a language. We do not speak to ourselves alone. A daydream is enough to satisfy our need for inner impression, and for intimate and subjective figurative imagery and expression; any outward manifestation presupposes and implies external relations, a response to the call of something outside ourselves. This in itself means that the outside world has an inescapable, deterministic effect on the artist. He has every right to think his own thoughts and to render them in his own way, but only so long as his language is accessible and comprehensible to those whom he addresses—for he needs must address someone.

Art, then, is a language; we may also liken it to a plant, and say that it has roots, which it sends down into a soil that nourishes it and supplies the fluids necessary for its continued existence. Its leaves, for their part, breathe the ambient air.

What is true of all art will be true, *a fortiori,* of any art that has a specific application: in other words, the decorative arts. If pure art, left to its own devices within such wide limits, may be likened to a plant or a tree, then the decorative arts are like espaliered plants. The term *decorative* implies subordination: the need to remain within a preordained framework, in conformity with the nature and character of the object that is to be *adorned.*

Not only are the decorative arts subject to this logical dependency but, as we have said, they are also applied arts; and this imposes an additional constraint, expressed by the other appellation sometimes bestowed on them, that of *industrial arts.*

Industrial! This makes them subject to the law of supply and demand. They must keep equidistant from two poles—those of Industry and Commerce—and from a zenith, which is Art. They evolve at the center of an equilateral triangle defined by these three points of attraction.

Far from injuring art, the fact that it is applied often stimulates it, playing the part of those damp patches on a wall that Leonardo da Vinci advises us to take as a starting-point for experimentation, for groping toward form: a springboard, as it were, for the imagination.[1] The statement that begins the preceding sentence is corroborated from a different angle by Michelet, who writes, in *Nos fils:*

> On close scrutiny, even the supposedly inferior handicrafts often prove to have individual aspects that are, or lead to, art. An able little shoemaker, known to me from the age of fifteen, realized that his craft verged on sculpture; that it implied a powerful feeling for the subtle molding of living, mobile form, and a sense of movement. This carried him into the arts of design. He is now one of our most delightful artists.
>
> But, even without going out of one's way, even without looking beyond one's own art, in the course of time one acquires easier, often quicker, and infinitely simpler ways of doing things. Simplicity of execution adds an astonishing degree of force, and the effects are often magnificent.[2]

Magnificent effects and *force* produced by *simplicity of execution:* we shall return to Michelet's penetrating insight into the virtues of industrial production, when it has the good sense to remain industrial. But, for the moment, let us speak of another, more prosaic virtue: the necessary benefit of commerce. All production is meant for consumption. Outside this area of possible consumption, there is nothing for the decorative arts but a void. To use the scholastic jargon of the economists, let us say that they must be productive of *utility*.

Decorative works, productions of the applied arts, are not only designed to answer to a specific function: they are also made for someone. They offer themselves on the market to meet a certain demand. And that demand introduces the fateful issue of money, venal benefit, cash value; that is to say, given the industrial "*struggle for life*," they must meet the *vital* condition of cheapness.[3]

The machine comes onto the scene in response to these economic conditions.

Let us once more quote Michelet, who writes, this time in *Le Peuple:* "The machine, because it necessitates the centralization of capital, would appear to be an entirely aristocratic force; and yet the cheapness of its products makes it a powerful agent of democratic progress. It gives the poor access to numerous objects of utility—even of luxury and of art—that would otherwise have remained beyond their reach."[4]

Utility, luxury, and *even art:* whether directly or as an intermediary, the machine generalizes utility, luxury, and art, and puts them within the reach of the greatest number. Conversely, by a just balance in human affairs, it provides the public with a reservoir of possible, virtual, latent artists, which is that same greatest number raised to a higher aesthetic power—still static for the moment, but potentially dynamic.

All this would be too good to be true, if there were no shadows in the picture. And some shadows there are. Michelet continues:

"But, at the same time, how galling it is to see man sunk so low in relation to the machine! . . . The head reels, and the heart misses a beat, when first we enter those enchanted palaces where glittering, polished iron and brass seem to move of their own accord, as if they had thoughts and a will of their own. Man is a poor, weak, pallid thing by comparison, a humble servant to those giants of steel."[5]

We have formed the consumer, it is true, but at the cost of deforming the producer. The machine mechanizes the workman and kills the man. What survives—or lingers on, twitching galvanically—is an automaton, chained to an unvarying, mechanical action, from which reason and thought are excluded. This ends only with death: the death of a machine, which is merely the end of motion and not of any real life.

A Socialist economist, a man of genius in his own way, P.-J. Proudhon, covers much the same ground in his *Système des contradictions économiques*. There he writes:

"The machine is the symbol of human liberty, the banner of our dominion over Nature, the attribute of our power, the expression of our right, the emblem of our personality."

But:

"Destitution or degradation: that is the alternative that the machine offers the worker. Because a machine is like an artillery piece: aside from the captain, its crew are there to serve it, to be its slaves.

How are we to resolve this disconcerting paradox: How is a man whose labor has made him a slave—that is to say, a piece of furniture, a thing—how is he to become a person once more by means of that very same labor, or while continuing to do the same thing?"[6]

How is he to turn back into an individual who has sensations and is capable of expressing through a given piece of work the inner state evoked in him by those sensations? How, in a word, can he once more become a potential artist? For this is the aspect of the problem that we must consider here.

At the same time (for the problem is twofold), how are we to reach the point where an industrialized art exerts an aesthetic, artistically educative effect on the purchaser, and thereby engenders a public capable of influencing production? Such a public will appreciate and reward with its patronage—and thus encourage and motivate—artists who, as things are, have dwindled into mere economic factors: cogs in a moral and social mechanism, like the very machines with which they work.

It would be rash indeed to expect machines to assist in sustaining an *intensive* artistic culture. But an *extensive* culture is another thing. It is the dissemination that puts art within the reach of the greatest number: the *primary education* that takes place at every instant, at every contact with an everyday life that has been simultaneously beautified and bettered. It is the refinement of the eye that takes place when the outlines of the most trivial objects correspond aesthetically to their functions. This ever-widening teaching process, conducted through the constant repetition of what modern educators call *object lessons,* is what the machine can achieve, if we desire it and are consistent in that desire. This is no means ambition. It aims to democratize art, just as physical well-being is now being democratized, and to bring art into that physical well-being as its legitimate expression. For beauty, no less than truth, goodness, and justice, is a need and a profound aspiration of human nature.

. . .

The use of mechanical techniques to produce art is almost as old as the world itself. At the risk of incurring the celebrated rebuke issued by Judge Dandin, in Racine's comedy *Les Plaideurs* (when he tells the attorney, "Counselor, I think we can skip as far as the Flood"), let us go back to the dawn of earthly existence.[7] The earth revolves, and to this rotation it owes its rounded shape; man took his cue from the great, primordial law of cosmic gravitation and put clay on a turntable in order to obtain vessels and utensils of a rounded shape.

The turntable, the potter's wheel, was perhaps the earliest industrial machine to impinge on art. The wheel facilitates art, serves it, and offers it an aid that is not to be despised.

. . .

The wheel, turntable, or lathe has a number of productive industrial uses. The English and the Americans, practical folk that they are, make significant use of it in producing wooden parts for furniture. Our own manufacturers would do well to study the results.

There is some of this furniture in which only the work of assembly is done by hand. The machine has done all the rest. We are not saying that such furniture is always in the best possible taste. But when it falls short in this respect, the blame lies not so much with the machines as with the cranial configuration of the designer. The aesthetic errors here are Anglo-Saxon, not mechanical.

The Anglo-Americans are artists only in this one respect: that they are superb industrialists. They are eminently practical people. This leads them to find

P. Rioux de Maillou {187}

the form that is correct in its logical relationship with the function that it manifests. They make good things when—and because—they make comfortable things.

The editor of the *Revue des Arts Décoratifs*, on a visit to the United States during the Chicago Exposition, found himself one day in the showrooms of one of the greatest furniture manufacturers in the New World, when a client arrived.[8] He was privileged to witness the highly characteristic little scene which he recounted to us, and which we crave his permission to retail here.

The client was an hotelier, engaged in fitting out one of those vast hives for travelers that exist only in great American cities. He had come to choose some furnishings, including some *rocking chairs:* an item, still comparatively unfamiliar to us, in which every good American spends every moment of what passes for leisure. This man had no time for questions of good or bad taste. *Comfort* was the sole theme of his remarks to the manufacturer, in the course of his inspection of the goods before he made up his mind to buy.

One chair had arms that did not permit a sufficiently relaxed position of the elbows. The back of another did not slope at the right angle to relax the lumbar region. Another chair had a back that went up too high, obstructing any *flirtation* with a chair behind; and so on.

Well, as it turned out, the chair that best answered the hotelier's requirements, the one best fitted to its use, and the one he decided on, was the very chair whose lines came closest to aesthetic perfection. The principle of the relationship between form and function, as a basis for beauty, had been utterly vindicated by the facts.

To tell us—in logical lines, expressively and not arbitrarily chosen—what it is and what it is for: such is the true character of any production of decorative art. A piece of furniture must express and intimate its use. But the design of industrial art is subject to a second and no less important rule: not content with manifesting its function, the piece must explain frankly, and in appropriate language, what it is and wherein and whereby it exists.

A piece of wooden furniture must look like wood. A piece that is partly turned on a lathe must permit the parts in question to reveal how they were made. For that, in a sense, is what makes them *sui generis*. No hybrids in art.

Honesty is the best workmate.

II

We therefore need not hesitate to enlist the aid of the lathe—always provided that we acknowledge that aid, allow the lathe its aesthetic place in the sun, and make no attempt to conceal its inexorable automatism beneath a mask of mendacious ornament.

Proudhon—who cannot be quoted too often on this topic, for his penetrating, abstract intelligence illuminates it, as it were, both within and without, both in depth and to the full extent of its surface—Proudhon wrote as follows: "In human undertakings, the farther man extends his reach, while delegating to others the tedium of execution and the care of details, the stronger his reason becomes, and the more his genius soars and dominates."[9]

In industry this is an undeniable truth: a man elevates himself and ennobles his work by rendering it less manual and more cerebral: by rising from laborer to skilled workman, and from workman to foreman and to manager. That is to say, the machine, the mechanism that is placed at our disposal, is capable in certain respects of serving the mind and facilitating its ascent toward the best— in other words, toward the ideal. In this sense, machines are favorable to aesthetic progress, since beauty is necessarily a category of the ideal. The machine exerts an indirect spiritualizing effect: because it deals with matter by material means, it frees man from mechanical tension and muscular effort, and thus liberates the mind to assume its rightful pride of place.

Back to the lathe, around which we have just taken a speculative *turn*. Our excursion may have been justified by the observations arising from it; but the machine hauls us back by centripetal force. It is not enough for us to circle round it: we must attend to the center, where it *operates in itself*. There lies the starting point, the solid base that legitimizes all our induction and generalization. Like the mythical Antaeus, we gain new strength every time we touch the earth in which our speculations take root.[10] The fact is, and always will be, the generator of the idea. The abstract presupposes the concrete, from which it derives.

The primitive lathe exploits a rotary force, with the aid of a tool placed at a greater or lesser distance and at a calculated angle to the material, which is whirled around its own axis in a sort of rapid waltz. Under these conditions, the greatest importance attaches to the skill of the turner's hand. This is an art in which the manual operation ranks as high as the original conception. In a word, the involvement of the workman, the artisan, sets his own personal seal on the product and makes it his own. It is as good as he is. The invention of the "carriage," which supports and steadies the hand, is a first step toward the eclipse of the workman by the machine. The carriage will be—has been— perfected, made more flexible, more adaptable. But its limitations are already apparent. The tool has to cut into the material at a number of different depths and angles. Time is lost in adjusting the position and angle of the carriage. It holds the tool steady; leave it to do that, and bypass this problem along with so many others. Hence the lathe with multiple carriages: one carriage and one tool for every distance and for every different curve. The piece to be turned, the rotating raw material, is raised and lowered to present itself in the requisite position for a cutting operation that has been mapped out in advance and logically prepared.

By this time the worker and the artisan have been absorbed: only the manager remains. The brain decides, and the docile mechanism executes. Proudhon's conditions for moral progress have been realized.

The producer has gained; can the same be said of the product and, indirectly, of the consumer? Aesthetically speaking, will the consumer gain by this new method of manufacture?

The question is a complex one, which therefore needs to be taken in stages. It needs to be examined in the unavoidable, and therefore the only true, light of its economic and social aspect.

The individual work of art, which enshrines the vibrant presence of the artist, which lives as it were by an extension of his life, which preserves the pulsating warmth of his breath, which bears his mark, is inevitably aristocratic. The division of labor—that inescapable economic law that brings production within the reach of all—is democratic, and therefore represents the death warrant of the individual work of art. M. de la Palisse formulates the contradiction that is implicit in the problem: *That which is individual can never be done by more than one.*[11]

The converse is no less true: *That which is done by more than one can never be—materially speaking (for the idea itself transcends the modes of realization and may syncretize them)—can never be materially individual.*

Now, the greatest number, the masses, can acquire only such products as are cheap: that is, placed within their reach, in proportion to the budgets available to the social units concerned. In a word: democratic products.

The question may thus be reduced to the following terms: which is preferable, a genuine *mechanical* art, or a simulated personal art?

For our own part, we have not a moment's hesitation. Simulation is art's worst enemy. It falsifies taste; it sows the seeds of kinds of knowledge of which the fruits are all too evident: we have only to look around us at what remains of the pioneering efforts made by the lower middle classes in Louis-Philippe's day.[12] Anything but simulation.

Since this particular blind alley is not available to us, and since at the same time the democratic imperatives of our age give us no option but to produce as cheaply as possible, we have no alternative but to use machines. It remains only to exact the best possible results from those machines. To do this, we must be honest about the way in which things are made. The machine does the work, and so the machine must leave its mark: it must impress its own mode of expression on the finished article.

There is a new decorative aesthetic to be extracted from this, the artistic dawn of industrialization. This is no time to mesmerize ourselves by gazing into the past. We must single out what is fruitful in the present, and cultivate it intelligently. We must allow the seeds to germinate. From this virgin soil will spring an unknown flower that will be our recompense, and also the defining artistic achievement of modern times.

. . .

To summarize: the use of machines deprives us of the *living* quality of execution that passes from the hand through the tool into the work; but it can instill an abstract beauty into its products through the affirmation, not of effort, but of the operator's *knowing*, conscious, sovereign will, which has used material means to impose the generative idea on matter, solely by virtue of being idea and will.

Idealism and *machine* are thesis and antithesis: in scholastic terms, it is for us to bring about their synthesis. If the application of machinery to the arts is to have a future, it must adopt as its mission the *higher reconciliation* of these two contradictory terms.

Because architecture is the most abstract of the arts, mechanized decorative production must direct its efforts—which are also abstract in their tendency—toward architectural qualities.

The charm, the grace, the picturesque quality of ornamental detail is all very well; but the expressive beauty of the whole—of the structure—and the logic of the lines of the composition are better still, for these dominate and command the rest. Even the most wondrous decoration does not redeem a work, if its architecture is bad. For then the decoration does not appear to be an intrinsic part of the structure: it seems to cover it, ineptly, and that is all. On the other hand, good proportions and a successful ensemble often suffice to make us overlook flaws of detail. In a word, architectural simplicity is sufficient in itself; but aesthetic decoration cannot exist without the support of an architecture. An ornamented piece must first of all be a piece: an object, an item of furniture, a work of art, or what not. Art is right to entertain high hopes of what machines can do, and to ask much of them; and, accordingly, to make much use of them in their legitimate sphere.

. . .

A perennial objection is raised against the mechanical shaping of sculptural form that is implicit in the technique [of using a machine to reproduce three-dimensional form]. This is that art is one of the expressive forms of life; that there is no art without life, and no life without humanity—which is to say, without the direct presence of the artist who is embodied in his work; there can consequently be no intermediary.

There are several answers to this. The most relevant in the present context runs as follows. As we have emphasized, this is all about reproduction and not about production. Where reproduction is concerned, to speak of life, personality, and humanity is to speak of interpretation: the involuntary substitution of one intellect, one temperament, etc., for another. And here it is surely the creative artist who interests us, not the artist who follows in his wake. Three studies of the same corner of landscape by three different artists may well bear no resemblance to each other; and it is equally true that, say, three etchings after the same painting will differ vastly. Quite apart from any qualitative distinctions among the three etchers concerned, this leaves us unable to claim that we possess a reproduction of the original. Photogravure, with its chemical sensibility, its mechanical operation, will come a thousand times closer.

Now, machines that reproduce and reduce sculptural form constitute photogravure in three dimensions. Their value in their own kind is neither superior nor inferior. No need to labor the point: the importance and the efficacy of photogravure are well recognized, and need no advocacy here. That would be pushing at an open door. The door is open: let us cross the threshold and enter.

There is, however, one danger with machines: the temptation to take them beyond the normal scope of their operation, and to believe that, because they can do so much, they can do everything. They must always respect the nature of the raw material on which they work. Metal is fusible, and can be struck, or forged, or cast in a mold. Wood cannot. When stamped, compressed, or tortured, wood is wood no longer. Whatever you do, it will never look like anything but papier-mâché. Its special character, its aesthetic beauty, resides in the affirmation of its fibrous identity, and in the felicitous working of the tool that works the fibrous substance. Crush those fibers, and you kill your material. Wood that is stamped or compressed is nothing but the corpse of wood. It has not been worked, but murdered.

The same applies to iron when it is laminated instead of wrought: when it no longer owes its form to the hammer striking the anvil. The results are as embarrassing as the work of those misguided silversmiths who impose on silverware the slender forms and designs of the Renaissance locksmiths.

Each raw material has its own method of working. Each has a language of its own; the mission of art is not to distort this, but to reinforce it through the use of appropriate form.

To sum up: machines can do a great deal for decorative art, and in general for the development of taste, on condition that we do not lose sight of what they are, what they operate on, and where their social influences lie. As economic phenomena, they may be turned to the advantage of art in two ways: by elevating the worker, on one hand, and by increasing the size of the public that is receptive to aesthetic impressions, on the other.

Never forget that we live in a democracy, that this is a democratically minded century, and that there can be no art without a society that enjoys it and desires—and thereby permits—its production.

In a word, *art is social.* Let us therefore accept it, conceive it, and pursue it in terms of our democratic society. Press on!

NOTES

1. Cf. *The Notebooks of Leonardo da Vinci,* ed. and trans. by E. MacCurdy (London, 1939), pp. 873–74.

2. From the French historian Jules Michelet (1798–1874), who wrote *Nos fils* (Paris, 1877).

3. In English in the original.

4. Jules Michelet, *Le Peuple* (Bruxelles, 1846).

5. Ibid.

6. See Pierre Joseph Proudhon, *Système des contradictions économiques ou Philosophie de la misère* (Paris, 1846); Proudhon (1809–1865) was an extremely influential socialist writer and theorist, who broke with Marx, adopting the name of Mutualisme for his own form of anarchism.

7. Maillou is here invoking the famous seventeenth-century French playwright Jean Racine, whose *Les Plaideurs* (1668) is his only comedy.

8. The editor would have been Victor Champier, attending the famous Chicago Universal Exhibition of 1892.

9. See note 2 above.

10. Antaeus was a demi-god whom Hercules defeated by detaching him from his mother, Earth, who was giving him strength.

11. M. de la Palisse seems to be a mythical, comical character of French folklore, known for formulating truisms, such as "a quarter of an hour before he died, he was still alive."

12. Louis-Philippe (1773–1850) was King of France from 1830 to 1848, establishing a constitutional monarchy after the July Revolution. He was known as the "citizen king" because of his bourgeois manner and dress.

HENRY VAN DE VELDE

Observations Toward a Synthesis of Art

It falls to our lot to live in an age in which art has collapsed like a great tree; the shattered remnants of its limbs and branches lie around us. Our first surmise is that some mighty foe, a bolt of lightning, has shattered it with anni-hilating power. In fact, however, there was no glory and no grandeur in the manner of its fall; it was worms that laid it low.

. . .

It must be stated, right at the outset, that all such terms as "low art" [*niedere Kunst*], "second-rank art" [*Kunst zweiten Ranges*], "industrial art" [*Kunstin-dustrie*], "applied art" [*angewandte Kunst*], or "art handicraft" [*Kunsthand-werk*], have no validity except insofar as a consensus exists to describe certain things in such a way. It cannot be conceded that such terms are in any sense ac-curate—or even that the things to which they refer have any real existence.

In art, we can admit of no distinction that assigns to any *one* of its many manifestations and expressive resources a higher rank than the others: which is precisely the end pursued by any separation of visual art into a high art and a second-rate, lower, industrial art. Such a distinction is entirely arbitrary and was introduced, in a wholly unjust and partisan fashion, by the fine arts, which needed such a device to stave off their own impending downfall. All institu-tions and all ideas eventually find themselves in such a phase. This is an uncon-scious attempt to defend oneself and deny the end—as if that were a way to stave off the facts that make the end inevitable.

Fundamentally, there is nothing here but an abusive attempt to establish a hierarchy, to preempt the first place by main force, to belittle those areas in art which are active and lively—namely the minor arts—and to do so at the very moment when a new means of expression has emerged: in industry. The fine arts perceived this as a threat: hence the declaration that this new form was in-ferior and second-rate.

One thinks of grey-haired old men, trying to cuff a child into accepting a lifelong position of inferiority to themselves: they forget how much closer they are to the end than the child. Dismissed as inferior, industrial art has nevertheless slowly gained in the awareness of its own strength, vitality, and future prospects—though it took long enough, in all conscience, to realize that its own allegedly inferior status is a myth.

Surely, if we are ever to speak of art at all, we must assume the existence of shared aspirations, a shared sense of purpose, and equal recognition and respect for all of its underlying objectives. But the "fine arts" in their overweening pride, have deliberately destroyed this sense of unity and community, both through self-aggrandisement and through their plainly announced contempt for any art that is executed in wood, clay, metal, glass, or textile.

Such an attempt to establish a hierarchy of the different realms of art is a new phenomenon, unknown in earlier periods of decline. There is a degree of ignorance in any attempt to apply such a hierarchy to the art of antiquity or of the Gothic age. The distinction is a recent one: it would no more have occurred to the ancients than it would, say, to the primitives.

For them, there was only *one* art, or—not to mince words—Art itself, which they revered in all its manifold manifestations, without any idea of creating hierarchies of value for those who worked in its several fields of activity. All were regarded as equal in vocation and equally honored, because each devoted himself, to the extent of his individual ability, to the same idea of the beautiful, as visualized in each individual age and country.

The division within art has been with us for some time now, but it is as transitory as the current mood of decadence. Its dismal work of fragmentation will last no longer than the appellations foisted upon those "minor arts" [*kleinere Künste*]" that have been cut adrift from "major art." It fluctuates and changes and transforms itself and expands; and on close scrutiny we can undoubtedly see a certain tendency, however slight, toward a return to the former unified definition of all the arts.

Initially, those arts that were officially relegated to a subordinate status had to content themselves with the appellation "arts of the second rank." Later they became "Decorative Arts" [*Dekorative Künste*], a term otherwise undefined and entirely uninformative; then "*Arts Mineurs*," which is as much as to say arts that have yet to reach years of discretion—but who or what was to be their guardian? And finally, "Industrial Arts."

If industry succeeds in restoring the separated arts to a new unity, we ought to be glad and thankful. And, in fact, the changes dictated by industry are none other than a natural development of the materials and techniques of the arts concerned, and an adaptation to the demands of the present day.

Industrial production itself, of course, is one of those demands, and is as natural an evolutionary form of human labor as any other: for without labor, and its whole organism, neither amalgamation nor dissemination would have been possible.

By imposing uniform demands and laws on arts that had previously been flying apart in all directions, industry has endowed them with a shared aesthetic that leads them all toward the same goal, while leaving each individual art to take its own chosen path. That is how a wise shepherd conducts his flock.

Industry has introduced metallic construction, and even the construction of machinery, into the realm of art. It has thus abruptly promoted the engineer to the status of artist, and has enriched the whole field of art with all that is implied by the proud designation "The Arts Applied to Industry."

But the aspiration toward a still more comprehensive union and still greater clarity of expression persists. It will probably not be long before we hear of the "Arts of Industry and Construction": a designation that embraces the art of architecture, currently—and almost reluctantly—a member of the triad of fine arts. Why should the artists who build palaces in stone hold a higher rank than those who build them in metal? And, if the numerous visual manifestations of painting and sculpture aim to be ornamental, not mere illusions—which they cannot be—then this union is only a question of time. Sooner or later, we shall be forced to acknowledge it under the name of "Arts of Industry, Construction, and Ornamentation."

.   .   .

To find the lost sense of living, bold, clear color, of strong and powerful forms, and of rational construction, we must seek it where the "fine arts" have never penetrated. We must look in places where artistic purpose is directed only toward necessary, useful things: as in our clothing—or in our houses.

A village street comes far closer to the characteristics of pure beauty than a street in a city—simply because in it every house, every object, stands out clearly, full of taste and often even full of artistic feeling. However, these qualities would seem to have been inherited only by farm and fishing people. What we like, in all this, is unfortunately no more than its traditional aspect; and, all too soon, farm people, too, will be infatuated with the artificial element in tradition.

The artistic sense—at least in its unadulterated, creative essence—will soon be found only among primitive peoples. To beautify their own lives and the implements that they need is their sole business in life. Forbid one of them to tattoo himself, or to decorate the mat he lies on, or the knife he uses to get his food or to defend himself, and he, child as he is, will conclude that nothing remains for him but to die—or else that this life is not the real life at all.

Art is the wondrous ornament of life. It cannot be otherwise, because ornament is the essence of all the arts. Music and poetry are the ornament of language; dance is the ornament of walking; painting and sculpture are the ornament of thought—as applied to blank walls.

In the last resort, it is perfectly possible to live without language, without walking, without thought, and without adorning one's house accordingly. But anyone who lives in such a way is sacrificing the best part of his life, and neglecting the sacred pledge that is entrusted to every one of us to make it grow. A life without ornament is no more a true life than the life they lead in monastic communities, where men or women vegetate in a constant denial of their natural destiny.

Herein lies a confusion between emotion and morality that inadequately shelters itself behind the name of an ideal—an ideal that itself derives only from an age of decline. Only the ideal of a decadent age could possibly tell us that we become holy by renouncing life itself; by seeing death as the sole hope of the righting of wrongs; by waiting with arms folded—or uplifted in prayer—for everyone to become equal in death.

The craft content clearly derives from that ancient art; the spiritual content does not. I would like to emphasize this. For the truth is—and I will hear no objections here—that the fine arts, as practiced today, have nothing mental or spiritual, but only the outward quality of craftsmanship, in common with art.

The means with which they operate are the same means that true, spiritual art adopts in order to adorn; but they do not adorn, because they are no longer conscious of that purpose and that function. The Arts of Industry and Ornamentation, on the other hand, have little to do with art in handicraft terms, because the craftspeople have lost the awareness of their calling, but the spiritual element has remained intact. And this is why even the most repulsive industrialist will drape the things he makes with a certain amount of ornament; it is hideous, for the most part, but he does not consider his products to be finished without it.

In common parlance, the most elementary and the most correct—but also the most brutal—definition of the distinction between works of Fine Art and those of the Art of Industry and Ornamentation goes roughly like this: those in one category are useful, and those in the other are not.

This is the issue that decides whether a work belongs to the aristocratic fine arts or to the democratic minor arts. The old humiliation endures, however: the artist is a superior being, and the craftsman is a day-laborer.

This view springs from a state of society in which the least useful individuals are the most honored, and the idlest the most respected. If a civilization classifies itself in this way, it is only natural that all those who dream of honor and high status will aspire to have as little to do as possible; that is the only way to attain their goal. Suppose it is decreed that there are two classes within art:

one is Fine Art, and those who practice it are members of the nobility; the other is the Art of Industry and Ornamentation, and those who practice it are day-laborers. Given this choice, it is obvious that everyone will go for the aristocratic option. Those who prefer to remain among the common people will always be very few.

The result of this was that all talent thronged onto the same path. All efforts were directed toward those areas in which the greatest prospects of success seemed to lie. Everyone became a painter or a sculptor or an architect. There appeared to be no alternative.

The artists of the old school dismissed our century as an age obsessed with practical utility. They were incorrigible, unproductive dreamers, who saw nothing in life but what appealed to their own vanity, and who were far removed from all that we consider to be our mission in life: to do our earthly duty. That duty, in turn, consists in making ourselves useful to other people by making works—making them to the best of our ability and as pure and as beautiful as possible.

Life is utilitarian—a truth that none can regret, save those who themselves are good for nothing.

To see Realism and Naturalism simply as new movements in art—dreamed up by some artist or other with no other motive than to set himself apart from the prevailing artistic ideal, and to exhort the young to dethrone the gods of the age and set themselves up in their stead—is to deceive ourselves as to the true nature of the movement; just as we deceive ourselves as to the nature of all other movements, if we fail to trace them to their logical sources.

For the artist, Realism and Naturalism signify finding the way back to life itself. But we have a long way to go before we reach a true union of Art and Life. The innovators believe that they can achieve this through absolute truth to Nature, and through an uncompromising statement of our morality and our outward existence.

To date, however, they have never progressed beyond good intentions. They have spoken a dead language, inaccessible to the public at large; they have elected to use forms—paintings and statues—that can have no effect on life itself. Where they have succeeded in producing such an effect, this has been limited to the few individuals wealthy enough to purchase the painting or statue in question for themselves.

Then, as now, artists sacrificed their lives and their talents, day in and day out, on works destined to find their resting place—without ever giving enjoyment to any but a tiny minority—in some locality quite unknown to the artist at the moment of creation.

The artist has, as it were, forged a chain-link at random and cast it from him, equally at random, so that somewhere it might fit into a chain.

* * *

For the moment, suffice it to say that art is on the brink of a transformation, because society itself is in the same position; and that art is changing its shape, because society is changing its shape. The Socialist writers have ably mined this vein of ideas. The coincidence of the dissemination of Socialist ideas with the blossoming of a new art is undeniable—but the connection between these two facts is not necessarily so close as to prove that they have influenced each other. It is quite possible to be a good Socialist while having no notion of the beauty of outward things; and, conversely, a consistent worshiper of the beauty of all those things that pertain to Life need not also be a Socialist.

Beauty and happiness have a life of their own, on which social circumstances impinge only in relation to social beauty and social happiness. The individual keeps his plot of land, even when his country falls into enemy hands. Upon it, he can cultivate fruits to feed his hunger and blossoms to give him joy.

Beauty and happiness descend to the depths of the heart and the spirit. There, they arouse an imperishable longing and thus form the first and the strongest link between ourselves and eternity. They arouse the curiosity to know the past, and the ardent wish to know the future—all that depends on happiness and beauty for the future.

Only fools take no heed of time, or of the things that lie between those twin poles of endlessness. Beauty and happiness, however, are better able to fill that gigantic span of time than all the assorted dogmas of faith, which are merely the formulas and illusions to which humanity has clung in response to immediate needs.

Beauty and happiness existed on earth long before any deities were believed in; it follows that, if everyone stopped believing in any god tomorrow, beauty and happiness would still be there. In modern life, both are most visibly present in the homes of the working class. In itself, however, Socialism will influence our architecture even less than the Christian faith influenced the wonders of Gothic art.

The current reawakening of art corresponds to a resurgence of the heart and mind—a resurgence in which we shall put into practice the knowledge we have acquired, and activate those materials that now, as never before, are freely available to us.

Both must necessarily lead us to remodel all of the expressive resources of art. Of course, there can be no question of a total breach with the older traditions. I see no reason for such a universal upheaval.

The sap and the strength of beauty are rising again; for we have discovered that it never withered after all, but that its vital force is eternally indestructible and can always bloom afresh. It was naive of us to expect something to appear from outside, and to suppose that only a new religion could reawaken art. And how we have wearied and tormented ourselves by waiting for something that never came and never could have come!

True enough, the old artistic ideal is a thing of the past. It lies embalmed in our museums; and all those who thirst for real life are distressed to find that so many incontestably great and supreme masterpieces can no longer give them full satisfaction.

They visit the museums as one visits a cemetery. They know in advance that, when they return, they will be neither greater nor stronger than before; but they make their pilgrimage through the museums of the world, because they still feel some reverence even for the withered flowers of beauty.

One thing helps us to recognize another. From the things that are stored in those places, we derive an understanding of those things that are evolving before our very eyes, in whatever field of human talent.

Beauty has power over every activity, the lowest as well as the highest. Beauty draws all actions, all previously unknown productions, into its ambit. It pervades them; it transforms itself along with them; it embodies itself in the respective works of our hands and our heads take possession of them.

Those souls who thirst after life and beauty hope that beauty's all-pervasive power will enable all of humanity to match their own evolution, just as soon as it attains self-awareness. They hope for an inexhaustible harvest from all those fragments of beauty that dwell within every scientific discovery and every new practical application. They observe this power with satisfaction or with concern, as the fragments germinate and thrive or are lost. And so they rejoice in the eternal burgeoning and growth of beauty that is constantly reawakened by our needs and by our desire for the most perfect and undiminished life and thought.

The Art and Craft of the Machine

As we work along our various ways, there takes shape within us, in some sort, an ideal—something we are to become—some work to be done. This, I think, is denied to very few, and we begin really to live only when the thrill of this ideality moves us in what we will to accomplish. In the years which have been devoted in my own life to working out in stubborn materials a feeling for the beautiful, in the vortex of distorted complex conditions, a hope has grown stronger with the experience of each year, amounting now to a gradually deepening conviction that in the machine lies the only future of art and craft—as I believe, a glorious future; that the machine is, in fact, the metamorphosis of ancient art and craft; that we are at last face to face with the machine—the modern Sphinx—whose riddle the artist must solve if he would that art live—for his nature holds the key. For one, I promise "whatever gods may be"[1] to lend such energy and purpose as I may possess to help make that meaning plain; to return again and again to the task whenever and wherever need be; for this plain duty is thus relentlessly marked out for the artist in this, the Machine Age, although there is involved an adjustment to cherished gods, perplexing and painful in the extreme the fire of many long-honored ideals shall go down to ashes to reappear, phoenix-like, with new purposes.

The great ethics of the machine are as yet, in the main, beyond the ken of the artist or student of sociology; but the artist mind may now approach the nature of this thing from experience, which has become the commonplace of his field, to suggest, in time, I hope, to prove, that the machine is capable of carrying to fruition high ideals in art—higher than the world has yet seen!

Disciples of William Morris cling to an opposite view. Yet William Morris himself deeply sensed the danger to art of the transforming force whose sign and symbol is the machine, and though of the new art we eagerly seek he sometimes despaired, he quickly renewed his hope.

He plainly foresaw that a blank in the fine arts would follow the inevitable abuse of new-found power and threw himself body and soul into the work of bridging it over by bringing into our lives afresh the beauty of art as she had been, that the new art to come might not have dropped too many stitches nor have unraveled what would still be useful to her.

That he had abundant faith in the new art his every essay will testify.

That he miscalculated the machine does not matter. He did sublime work for it when he pleaded so well for the process of elimination its abuse had made necessary, when he fought the innate vulgarity of theocratic impulse in art as opposed to democratic, and when he preached the gospel of simplicity.

All artists love and honor William Morris.

He did the best in his time for art and will live in history as the great socialist, together with Ruskin the great moralist; significant fact worth thinking about, that the two great reformers of modern times professed the artist.

The machine these reformers protested, because the sort of luxury which is born of greed had usurped it and made of it a terrible engine of enslavement, deluging the civilized world with a murderous ubiquity, which plainly enough was the damnation of their art and craft.

It had not then advanced to the point which now so plainly indicates that it will surely and swiftly, by its own momentum, undo the mischief it has made, and the usurping vulgarians as well.

Nor was it so grown as to become apparent to William Morris, the grand democrat, that the machine was the great forerunner of Democracy.

The ground plan of this thing is now grown to the point where the artist must take it up no longer as a protest: genius must progressively dominate the work of the contrivance it has created; to lend a useful hand in building afresh the "Fairness of the Earth."

That the Machine has dealt Art in the grand old sense a death blow, none will deny.

The evidence is too substantial.

Art in the grand old sense—meaning Art in the sense of structural tradition, whose craft is fashioned upon the handicraft ideal, ancient or modern; an art wherein this form and that form as structural parts were laboriously joined in such a way as to beautifully emphasize the manner of the joining: the million and one ways of beautifully satisfying bare structural necessities, which have come down to us chiefly through the books as "Art."

For the purpose of suggesting hastily and therefore crudely wherein the machine has sapped the vitality of this art, let us assume Architecture in the old sense as a fitting representative of Traditional art and Printing as a fitting representation of the Machine.

What printing—the machine—has done for architecture—the fine art—will have been done in measure of time for all art immediately fashioned upon the early handicraft ideal.

. . .

So the Artist craft wanes.

Craft that will not see that "human thought is stripping off one form and donning another," and artists are everywhere, whether catering to the leisure class of old England or ground beneath the heel of commercial abuse here in the great West, the unwilling symptoms of the inevitable, organic nature of the machine, they combat, the hell-smoke of the factories they scorn to understand.

And, invincible, triumphant, the machine goes on, gathering force and knitting the material necessities of mankind ever closer into a universal automatic fabric; the engine, the motor, and the battleship, the works of art of the century!

The Machine is Intellect mastering the drudgery of earth that the plastic art may live; that the margin of leisure and strength by which man's life upon the earth can be made beautiful, may immeasurably widen; its function ultimately to emancipate human expression!

It is a universal educator, surely raising the level of human intelligence, so carrying within itself the power to destroy, by its own momentum, the greed which in Morris' time and still in our own time turns it to a deadly engine of enslavement. The only comfort left the poor artist, sidetracked as he is, seemingly is a mean one; the thought that the very selfishness which man's early art idealized, now reduced to its lowest terms, is swiftly and surely destroying itself through the medium of the Machine.

The artist's present plight is a sad one, but may he truthfully say that society is less well off because Architecture, or even Art, as it was, is dead, and printing, or the Machine, lives?

Every age has done its work, produced its art with the best tools or contrivances it knew, the tools most successful in saving the most precious thing in the world—human effort. Greece used the chattel slave as the essential tool of its art and civilization. This tool we have discarded, and we would refuse the return of Greek art upon the terms of its restoration, because we insist now upon a basis of Democracy.

Is it not more likely that the medium of artistic expression itself has broadened and changed until a new definition and new direction must be given the art-activity of the future, and that the Machine has finally made for the artist, whether he will yet own it or not, a splendid distinction between the Art of old and the Art to come? A distinction made by the tool which frees human labor, lengthens and broadens the life of the simplest man, thereby the basis of the Democracy upon which we insist.

The Art of old idealized a Structural Necessity—now rendered obsolete and unnatural by the Machine—and accomplished it through man's joy in the labor of his hands.

The new will weave for the necessities of mankind, which his Machine will have mastered, a robe of ideality no less truthful but more poetical, with a rational freedom made possible by the machine, beside which the art of old will be as the sweet plaintive wail of the pipe to the outpouring of full orchestra.

It will clothe Necessity with the living flesh of virile imagination, as the living flesh lends living grace to the hard and bony human skeleton.

The new will pass from the possession of kings and classes to the everyday lives of all—from duration in point of time to immortality.

This distinction is one to be felt now rather than clearly defined.

The definition is the poetry of this Machine Age, and will be written large in time; but the more we, as artists, examine into this premonition, the more we will find the utter helplessness of old forms to satisfy new conditions, and the crying need of the machine for plastic treatment—a pliant, sympathetic treatment of its needs that the body of structural precedent cannot yield.

To gain further suggestive evidence of this, let us turn to the Decorative Arts—the immense middle ground of all art now mortally sickened by the Machine—sickened that it may slough the art ideal of the constructural art for the plasticity of the new art—the Art of Democracy.

Here we find the most deadly perversion of all—the magnificent prowess of the machine bombarding the civilized world with the mangled corpses of strenuous horrors that once stood for cultivated luxury—standing now for a species of fatty degeneration simply vulgar.

Without regard to first principles or common decency, the whole letter of tradition—that is, ways of doing things rendered wholly obsolete and unnatural by the machine—is recklessly fed into its rapacious maw until you may buy reproductions for ninety-nine cents at "The Fair" that originally cost ages of toil and cultivation, worth now intrinsically nothing—that are harmful parasites befogging the sensibilities of our natures, belittling and falsifying any true perception of normal beauty the Creator may have seen fit to implant in us.

The idea of fitness to purpose, harmony between form, and use with regard to any of these things, is possessed by very few, and utilized by them as a protest chiefly—a protest against the machine!

As well blame Richard Croker for the political iniquity of America.[2]

As "Croker is the creature and not the creator" of political evil, so the machine is the creature and not the creator of this iniquity; and with this difference—that the machine has noble possibilities unwillingly forced to degradation in the name of the artistic; the machine, as far as its artistic capacity is concerned, is itself the crazed victim of the artist who works while he waits, and the artist who waits while he works.

There is a nice distinction between the two.

Neither class will unlock the secrets of the beauty of this time.

They are clinging sadly to the old order and would wheedle the giant frame of things back to its childhood or forward to its second childhood, while this Machine Age is suffering for the artist who accepts, works, and sings as he works, with the joy of the *here* and *now!*

We want the man who eagerly seeks and finds, or blames himself if he fails to find, the beauty of this time; who distinctly accepts as a singer and a prophet; for no man may work while he waits or wait as he works in the sense that William Morris' great work was legitimately done—in the sense that most art and craft of today is an echo; the time when such work was useful has gone.

Echoes are by nature decadent.

Artists who feel toward Modernity and the Machine now as William Morris and Ruskin were justified in feeling then, had best distinctly wait and work sociologically where great work may still be done by them. In the field of art activity they will do distinct harm. Already they have wrought much miserable mischief.

If the artist will only open his eyes he will see that the machine he dreads has made it possible to wipe out the mass of meaningless torture to which mankind, in the name of the artistic, has been more or less subjected since time began; for that matter, has made possible a cleanly strength, an ideality and a poetic fire that the art of the world has not yet seen; for the machine, the process now smooths away the necessity of petty structural deceits, soothes this wearisome struggle to make things seem what they are not, and can never be; satisfies the simple term of the modern art equation as the ball of clay in the sculptor's hand yields to his desire—comforting forever this realistic, brain-sick masquerade we are wont to suppose art.

William Morris pleaded well for simplicity as the basis of all the art. Let us understand the significance to art of that word—SIMPLICITY—for it is vital to the Art of the Machine.

We may find, in place of the genuine thing we have striven for, an affectation of the naive, which we should detest as we detest a full-grown woman with baby mannerisms.

English art is saturated with it, from the brand-new imitation of the old house that grew and rambled from period to period to the rain-tub standing beneath the eaves.

In fact, most simplicity following the doctrines of William Morris is a protest; as a protest, well enough, but the highest form of simplicity is not simple in the sense that the infant intelligence is simple—nor, for that matter, the side of a barn.

A natural revulsion of feeling leads us from the meaningless elaboration of today to lay too great stress on mere platitudes, quite as a clean sheet of paper is a relief after looking at a series of bad drawings—but simplicity is not merely a neutral or a negative quality.

Simplicity in art, rightly understood, is a synthetic, positive quality, in which we may see evidence of mind, breadth of scheme, wealth of detail, and withal a sense of completeness found in a tree or a flower. A work may have the delicacies of a rare orchid or the stanch fortitude of the oak, and still be simple. A thing to be simple needs only to be true to itself in organic sense.

With this ideal of simplicity, let us glance hastily at a few instances of the machine and see how it has been forced by false ideals to do violence to this simplicity; how it has made possible the highest simplicity, rightly understood and so used. As perhaps wood is most available of all homely materials and therefore, naturally, the most abused—let us glance at wood.

Machinery has been invented for no other purpose than to imitate, as closely as possible, the wood carving of the early ideal—with the immediate result that no ninety-nine-cent piece of furniture is salable without some horrible botchwork meaning nothing unless it means that art and craft have combined to fix in the mind of the masses the old hand-carved chair as the *ne plus ultra* of the ideal.

The miserable, lumpy tribute to this perversion which Grand Rapids alone yields would mar the face of art beyond repair; to say nothing of the elaborate and fussy joinery of posts, spindles, jig-sawed beams and braces, butted and strutted, to outdo the sentimentality of the already overwrought antique product.

Thus is the woodworking industry glutted, except in rarest instances. The whole sentiment of early craft degenerated to a sentimentality having no longer decent significance nor commercial integrity; in fact all that is fussy, maudlin, and animal, basing its existence chiefly on vanity and ignorance.

Now let us learn from the Machine.

It teaches us that the beauty of wood lies first in its qualities as wood; no treatment that did not bring out these qualities all the time could be plastic, and therefore not appropriate—so not beautiful, the Machine teaches us, if we have left it to the machine that certain simple forms and handling are suitable to bring out the beauty of wood and certain forms are not; that all wood carving is apt to be a forcing of the material, an insult to its finer possibilities as a material having in itself intrinsically artistic properties, of which its beautiful markings is one, its texture another, its color a third.

The machine, by its wonderful cutting, shaping, smoothing, and repetitive capacity, has made it possible to so use it without waste that the poor as well as the rich may enjoy today beautiful surface treatments of clean, strong forms that the branch veneers of Sheraton and Chippendale only hinted at, with dire extravagance, and which the Middle Ages utterly ignored.[3]

The machine has emancipated these beauties of nature in wood; made it possible to wipe out the mass of meaningless torture to which wood has been subjected since the world began, for it has been universally abused and mal-treated by all peoples but the Japanese.

Rightly appreciated, is not this the very process of elimination for which Morris pleaded?

Not alone a protest, moreover, for the machine, considered only technically, if you please, has placed in artist hands the means of idealizing the true nature of wood harmoniously with man's spiritual and material needs, without waste, within reach of all.

And how fares the troop of old materials galvanized into new life by the Machine?

Our modern materials are these old materials in more plastic guise, rendered so by the Machine, itself creating the very quality needed in material to satisfy its own art equation.

We have seen in glancing at modern architecture how they fare at the hands of Art and Craft; divided and subdivided in orderly sequence with rank and file of obedient retainers awaiting the master's behest.

Steel and iron, plastic cement, and terra-cotta.

Who can sound the possibilities of this old material, burned clay, which the modern machine has rendered as sensitive to the creative brain as a dry plate to the lens—a marvelous simplifier? And this plastic covering material, cement, another simplifier, enabling the artist to clothe the structural frame with a sim-ple, modestly beautiful robe where before he dragged in, as he does still drag, five different kinds of material to compose one little cottage, pettily arranging it in an aggregation supposed to be picturesque—as a matter of fact, millinery, to be warped and beaten by sun, wind, and rain into a variegated heap of trash.

There is the process of modern casting in metal—one of the perfected mod-ern machines, capable of any form to which fluid will flow, to perpetuate the imagery of the most delicately poetic mind without let or hindrance—within reach of everyone, therefore insulted and outraged by the bungler forcing it to a degraded seat at his degenerate festival.

Multitudes of processes are expectantly awaiting the sympathetic interpretation of the mastermind; the galvano-plastic and its electrical brethren, a prolific horde, now cheap fakirs imitating real bronzes and all manner of the antique, secretly damning it in their vitals.

Electro-glazing, a machine shunned because too cleanly and delicate for the clumsy hand of the traditional designer, who depends upon the mass and blur of leading to conceal his lack of touch.

That delicate thing, the lithograph—the prince of a whole reproductive province of processes—see what this process becomes in the hands of a master like Whistler.[4] He has sounded but one note in the gamut of its possibilities, but that product is intrinsically true to the process, and as delicate as the butterfly's wing. Yet the most this particular machine did for us, until then in the hands of Art and Craft, was to give us a cheap, imitative effect of painting.

So spins beyond our ability to follow tonight, a rough, feeble thread of the evidence at large to the effect that the machine has weakened the artist; all but destroyed his handmade art, if not its ideals, although he has made enough miserable mischief meanwhile.

These evident instances should serve to hint, at least to the thinking mind, that the Machine is a marvelous simplifier; the emancipator of the creative mind, and in time the regenerator of the creative conscience. We may see that this destructive process has begun and is taking place that art might awaken to that power of fully developed senses promised by dreams of its childhood, even though that power may not come the way it was pictured in those dreams.

Now, let us ask ourselves whether the fear of the higher artistic expression demanded by the Machine, so thoroughly grounded in the arts and crafts, is founded upon a finely guarded reticence, a recognition of inherent weakness or plain ignorance!

Let us, to be just, assume that it is equal parts of all three, and try to imagine an Arts and Crafts Society that may educate itself to prepare to make some good impression upon the Machine, the destroyer of their present ideals and tendencies, their salvation in disguise.

Such a society will, of course, be a society for mutual education.

Exhibitions will not be a feature of its programme for years, for there will be nothing to exhibit except the shortcomings of the society, and they will hardly prove either instructive or amusing at this stage of proceedings. This society must, from the very nature of the proposition, be made up of the people who are in the work—that is, the manufacturers—coming into touch with such of those who assume the practice of the fine arts as profess a fair sense of the obligation to the public such assumption carries with it, and sociological workers whose interest are ever closely allied with art, as their prophets Morris, Ruskin, and Tolstoy evince, and all those who have as personal graces and accomplishment perfected handicraft, whether fashion old or fashion new.

Without the interest and cooperation of the manufacturers, the society cannot begin to do its work, for this is the cornerstone of its organization.

All these elements should be brought together on a common ground of confessed ignorance, with a desire to be instructed, freely encouraging talk and opinions, and reaching out desperately for anyone who has special experience in any way connected to address them.

. . .

Surely a thing like this would be worthwhile—to alleviate the insensate numbness of the poor fellows out in the cold, hard shops, who know not why nor understand, whose dutiful obedience is chained to botch work and bungler's ambition; surely this would be a practical means to make their dutiful obedience give us something we can all understand, and that will be as normal to the best of this machine age as a ray of light to the healthy eye; a real help in adjusting the *Man* to a true sense of his importance as a factor in society, though he does tend a machine.

Teach him that that machine is his best friend—will have widened the margin of his leisure until enlightenment shall bring him a further sense of the magnificent ground plan of progress in which he too justly plays his significant part.

If the art of the Greek, produced at such cost of human life, was so noble and enduring, what limit dare we now imagine to an Art based upon an adequate life for the individual?

> The machine is his!
> In due time it will come to him!
> Meanwhile, who shall count the slain?

From where are the trained nurses in this industrial hospital to come if not from the modern arts and crafts?

Shelley says a man cannot say—"I will compose poetry."[5] "The greatest poet even cannot say it, for the mind in creation is as a fading coal which some invisible influence, like an inconstant wind awakens to transitory brightness; this power arises from within like the color of a flower which fades and changes as it is developed, and the conscious portions of our nature are unprophetic either of its approach or its departure"; and yet in the arts and crafts the problem is presented as a more or less fixed quantity, highly involved, requiring a surer touch, a more highly disciplined artistic nature to organize it as a work of art.

The original impulses may reach as far inward as those of Shelley's poet, be quite as wayward a matter of pure sentiment, and yet after the thing is done, showing its rational qualities, are limited in completeness only by the capacity of whoever would show them or by the imperfection of the thing itself.

This does not mean that Art may be shown to be an exact Science.

"It is not pure reason, but it is always reasonable."

It is a matter of perceiving and portraying the harmony of organic tendencies; is originally intuitive because the artist nature is a prophetic gift that may sense these qualities afar.

To me, the artist is he who can truthfully idealize the common sense of these tendencies in his chosen way.

So I feel conception and composition to be simply the essence of refinement in organization, the original impulse of which may be registered by the artistic nature as unconsciously as the magnetic needle vibrates to the magnetic law, but which is, in synthesis or analysis, organically consistent, given the power to see it or not.

And I have come to believe that the world of Art, which we are so fond of calling the world outside of Science, is not so much outside as it is the very heart quality of this great material growth—as religion is its conscience.

A foolish heart and a small conscience.

A foolish heart, palpitating in alarm, mistaking the growing pains of its giant frame for approaching dissolution, whose sentimentality the lusty body of modern things has outgrown.

Upon this faith in Art as the organic heart quality of the scientific frame of things, I base a belief that we must look to the artist brain, of all brains, to grasp the significance to society of this thing we call the Machine, if that brain be not blinded, gagged, and bound by false tradition, the letter of precedent. For this thing we call Art is it not as prophetic as a primrose or an oak? Therefore, of the essence of this thing we call the Machine, which is no more or less than the principle of organic growth working irresistibly the Will of Life through the medium of Man.

Be gently lifted at nightfall to the top of a great downtown office building, and you may see how in the image of material man, at once his glory and menace, is this thing we call a city.

There beneath, grown up in a night, is the monster leviathan, stretching acre upon acre into the far distance. High overhead hangs the stagnant pall of its fetid breath, reddened with the light from its myriad eyes endlessly everywhere blinking. Ten thousand acres of cellular tissue, layer upon layer, the city's flesh, outspreads enmeshed by intricate network of veins and arteries, radiating into the gloom, and there with muffled, persistent roar, pulses and circulates as the blood in your veins, the ceaseless beat of the activity to whose necessities it all conforms.

Like to the sanitation of the human body is the drawing off of poisonous waste from the system of this enormous creature; absorbed first by the infinitely ramifying, threadlike ducts gathering at their sensitive terminals matter destructive to its life, hurrying it to millions of small intestines, to be collected in turn by larger, flowing to the great sewer, on to the drainage canal, and finally to the ocean.

This ten thousand acres of fleshlike tissue is again knit and interknit with a nervous system marvelously complete, delicate filaments for hearing, knowing, almost feeling the pulse of its organism, acting upon the ligaments and tendons for motive impulse, in all flowing the impelling fluid of man's own life.

Its nerve ganglia!—the peerless Corliss tandems whirling their hundred ton fly-wheels, fed by gigantic rows of water-tube boilers burning oil, a solitary man slowly pacing backward and forward, regulating here and there the little feed valves controlling the deafening roar of the flaming gas, while beyond, the incessant clicking, dropping, waiting—lifting, waiting, shifting of the governor gear controlling these modern Goliaths seems a visible brain in intelligent action, registered infallibly in the enormous magnets, purring in the giant embrace of great induction coils, generating the vital current meeting with instant response in the rolling cars on elevated tracks ten miles away, where the glare of the Bessemer steel converter makes a conflagration of the clouds.

More quietly still, whispering down the long, low rooms of factory buildings buried in the gloom beyond, range on range of stanch, beautifully perfected automatons, murmur contentedly with occasional click-clack, that would have the American manufacturing industry of five years ago by the throat today manipulating steel as delicately as a mystical shuttle of the modern loom manipulates a silk thread in the shimmering pattern of a dainty gown.

And the heavy breathing, the murmuring, the clangor, and the roar!—how the voice of this monstrous thing, this greatest of machines, a great city, rises to proclaim the marvel of the units of its structure, the ghastly warning boom from the deep throats of vessels heavily seeking inlet to the waterway below, answered by the echoing clangor of the bridge bells growing nearer and more ominous as the vessel cuts momentarily the flow of the nearer artery, warning the current from the swinging bridge now closing on its stately passage, just in time to receive in a rush of steam, as a streak of light, the avalanche of blood and metal hurled across it and gone, roaring into the night on its glittering bands of steel, ever faithfully encircled by the slender magic lines tick-tapping its invincible protection.

Nearer, in the building ablaze with midnight activity, the wide white band streams into the marvel of the multiple press, receiving unerringly the indelible impression of the human hopes, joys, and fears throbbing in the pulse of this great activity, as infallibly as the gray matter of the human brain receives the impression of the senses, to come forth millions of neatly folded, perfected news sheets, teeming with vivid appeals to passions, good or evil; weaving a web of intercommunication so far-reaching that distance becomes as nothing, the thought of one man in one corner of the earth one day visible to the naked eye of all men the next; the doings of all the world reflected as in a glass, so marvelously sensitive this wide white band streaming endlessly from day to day becomes in the grasp of the multiple press.

If the pulse of activity in this great city, to which the tremor of the mammoth skeleton beneath our feet is but an awe-inspiring response, is thrilling, what of this prolific, silent obedience?

And the texture of the tissue of this great thing, this Forerunner of Democracy, the Machine, has been deposited particle by particle, in blind obedience to organic law, the law to which the great solar universe is but an obedient machine.

Thus is the thing into which the forces of Art are to breathe the thrill of ideality! A SOUL!

NOTES

1. From *Invictus*, by William Ernest Henley. [B. B. Pfeiffer]

2. Richard Croker (1841–1922) a New York politician of Irish birth, who rose to Tammany leadership in the mid-1880s. [B. B. Pfeiffer]

3. Wright is referring to the Chippendale firm of cabinetmaker and design, established by Thomas Chippendale in the 1750s, and to Thomas Sheraton, a contemporary eighteenth-century cabinetmaker and designer.

4. See Crane excerpt, note 2.

5. The citation is from the only prose work by the English Romantic poet, Percy Shelley (1792–1822), *Defence of Poetry* (1821) §284.

LE CORBUSIER

The Decorative Art of Today

The decorative art of today! Am I plunging into paradox?—a paradox
that is only apparent. To include under this rubric everything that is free from
decoration, whilst making due apology for what is simply banal, indifferent, or
void of *artistic intention,* to invite the eye and the spirit to take pleasure in the
company of such things and perhaps to rebel against the flourish, the stain, the
distracting din of colours and ornaments, to dismiss a whole mass of artefacts,
some of which are not without merit, to pass over an activity that has sometimes been disinterested, sometimes idealistic, to disdain the work of so many
schools, so many masters, so many pupils, and to think thus of them: 'they are
as disagreeable as mosquitoes'; and thence to arrive at this impasse: *modern
decorative art is not decorated.* Have we not the right? A moment's thought will
confirm it. The paradox lies not in reality, but in the words. Why do the objects
that concern us here have to be called *decorative art?* This is the paradox: why
should chairs, bottles, baskets, shoes, which are all objects of utility, all *tools,* be
called *decorative art?* The paradox of making art out of tools. Let's be clear. I
mean, the paradox of making *decorative* art out of tools. To make art out of
tools is fair enough, if we hold with Larousse's definition, which is that ART is
the application of knowledge to the realisation of an idea.[1] Then yes. We are indeed committed to apply all our knowledge to the perfect creation of a tool:
know-how, skill, efficiency, economy, precision, the sum of knowledge. A good
tool, an excellent tool, the very best tool. This is the world of *manufacture,* of
industry; we are looking for a standard and our concerns are far from the personal, the arbitrary, the fantastic, the eccentric; our interest is in the norm, and
we are creating type-objects.

So the paradox certainly lies in the terminology.

But we are told that decoration is necessary to our existence. Let us correct
that: art is necessary to us; that is to say, a disinterested passion that exalts us.
Decoration: baubles, charming entertainment for a savage. (And I do not deny
that it is an excellent thing to keep an element of the savage alive in us—a small
one.) But in the twentieth century our powers of judgement have developed
greatly and we have raised our level of consciousness. Our spiritual needs are
different, and higher worlds than those of decoration offer us commensurate

experience. It seems justified to affirm: *the more cultivated a people becomes, the more decoration disappears.* (Surely it was Loos who put it so neatly.)[2]

So, to see things clearly, it is sufficient to separate the satisfaction of disinterested emotion from that of utilitarian need. Utilitarian needs call for tools brought in *every respect* to that degree of perfection seen in industry. This then is the magnificent programme for *decorative art* (decidedly, an inappropriate term!).*

To provoke elevated sensations is the prerogative of proportion, which is a sensed mathematic; it is afforded most particularly by architecture,† painting, and sculpture—works of no immediate utility, disinterested, exceptional, works that are plastic creations invested with passion, the passion of a man— the manifold drama that arrests us, jolts us, rouses us, moves us.‡ Now and always there is a hierarchy. There is a time for work, when one uses oneself up, and also a time for meditation, when one recovers one's bearing and rediscovers harmony. There should be no confusion between them; we are no longer in the age of the dilettante, but at an hour that is harsh and epic, serious and violent, pressured and productive, fertile and economic. Everything has its classification; work and meditation.

The classes too have their classification: those who struggle for their crust of bread have the simple ideal of a decent lodging (and they love to see the fanciest furniture, Henry II or Louis XV, which gives them the feeling of wealth—an elementary ideal). And those well-enough endowed to have the ability and the duty to think (and they aspire to the wisdom of Diogenes).[3]

Previously, decorative objects were rare and costly. Today they are commonplace and cheap. Previously, plain objects were commonplace and cheap; today they are rare and expensive. Previously, decorative objects were items for special display: the plate which the peasant family hung on the wall and the embroidered waistcoat for holidays; grist for the propaganda of princes. Today decorative objects flood the shelves of the Department Stores; they sell cheaply to shop-girls. If they sell cheaply, it is because they are badly made and because

*It has to be said that for thirty years no one has been able to find an accurate term. Is that not because the activity lacks precision, lacks direction, and that as a result it is impossible to define it? The Germans invented the word *Kunstgewerb* (industrial art); that is even more equivocal! I was forgetting that pejorative term *applied art.*

†Architecture begins where calculation ends.

‡And without doubt furniture can lead us towards architecture, and in place of decoration we shall see the rise of architecture.

decoration hides faults in their manufacture and the poor quality of their materials: decoration is disguise. It pays the manufacturer to employ a decorator to disguise the faults in his products, to conceal the poor quality of their materials and to distract the eye from their blemishes by offering it the spiced morsels of glowing gold-plate and strident symphonies. Trash is always abundantly decorated; the luxury object is well made, neat and clean, pure and healthy, and its bareness reveals the quality of its manufacture. It is to industry that we owe this reversal in the state of affairs: a cast-iron stove overflowing with decoration costs less than a plain one; amidst the surging leaf patterns flaws in the casting cannot be seen. And the same applies generally. Take some plain calico and soak it in colour; the printing machine will instantly cover it in the most fashionable patterns (for example, copies of Spanish mantillas, Bulgarian embroidery, Persian silks, etc.) and without incurring much expense one can double the sale price. I quite agree that it can be as charming, as gay, and as shop-girl-like as you could want, and I would want that to continue. What would spring be without it! But this surface elaboration, if extended without discernment over absolutely everything, becomes repugnant and scandalous; it smells of pretence, and the healthy gaiety of the shop-girl in her flower-patterned cretonne dress, becomes rank corruption when surrounded by Renaissance stoves, Turkish smoking tables, Japanese umbrellas, chamber pots and bidets from Lunéville or Rouen, Bichara perfumes, bordello lamp-shades, pumpkin cushions, divans spread with gold and silver *lamé*, black velvets flecked like the Grand Turk, rugs with baskets of flowers and kissing doves, linoleum printed with Louis XVI ribbons. The pretty little shepherdess shop-girl in her flowery cretonne dress, as fresh as spring, seems, in a bazaar such as this, like a sickening apparition from the show-cases of the costume department in the ethnographic museum.

Not only is this accumulation of false richness unsavoury, but above all and before all, this taste for decorating everything around one is a false taste, an abominable little perversion. I reverse the painting; the shepherdess shop-girl is in a pretty room, bright and clear, white walls, a good chair—wickerwork or Thonet; table from the *Bazaar de l'Hotel de Ville* (in the manner of Louis XIII, a very beautiful table) painted with ripolin.[4] A good well-polished lamp, some crockery of white porcelain; and on the table three tulips in a vase can be seen lending a lordly presence. It is healthy, clean, decent. And to make something attractive, as little as that is enough.

Certainly, the modern decorative art of the decorators has different objectives, and it is fair to say that the picture I painted above was no more than the vulgarisation of much worthier intentions. So at this point in our search for a guiding principle, we arrive at the impasse of decorative art: decorative art that is not decorated. And we assert that this art without decoration is made not by artists but by anonymous industry following its airy and limpid path of economy.

The guiding principle of decorators with serious intentions is to cater for the enjoyment of life by a sophisticated clientele. As a result of fashions, the publication of books, and the assiduous efforts of a whole generation of decorators, this clientele has seen its tastes sharply awakened to matters connected with art. Today there is a lively aesthetic awareness and a taste for a contemporary art responding to very much more subtle requirements and to a new spirit. As a result there is a distinct evolution towards ideas reflecting the new spirit; the experience of decoration as art from 1900 to the war has illustrated the impasse of decoration and the fragility of the attempt to make our tools expressive of sentiment and of individual states of mind. There has been a reaction to this obtrusive presence, and it is being rejected. Day after day, on the other hand, we notice among the products of industry articles of perfect convenience and utility, that soothe our spirits with the luxury afforded by the elegance of their conception, the purity of their execution, and the efficiency of their operation. They are so well thought out that we feel them to be harmonious, and this harmony is sufficient for our gratification.

And so, having opened our eyes and rid ourselves of the romantic and Ruskinian baggage that formed our education, we have to ask ourselves whether these new objects do not suit us very well, and whether this rational perfection and precise formulation in each does not constitute sufficient common ground between them to allow the recognition of a *style!*

We have seen that, freed from all reminiscence and traditional preconception, a rational and reassuring rigour has been applied to their design. Their choice of material, first of all, has been dictated by considerations of strength, lightness, economy and durability alone; objects for centuries made of wood have been adapted to metal and steel—objects such as office furniture, from which an entirely new precision of operation is demanded. Thus the 'Voltaire' low armchair has become a totally different machine for sitting in since it was covered in leather.

As a result of this adaptation to new materials, the structure has been transformed, often radically; for a long time these new forms offended us and, by a fatal process of reasoning, provoked a violent *nationalist* (that is to say, regionalist) reaction, an appeal to handicraft as opposed to the machine, seen as a modern hydra. A sterile reaction: one cannot swim back against the current, and the machine which does its work with purity and exactitude is from today dispelling this anachronistic backwash. Let us allow one or two generations brought up in the religion of patina and the 'handmade' to fade away quietly.

The young generations are born to the new light and turn naturally and with enthusiasm to the simple truths. When an electric light bulb is at last *weighed*, one fine day, in the design office of a manufacturer of chandeliers, its 50 grams will weigh heavily in the scales that determine the fate of industries doomed to disappearance; the technological firm will replace the artistic: so it is written.

Thus, as new materials and forms were inevitably introduced into the decorative art industries, at the dictate of the all-powerful gods of price and performance, some alert and enquiring minds noted the unvarying laws that were shaping the new products. These laws endowed everything with a common character, and the confidence that they gave to the mind constituted the basis of a new sense of harmony.

If we pause to consider the situation, we are bound to admit that there is no need to wait any longer for objects of utility.

Without a revolution, barricades, or gun-fire, but as a result of simple evolution accelerated by the rapid tempo of our time, we can see decorative art in its decline, and observe that the almost hysterical rush in recent years towards quasi-orgiastic decoration is no more than the final spasm of an already forseeable death.

In face of this unbroken and continuing evidence, good sense has gradually rejected the tendency to luxuriousness as inappropriate to our needs. Its last popular resort has been a devotion to *beautiful materials,* which leads to real byzantinism. The final retreat for ostentation is in polished marbles with restless patterns of veining, in panelling of rare woods as exotic to us as hummingbirds, in glass pastes, in lacquers copied from *the excesses* of the Mandarins and thence made the starting point for further elaboration. At the same time, the Prefecture of Police has set about pursuing the pedlars of cocaine. This is all of a piece: feverish pulses and nerves shattered in the aftermath of war like to cool themselves by contact with these inhuman materials that keep us at a distance; in other circumstances they could well offer us a delicate slice of the miracle of nature; but the matrix of amethyst split and polished, or a lump of rock crystal set on my desk is just as expressive, and a great deal more comfortable as an exemplar of the glittering geometries that enthrall us and that we discover with delight in natural phenomena. When we have occasion to enter one of these troubled sanctuaries where so many artful reflections flit about amongst the black or white marbles, the gilt, the red or blue lacquers, we are seized by malaise, by anguish: we long to leave this den, to escape to the open air, and there, reassured and confident, to seat ourselves in a cell such as that in the convent of Fiesole, or better still, to get down to work in the superb office of a modern factory, which is clear and rectilinear and painted with white ripolin and in which healthy activity and industrious optimism reign.

The religion of beautiful materials is now no more than the final spasm of an agony.

During these last years we have witnessed the successive stages of a development: with metallic construction, the *separation of decoration from structure*. Then the fashion for *expressing the construction,* the sign of a new construction. Then the ecstasy before *nature,* showing a desire to rediscover (by however circuitous a path!) the laws of *the organic.* Then the craze for the *simple,* the first contact with the truths of the machine leading us back to good sense, and the instinctive manifestation of an aesthetic for our era.

To tie up the final strand: a triggering of our consciousness, a classification, and a normal perception of the objects in our life will emerge, which distinguishes the highly practical things of work from the intensely free, living, ideal things of the mind.

NOTES

1. See note 1 of Le Corbusier's "Type-Needs: Type-Furniture" in this volume.

2. See Loos's "Ornament and Crime" in this volume.

3. The Greek philosopher Diogenes (died c. 320 BCE) rejected social conventions and founded a philosophy of Cynics.

4. The Bazaar de l'Hotel de Ville (founded 1857) was one of the new department stores built in the second half of the nineteenth century in Paris; it moved to a building designed by Auguste Roy on the rue de Rivoli in 1913.

GOTTFRIED SEMPER

Introduction to *Style in the Technical and Tectonic Arts*

CHAPTER 1: INTRODUCTION

§1: General

Art has a language of its own, which consists of formal types and symbols. In the course of the history of culture, this has undergone so many and such disparate transformations that it now affords almost as many different ways to make oneself understood as do the varieties of language proper. Modern philology sets out to demonstrate the affiliations among human languages, and to trace the changes in individual words back through the centuries to the single or multiple points at which they coalesce in shared ancestral forms. In this way, it has succeeded in elevating the study of language to the status of a true science—and even in facilitating the purely practical study of languages—and has cast light on the dark and distant past of nations. An analogous endeavor in the realm of art scholarship is similarly justified, for it devotes attention to the evolution of art forms, their seeds and roots, their transitions and ramifications, that it undoubtedly deserves.

This initial statement would seem superfluous, had not all investigation of the origin of basic architectural forms and symbols been rendered suspect by a long line of futile speculations, some of which have given rise to positively dangerous errors and false theories. It suffices to mention the attempt, first made by Vitruvius and repeated a hundred times after him, to deduce the Doric temple, in all of its parts and members, from a wooden hut; or the erroneous notion, to which even such a man as Gau subscribed, that Egyptian temple architecture had its origins in a troglodyte culture.[1] This last error resulted in totally fallacious theories of the history of Egyptian civilization, according to which it spread down the Nile Valley from the sources of the river; whereas all the historical and monumental evidence, and the very nature of the subject, indicate that its diffusion took place in the opposite direction. Indian architecture, too, was alleged to derive from cave structures (an idea that sounds, if possible, even more unlikely); and the Mongol tent was named as the source of the curved roofs of the Chinese.

All these conjectures were based on a just assessment of the importance of the primal affinities between art forms; but those who framed them acted as if they were trying to trace the various languages of humanity back to the sounds made by small children, or the inarticulate voices of animal Nature, or the gibberish of savage tribes—which I believe has also been tried in the past.

Comparative philology has shown us that the source to which all or most Old World languages, living and dead, can be directly or indirectly traced is the richest in vocabulary, and the most flexible, of all languages. Linguistic impoverishment is not a product of the infancy of the human race but represents the decline, degeneracy, or violent mutilation of what were previously richer and more authentic linguistic organisms. In the linguistic forms used by certain peoples, we even find an artificial illusion of primitivism, promoted or at least fostered by social and political systems: as for example among the Chinese, who have no verbal inflections, and whose language consists of elements strung together without inflection or connection. And yet this simplicity has more to do with the infantilization imposed by priestcraft than with childlike spontaneity.

The same is true of the language of artistic forms. Often, if not always, when we seem to be hearing the prattle of infancy, this represents a decadent form of earlier and more highly evolved states. The same applies to the nature of social relations among those peoples in whom these supposedly primordial forms of art are observed. At all events, this is demonstrably true of the inhabitants of the Old World, or of such as have left traces of their existence behind them. The most primitive tribes known to us do not represent the primal state of humanity but rather a state of impoverishment and aridity. There is much in them to suggest a relapse into savagery, or rather a dissolution of the living organism of society into its constituent elements.

· · ·

If this be so, as all the evidence suggests it is, then it is vain to attempt to recapture society in its earliest formative processes on Old World soil, and impossible to trace architecture—which both expresses and houses the social organisms—back to its origins. Thus, for example, the seemingly primordial art of Egypt proves on close scrutiny to be secondary at best, and—in evolutionary terms—posterior to cultures that are thousands of years more recent in chronological terms and offer far more complex combinations. One case in point is the culture of Assyria, whose true nature and historical and cultural significance we have realized only as a result of recent discoveries.

It will be necessary to pursue this difficult theme in Part II of this book; here, however, two theses will be put forward in this connection, to be pursued in the text directly following.

1. The attentive observer who encounters the monumental remains of extinct social organisms will everywhere find certain basic forms or types of art. Clear and unclouded in some cases, these manifest themselves elsewhere in the indistinct form of a secondary or tertiary metamorphosis. But the types are always the same; it follows that they are older than all the social organisms whose monumental remains have been preserved, or of whose art we possess other evidence.

2. These types derive from the various technical arts, which—be they primitive or advanced—were conceived as the primordial protectors of the sacred hearth-flame (the earliest symbol of society, and of humanity in general). At a very early stage, these acquired a symbolic significance (both in a hieratic, rhetorical sense and in an aesthetic, formal sense), but were never entirely abandoned in their original technical and spatial function. In this respect, also, they operated as important agencies in the later transformations of architectural forms.

Without an appreciation of this early influence of the technical arts on the genesis of traditional forms and types in architecture, no proper understanding of architecture is possible. Etymological roots hold good and reemerge, in their basic form, in spite of all subsequent remodelings and extensions of the concepts with which they are associated; and it is impossible to find an entirely new word for a new concept without failing in the prime purpose of making oneself understood. In the same way, these earliest types and roots of artistic symbolism must not be discarded or ignored. The viewing public, and with it the majority of executant architects, follow tradition more or less unconsciously. But, just as today's artist with words [*Redekünstler*] derives profit from comparative philology and from the study of the primordial filiations of languages, so is there an equal profit in store for the architect who is familiar with the primordial meanings of the most ancient symbols of *his* language, and with the historical transformations that they and the art itself have undergone. The time, I believe, is not far distant when the study of linguistic forms and that of artistic forms will enjoy a reciprocal relationship that must inevitably lead to the most remarkable insights within both disciplines.

The structural and technical approach to the origins of basic architectural forms, as set out above and as argued below, has nothing in common with the crudely materialistic view that the essence of architecture is nothing but the elaboration of construction. The notion that architecture is a kind of illustrated and illuminated statics and mechanics, a mere proclamation of matter, was first developed in Roman times and was systematically pursued in the so-called Gothic style of architecture. It has, however, never been openly professed until recently. As will be shown in due course, it is sustained only by relegating to oblivion those ancient, traditional types that spring from the joint operation of the technical arts in a primitive architectural arrangement.

§2: Every Technical Product a Resultant of Function and Material

My self-imposed task has required me to divide the technical arts into categories and consider each of these in isolation, insofar as this is necessary to demonstrate the influence on the emergence of artistic symbols in general, and of architectural symbols in particular. It transpires that the fundamental laws of style in the technical arts are identical with those of architecture; that these principles appear here in their simplest and clearest form; and that it was here that those principles were first established.

In what follows, in accordance with the program of this essay, the various technical arts will be treated—in terms of their earliest connection with architecture, when they influenced the evolution of basic architectural forms—as evolving entities in their own right. Each will therefore be discussed in turn from the two following viewpoints:

1. The work as the resultant of the *material service* or *use* for which it is intended, whether this be real and literal, or implicit and symbolic.

2. The work as the resultant of the *material* used in its production, and of the *tools* and *procedures* employed therein.

By its very nature, the purpose for which any technical product is made remains the same for all time, insofar as it is founded on the general needs of humanity, and on universally and permanently valid natural laws that seek expression through form. However, the materials that are required to make the product, and more especially the ways of working those materials, are subject to radical change, both in the course of time and as a result of changes in local and other circumstances. It is therefore appropriate to link my more general remarks on form and aesthetics with those that concern material. However, it cannot be expected that this principle will be pursued with total consistency, since function commonly demands, a priori, the use of certain materials and techniques rather than others. General considerations of form and aesthetics therefore lead us directly into the realm of material.

A *band*, for instance, is defined by its purpose as a strip that encircles an object or extends along its length; its character becomes more sharply defined when the band is twisted, like a cord, or shows on its surface the pattern of an interlaced or woven material. This, however displays the binding material only in its abstract properties, as it were; the question of how different such a band would look if expressed in linen, wool, or silk, in wood, clay, stone, or metal is a separate one that concerns the *history of style*.

§3: *Four Categories of Raw Materials*

There are four main categories to which raw materials may be assigned in terms of the technical uses to which they are put. These are classified by their specific physical properties:

1. Flexible, tough, with high tensile strength and great *absolute* firmness.

2. Soft, readily formed (plastic), capable of hardening, lending itself to molding and shaping in many forms, and, once hardened, holding its form permanently.

3. Rod-shaped, elastic, and of predominantly *relative* firmness—i.e., resistant to forces exerted at right angles to its length.

4. Firm, *densely aggregated,* resistant to crushing and buckling, and thus of considerable *reactive* firmness and thus well suited to being worked by the removal of parts of the mass in any chosen form, and to being combined in regular pieces into stable systems, in which reactive firmness is the principle of the construction.

In accordance with these four categories, four principal classes of artistic operation serve, with varying degrees of labor and technical ingenuity, to adapt the raw material to appropriate ends.

These classes are as follows:

1. Textile art
2. Ceramic art
3. Tectonics (carpentry, framed structure)
4. Stereotomy (masonry, etc.)

To this classification must be added the rider—a highly necessary one, as will be seen—that each division must be interpreted with the greatest possible latitude. There are, in consequence, many reciprocal relationships between them, which it will be our business to trace. Each of the four technical classes has its own specific realm within the domain of forms in general, and the production of such forms is, as it were, the natural and basic preoccupation of that technique. Furthermore, for every technique there is a specific "primary" material that offers the most convenient route to the forms that belong to its original field of operation. In the course of time, it has become possible to create these forms from other materials, and to use these materials for forms derived from other departments of art. Stylistically, such work belongs to two different technical realms: one for its form and the other for its material.

Taken in its widest sense, ceramics is not restricted to earthen vessels: it embraces the whole study of vessels of all kinds, including related ware in glass, stone, and metal. Some articles made of wood, such as barrels and wooden pails, also belong here in stylistic terms. Even textile works such as baskets are stylistically related to ceramics in this respect.

On the other hand, certain objects that belong to the ceramic arts in material terms—in that they are formed from a soft material which is subsequently hardened and made permanent—can be assigned to the ceramic arts only in the second degree, because in formal terms they belong elsewhere. These include bricks, roof tiles, terra-cotta, and the glazed tiles that are used to line walls and pave floors; likewise the tesserae of glass and colored clay that are used for inlays, and other ceramic products. In stylistic terms, these articles belong more properly either to stereotomy or to textile art, since the result is either an inlay, and thus related to masonry, or a covering for walls and the like.

Textile art is thus not limited to woven fabrics, as will be evident from what follows.

Tectonics too has a wide scope. Besides timber roof frames and their supports, this category also includes a considerable proportion of our domestic furnishings. In some respects it also embraces one aspect of masonry and one variety of metal construction.

Stereotomy extends beyond the art of the mason and the excavator: the mosaicist and the carver in wood, ivory, or metal are also stereotomists. Even the jeweler's trade derives some of its stylistic laws from this technique.

Highly significant in this respect is the existence of overlaps and transitional areas between the four classes of art handicraft. Thus, textile art unites with ceramics in the tiling of walls and floors, and with tectonics in wainscoting. Other and stylistically even more important associations between tectonics and the cladding or siding principle of textiles will emerge in what follows. (*Tubular constructions* and *grilles:* in the former, textile material associates with tectonic form; whereas in the latter—grilles—tectonic material associates with textile form.)

Other examples of a mixed style are goldsmith's work and—besides many other instances to be cited in what follows—those stone constructions, inspired by antiquity, in which stereotomy makes its appearance in conjunction with tectonics and the textile cladding principle.

Of all the materials that are used to serve human ends, it is metal that unites all the properties listed above. It can be made plastic and then hardened; it is flexible and tough, with a high tensile strength. It is extremely elastic and of considerable relative firmness (although elasticity and flexibility are its weakest point), and therefore highly useful for frame structures. Finally, it is firm, homogeneous, dense, and immensely resistant to pressure, all of which properties make it better suited than other materials to be reduced to a preordained shape and assembled into stable systems.

As a result of this versatility, metalwork combines all four technical classes within itself. Metal gives rise to a greater number of borderline or transitional techniques than any other material. Thus, for example, the malleability of metals leads to the important technique of *repoussé*.[2] This is distinct from forging, a technique that marks the transition between treating the metal as a tough, flexible mass and dealing with it stereotomically as a dense solid. Other techniques, each with its own stylistic peculiarities, are stamping and minting, soldering, welding, and riveting. There are also composite techniques such as enamel, niello, gilding, and many others, all of which require separate consideration. These are of the greatest significance by virtue of their influence on the fine arts, and on that of architecture in particular.

Because of the great artistic importance of metal working, and the difficulties that might arise in assigning the techniques just named, and others, to any of the four general classes established above, it will be necessary to devote a separate section to this topic.

NOTES

1. Vitruvius, *The Ten Books of Architecture*, Book 4, chap. 2, pp. 107–09; Krubsacius's text provides a good example of just such an interpretation in Part III of this anthology. The architectural historian is probably Charles Francois Gau (1790–1854).

2. "Repoussé" work is relief decoration on metal, produced by hammering from the underside so that the decoration projects; for Semper this technique is closer to sculpture and modeling than to forging.

ALOIS RIEGL

Introduction to *Problems of Style*

The subtitle of this book announces its theme: "Foundations for a History of Ornament." How many of you are now shrugging your shoulders in disbelief merely in response to the title? What, you ask, does ornament also have a history? Even in an era such as ours, marked by a passion for historical research, this question still awaits a positive, unqualified answer. Nor is this purely the reaction of radicals who consider all decoration original and the direct result of the specific material and purpose involved. Alongside these radical extremists, there are also those of a more moderate bent, who would accord to the decorative arts some degree of historical development from teacher to pupil, from generation to generation, and from culture to culture, at least insofar as they have to do with so-called high art, devoted to the representation of man, his achievements, and struggles.

Certainly, from the very inception of art historical research, there have always been some scholars in the field who also conceived of pure decoration in terms of a progressive development, i.e., according to the principles of historical methodology. But these were, of course, mainly learned academicians who adapted the rigorous training in philology and history acquired at gymnasia and universities to the study of ornamental phenomena as well. However, the drastic impact of this more extremist position upon the general attitude toward the decorative arts is revealed by the way in which historical methodology has been applied to the study of ornament up to now. For example, scholars have been extremely reticent to propose any sort of historical interrelationships, and even then, only in the case of limited time periods and closely neighboring regions. Their courage seems to fail them completely the moment an ornament ceases to have any direct relationship with objective realities—to organic, living creatures or to works fashioned by the human hand. As soon as they deal with the so-called Geometric Style, which is characterized by the mathematical expression of symmetry and rhythm in abstract lines, all consideration of artistic, mimetic impulses or of variation in the creative abilities of various cultures immediately ceases. The degree to which the terrorism of extremists has successfully intimidated even the "historians" involved in the study of ornament emerges clearly in the haste of scholars to assure us that they would never be so foolish and naive as to believe, for example, that one culture could have ever copied a "simple" meander band from another, or by their repeated apologies whenever they do venture to assert even a loose connection between, shall we say, the stylized two-dimensional vegetal motifs current in two geographic areas.

What led to this situation, which has had such a decisive and, in many respects, paralyzing effect upon all art historical research in the last twenty-five years? The blame can be placed squarely on the materialist interpretation of the origin of art that developed in the 1860s, and which succeeded in winning over, virtually overnight, everyone concerned with art, including artists, art lovers, and scholars. The theory of the technical, materialist origin of the earliest ornaments and art forms is usually attributed to Gottfried Semper. This association is, however, no more justified than the one made between contemporary Darwinism and Darwin. I find the analogy between Darwinism and artistic materialism especially appropriate, since there is unquestionably a close and causal relationship between the two: the materialist interpretation of the origin of art is nothing other than Darwinism imposed upon an intellectual discipline. However, one must distinguish just as much and just as sharply between Semper and his followers as between Darwin and his adherents. Whereas Semper did suggest that material and technique play a role in the genesis of art forms, the Semperians jumped to the conclusion that all art forms were always the direct product of materials and techniques. "Technique" quickly emerged as a popular buzzword; in common usage, it soon became interchangeable with "art" itself and eventually began to replace it. Only the naive talked about "art"; experts spoke in terms of "technique."

It may seem paradoxical that so many practicing artists also joined the extreme faction of art materialism. They were, of course, not acting in the spirit of Gottfried Semper, who would never have agreed to exchanging free and creative artistic impulse [Kunstwollen] for an essentially mechanical and materialist drive to imitate. Nevertheless, their misinterpretation was taken to reflect the genuine thinking of the great artist and scholar. Furthermore, the natural authority that practicing artists exert in matters of technique resulted in an environment where scholars, archaeologists, and art historians swallowed their pride and beat a hasty retreat whenever the question of technique arose. For they—mere scholars that they were—could have little or no competence in this regard. Only recently have scholars become bolder. The word "technique" proved to be extremely flexible: first came the discovery that most ornamental motifs could be (and had actually been) rendered in a variety of techniques; then came the pleasant realization that techniques were an excellent source of controversy. In time, archaeological publications, as well as journals devoted to arts and crafts, joined in the wild chase for techniques, a pastime that will probably continue until all the technical possibilities for each and every humble motif have been exhausted, only to return—one may be sure—precisely to the point where it all began.

In the midst of such a spirited intellectual atmosphere, this book ventures to come forward with foundations for a history of ornament. The wisdom of beginning with foundations that pretend to be nothing more than that is obvious. In a situation where not only the field of action is hotly contested at every step along the way but even the groundwork itself is constantly in dispute, our first concern is to secure a few positions, a connected series of strongholds from which a comprehensive, systematic, and complete offensive can later be launched. The nature of the situation militates further that "negative arguments" take up a far greater portion of this book than is customary in a positive, pragmatic description of history. Here our most immediate and urgent objective is to address the most fundamental and harmful of the misconceptions and preconceptions that still hinder research today. This is another reason why, for the present, the concepts of this study are presented in the form of "foundations."

Having said this, I still feel compelled to justify the existence of this book. However, anything one might say in this regard will sound unconvincing as long as the technical-materialist theory of the origin of the earliest primeval art forms and ornamental motifs remains unchallenged, even though it has failed to define the precise moment when the spontaneous generation of art ends, and the historical development effected by laws of transmission and acquisition begins. The first chapter, therefore, is devoted to challenging the validity of the technical-materialist theory of the origin of art. As its title indicates, it deals with the nature and origin of the Geometric Style. Here, I hope to demonstrate that not only is there no cogent reason for assuming a priori that the oldest geometric decorations were executed in any particular technique, least of all weaving, but that the earliest, genuinely historical artistic monuments we possess in fact contradict this assumption. Similar conclusions will also emerge from deliberations of a more general nature. It will become evident, namely, that the human desire to adorn the body is far more elementary than the desire to cover it with woven garments, and that the decorative motifs that satisfy the simple desire for adornment, such as linear, geometric configurations, surely existed long before textiles were used for physical protection. As a result, this eliminates one principle that has ruled the entire field of art theory for the past quarter century: the absolute equation of textile patterns with surface decoration or ornament. The moment it becomes untenable to assume that the earliest surface decoration first appeared in textile material and technique, then the two can no longer be considered identical. Surface decoration becomes the larger unit within which woven ornament is but a subset, equivalent to any other category of surface decoration.

In general then, one of the main objectives of this book is to reduce the importance of textile decoration to the level it deserves. At the same time, I must admit that this medium has been the point of departure for all the research that I have gathered from eight years of service in the textile collection of the k. k. Österreichisches Museum für Art und Industrie [Österreichisches Museum für Angewandte Kunst]. At the risk of ridiculous sentimentality, I cannot help feeling some regret at robbing textile art of its nimbus, in view of the personal relationship which I acquired with textiles in the course of curating the museum's collection for so many years.

Once the momentous proposition about the original identity of surface decoration and textile ornament had become accepted, there were almost no limits placed on its application. Beginning with rectilinear geometric shapes, it quickly expanded to include artistic representations of even the most complex natural forms, namely, human beings and animals. For example, the origin of motifs consisting of two figures symmetrically arranged to either side of a central axis was attributed to tapestry weaving. The Heraldic Style, as this type of decorative arrangement has come to be known, is so common that it warrants its own separate discussion. In the second chapter, therefore, I explain why there is neither proof nor even a possibility that heraldic motifs resulted from tapestry weaving, since the advanced technical knowledge necessary to produce such complicated forms simply did not exist during the period when the earliest heraldic motifs originated. And, at any rate, we shall see that there are other, albeit less tangibly materialist explanations for the Heraldic Style.

As a result, the basic tone of the first two chapters is somewhat negative, even though I have made every effort to replace the things that were discredited with something new and positive. In the case of the Geometric Style, it is especially necessary to dispel once and for all the misconceptions surrounding its purely technical, material origin and the allegedly ahistorical nature of its development. Yet one fact enormously complicates any historical approach to the Geometric Style: whereas organic nature and the handicrafts inspired by it allow the artist manifold alternatives, the mathematical laws of symmetry and rhythm that govern the simple motifs of the Geometric Style are more or less the same the world over. Spontaneous generation of the same geometric decorative motifs in different parts of the world is, therefore, not out of the question; but even so, one can take specific historical factors into account with complete objectivity. Certainly, some cultures were always leading the way for others, just as more talented individuals have always distinguished themselves from their peers. And surely it was just as true in the remote past as it is today that the vast majority of people find it easier to imitate than to invent.

Once plants are used as decorative motifs, the study of ornament finds itself on more solid ground. There are infinitely more species of plants that can be used as the basis for patterns than there are abstract, symmetrical shapes, limited as these are to the triangle, the rectangle, the rhombus, and only a few others. This is the point where classical archaeology begins to take an interest in vegetal ornament; in particular, the connection between Greek plant motifs and their ancient Near Eastern prototypes, which mark the beginning of art history proper, has already provided the subject of intense study and extensive debate. Nevertheless, German archaeology has not yet attempted a systematic description of the history of the vegetal ornament that was so crucial to antique art from ancient Egyptian to Roman times; this is a consequence of the enormous resistance to making "mere ornament" the basic theme of a more ambitious historical study. However, an American, has recently taken the step that German-trained scholars timidly avoided. W. G. Goodyear, in his book, *The Grammar of the Lotus*, was the first to argue that all antique vegetal ornament, and a good deal more, was a continuation of ancient Egyptian lotus ornament. The driving force behind the ubiquitous diffusion of this ornament was, in his opinion, the sun cult. This American scholar is apparently no more concerned with the technical-materialist theory of the origin of art than he is with Europe's crumbling castles and basalt deposits—unless I am mistaken, Gottfried Semper's name is not mentioned once in the entire book.

Strictly speaking, Goodyear's main thesis is not completely new; what is indisputably unique, however, is his radical determination to accord his ideas a universal significance, as well as the motivation that he cites for the entire development.

As far as the latter is concerned, however, the idea that the sun cult had such an overwhelming influence on decoration is surely erroneous. It is not even certain whether sun-cult symbolism played such a preponderant role in ancient Egyptian ornament, much less outside of Egypt, where there is absolutely no proof and, moreover, no likelihood that it did. Symbolism was unquestionably one of the factors that contributed to the gradual creation of a wealth of traditional ornament. However, by proclaiming symbolism the sole and decisive factor, Goodyear makes the same mistake as the materialists who single out technique in this way. Moreover, both interpretations share an obvious desire to avoid at all costs the purely psychological, artistic motivation behind decoration. In cases where the artist is obviously responding to an immanent, artistic, creative drive, Goodyear sees symbolism at work, just as the artistic-materialists in the same instance utilize technique as their incidental, lifeless objective.

Moreover, Goodyear places almost no limitations on the influence that the lotus motif exerted as a model for all sorts of ancient ornament, including even the prehistoric zigzag, and this amounts to the same kind of overstatement indulged in by artistic-materialists and Darwinists. As a result, Goodyear often makes historical connections that a more dispassionate observer would flatly reject. Since he seizes only upon those things which serve his purpose, he has become willfully blind to finer distinctions. Therefore, it is not surprising that he overlooked, among other things, the genuinely Greek core of Mycenaean ornament, thereby missing what may well have been the most important point of the entire development of classical ornament.

As many a scholar before him, Goodyear clearly recognized the vital importance of vegetal decoration in ancient ornament, not only for its own sake but also for the proper assessment and appreciation of ancient ornament within the overall history of the decorative arts. My lectures on the history of ornament, delivered during the winter term of 1890–91 at the University of Vienna, gave special emphasis to the development of the vegetal ornament that began in the earliest period of antiquity. A part of the content of these lectures appears in the third chapter along with a few minor additions; it consists mainly of responses to Goodyear's work, which had since appeared. I would agree with him that the Greeks borrowed motifs extensively from the ancient Near East; moreover, the way that they infused such forms with formal beauty has long been acknowledged as a Greek accomplishment. However, Goodyear, along with other scholars interested in determining the essentially Western elements and impulses in early Greek art, ignored the Greeks' most characteristic, autonomous, and influential invention, namely the tendril. One seeks in vain for dynamic, rhythmic vegetal tendrils among the various ancient Near Eastern styles, though they already appear fully developed in Mycenaean art on what would later become Greek soil. While Greek blossom motifs have a Near Eastern origin, the lovely undulating lines connecting them are specifically Greek. From this point on, the development of the tendril is a major aspect of the subsequent history of ornament. The tendril begins as an undulating band emitting spirals within a narrow border; by the late Hellenistic period, it has turned into an elaborately branching, leafy vine capable of spreading out over large areas. In this form it continues in Roman art and beyond to the Middle Ages, in the West as well as in the East, in Islamic no less than in Renaissance art. The curling foliage of the Little Masters of the sixteenth century is as much a direct descendant of antique classical tendril ornament as late Gothic crocket-work. By tracing vegetal decoration throughout the centuries from its first appearance up to the present day, it becomes evident that ornament experiences the same continuous, coherent development that prevails in the art of all periods, as in the historical relationship between antique mythological imagery and Christian iconographic types. But this is too vast a theme to take up in depth within the framework of this book. Therefore, I will concentrate solely on describing in detail the development of tendril ornament from its origins down through the Hellenistic and Roman periods. Chapter 3, because it deals with a topic of such obvious importance, represents a truly significant "foundation" for the history of ornament.

It is very easy to trace the historical development of traditional stylized vegetal motifs. The same is not true, however, the moment that man attempts to produce ornament related to the natural appearance of an actual vegetal prototype. For example, the projection of the palmette found in Egypt and Greece cannot have been invented independently in both places, since the motif bears no resemblance to the actual plant. One can only conclude, therefore, that it originated in one place and was subsequently transmitted to the other. It is quite another matter, however, in the case of two ornamental works of differing origin that depict a rose, for instance, as it appears in nature; since the natural appearance of the rose is generally the same even in the most diverse countries, it is conceivable that similar depictions could arise independently. It becomes readily apparent from the study of vegetal ornament as a whole, however, that realistic renderings of flowers for decorative purposes, as is nowadays the vogue, is a recent phenomenon. The naive approach to art characteristic of earlier cultures insisted adamantly on symmetry, even in the case of reproductions of nature. Representations of humans and animals soon departed from symmetry by way of the Heraldic Style and other similar arrangements. Yet plants—subordinate and seemingly lifeless as they are—remained symmetrical and stylized throughout the centuries even in the most sophisticated styles, particularly as long as they functioned as pure decoration and had no representational value. The transition from ancient stylization to modern realism, of course, did not come about in a day. Naturalism, the tendency to make ornamental forms resemble actual plants seen in perspective, crops up repeatedly in the history of vegetal ornament. Indeed, there was even a period in antiquity when naturalism was quite advanced; however, it represents only a brief interlude in the otherwise constant use of traditional, stylized forms. Generally speaking, the naturalistic vegetal motifs of antiquity and of almost the entire medieval period were never copied directly from nature.

The acanthus motif provides us with the best, and probably most crucial, insight into how naturalized vegetal motifs were understood and executed in antiquity. Nevertheless, Vitruvius's story that decorative acanthus motifs were originally based directly upon the actual plant is still accepted without question today.[1] No one seems disturbed by the improbable suggestion that a common ordinary weed could suddenly and miraculously be transformed into an artistic motif. Seen within the context of the history of ornament as a whole, the situation is unprecedented, without parallel, and downright absurd. Furthermore, it is the earliest acanthus motifs that least resemble the actual plant. Only in the course of time did the stylized motifs begin to acquire the characteristics of the acanthus plant itself; obviously, no one referred to them as acanthus motifs until much later in their development, when they actually began to resemble the plant. Chapter 3 will prove that the earliest acanthus ornaments are nothing more than palmettes that were either executed in sculpture or else conceived sculpturally. As a result, the acanthus motif, by far the most important vegetal ornament of all time, makes its debut in art history not as a *deus ex machina* but with a role that is fully integrated into the coherent course of development of antique ornament.

From the time it first fell under the influence of the more refined culture and art of Greece, the Orient resisted the naturalizing tendencies of Western art epitomized in the development of acanthus motifs and the like. Nevertheless, it fully accepted Hellenistic forms; surely no one doubts this anymore except those stubbornly committed to upholding a cherished theory. That there should be any question at all today in this regard, in view of the convincing evidence offered by the monuments themselves, is due primarily to the deeply-rooted antihistorical attitudes in evaluating decorative forms. In actual fact, however, the stylized blossom forms of Late Hellenistic and Alexandrian art occur frequently on Oriental works from the Roman Imperial period side by side with the naturalistic forms of the Roman West. Byzantine decoration is in part directly related to the Hellenistic forms that were clearly still in use in Greece and Asia Minor even during the Roman Empire. The same is true of Islamic art, though less obviously, since there were so many intervening stages.

A strong Byzantine element has long been recognized as a factor in the origin of Islamic ornament, in fact, even more so in the 1840s and 50s than today, a circumstance once again attributable to the ill-advised technical-materialist theory that doggedly insists upon the spontaneous, autochthonous origin of the art of different cultures. In contrast, the Arabesque remains uncontested as a special creation of the Orient, and particularly of the Arabs. And yet the history of antique ornament demonstrates clearly that the tendrils basic to Arabesque decoration were unknown in the ancient Near East and therefore could only have been adopted from the Hellenistic West. In addition, a closer look at the dense entanglements of Arabesque decoration discloses a number of more conspicuous motifs whose volute-shaped calyces and leaf-fans clearly betray their connection to ancient palmette ornament. What does appear as an entirely new feature of the Arabesque, and completely unattested in the decorative approach to plants in classical antiquity, however, is the peculiar placement of Islamic blossoms. These occur not only at the ends of tendrils, as they are in nature and in Western decoration in general, but they often appear integrated within the tendril. This arrangement suppresses the character of the blossom and obscures the concept of the tendril as a stem, so much that it is sometimes difficult to recognize the Arabesque as a form of vegetal tendril ornament at all.

However, even these fundamental and characteristic idiosyncracies of the Arabesque, in which the antinaturalistic and abstract quality of all early Islamic art emerges so perfectly, have their antecedents in ancient tendril ornament, as the conclusion of the third and the fourth chapters will demonstrate. Here I am able to address a number of additional issues that could not be accommodated in my *Altorientalische Teppiche*, mostly because of the limitations on space. I am happy for the opportunity to expand upon the subject since I realize that many are still unconvinced that antique art was also the evident point of departure for the early medieval art of the Near East. This shows how profoundly modern thinking has been biased by the ahistorical attitude that maintains that art must have originated here and there spontaneously and autochthonously, yet even so the Occident must be a passive recipient, with the Orient always on the giving end. The Orient, of course, represents a land of fable and enchantment, not only for poets but also for art historians, who blithely attribute to it the invention of every imaginable "technique," particularly those that have anything to do with surface decoration. And once a particular "technique" is declared indigenous to the East, one can be certain, according to this viewpoint, that its corresponding artistic progeny is following close behind it.

Conditions are more favorable for an historical approach to vegetal tendril ornament in Western medieval art. This is not to say that the effects of artistic materialism have not taken their toll; on the contrary, they are apparent everywhere. Their pernicious influence is undoubtedly responsible for our vague, contradictory, and fragmented understanding of what transpired during the early stages of medieval art, the so-called Migration Period, and even later in the Carolingian and Ottonian periods, despite the relatively abundant material that has survived. Nevertheless, I am convinced that there are still fewer deep-seated preconceptions and less blind resistance to impede an attempt at treating the historical development of Western medieval vegetal decoration from the twilight of classical antiquity up through the beginning of the Renaissance. Since the present context does not permit me to touch upon everything related to the historical development of vegetal tendril ornament, I have concentrated on the aspects that seemed to require clarification most urgently, and that could, once clarified, provide a firm foundation upon which a history of ornament could continue to build. This involves, as stated above, antique tendril ornament, along with its most faithful follower in the conservative Orient, the Arabesque. Even in the scholarly literature dealing with the history of medieval art, one often encounters certain decorative motifs referred to vaguely as an "ornament," which then have to be described at greater length. This procedure would be totally superfluous if the motif involved had already been assigned its proper place within the overall historical development. Since the creation of this historical order is not without its difficulties, at least in the case of antique and Islamic tendril ornament, the main purpose of the third and fourth chapters will be to establish the historical foundations that will make this possible.

Even though the principle task of historical and art historical research is usually to make critical distinctions, this book tends decidedly in the opposite direction. Things once considered to have nothing in common will be connected and related from a unified perspective. In fact, the most pressing problem that confronts historians of the decorative arts today is to reintegrate the historical thread that has been severed into a thousand pieces.

Since this book threatens to undermine so many deeply-ingrained and fondly-cherished opinions, it is bound to create a storm of protest. I am acutely aware of this. However, I also know that there are many who already share my views, and still others who may be in tacit agreement but who are not yet ready to speak out. And as for those who remain unpersuaded by my arguments, I shall have accomplished something even if I succeed only in compelling them to realize that they must go back and reexamine their premises and seek better and stronger evidence to support their cherished theories. For even limited success is worth the effort, if it sheds some light on the fundamental issues that concern us in this book. Only through trial and error can one approach the truth.

NOTE

1. Vitruvius, *Ten Books of Architecture*, Book 4, chap. 1, p. 104.

R. G. COLLINGWOOD

II. *Art and Craft*

§1. THE MEANING OF CRAFT

The first sense of the word 'art' to be distinguished from art proper is the obsolete sense in which it means what in this book I shall call craft. This is what *ars* means in ancient Latin, and what τέχνη means in Greek: the power to produce a preconceived result by means of consciously controlled and directed action. In order to take the first step towards a sound aesthetic, it is necessary to disentangle the notion of craft from that of art proper. In order to do this, again, we must first enumerate the chief characteristics of craft.

(1) Craft always involves a distinction between means and end, each clearly conceived as something distinct from the other but related to it. The term 'means' is loosely applied to things that are used in order to reach the end, such as tools, machines, or fuel. Strictly, it applies not to the things but to the actions concerned with them: manipulating the tools, tending the machines, or burning the fuel. These actions (as implied by the literal sense of the word means) are passed through or traversed in order to reach the end, and are left behind when the end is reached. This may serve to distinguish the idea of means from two other ideas with which it is sometimes confused: that of part, and that of material. The relation of part to whole is like that of means to end, in that the part is indispensable to the whole, is what it is because of its relation to the whole, and may exist by itself before the whole comes into existence; but when the whole exists the part exists too, whereas, when the end exists, the means have ceased to exist. As for the idea of material, we shall return to that in (4) below.

(2) It involves a distinction between planning and execution. The result to be obtained is preconceived or thought out before being arrived at. The craftsman knows what he wants to make before he makes it. This foreknowledge is absolutely indispensable to craft: if something, for example stainless steel, is made without such foreknowledge, the making of it is not a case of craft but an accident. Moreover, this foreknowledge is not vague but precise. If a person sets out to make a table, but conceives the table only vaguely, as somewhere between two by four feet and three by six, and between two and three feet high, and so forth, he is no craftsman.

(3) Means and end are related in one way in the process of planning; in the opposite way in the process of execution. In planning the end is prior to the means. The end is thought out first, and afterwards the means are thought out. In execution the means come first, and the end is reached through them.

(4) There is a distinction between raw material and finished product or artifact. A craft is always exercised upon something, and aims at the transformation of this into something different. That upon which it works begins as raw material and ends as finished product. The raw material is found ready made before the special work of the craft begins.

(5) There is a distinction between form and matter. The matter is what is identical in the raw material and the finished product; the form is what is different, what the exercise of the craft changes. To describe the raw material as raw is not to imply that it is formless, but only that it has not yet the form which it is to acquire through 'transformation' into finished product.

(6) There is a hierarchical relation between various crafts, one supplying what another needs, one using what another provides. There are three kinds of hierarchy: of materials, of means, and of parts. (*a*) The raw material of one craft is the finished product of another. Thus the silviculturist propagates trees and looks after them as they grow, in order to provide raw material for the felling-men who transform them into logs; these are raw material for the sawmill which transforms them into planks; and these, after a further process of selection and seasoning, become raw material for a joiner. (*b*) In the hierarchy of means, one craft supplies another with tools. Thus the timber-merchant supplies pit-props to the miner; the miner supplies coal to the blacksmith; the blacksmith supplies horseshoes to the farmer; and so on. (*c*) In the hierarchy of parts, a complex operation like the manufacture of a motor-car is parcelled out among a number of trades: one firm makes the engine, another the gears, another the chassis, another the tyres, another the electrical equipment, and so on; the final assembling is not strictly the manufacture of the car but only the bringing together of these parts. In one or more of these ways every craft has a hierarchical character; either as hierarchically related to other crafts, or as itself consisting of various heterogeneous operations hierarchically related among themselves.

Without claiming that these features together exhaust the notion of craft, or that each of them separately is peculiar to it, we may claim with tolerable confidence that where most of them are absent from a certain activity that activity is not a craft, and, if it is called by that name, is so called either by mistake or in a vague and inaccurate way.

· · ·

(1) The first characteristic of craft is the distinction between means and end. Is this present in works of art? According to the technical theory, yes. A poem is means to the production of a certain state of mind in the audience, as a horse-shoe is means to the production of a certain state of mind in the man whose horse is shod. And the poem in its turn will be an end to which other things are means. In the case of the horseshoe, this stage of the analysis is easy: we can enumerate lighting the forge, cutting a piece of iron off a bar, heating it, and so on. What is there analogous to these processes in the case of a poem? The poet may get paper and pen, fill the pen, sit down and square his elbows; but these actions are preparatory not to composition (which may go on in the poet's head) but to writing. Suppose the poem is a short one, and composed without the use of any writing materials; what are the means by which the poet composes it? I can think of no answer, unless comic answers are wanted, such as "using a rhyming dictionary," "pounding his foot on the floor or wagging his head or hand to mark the metre," or "getting drunk." If one looks at the matter seriously, one sees that the only factors in the situation are the poet, the poetic labour of his mind, and the poem. And if any supporter of the technical theory says "Right: then the poetic labour is the means, the poem the end," we shall ask him to find a blacksmith who can make a horseshoe by sheer labour, without forge, anvil, hammer, or tongs. It is because nothing corresponding to these exists in the case of the poem that the poem is not an end to which there are means.

Conversely, is a poem means to the production of a certain state of mind in an audience? Suppose a poet had read his verses to an audience, hoping that they would produce a certain result; and suppose the result were different; would that in itself prove the poem a bad one? It is a difficult question; some would say yes, others no. But if poetry were obviously a craft, the answer would be a prompt and unhesitating yes. The advocate of the technical theory must do a good deal of toe-chopping before he can get his facts to fit his theory at this point.

So far, the prospects of the technical theory are not too bright. Let us proceed.

(2) The distinction between planning and executing certainly exists in some works of art, namely those which are also works of craft or artifacts; for there is, of course, an overlap between these two things, as may be seen by the example of a building or a jar, which is made to order for the satisfaction of a specific demand, to serve a useful purpose, but may none the less be a work of art. But suppose a poet were making up verses as he walked; suddenly finding

a line in his head, and then another, and then dissatisfied with them and altering them until he had got them to his liking: what is the plan which he is executing? He may have had a vague idea that if he went for a walk he would be able to compose poetry; but what were, so to speak, the measurements and specifications of the poem he planned to compose? He may, no doubt, have been hoping to compose a sonnet on a particular subject specified by the editor of a review; but the point is that he may not, and that he is none the less a poet for composing without having any definite plan in his head. Or suppose a sculptor were not making a Madonna and child, three feet high, in Hoptonwood stone, guaranteed to placate the chancellor of the diocese and obtain a faculty for placing it in the vacant niche over a certain church door; but were simply playing about with clay, and found the clay under his fingers turning into a little dancing man: is this not a work of art because it was done without being planned in advance?

All this is very familiar. There would be no need to insist upon it, but that the technical theory of art relies on our forgetting it. While we are thinking of it, let us note the importance of not over-emphasizing it. Art as such does not imply the distinction between planning and execution. But (*a*) this is a merely negative characteristic, not a positive one. We must not erect the absence of plan into a positive force and call it inspiration, or the unconscious, or the like. (*b*) It is a permissible characteristic of art, not a compulsory one. If unplanned works of art are possible, it does not follow that no planned work is a work of art. That is the logical fallacy* that underlies one, or some, of the various things called romanticism. It may very well be true that the only works of art which can be made altogether without a plan are trifling ones, and that the greatest and most serious ones always contain an element of planning and therefore an element of craft. But that would not justify the technical theory of art.

(3) If neither means and end nor planning and execution can be distinguished in art proper, there obviously can be no reversal of order as between means and end, in planning and execution respectively.

(4) We next come to the distinction between raw material and finished product. Does this exist in art proper? If so, a poem is made out of certain raw

---

*It is an example of what I have elsewhere called the fallacy of precarious margins. Because art and craft overlap, the essence of art is sought not in the positive characteristics of all art, but in the characteristics of those works of art which are not works of craft. Thus the only things which are allowed to be works of art are those marginal examples which lie outside the overlap of art and craft. This is a precarious margin because further study may at any moment reveal the characteristics of craft in some of these examples. See R. G. Collingwood, *Essay on Philosophical Method* (Oxford, 1933).

material. What is the raw material out of which Ben Jonson made *Queene and Huntresse, chaste, and faire?*[1] Words, perhaps. Well, what words? A smith makes a horseshoe not out of all the iron there is, but out of a certain piece of iron, cut off a certain bar that he keeps in the corner of the smithy. If Ben Jonson did anything at all like that, he said: "I want to make a nice little hymn to open Act v, Scene vi of *Cynthia's Revels.* Here is the English language, or as much of it as I know; I will use *thy* five times, *to* four times, *and, bright, excellently,* and *goddesse* three times each, and so on." He did nothing like this. The words which occur in the poem were never before his mind as a whole in an order different from that of the poem, out of which he shuffled them till the poem, as we have it, appeared. I do not deny that by sorting out the words, or the vowel sounds, or the consonant sounds, in a poem like this, we can make interesting and (I believe) important discoveries about the way in which Ben Jonson's mind worked when he made the poem; and I am willing to allow that the technical theory of art is doing good service if it leads people to explore these matters; but if it can only express what it is trying to do by calling these words or sounds the materials out of which the poem is made, it is talking nonsense.

But perhaps there is a raw material of another kind: a feeling or emotion, for example, which is present to the poet's mind at the commencement of his labour, and which that labour converts into the poem. "Aus meinem grossen Schmerzen mach' ich die kleinen Lieder," said Heine;[2] and he was doubtless right; the poet's labour can be justly described as converting emotions into poems. But this conversion is a very different kind of thing from the conversion of iron into horseshoes. If the two kinds of conversion were the same, a blacksmith could make horseshoes out of his desire to pay the rent. The something more, over and above that desire, which he must have in order to make horseshoes out of it, is the iron which is their raw material. In the poet's case that something more does not exist.

(5) In every work of art there is something which, in some sense of the word, may be called form. There is, to be rather more precise, something in the nature of rhythm, pattern, organization, design, or structure. But it does not follow that there is a distinction between form and matter. Where that distinction does exist, namely, in artifacts, the matter was there in the shape of raw material before the form was imposed upon it, and the form was there in the shape of a preconceived plan before being imposed upon the matter; and as the two coexist in the finished product we can see how the matter might have accepted a different form, or the form have been imposed upon a different matter. None of these statements applies to a work of art. Something was no doubt there before a poem came into being; there was, for example, a confused excitement in

the poet's mind; but, as we have seen, this was not the raw material of the poem. There was also, no doubt, the impulse to write; but this impulse was not the form of the unwritten poem. And when the poem is written, there is nothing in it of which we can say, "this is a matter which might have taken on a different form," or "this is a form which might have been realized in a different matter."

When people have spoken of matter and form in connexion with art, or of that strange hybrid distinction, form and content, they have in fact been doing one of two things, or both confusedly at once. Either they have been assimilating a work of art to an artifact, and the artist's work to the craftsman's; or else they have been using these terms in a vaguely metaphorical way as means of referring to distinctions which really do exist in art, but are of a different kind. There is always in art a distinction between what is expressed and that which expresses it; there is a distinction between the initial impulse to write or paint or compose and the finished poem or picture or music; there is a distinction between an emotional element in the artist's experience and what may be called an intellectual element. All these deserve investigation; but none of them is a case of the distinction between form and matter.

(6) Finally, there is in art nothing which resembles the hierarchy of crafts, each dictating ends to the one below it, and providing either means or raw materials or parts to the one above. When a poet writes verses for a musician to set, these verses are not means to the musician's end, for they are incorporated in the song which is the musician's finished product, and it is characteristic of means, as we saw, to be left behind. But neither are they raw materials. The musician does not transform them into music; he sets them to music; and if the music which he writes for them had a raw material (which it has not), that raw material could not consist of verses. What happens is rather that the poet and musician collaborate to produce a work of art which owes something to each of them; and this is true even if in the poet's case there was no intention of collaborating.

Aristotle extracted from the notion of a hierarchy of crafts the notion of a supreme craft, upon which all hierarchical series converged, so that the various "goods" which all crafts produce played their part, in one way or another, in preparing for the work of this supreme craft, whose product could, therefore, be called the "supreme good."* At first sight, one might fancy an echo of this in Wagner's theory of opera as the supreme art, supreme because it combines the beauties of music and poetry and drama, the arts of time and the arts of space, into a single whole. But, quite apart from the question whether Wagner's opin-

*Nicomachean Ethics, beginning: 1094 a1–b10.

ion of opera as the greatest of the arts is justified, this opinion does not really rest on the idea of a hierarchy of arts. Words, gestures, music, scenery are not means to opera, nor yet raw materials of it, but parts of it; the hierarchies of means and materials may therefore be ruled out, and only that of parts remains. But even this does not apply. Wagner thought himself a supremely great artist because he wrote not only his music but his words, designed his scenery, and acted as his own producer. This is the exact opposite of a system like that by which motorcars are made, which owes its hierarchical character to the fact that the various parts are all made by different firms, each specializing in work of one kind.

NOTES

1. The line is from *Cynthia's Revels* (1601) written by the British dramatist Ben Jonson (1572–1637).

2. Collingwood cites poem 36 of "Lyrisches Intermezzo," in *Buch der Lieder* (1827) by the German poet, H. Heine (1797–1856): "Out of my great sorrow I [shall] make small songs."

III

ORNAMENT AND STYLE IN THE DECORATIVE ARTS

INTRODUCTION

ORNAMENT AND ITS PRINCIPLES

It is difficult to write about ornament in a way that does justice to its special position within the theory of decorative art. As we have already seen, the artistic reputation of ornament varied considerably from the late-eighteenth to the mid-twentieth centuries: for some it was an applied element, subordinate to the other arts (especially that of architecture); for others it was *the* element that expressed an object's style; and for a small minority, ornament was itself a pure, abstract carrier of beauty. To compound the problem, ornament's artistic status rapidly declined during this period: considered a crucial element of decorative art and architecture in the eighteenth and early-nineteenth centuries, it was banned from both in the early-twentieth century.

The dramatic change in ornament's fortunes, along with its present marginal position, has attracted the attention of some contemporary critics and historians. They have examined the competing claims made on its behalf by earlier writers, treating the development of a theory of ornament as a separate and independent history.[1] In addition, architectural historians have continued to debate ornament's relative merits within the confines of architectural theory and practice. Such studies, however, are not concerned with ornament's crucial role within an emerging theory of decorative art.

The selections presented in this part of the anthology, in contrast, shed light on how ornament is able to interact with function, material, and technique in order to produce an object that is imbued with an identifiable artistic style. These writers believe that ornament must be subordinated to the object's overall purpose and materials, while recognizing its dominating influence on an object's style. Many of them puzzle over this vexing question of ornament's relation to its object, or ornament-bearer, attempting to clarify it through ever-more elaborate rules of design. These rules are sometimes abstract and theoretical, like the eighteenth-century ones of Moritz, extremely practical, like those of Jones, or even condemnatory, like those of Adolf Loos. But common to all is the growing conviction that ornament as *the* vehicle of artistic style in the decorative arts should not be left to develop on its own.

The little-known treatise by Friedrich August Krubsacius, *Reflections on the Origin, Growth, and Decline of Decoration in the Fine Arts* [Gedanken von dem Ursprung, Wachstum und Verfall der Verzierungen in den schönen Künsten] of 1759, contains one of the earliest published proposals for improving decoration.[2] Although the title suggests that Krubsacius's focus is *fine art,* the treatise in fact offers a general rule for achieving beauty in decorative art, supported by a brief overview of this principle seen throughout the history of design. The principle in question is that of asymmetry, which for Krubsacius is the source of beauty in art. Written at the height of the Rococo style, Krubsacius's pamphlet participates in the contemporary quarrel about the Rocaille. His position is one of moderation, condemning the excessive distortion of late-sixteenth-century Mannerist paintings, while praising Hogarth's *Analysis of Beauty* (1753) and his "line of beauty."[3] Krubsacius, however, adds a historical dimension to this quarrel, tracing the ideal of asymmetry back to the *contrapposto* of Greek statues. Of great interest is that decoration (*Verzierung*) in this passage can refer both to a statue's posture as well as to a vase's ornamental details; the specific definition of decoration or ornament therefore remains unclear, best understood as that element which adds beauty to an object, be it a free-standing statue or a sculpted garland.

Krubsacius's treatise contributes to the Rococo *querelle* while also proposing a transcendent principle of artistic beauty. Forty years later, the philosopher Moritz theorizes about ornament's functional and visual role in a publication free of these polemics. Moritz's writings on ornament consist of preliminary notes intended for an unfinished study, *Preliminary Ideas to a Theory of Ornament* (Vorbegriffe zu einer Theorie der Ornamente [1793]).[4] Although only fragments, Moritz's comments are nonetheless of great interest. For one, Moritz (like his contemporary Kant) there examines the nature of beauty and visual pleasure in the decorative as well as the fine arts. Moreover, like Kant, Moritz uses the notion of the frame to explain his understanding of ornament as both a necessary and yet superfluous element; for Moritz, ornament, like a frame, serves primarily to *contain* that which it surrounds (in contrast to Kant who sees the frame and ornament as presenting that which is inside).[5] In certain cases, an object has no need of applied ornament if its entire form expresses the idea of containment. For example, the shape of an undecorated vase can function as ornament when the shape unequivocally articulates the concept of containing. By defining it as the visual manifestation of an intended function, such as containing, Moritz elevates ornament from the material realm to the loftier domain of abstract ideas.

Moritz's observations on Roman ornament also led him to unexpected conclusions. Examining ancient as well as Renaissance and Baroque art, he suggests that there are two types of ornament: the first is found on three-dimensional objects, like a building or a boat, and reflects the object's movement and direction; the other appears on a large, flat surface, such as a wall, and simply represents the artist's creative inventions. In the first case, decoration is subordinate to the object's purpose (curved lines for a boat, rectilinear ones for a table), whereas in the second, it manifests our shared impulse toward beauty, conveying visual pleasure to others. Moritz's insightful musings touch upon three themes that are to dominate the debate about ornament over the next century and a half: ornament as the visual expression of an object's function; ornament as undecorated form; and ornament as a joyful product of artistic creativity.

Thoughout the nineteenth century, the first of these themes—ornament's relation to function—overshadows the other two. Troubled by the thoughtless, industrial production of ornament, art theorists and reformers search with increasing fervor for corrective principles with which to contain this wayward art. Even Ruskin, though extremely critical of design schools and of such principles in general, is nonetheless ready to offer his own prescriptive advice.

In two excerpts from *Seven Lamps of Architecture* (1849), Ruskin criticizes the current use of ornament from a perceptual point of view. Certain types of ornament, he explains, are suited to being seen from afar and others from nearby. His notion of suitability includes not only placement, size, and quantity but also the rendering of the ornament: refined and delicate ornamentation should not be placed on external façades, for instance, because there their fineness evokes a sense of waste and even of suffering. Ruskin's exploration of the psychology of human perception results in influential and insightful observations on the intertwining of visual perception and human emotions in the reading of even abstract artistic forms. The second excerpt, in contrast, reveals Ruskin at his most dogmatic. Convinced that all good art must be modeled after nature, Ruskin here argues that ornament too must be drawn from the natural world. In a futile attempt to reconcile natural objects (eggs and plants) with ornamental motifs, he resorts to fabricating lineages for ornaments he likes, while arbitrarily dismissing others for being completely abstract. Ruskin unintentionally demonstrates the difficulties of applying the same yardstick, in this case natural representation, to both decorative art and fine art.

Ruskin's writings, of course, were not meant to provide students with hard-and-fast principles, but rather to point out misuses of ornament in general. For an exhaustive set of such rules one must turn instead to Jones's *Grammar of Ornament* (1856). Jones believed that his thirty-seven "general principles" encompassed all the necessary laws of good design. Although seemingly narrow and restrictive, Jones's rules are in fact quite ambitious. In the first one, for instance, he states that beauty of form depends upon there being nothing that "could be removed and leave the design equally good or better."[6] The successive principles enable ornament to achieve this beauty of form, through composition, shading, style, and color harmony. His illustrations, principles, and commentary work together to endow ornament with universal rules of beauty that can be applied regardless of material, purpose, and technique.

The impact of such works was felt even across the Atlantic Ocean. Writing in 1880, American art critic Mariana Griswold Van Rensselaer laments the influence of these principles of design on the American upper-middle class. So diligently have these books been studied, she complains, that their rules have become eternal standards of beauty. In her article here, Van Rensselaer reminds readers that such principles are merely remedial measures, which cannot lead to the fruition of the highest beauty.

Whereas Van Rensselaer articulates the concerns of the American upper-middle class, tied to British dictates on taste, Louis Sullivan in contrast expresses the innovative opinions of a major American architect. Sullivan's article on ornament (1892) is often read as a diatribe against ornament. But it is also the reverse—a last attempt to salvage ornament from its own demise. Like Moritz and Ruskin, Sullivan considers architecture to be a spiritual form, whose meaning ornament must in turn convey to the viewer. Because ornament has lost this ability, Sullivan proposes that architects refrain from using ornament until its organic relation to architecture has been reestablished. This process, Sullivan believes, will entail the creation of an entirely new form of ornament, bearing no relation to those of the past. Concluding on a patriotic note, he explains that this new ornament can emerge only in the United States, a country free from the burden of European historical styles.

Although Sullivan wrote exclusively about ornament in architecture, not in the decorative arts, his numerous followers applied his ideas to ornament and decoration as well. The most famous of these was the Viennese architect Loos, whose equation of ornament with crime, in "Ornament and Crime" (1910), still reads as a manifesto of the Modernist movement.[7] Intending to épater le bourgeois, Loos traces the creation of decoration (including the crucifix) back to the human erotic urge, linking the present production of ornament to criminal behavior. Mixing politics, economics, and his own brand of Darwinism, he claims that progress in civilization is directly related to the disappearance of ornament. Beneath Loos's polemical tone, one also recognizes arguments proffered by others in more moderate ways. Like Sullivan, he celebrates America's unfettered past; like Morris, he chaffs at the commercial interests vested in the production of ornament; like Ruskin, he condemns cheap imitations; and like Maillou and Wright, he believes in a machine aesthetics. But Loos's combination of all these elements, along with his own incendiary comments, transform the article into a virulent statement.

Loos himself did not necessarily follow what he preached; just as important, neither did his contemporaries. A 1912 article by art critic George Grosz reveals the tenacious influence of the Arts and Crafts movement on Continental designers; like Muthesius, Van de Velde, and Bing, Grosz believes in the possibility of a handcrafted, ornamented art. Writing for an organ of the German Werkbund (founded by Muthesius), Grosz launches a valiant defense of handmade crafts. Repeating what must have been commonplace by then, he concedes that form and material can be ornaments, while still calling for the rejuvenation of ornament—by then a moribund art.

THE THEORY OF STYLE

As the search for design principles was dying out with the demise of ornament itself, the study of the history of ornament was coming into its own. These two strands of writing initially developed together: Krubsacius's pamphlet, for example, presents a history of ornament as well as corrective principles, just as Jones's *Grammar of Ornament* offers pragmatic rules of design, explaining their importance with a lavishly illustrated encyclopedic survey of ornament. Although in both cases the historical sections merely support the principle or principles presented, they nonetheless end up dominating the respective publications.

Jones's *Grammar*, in particular, straddles the worlds of artistic practice and of scholarly investigation. Because his writings lacked traditional academic rigour, they are often dismissed today; yet they challenged, and transformed, some of the aesthetic assumptions that lay at the heart of the nineteenth-century studies of art.[8] For one, Jones's survey expands beyond the normal confines of ancient and European art to include tribal, Turkish, Persian, and Asian decoration. Even more startling, he argues that perfect ornamental style—the ideal—is reached in Islamic, or what he calls Moorish, art rather than in Greek or Roman. According to Jones, the abstract forms of Moorish ornament embody all of his design principles, while the representational qualities of Classical decoration earn it only second place within his ranking of historic styles. For the first time in a European history of art, abstract, non-Western art forms serve as models of artistic perfection.

More of a scholar than Jones, Semper was able to free his study of ornament from the debate about the current production of ornament. His search for the roots of all artmaking ultimately took him outside the traditional limits of European art history, into the history of technology. He believed that he could reconstruct the development of the earliest forms of art by studying the tools and materials used to make it. In the introduction to *Style in the Technical and Tectonic Arts* (in Part II), he suggests that four basic materials conditioned the evolution of art and ornament. The volume itself then presents a history of art based on Semper's understanding of the material and technical evolution of early man.

For Semper textile art was the first to develop, and therefore influenced the forms and motifs of the other three. In the passage on textile art here, he carefully classifies the physical properties of textile art and then connects each material (vegetal stems or leather), based on its formal qualities (knotted or twisted), to a specific technique (spun or woven, embroidered or stitched). Finally, he argues that a given technique and material results in the creation of a specific ornament, such as the knot or the net. Moreover, once the motif emerges because of physical manipulation of material, the craftsman recognizes it to be a pleasing decoration and can intentionally reproduce it in another art, regardless of technique and material. This explains, therefore, the promiscuous appearance of knot or interlace designs in various forms of art throughout the ages. However, Semper cannot account for the continuous evolution of a motif throughout the technical arts, or for a culture's favoring one motif over another. At best, he has illuminated the source of certain ornamental motifs, but he has not constructed a theory of style in the decorative or technical arts.

Semper's near contemporary, the French architect Eugène-Emmanuel Viollet-le-Duc, exemplifies a more traditional approach to the question of style in the decorative arts. Like Semper and Jones, Viollet-le-Duc was an architect not a historian, and he grappled with the question "What is style?" in one of his rambling lectures (published in 1872). There he first criticizes the current usage of the word "style," reminding readers of its original association with artistic superiority and excellence *tout court*. For him, style is not simply the hallmark of different artistic ages, but rather that which elevates good art above all other, regardless of periods and taste. Style here becomes an ineffable mark of distinction, visible only to the true connoisseur. Taking a vessel as his example, he stipulates that the form must express its purpose, that it be fashioned in accordance with the material, and that it be suited to its function for it to possess what he calls style. Viollet-le-Duc's brief definition is clearly colored by functionalist and technical tenets first aired by Pugin and Ruskin, but unlike them he here does not champion a particular historical style or type of ornament. Nor, like Jones and Semper, doe he try to ground the notion of good style in a set of formal features or to a hierarchy of materials. Rather, as a term of praise, style can appear in all human artifacts, be they dresses, buildings, ancient vessels, or current paintings. It is in such theoretical passages on style and decoration that the reformist writings of architects merge with the budding tradition of scholarly writings.

Riegl and Wölfflin, it is fair to say, are among the few professional art historians to cross over into the domain of decorative art theory in the nineteenth century. Both scholars believed ornament to be a crucial vehicle of artistic style, and to be the direct result of human creativity. Each was looking for an alternative to Semper's materialistic interpretation of style based on technique, medium, and function. But whereas Wölfflin turned to psychology, and to a more perceptual, psychological reading of art, Riegl elaborated his new concept of artistic volition.

Wölfflin's interest in ornament first appears in his 1886 dissertation on the psychology of architecture. There he defines ornament as the expression of architecture's innate force. Like Moritz and Riegl, Wölfflin reads columns, architraves, and capitals in terms of opposing thrusts and even of creative will. But while the first two believe that this impulse emanates from the artist, Wölfflin sees this force as an excess energy radiating out of the architectural form itself. Even more important, he argues that the viewer unconsciously responds with his own body to this play of forces; the human form literally becomes the measure of architecture, vibrating to the perpendicular and horizontal forces of architectural forms.[9]

In his conclusion, Wölfflin suggests how and why ornament also functions as a carrier of period style. Drawing on contemporary theories of psychology and of zeitgeist (spirit of the time), he reasons that if the human body, and its directional forces, somehow inform the look and feel of buildings, then architectural style should reflect the different ways society relates to its own directional forces. Moreover, he continues, since each historic period does possess a distinctive zeitgeist, the arts will naturally reflect this in a distinctive *Formgefühl*, or sense of form. In the Gothic period, as Wölfflin famously puts it, the shoes are pointed, the lettering is sharp, the faces are elongated, and the architecture is vertical. Thus for Wölfflin the ornamental details of clothes, furniture, and illuminated manuscripts betray a shared period style, but only when examined through the lens of psychology of form.

In his chapter on Geometric style from *Problems of Style* (1893), Riegl also sees a psychological, creative force as the source of *all* art. For Riegl, this creative force is an inner urge (which he later terms *Kunstwollen*); it is best described as a human need to refashion the external, natural world in symbolic representations. Unintentionally, these artistic forms express a society's relation to the outside world as a whole (*Weltanschauung*), one that varies according to historical period and regional culture. By linking the evolution of decoration to the history of human culture (or world views), Riegl can posit the existence of a continuous and evolving history of ornamental style, connected, but not subordinate, to that of fine art.

The ideas of Riegl and Wölfflin represent exceptions within the theory of art history. Although some of their students explored the theoretical implications of their writings on ornament and decorative art, most remained within the confines of the fine arts (to which Riegl and Wölfflin themselves returned). Only in cultures for which the traditional notion of fine art was not appropriate or relevant did historians continue to explore the significance of ornament in such art objects as porcelain, calligraphy, or carpets, still considered as decorative art within the discipline of art history.

The final excerpt by the French art historian Henri Focillon is therefore an exception to this tendency. Writing in 1934, Focillon is here less concerned with understanding the inner workings of ornamental style than with ornament's power of abstraction and the breadth of its imaginary realm. In contrast to his predecessors, Focillon offers a poetics of ornament rather than an interpretation of its rational development. He neither defends the status of ornament within the history of art nor does he feel the need to defend contemporary ornament in the face of its theoretical demise. Instead, at the height of Modernism, Focillon simply celebrates ornament of the past, invoking, as had Moritz a century and a half before, the joyful, inventive richness of these abstract forms.

NOTES

1. See Kroll, *Das Ornament in der Kunsttheorie,* Grabar, *Mediation of Ornament,* and Harries, *Ethical Function;* Derrida's *La Verité en peinture* has inspired responses such as Scheffer's *L'Art de l'âge moderne.* See note 8 of the general Introduction in this volume for social and cultural histories of ornament.

2. Written a few years after Winckelmann's *Reflections on the Imitation of Greek Works in Painting and Sculpture* (1755), Krubsacius's treatise covers art from the Greeks down to the early modern period.

3. Hogarth, *Analysis of Beauty.*

4. This treatise was put together at the end of Moritz's life, partly from previously published pieces. For this reason it is not usually considered a separate publication, although Moritz there was attempting to fashion a separate theory of ornament. See the introduction by Kruft to Karl Philipp Moritz, *Vorbegriffe zu einer Theorie der Ornamente.*

5. See Derrida's *La Verité en peinture,* for an exhaustive discussion of Kant's use of the frame as an example of dependent beauty.

6. One recognizes here echoes of Alberti's famous definition of beauty in architecture: "Beauty is that reasoned congruity of all the parts within a body, so that nothing may be added, taken away, or altered but for the worse." As cited by Leon Battista Alberti in *Leon Battista Alberti, On the Art of Building,* p. 156 [*De re aedificatoria,* chap. 6, p. ii].

7. This article, originally dated to 1908, is now thought to have been written in 1910; see, for instance, Rukschcio and Schachel, *Adolf Loos, Leben und Werk.*

8. Jones was read seriously by at least one founding father of art history, as argued in I. Frank, "Das körperlose Ornament."

9. For a discussion of the theories of Fiedler and Wölfflin, see H. F. Mallgrave's and E. Ikonomou's introduction to *Empathy, Form and Space: Problems in German Aesthetics,* especially pp. 29–50.

FRIEDRICH AUGUST KRUBSACIUS

from *Reflections on the Origin, Growth, and Decline of Decoration in the Fine Arts*

"BRIEF EXAMINATION OF THE ORIGINS OF ORNAMENT"

How did asymmetrical ornament ever come to gain the approval of persons of understanding, taste, and insight, and even of artists themselves? I shall attempt to explain.

Taking the human body as the pattern of all symmetry, we observe that a particular kind of posture confers new luster upon its natural beauty and even lends a good appearance to a body that is ugly in itself. Such a posture consists in an unforced attitude and movement of the body and limbs, in accordance with the laws of gravity and motion. Let a human being adopt only strictly symmetrical positions: for example, face forward, neck likewise, shoulders and trunk straight, arms hanging down, legs and feet rigidly together. Would not a statue in this posture—even an Apollo or a Venus—be displeasing? And yet the most perfect symmetry prevails throughout! Or else spread the legs to either side in a straight line, and raise both arms to the same height, or stretch them out horizontally: surely both postures would be universally decried as too uniform or too simple? Not only these, but every conceivable posture that displays a commonplace symmetry will incur the same reproach. We have only to reflect how rarely such symmetrical postures are seen in our own daily activities—albeit in some individuals more than others.

The earliest Egyptian sculptors made their figures like this, as can be seen from their extant works; the Greeks then showed their figures stepping forward, seated, or reclining. Eventually they devised rules to obtain postures that were natural, unforced, and suited to the expression of all the passions. The principal rule is the precise opposite of the former one: namely, asymmetry. With the head looking slightly to one side, the shoulder toward which it turns is raised, the breast thrust out, the hips turned, and the body curved, as Lairesse shows in his manual of painting and drawing.[1] One leg must be advanced, the corresponding arm drawn back, and the other arm advanced, in such a way that the directional line always passes through the ground of the figure, and the latter never loses its equilibrium. Such a posture will be found pleasing to all;

and yet its two sides are unequal throughout. If a number of figures with accessories appear together, then every horizontal projection in their collective outline must be matched by a recession elsewhere, alternating from head to foot: in which process the accessories prove extremely helpful.

By accessories, I mean all those things with which the figures appear to occupy themselves: in the case of gods and goddesses, these are their attributes, and, where none are present, their garments and hair. Although these last may in themselves be disposed symmetrically, they must nevertheless display asymmetry in their respective folds and locks. All of this must be visible not only in a frontal view but also from the back and to either side. This is what the sculptors call "contrast," [contrapposto] and in their works they regard it as the supreme art and the greatest mystery. It is this, together with the beautiful proportions of the limbs, and the close attention to finish, that makes the figures of the Greeks and Romans inimitable. It amounts, in fact, to a pleasing and natural asymmetry of posture.

For still more evidence of this natural asymmetry of posture, we have only to look at flowers. Delightful creations indeed, which Nature produces in obedience to the strictest symmetry! And yet it will be observed that in everything, from leaves and stalks to calyx, there is a "contrast." Look closely at two flowers of the same species: what a difference is here! And it has long been established in natural history that no two things in the world are perfectly equal and similar. From this source the sculptors and decorators of our own day have derived their new manner of ornamentation, and persons of understanding have acknowledged the unforced and natural quality of their work.

However, anything may be carried to excess; and so it has proved in this case. Too regular a posture may make a human figure look like a jumping jack; but too irregular a posture will make it look like a harlequin. And, just as an excessively symmetrical flower would look stiff and wooden, so an excessively asymmetrical one would seem withered. Golz [Goltzius] and Spranger,[2] two great German painters of the sixteenth century, exaggerated postures in this way, and made them too violent in pictorial expression.* And so, in the name of free, bold drawing, we have spoilt our ornaments by inserting contrast [contrapposto] into works that cannot accommodate it: for they cannot be ornaments except by virtue of art and order. They are intended to give pleasure not only to the eye but also to the mind, and even to display our skill to later generations. Can this be possible, where the utmost disorder is allowed to prevail? I

---

*The very same contorted posture can be seen in the engraving of Madame de Maintenon, in both French and German editions. [Mme. de Maintenon (1635–1719) was mistress and then second wife of Louis XIV of France.]

think not—any more than furnishings in disarray are an ornament to a best parlor, or asymmetry can be regarded as a beauty in the appearance of a house.

The rule for the avoidance of exaggeration is the following: never bend any limb as far as a right angle, let alone further. As Borellus [Borelli] has shown, the whole human body is made up of levers; because all our movements are mechanical, it follows that the force, in order to operate, must be kept as far as possible from the load.[3] This cannot be the case if it makes an acute angle with the line of direction; consequently, the motion is exaggerated. Nature herself teaches us how to husband our strength in our bodily movements, if only we pay attention to ourselves. This is precisely what Mr. Marseille, a celebrated dancing-master to the youth of Paris, preaches under the name of *bonne grâce,* i.e., good grace. Mr. Hooghard [Hogarth], a great painter and draftsman in London, explains it still better, in his work on the *Analysis of Beauty,* through his pleasing serpentine line.[4] Here we have before us a number of good rules that can preserve us both from undue simplicity and from exaggeration. I intend to go still farther, and to see whether yet more rules may be extracted from the origins and history of ornament.

The earliest ornaments originated simultaneously with architecture. For, as soon as the shepherds had built their cabins from tree trunks, boughs, and twigs, they wanted to ornament them. Flowers and fruits were the first choices on offer from a kind Nature. Their sweet scent, their pleasing color, their lovely shapes, their good taste, and the manifold variety and successive changes that they afforded, prompted the shepherds to wear them, adorn themselves with them, and finally ornament their dwellings with them. The idea will readily have presented itself to their minds that they could twine them around their tree trunks or columns, or pile a few seed grains at the bases, or hang and string all manner of such things over their doors and windows. How joyously a shepherd will have strung up the garland of his beloved shepherdess! And is it so unusual to see such natural ornaments in the houses of country folk to this day?

The second source of material lies in the necessary implements of life. A shepherd's crook, a pitcher, a wallet, a reed pipe, hung with flowers and garlands; were these not in themselves the neatest, prettiest decoration for a wall? I have no idle shepherds in mind, for I like to think that during their courtships, and while they sang, they carved their own crooks and their mostly wooden household utensils. They carved, as shepherds still do today. Must they not have carved their crooks with flowers taken directly from Nature? Or did they only learn to carve their sweethearts' names, by means of signs, in the barks of trees? I believe that they did both; and, what is more, that they used bark to put inscriptions on their houses. The architecture of later times, its cornices and other features still bearing the age-old ornamentation of flowers and leaves, induces me to think so. I seek the origins of ornament among those peoples that were destined not merely to invent but to improve and ultimately to perfect the arts; and I leave it to the Hottentots to make their ornaments with animal entrails and to the American Indians ones with feathers.

As human beings multiplied, so did the arts. And when, for company's sake or for protection, people began to build cities, and to build their houses durably in stone, they retained the tree trunks and beams of their cabins—as the Greek terms of art, and their meanings, indicate—in remembrance of their age-old, contented, innocent way of life. And so they reproduced their old wooden cabins in stone, not omitting the leaves, flowers, and other ornaments that they had suspended on them and carved into them. The first to do this were the ancient Chaldeans, Phoenicians, and Egyptians. Baron von Erlach, chief architect to the Emperor, gives a number of instances of this in his treatise on historical architecture.[5] From the Greeks, architecture passed to the Romans—not without a sensible decline: for the Romans were never able to copy, let alone surpass the magnificent works of Greek sculpture.

The same applied to the three Greek orders of columns, Doric, Ionic, and Corinthian. The Romans proved incapable of adding a fourth that should improve upon these. For the Tuscan is no more than a debased Doric, and the Roman is a composite of Ionic and Corinthian. Nor was their taste in ornament as pure as that of the Greeks. Vitruvius condemned it as early as the reign of the Roman Emperor Augustus; and so architecture, sculpture, painting, drawing, and consequently also ornament, declined from age to age.

Here I regard it as highly necessary to insert the whole fifth section of Book Seven of Vitruvius' Architecture, in German translation, for the benefit of those artists who are unacquainted with this great architect.* [6]

NOTES

1. Gérard de Lairesse (1640–1711), *Grondlegginge der teekenkunst* [Principles of Design] (Amsterdam, 1701).

2. Bartholomaus Spranger (1546–1611) worked in Rome, Vienna, and Prague; Hendrick Goltzius (1558–1617) was first influenced by Spranger and then by the late Renaissance Italian painters.

3. Giovanni Alfonso Borelli (1608–1679), *De motu animalium* (1680–81), in which he sought to explain the movements of the animal body on mechanical principles.

*This will shame those superstitious worshipers of antiquity who regard every piece of work produced under the early Roman Emperors, without exception, as an immaculate masterpiece. Such a fanatical view runs counter to human nature; and Vitruvius, like Horace, has some harsh home truths to tell his Roman contemporaries.

4. William Hogarth (1697–1764), *Analysis of Beauty* (London, 1753).

5. Johann Bernhard Fischer von Erlach, *Entwurff einer historischen Architecktur* (Vienna, 1721–25), was architect to the Holy Roman Emperors Joseph I (reg. 1705–11) and Charles VI (reg. 1711–40).

6. Krubsacius cites the entire chapter 5 of Book 7 of Vitruvius, *Ten Books of Architecture.*

KARL PHILIPP MORITZ

from *Preliminary Ideas on the Theory of Ornament*

APPLICATION OF THE CONCEPT OF ISOLATION TO ORNAMENT

The frame adorns a painting because it isolates it, sets it apart from the surrounding mass of other objects, and commends it to our attention as an exceptional object. All *settings* adorn by containing and isolating the thing they set apart, by detaching it from the surrounding mass of objects, and by presenting it as something exceptionally worthy of our attention. Thus, the hem adorns the dress, the ring the finger, the garland the head.

The vase, the container par excellence, is thus an ornament in itself—because it embodies the idea of *the thing that isolates and contains within itself.* The form of the vase emerges of its own accord from the natural idea of containing. A thing that is to contain will open and widen gradually—for, if it were as wide below as it is above, it would appear to be passive rather than active; it would not stand for the *living* idea of containment. This idea of containment is most clearly manifest in the calyx of a flower, which curls back over itself to catch the falling dewdrops with its outermost rim, and to let nothing escape that approaches it from above.

For the ancients, as for ourselves, it was the most natural and obvious idea to build vases up from the base, in shapes that resemble the calyces of flowers. Just as the container gradually widens and opens from below, it is natural for it to contract a little towards the top, in order to conserve the contents and protect them from above. If the vase's character is that of conserving, the form must contract still farther up beneath its rim, which represents its completion. If it is made for dipping, it must slightly retreat into itself beneath its rim; if it is of the offering kind, its wider rim needs not give way to a contraction.

"BORROMINO" [sic] [1]

Certainly, the principles of taste reside in our intellect as much as in our feelings. We believe that we feel a thing to be beautiful; we feel it by way of the thought. And that, presumably, is why taste can be discussed—

Curves and bends are not beautiful on a building, because they are not in keeping with the concept of a building, in which the entablature, resting on columns, lies in a straight line. Curved lines in architecture offend not so much the eye as the intellect. The undulating line is not beautiful in itself, but by virtue of the idea of motion that is associated with it.

A path that meanders, a river that meanders, are charmingly poetic images because their curves are in harmony with the idea of motion, and this is the dominant idea both in a river and in a path. Similarly, undulating lines in the bodies of animals are beautiful because here the idea of motion is dominant. In plants they would not be so beautiful, for there the dominant idea is that of stasis.

In buildings the idea of stasis is altogether dominant—and an undulating line is entirely out of harmony with this.

In a ship, on the other hand, the curved line is beautiful, because it harmonizes with the idea of motion, which is the main one in a ship.

The most repellent form for a boat would be that of a trough—in which nothing would express the idea of mobility.

In chairs and tables, in which the idea of stability is dominant, undulating lines are therefore always inappropriate. Where the ancients employed them, they combined them with animal forms. A table-top was supported by a griffin or a centaur.—The chair stood on bear's paws.—The improved taste in furniture began when the straight line supplanted the curve.

ORNAMENTS (ON VIEWING THE LOGGIAS OF RAPHAEL)[2]

(Rome, April 6)

Delicacy of form is used to counteract the ungainliness of heavy masses. The human mind is always busy; it cannot endure uniform, dead masses; it seeks to breathe life into them; it creates and forms things in its own image—from the poor savage who whittles his bow and steers his canoe to the supreme artist. What can this be but one more manifestation of the inner impulse toward perfection, which takes a thing that has no termination, no boundaries of its own, and seeks to give it some kind of completion that will make it into a whole?

The finest capital is no better as a support than the bare shaft—

The most precious cornice affords no more shelter or warmth than a blank wall—

Man not only wants to live in a building with pleasure—he wants to look on it with pleasure too—and almost as many hands are at work for the nourishment of the eye as for the nourishment of the body.

Art can therefore proliferate without pause; for the eye never tires of look-ing, nor the ear of listening.

Perceived in tranquillity, the mere sight of the vault of heaven, the verdant meadows, and the leaf on the tree, imperceptibly elevates and ennobles the soul; so too can the slightest, well-chosen ornament delight the soul through the eye, imperceptibly refining the taste and educating the mind.

The urge to decorate is, therefore, a noble drive of the human soul, one that distinguishes man from the beast, which only satisfies its needs. And if this drive is not led astray, it is just as beneficial to man as is his drive for knowledge and high art.

The true strength of the instinct for beauty appears in this: even where beauty no longer finds a place, humans seek at least to find a place for orna-ment—

THE ARABESQUES IN RAPHAEL'S LOGGIAS

Horace's saying, "Painters and poets have always had license to take any risk," seems to be the law that governs arabesque.[3] In the reign of Augustus there lived in Rome a certain Ludius, who, as Pliny the Elder tells us, was the first to paint the walls of rooms with little landscapes, in which women bearing loads waded through swamps with their skirts tucked up, and were afraid of losing their footing, and with all other manners of quaint objects which de-tracted from the seriousness of ancient art.[4]

Vitruvius condemns this as an unpardonable abuse of art: the ancients, he says, painted only true and serious subjects. The moderns, he complains, paint a thin reed instead of columns—they represent figures standing on tall cande-labra—delicate, intertwined stalks sprout forth, and on them dance fantastic creatures from who knows where—heads, half human, half animal, grow out of flowers, etc.[5]

All this invective from art connoisseurs did no good, for the human imagi-nation was inclined to play.

Under Pope Leo X, walls decorated with encaustic paintings were discov-ered in the ruins of the Palace and Baths of Titus. Everyone went there to ad-mire them. Raphael was there, with his pupil Giovanni da Udine, and he stands accused of destroying some of the ancient paintings in order to take credit for their originality.[6]

This discovery was perfectly suited to the human addiction to novelty and fashion, and to the free play of taste.

There appeared a new branch of art, which took its name of *grotesque* from the accident that these caprices of the imagination were discovered in buried, subterranean apartments or *grottoes*. The word later became a general term of art, and also served to denote a specific category of the comic in general, which is now called grotesque whenever it strays into the absurd and the fantastic.

The loggias, or open, vaulted passages, which line the upper story of the inner courtyard of the Vatican palace, had been left unfinished by Bramante, and Raphael now decorated the fourteen piers that support the thirteen compartments of the vault.[7]

Animals—masks—foliage—cameos—vases—trophies—mermaids—terms and terminets—satyrs—little shields—moldings—pavilions—weaponry—insects—etc. appear in these clusters in the most wonderful mixture.—

Nevertheless, even here everything still falls into a certain unity—we are, as it were, climbing the ladder of creation—a beauteous labyrinth in which the eye loses itself—

Except that we must to take care not to mistake this array of imagery for a type of hieroglyphics in which everything is subject to interpretation—in some of these combinations there is some sort of plan to be found—but much is the work of caprice, in which no interpretation is possible, and the quirks of the imagination simply spin on their own axis—

This is the essence of decoration, which observes no law, because it has no purpose but that of giving pleasure.—

NOTES

This chapter is made up of notes that eventually became part of Moritz's *Preliminary Ideas for a Theory of Ornament* (Vorbegriffe zu einer Theorie der Ornamente [1793]).

1. These remarks are inspired by buildings of Francesco Borromini (1599–1667), who, along with his rival Gianlorenzo Bernini, established the style of Roman High Baroque architecture.

2. Moritz is describing the private Vatican loggias of Pope Leo X, decorated by Raphael (1483–1520) and his assistants, Giovanni da Udine and Giulio Romano, from 1518–19. The pilasters and vaults were covered with "grotesques," an ornament type based on frescoed interiors of ancient Roman palaces and tombs.

3. The citation is from Horace, *Ars Poetica*, 9–10: "Picturibus atque poetis / quidlibet audendi semper fuit aequa potestas."

4. Pliny the Elder, *Natural History*, Book 35: 37, p. 116.

5. This is from Vitruvius, *Ten Books On Architecture*, Book 7, chapter 5, and is cited in full by Krubsacius.

6. Giovanni da Udine (1487–1564) was one of Raphael's main associates, see note 2

above. Moritz's story of their supposed vandalism of Roman frescoes is an interesting eighteenth-century view of Renaissance artists' relation to Roman art.

7. Donato Bramante (1443/4–1514) is considered the father of High Renaissance architecture; he is responsible for building the loggias added to the Vatican Palace, then painted by Raphael and his associates.

JOHN RUSKIN

"The Lamp of Sacrifice" and "The Lamp of Beauty"

THE LAMP OF SACRIFICE

xii. Visibility, however, we must remember, depends, not only on situation, but on distance; and there is no way in which work is more painfully and unwisely lost than in its over delicacy on parts distant from the eye. Here, again, the principle of honesty must govern our treatment; we must not work any kind of ornament which is, perhaps, to cover the whole building (or at least to occur on all parts of it) delicately where it is near the eye, and rudely where it is removed from it. That is trickery and dishonesty. Consider, first, what kinds of ornaments will tell in the distance and what near, and so distribute them, keeping such as by their nature are delicate, down near the eye, and throwing the bold and rough kinds of work to the top; and if there be any kind which is to be both near and far off, take care that it be as boldly and rudely wrought where it is well seen as where it is distant, so that the spectator may know exactly what it is, and what it is worth. Thus chequered patterns, and in general such ornaments as common workmen can execute, may extend over the whole building; but bas-reliefs, and fine niches and capitals, should be kept down; and the common sense of this will always give a building dignity, even though there be some abruptness or awkwardness in the resulting arrangements. Thus at San Zeno at Verona, the bas-reliefs, full of incident and interest, are confined to a parallelogram of the front, reaching to the height of the capitals of the columns of the porch.[1] Above these, we find a simple, though most lovely, little arcade; and above that, only blank wall, with square face shafts. The whole effect is tenfold grander and better than if the entire façade had been covered with bad work, and may serve for an example of the way to place little where we cannot afford much. So, again, the transept gates of Rouen* are covered with delicate bas-reliefs (of which I shall speak at greater length presently) up to about once and a half a man's height; and above that come the usual and more visible statues and niches.[2] So in the campanile at Florence, the circuit of bas-

*Henceforward, for the sake of convenience, when I name any cathedral town in this manner, let me be understood to speak of its cathedral church.

{264}

reliefs is on its lowest story; above that come its statues; and above them all is pattern mosaic, and twisted columns, exquisitely finished, like all Italian work of the time, but still, in the eye of the Florentine, rough and commonplace by comparison with the bas-reliefs.[3] So generally the most delicate niche work and best mouldings of the French Gothic are in gates and low windows well within sight; although, it being the very spirit of that style to trust to its exuberance for effect, there is occasionally a burst upwards and blossoming unrestrainably to the sky, as in the pediment of the west front of Rouen, and in the recess of the rose window behind it, where there are some most elaborate flower-mouldings, all but invisible from below, and only adding a general enrichment to the deep shadows that relieve the shafts of the advanced pediment. It is ob-servable, however, that this very work is bad flamboyant, and has corrupt re-naissance characters in its detail as well as use; while in the earlier and grander north and south gates, there is a very noble proportioning of the work to the distance, the niches and statues which crown the northern one, at a height of about one hundred feet from the ground, being alike colossal and simple; visibly so from below, so as to induce no deception, and yet honestly and well finished above, and all that they are expected to be; the features very beautiful, full of expression, and as delicately wrought as any work of the period.

XIII. It is to be remembered, however, that while the ornaments in every fine ancient building, without exception so far as I am aware, are most delicate at the base, they are often in greater effective *quantity* on the upper parts. In high towers this is perfectly natural and right, the solidity of the foundation being as necessary as the division and penetration of the superstructure; hence the lighter work and richly pierced crowns of late Gothic towers. The campanile of Giotto at Florence already alluded to, is an exquisite instance of the union of two principles, delicate bas-reliefs adorning its massy foundation, while the open tracery of the upper windows attracts the eye by its slender intricacy, and a rich cornice crowns the whole. In such truly fine cases of this disposition the upper work is effective by its quantity and intricacy only, as the lower portions by delicacy; so also in the Tour de Beurre at Rouen, where, however, the detail is massy throughout, subdividing into rich meshes as it ascends. In the bodies of buildings the principle is less safe, but its discussion is not connected with our present subject.

XIV. Finally, work may be wasted by being too good for its material, or too fine to bear exposure; and this, generally a characteristic of late, especially of renaissance, work, is perhaps the worst fault of all. I do not know anything more painful or pitiful than the kind of ivory carving with which the Certosa of Pavia, and part of the Colleone sepulchral chapel at Bergamo, and other such buildings, are incrusted, of which it is not possible so much as to think without exhaustion; and a heavy sense of the misery it would be, to be forced to look at it all.[4] And this is not from the quantity of it, nor because it is bad work—much of it is inventive and able; but because it looks as if it were only fit to be put in inlaid cabinets and velveted caskets, and as if it could not bear one drifting shower or gnawing frost. We are afraid for it, anxious about it, and tormented by it; and we feel that a massy shaft and a bold shadow would be worth it all. Nevertheless, even in cases like these, much depends on the accomplishment of the great ends of decoration. If the ornament does its duty—if it *is* ornament, and its points of shade and light tell in the general effect, we shall not be offended by finding that the sculptor in his fulness of fancy has chosen to give much more than these mere points of light, and has composed them of groups of figures. But if the ornament does not answer its purpose, if it have no distant, no truly decorative power; if, generally seen, it be a mere incrustation and meaningless roughness, we shall only be chagrined by finding when we look close, that the incrustation has cost years of labour, and has millions of figures and histories in it; and would be the better of being seen through a Stanhope lens.[5] Hence the greatness of the northern Gothic as contrasted with the latest Italian. It reaches nearly the same extreme of detail; but it never loses sight of its architectural purpose, never fails in its decorative power; not a leaflet in it but speaks, and speaks far off too; and so long as this be the case, there is no limit to the luxuriance in which such work may legitimately and nobly be bestowed.

xv. No limit: it is one of the affectations of architects to speak of overcharged ornament. Ornament cannot be overcharged if it be good, and is always overcharged when it is bad.

. . .

THE LAMP OF BEAUTY

III. Now, I would insist especially on the fact, of which I doubt not that farther illustrations will occur to the mind of every reader, that all most lovely forms and thoughts are directly taken from natural objects; because I would fain be allowed to assume also the converse of this, namely, that forms which are *not* taken from natural objects *must* be ugly. I know this is a bold assumption; but as I have not space to reason out the points wherein essential beauty of form consists, that being far too serious work to be undertaken in a bye way, I have no other resource than to use this accidental mark or test of beauty, of whose truth the considerations which I hope hereafter to lay before the reader may assure him. I say an accidental mark, since forms are not beautiful *because* they are copied from Nature; only it is out of the power of man to conceive beauty without her aid. I believe the reader will grant me this, even from the examples above advanced; the degree of confidence with which it is granted must attach also to his acceptance of the conclusions which will follow from it; but if it be granted frankly, it will enable me to determine a matter of very essential importance, namely, what *is* or is *not* ornament. For there are many forms of so called decoration in architecture, habitual, and received, therefore, with approval, or at all events without any venture at expression of dislike, which I have no hesitation in asserting to be not ornament at all, but to be ugly things, the expense of which ought in truth to be set down in the architect's contract, as "For Monstrification." I believe that we regard these customary deformities with a savage complacency, as an Indian does his flesh patterns and paint (all nations being in certain degrees and senses savage). I believe that I can prove them to be monstrous, and I hope hereafter to do so conclusively; but, meantime, I can allege in defence of my persuasion nothing but this fact of their being unnatural, to which the reader must attach such weight as he thinks it deserves. There is, however, a peculiar difficulty in using this proof; it requires the writer to assume, very impertinently, that nothing is natural but what he has seen or supposes to exist. I would not do this; for I suppose there is no conceivable form or grouping of forms but in some part of the universe an example of it may be found. But I think I am justified in considering those forms to be *most* natural which are most frequent; or, rather, that on the shapes which in the every-day world are familiar to the eyes of men, God has stamped those characters of beauty which He has made it man's nature to love; while in certain exceptional forms He has shown that the adoption of the others was not a matter of necessity, but part of the adjusted harmony of creation. I believe that thus we may reason from Frequency to Beauty, and *vice versâ;* that knowing a thing to be frequent, we may assume it to be beautiful; and assume that which is most frequent to be most beautiful: I mean, of course, *visibly* frequent; for the forms of things which are hidden in caverns of the earth, or in the anatomy of animal frames, are evidently not intended by their Maker to bear the habitual gaze of man. And, again, by frequency I mean that limited and isolated frequency which is characteristic of all perfection; not mere multitude: as a rose is a common flower, but yet there are not so many roses on the tree as there are leaves. In this respect Nature is sparing of her highest, and lavish of her less, beauty; but I call the flower as frequent as the leaf, because, each in its allotted quantity, where the one is, there will ordinarily be the other.

iv. The first so called ornament, then, which I would attack is that Greek fret, now, I believe, usually known by the Italian name Guilloche, which is exactly a case in point. It so happens that in crystals of bismuth, formed by the unagitated cooling of the melted metal, there occurs a natural resemblance of it almost perfect. But crystals of bismuth not only are of unusual occurrence in every-day life, but their form is, as far as I know, unique among minerals; and not only unique, but only attainable by an artificial process, the metal itself never being found pure. I do not remember any other substance or arrangement which presents a resemblance to this Greek ornament; and I think that I may trust my remembrance as including most of the arrangements which occur in the outward forms of common and familiar things. On this ground, then, I allege that ornament to be ugly; or, in the literal sense of the word, monstrous; different from anything which it is the nature of man to admire: and I think an uncarved fillet or plinth infinitely preferable to one covered with this vile concatenation of straight lines: unless indeed it be employed as a foil to a true ornament, which it may, perhaps, sometimes with advantage; or excessively small, as it occurs on coins, the harshness of its arrangement being less perceived.

v. Often in association with this horrible design we find, in Greek works, one which is as beautiful as this is painful—that egg and dart moulding, whose perfection, in its place and way, has never been surpassed. And why is this? Simply because the form of which it is chiefly composed is one not only familiar to us in the soft housing of the bird's nest, but happens to be that of nearly every pebble that rolls and murmurs under the surf of the sea, on all its endless shore. And that with a peculiar accuracy; for the mass which bears the light in this moulding is *not* in good Greek work, as in the frieze of the Erechtheum, merely of the shape of an egg. It is *flattened* on the upper surface, with a delicacy and keen sense of variety in the curve which it is impossible too highly to praise, attaining exactly that flattened, imperfect oval, which, in nine cases out of ten, will be the form of the pebble lifted at random from the rolled beach. Leave out this flatness, and the moulding is vulgar instantly. It is singular also that the insertion of this rounded form in the hollow recess has a *painted* type in the plumage of the Argus pheasant, the eyes of whose feathers are so shaded as exactly to represent an oval form placed in a hollow.

vi. It will evidently follow, upon our application of this test of natural resemblance, that we shall at once conclude that all perfectly beautiful forms must be composed of curves; since there is hardly any common natural form in which it is possible to discover a straight line. Nevertheless, Architecture, having necessarily to deal with straight lines essential to its purposes in many instances and to the expression of its power in others, must frequently be content with that measure of beauty which is consistent with such primal forms; and we may presume that utmost measure of beauty to have been attained when the arrangements of such lines are consistent with the most frequent natural groupings of them we can discover, although, to find right lines in nature at all, we may be compelled to do violence to her finished work, break through the sculptured and coloured surfaces of her crags, and examine the processes of their crystallisation.

VII. I have just convicted the Greek fret of ugliness, because it has no precedent to allege for its arrangement except an artificial form of a rare metal. Let us bring into court an ornament of the Lombard architects, . . . This ornament, taken from the front of the Cathedral of Pisa, is universal throughout the Lombard churches of Pisa, Lucca, Pistoja, and Florence; and it will be a grave stain upon them if it cannot be defended. Its first apology for itself, made in a hurry, sounds marvellously like the Greek one, and highly dubious. It says that its terminal contour is the very image of a carefully prepared artificial crystal of common salt. Salt being, however, a substance considerably more familiar to us than bismuth, the chances are somewhat in favour of the accused Lombard ornament already. But it has more to say for itself, and more to the purpose; namely, that its main outline is one not only of natural crystallisation, but among the very first and commonest of crystalline forms, being the primal condition of the occurrence of the oxides of iron, copper, and tin, of the sulphurets of iron and lead, of fluor spar, &c.; and that those projecting forms in its surface represent the conditions of structure which effect the change into another relative and equally common crystalline form, the cube. This is quite enough. We may rest assured that it is as good a combination of such simple right lines as can be put together, and gracefully fitted for every place in which such lines are necessary.

· · ·

XV. Thus far of what is *not* ornament. What ornament is, will without difficulty be determined by the application of the same test. It must consist of such studious arrangements of form as are imitative or suggestive of those which are commonest among natural existences, that being of course the noblest ornament which represents the highest orders of existence. Imitated flowers are nobler than imitated stones, imitated animals, than flowers; imitated human form, of all animal forms the noblest. But all are combined in the richest ornamental work; and the rock, the fountain, the flowing river with its pebbled bed, the sea, the clouds of Heaven, the herb of the field, the fruit-tree bearing fruit, the creeping thing, the bird, the beast, the man, and the angel, mingle their fair forms on the bronze of Ghiberti.[6]

Everything being then ornamental that is imitative, I would ask the reader's attention to a few general considerations, all that can here be offered relating to so vast a subject; which, for convenience sake, may be classed under the three heads of inquiry:—What is the right place for architectural ornament? What is the peculiar treatment of ornament which renders it architectural? and what is the right use of colour as associated with architectural imitative form?

NOTES

1. San Zeno, Verona, was built between 1120–1225.

2. Rouen Cathedral, rebuilding began in 1201 and finished in 1514.

3. Giotto designed the Florence Campanile shortly before his death in 1337; the greater part of the early sculptural work was done by Pisano and others.

4. The West Front of the Certosa of Pavia was built in 1499, with a superabundance of ornament; the Colleoni Chapel in Bergamo was built c. 1476.

5. The Stanhope lens, which allows one to see microscopically, was invented by Charles Stanhope (1753–1816).

6. Ruskin is referring to Lorenzo Ghiberti (1378–1455) and the famous sets of doors he sculpted for the Baptistry in Florence in the first part of the fifteenth century.

OWEN JONES

General Principles in the Arrangement of Form and Colour in Architecture and the Decorative Arts

General
principles.

PROPOSITION 1.

The Decorative Arts arise from, and should properly be attendant upon, Architecture.

PROPOSITION 2.

Architecture is the material expression of the wants, the faculties, and the sentiments, of the age in which it is created.

Style in Architecture is the peculiar form that expression takes under the influence of climate and materials at command.

PROPOSITION 3.

As Architecture, so all works of the Decorative Arts, should possess fitness, proportion, harmony, the result of all which is repose.

PROPOSITION 4.

True beauty results from that repose which the mind feels when the eye, the intellect, and the affections, are satisfied from the absence of any want.

PROPOSITION 5.

Construction should be decorated. Decoration should never be purposely constructed.

That which is beautiful is true; that which is true must be beautiful.

PROPOSITION 6.

Beauty of form is produced by lines growing out one from the other in gradual undulations: there are no excrescences; nothing could be removed and leave the design equally good or better.

On general form.

PROPOSITION 7.

The general forms being first cared for, these should be subdivided and ornamented by general lines; the interstices may then be filled in with ornament, which may again be subdivided and enriched for closer inspection.

Decoration of the surface.

PROPOSITION 8.

All ornament should be based upon a geometrical construction.

PROPOSITION 9.

As in every perfect work of Architecture a true proportion will be found to reign between all the members which compose it, so throughout the Decorative Arts every assemblage of forms should be arranged on certain definite proportions; the whole and each particular member should be a multiple of some simple unit.

Those proportions will be the most beautiful which it will be most difficult for the eye to detect.

Thus the proportion of a double square, or 4 to 8, will be less beautiful than the more subtle ratio of 5 to 8; 3 to 6, than 3 to 7; 3 to 9, than 3 to 8; 3 to 4, than 3 to 5.

PROPOSITION 10.

Harmony of form consists in the proper balancing, and contrast of, the straight, the inclined, and the curved.

PROPOSITION 11.

In surface decoration all lines should flow out of a parent stem. Every ornament, however distant, should be traced to its branch and root. *Oriental practice.*

PROPOSITION 12.

All junctions of curved lines with curved or of curved lines with straight should be tangential to each other.

Natural law. Oriental practice in accordance with it.

PROPOSITION 13.

Flowers or other natural objects should not be used as ornaments, but conventional representations founded upon them sufficiently suggestive to convey the intended image to the mind, without destroying the unity of the object they are employed to decorate. *Universally obeyed in the best periods of Art, equally violated when Art declines.*

PROPOSITION 14.

Colour is used to assist in the development of form, and to distinguish objects or parts of objects one from another.

PROPOSITION 15.

Colour is used to assist light and shade, helping the undulations of form by the proper distribution of the several colours.

PROPOSITION 16.

These objects are best attained by the use of the primary colours on small surfaces and in small quantities, balanced and supported by the secondary and tertiary colours on the larger masses.

PROPOSITION 17.

The primary colours should be used on the upper portions of objects, the secondary and tertiary on the lower.

On the proportions by which harmony in colouring is produced.

PROPOSITION 18.

(*Field's Chromatic equivalents.*)[1]

The primaries of equal intensities will harmonise or neutralise each other, in the proportions of 3 yellow, 5 red, and 8 blue,—integrally as 16.

The secondaries in the proportions of 8 orange, 13 purple, 11 green,—integrally as 32.

The tertiaries, citrine (compound of orange and green), 19; russet (orange and purple), 21; olive (green and purple), 24;—integrally as 64.

It follows that,—

Each secondary being a compound of two primaries is neutralised by the remaining primary in the same proportions: thus, 8 of orange by 8 of blue, 11 of green by five of red, 13 of purple by 3 of yellow.

Each tertiary being a binary compound of two secondaries, is neutralised by the remaining secondary: as, 24 of olive by 8 of orange, 21 of russet by 11 of green, 19 of citrine by 13 of purple.

PROPOSITION 19.

The above supposes the colours to be used in their prismatic intensities, but each colour has a variety of *tones* when mixed with white, or of *shades* when mixed with grey or black.

When a full colour is contrasted with another of a lower tone, the volume of the latter must be proportionally increased.

On the contrasts and harmonious equivalents of tones, shades, and hues.

PROPOSITION 20.

Each colour has a variety of hues, obtained by admixture with other colours, in addition to white, grey, or black: thus we have of yellow,— orange-yellow on the one side, and lemon-yellow on the other; so of red,—scarlet-red, and crimson-red; and of each every variety of *tone* and *shade*.

When a primary tinged with another primary is contrasted with a secondary, the secondary must have a hue of the third primary.

PROPOSITION 21.

In using the primary colours on moulded surfaces, we should place blue, which retires, on the concave surfaces; yellow, which advances, on the convex; and red, the intermediate colour, on the undersides; separating the colours by white on the vertical planes.

When the proportions required by Proposition 18 cannot be obtained, we may procure the balance by a

On the positions the several colours should occupy.

change in the colours themselves: thus, if the surfaces to be coloured should give too much yellow, we should make the red more crimson and the blue more purple,—*i.e.* we should take the yellow out of them; so if the surfaces should give too much blue, we should make the yellow more orange and the red more scarlet.

PROPOSITION 22.

The various colours should be so blended that the objects coloured, when viewed at a distance, should present a neutralised bloom.

PROPOSITION 23.

No composition can ever be perfect in which any one of the three primary colours is wanting, either in its natural state or in combination.

On the law of simultaneous contrasts of colours, derived from Mons. Chevruil.[2]

PROPOSITION 24.

When two tones of the same colour are juxtaposed, the light colour will appear lighter, and the dark colour darker.

PROPOSITION 25.

When two different colours are juxtaposed, they receive a double modification; first, as to their tone (the light colour appearing lighter, and the dark colour appearing darker); secondly, as to their hue, each will become tinged with the complementary colour of the other.

PROPOSITION 26.

Colours on white grounds appear darker; on black grounds lighter.

PROPOSITION 27.

Black grounds suffer when opposed to colours which give a luminous complementary.

PROPOSITION 28.

Colours should never be allowed to impinge upon each other.

PROPOSITION 29.

When ornaments in a colour are on a ground of a contrasting colour, the ornament should be separated from the ground by an edging of lighter colour; as a red flower on a green ground should have an edging of lighter red.

PROPOSITION 30.

When ornaments in a colour are on a gold ground, the ornaments should be separated from the ground by an edging of a darker colour.

PROPOSITION 31.

Gold ornaments on any coloured ground should be outlined with black.

On the means of increasing the harmonious effects of juxtaposed colours. Observations derived from a consideration of Oriental practice.

PROPOSITION 32.
Ornaments of any colour
may be separated from
grounds of any other colour
by edgings of white, gold, or
black.

PROPOSITION 33.
Ornaments in any colour, or
in gold, may be used on
white or black grounds,
without outline or edging.

PROPOSITION 34.
In "self-tints," tones, or
shades of the same colour, a
light tint on a dark ground
may be used without outline;
but a dark ornament on a
light ground requires to be
outlined with a still darker
tint.

PROPOSITION 35.
Imitations, such as the grain-
ing of woods, and of the various coloured marbles, allowable only, when the
employment of the thing
imitated would not have
been inconsistent.

PROPOSITION 36.
The principles discoverable
in the works of the past belong to us; not so the results.
It is taking the end for the
means.

PROPOSITION 37.
No improvement can take
place in the Art of the present generation until all
classes, Artists, Manufacturers, and the Public, are better
educated in Art, and the existence of general principles
is more fully recognised.

On imitations.

NOTES

1. George Field (1777–1854) was a leading color chemist, and his *Chromatography* (1835) was the standard English text on pigments and their uses.

2. See note 6 in Semper's "Concerning the Formal Principles of Ornament" in Part I of this volume.

MARIANA GRISWOLD VAN RENSSELAER

Decorative Art and Its Dogmas

It would be a pleasant task to retrace the history of twenty years and show how rapid and how creditable has been our recent progress in the cultivation of beauty. Whatever our actual rank may be as workers in art or judges of the artwork of others, our comparative rank as against our predecessors of the last generation is certainly high. We can confidently say that art is far better loved by us than it was by our fathers, far more accurately known, far more wisely criticised. In its actual practice, too, we have improved, and there are sure signs, I think, of a swifter and broader improvement in a future very near us.

Our most noteworthy advance in actual achievement has perhaps been made along the line of decorative art—that art which has been explained as "ornamenting a useful thing," in contrast with the art which "represents a beautiful thing." But though this is the department where past results have been greatest, it is, on the other hand, the department where the outlook seems least full of promise to the careful prophet—to him whose data are drawn from underlying principles as well as from results already wrought. It has been contended that this is so because decorative art is a lower, simpler thing than strictly creative art of any kind—a thing easier to fathom, master and exercise at the outset, less rich in capabilities of development and progress. But such an argument goes very wide of the mark. If we were true connoisseurs in our appreciation of ornament, if we were true artists in its application to every detail of our surroundings, it would become not only a pleasant atmosphere about us, but a potent educator as well. We should pass from each attained level to a higher one of subtler enjoyment and skilfuller design. The time would never come when we should necessarily stagnate, as we now show signs of doing amid the rather incongruous débris that marks where we have theorized and experimented for some fifteen years.

It is, therefore, not to the pleasant labor of praising our pretty interiors that we may most profitably address ourselves just now. It is not to the task of contrasting those interiors in a self-satisfied way with the ones where our fathers and mothers dwelt some thirty or forty years ago—abodes of grim provincial ugliness or gilt and gaudy copies of Parisian elegance, in itself a none too worthy model. It will not be quite so pleasant, but it may be more wholesome, to seek out such mistakes as mar the very good work we have most certainly done, and see how it is they threaten to limit or to maim our further possible achievements. Some of them have been inevitable, the result of inexperience or experiment. These will be outgrown or eliminated, and leave no progeny of vital error behind them. But others are the logical outcome of defective thinking, of one-sided judgments, or of provisional theories that bid fair to crystallize into narrow and absolute dogmas.

It was natural that when our interest in artistic things increased it should first be practically shown in the department of decoration. When we began to realize the very low grade of our art-instincts and perceive the very inferior character of our performance, it was natural that we should be most forcibly distressed by the things that lay nearest to us. Works of art in the strict sense we could, at the worst, do without entirely. Useful things we were obliged to have always with us—if not in beautiful shapes and colors, then in shapes and colors that were an incessant and unabatable annoyance. In our first enlightenment, then—an enlightenment that was merely the realization of our great ignorance—we were forced to attempt the actual exercise of decoration. It was a widespread popular wish and need that caused the almost simultaneous appearance of so many books on "household art" in this country and in England; as is proved, indeed, by the rapidity with which their teachings were assimilated and put in practice. To how many who were vaguely dissatisfied with their surroundings, acutely conscious of their stumbling inability to better them very materially, did Mr. Eastlake's *Hints,* for example, come as a deliverance![1] What was their joy at finding "beauty made easy," to all appearance, in his straightforward, confident pages! It is unnecessary to remind ourselves through how wide a circle his and kindred lessons have spread, nor how much good they have wrought. Yet they have not, as their students are apt to imagine, given us the broadest and truest possible ideas on the whole subject, much less caused our practice to be actually, as well as comparatively, admirable. The ostensible aim of the first apostles, at least, of the new cult was to pave the way for the entrance of originality into the fittings of our homes. Their lessons and the queerly exaggerated inferences of their devotees have in fact, however, only furnished us with a conventionality of a more desirable pattern than we knew before. It is not even conventionality of the most perfect possible type: still less is it apt to give place to the expression of original, characteristic taste. These shortcomings would not of necessity prophesy stagnation in the future: they might be merely temporary halting-places on our upward path. The threatening fact is that we do not see them as shortcomings, do not tolerate them as halting-places, but praise and admire them as ultimate goals. Our mistake has

come about very naturally. It has arisen from the fact that our defective practice has not always grown out of theoretical fallacies or utter blunders, but out
of half truths that were useful in the beginning of our reform. We see the good
they have wrought—we see that they were once indispensable to us. We do not
see that they must now be cast aside or broadened if we would continue to improve. The purest truth would have been wasted on us at first: we could not
have attempted to put its precepts into action. For, as I have said, decorative
art was preached to us as the very first chapter of our education, and the
preachers could not say in the beginning, "Leave your worship of ugliness and
pursue true beauty in its highest shapes, each man as it seems good to him."
They dared not say, "Shun conventionality: let each man express his own taste
in his own way." It was necessary first to demolish—to remove out of our sight
things which would for ever contaminate our eyes, to remove out of our minds
ideas that would for ever vitiate our judgments; and, secondly, to replace both
the things and the ideas with the best substitutes that could be immediately
comprehended by our blunt perceptions and executed by our clumsy hands.
The first preaching was of necessity negative. It began by forbidding styles of
work that had run into absurd exaggerations or been degraded into caricatures
of their true selves. The mistake we have made lay in accepting such negative
precepts as positive laws, and in looking upon the provisional reform which
followed as perfection absolutely attained. Our "working hypotheses," by a
very usual process, have been set up as unassailable axioms. In consequence,
we have come to condemn as alike wrong the perfectly artistic and admirable
use of the interdicted styles and that misuse of them which rightly led to their
interdiction. The only possible remedy for defective or mistaken theories is a
reference to the best practice of the past. Let us see, therefore, what are the
dogmas in which we believe just now, and whether they are in conformity with
or in opposition to the principles acted upon by the greatest artists and en-
dorsed by the most universally and spontaneously æsthetic peoples.

Let us ask our neighbor who is fashionably artistic what are the laws by
which he guides his taste, what are the rules to which he defers when beautifying his home; for be sure that such a one will be apt to think and work by law
and rule. The main points of his answer will be somewhat as follows: All articles must be "sincerely" made; bright colors as a rule should be avoided; a strict
line must be drawn between representative and decorative art, and all decoration, properly so called, must be "conventional." If we think back ten or fifteen
years, we shall agree that these principles were wise and useful for the reform of
then flagrant abuses, for the abolition of the detestable modes of work then
universally followed. Those who remember most acutely our homes at that
period—still more those who knew the typical interior of the British middle

class—will realize that the conscientious application of such rules must in all cases have resulted in a marvelous improvement. But if we think back farther still, or if we look abroad beyond the borders of the Anglo-Saxon race, we shall find that they are not laws of ultimate and universal necessity—that they have, in truth, been nowhere followed where the very highest results have been achieved. In a word, as negative, provisional, preparatory teaching they were valuable: as positive precepts for all future conduct they must prove most hurtful. Let us take them in detail, and note the abuses by which they were called forth, as well as the prejudicial way in which they now seem likely to exert their influence.

First, as to the necessity of "sincere" construction. Construction is indubitably the first and most important element in articles of furniture or use as distinguished from articles that exist primarily because of their beauty. There is no doubt, also, that at the time when the recent reform began construction was terribly degraded. It was not only lost sight of as a priceless means of producing beauty, but the highest beauty was thought to consist in its deliberate concealment or falsification. It is unnecessary to dilate on the special articles in use, with their bent and contorted outlines, their unmeaning angles and flourishes, their clumsy, superfluous legs, their pendants and urns and heads, and machine-turned ornaments of shapes impossible to describe. Be it noted—for this is the main point of my argument—that these perfunctory elaborations of structure were not beautiful in any sense. They were "false" and detestable, not by being unnecessary only, but by being hideous and inappropriate and mechanical. They were perfunctory, as I have just said, not spontaneous. They were not produced by that inextinguishable desire for beauty which among artistic peoples prompts the workman's hand to elaborate everything it touches, and shows him at the same time how to make elaboration in all cases truly decorative. They were produced simply by a resolve at all events to avoid plainness. We were incapable of producing or appreciating good simplicity, and fondly fancied that any article not plain was of necessity "decorated." Now, if we wished to bring about a better state of thinking and working, it was necessary to abolish together the notion of which I speak and the ugly products resulting from it. It was necessary to cut away, root and branch, the idea that elaboration and ornament were essential to beauty. It would have been folly to have said at the beginning, "Elaborate more skillfully—construct, design, carve like true artists, not like clumsy machines." How *could* we have done so when we were not able at first even to see the difference between good and bad? The virtues of simplicity of all kinds were preached through the gospel of "sincerity," for so bad had been our habits that elaboration and insincerity were indeed synonymous terms. Its preaching was valuable—nay, indispensable—at

Mariana Griswold Van Rensselaer {279}

the time, but it should have been regarded as preparatory only. Unfortunately, it came to be preached as a final and complete religion, and to be exaggerated, moreover, in plausibly dangerous ways. The doctrine that structure should not be falsified, nor the appearance of it feared, was cast into the dogma that it should always be visibly expressed. We are still told—though there has been, perhaps, very lately, a slight falling off in the vehemence of the telling—that nail-heads and rivets and hinges and supports and all similar means employed by the constructor to attain his ends *must* appear prominently to the eye. Truly, they *may,* and it is often wise to use them as the keynote of the ornamentation. But there is no artistic law—and, spite of Mr. Ruskin and Mr. Eastlake to the contrary, artistic laws are the only ones to be considered in art—why they should of necessity show, any more than all the stitches in our coatseams or all the dowels in a Greek column. The mediæval workman, so much quoted as authority, often, it is true, ornamented his constructive devices, because he was one of those who, wishing to elaborate everything they make, know by instinct just how to do it. But on occasions where he did not so wish he did his necessary devices with all complacency, and we may most assuredly do likewise. We are told that we must not have extension-tables, because they are "insincere." A better reason might be that they are certainly unbeautiful when extended. But as they are to be draped, this does not hold, and there is no possible artistic (or moral) reason why they should not pull out if convenient. There is no greater "insincerity" and affectation than to sacrifice a real convenience for the sake of something that does not do its work so well. Nor does this advocate the toleration of ugliness, for if we were true artists we should be able so to shape *anything* that it would not be unpleasant to the eye or jar with neighboring objects capable of still higher beauty.

Furniture upholstered throughout is another thing that has been forbidden. Here the complaint is that it looks as if it had no structure at all, because none is palpable. This is absurd, for the outlines and the mode of covering show the construction as distinctly as plump human flesh shows the bones of humanity beneath it. There is no more artistic necessity for the tangible exhibition of constructive devices in the one case than in the other. And there is, I reiterate, and can be, no question of morality and "sincerity" in the matter. The laws of art require that structure be indicated sufficiently to *satisfy the eye.* Surely, more is not a necessity on the small scale of interior fittings when more has never been demanded in architecture, the most constructive of the arts. The Gothic workman was quite content if his spire *looked* firm: no tender conscience impelled him to exhibit the true causes of its firmness. And no tender conscience, moreover, forbade his creating false ones to reassure the doubting eye—false ones which simulated the strength that was really obtained in quite other ways.

And the Venetian calmly plastered out the structural lines of his palace-front, and was satisfied when Giorgione laid his fresco without regard for them.[2] This very work of stuccoing, by the way, is another thing that has been most utterly condemned, especially in England, where it is far more usual than with us. But the true fact is forgotten. Stucco is not intrinsically immoral. English stucco is bad because utterly hideous, while Venetian stucco was admirable because more beautiful than stone or marble. Surely it was as artistic as a wall where every brick may be counted in unmitigated sincerity of shape and color.

As we have seen it to be with form, so has it also been with material. It was necessary at first to strongly advocate simplicity. We had no eye for intrinsic beauty, and we fondly thought to buy it with many ducats. Is not this belief, that costly things as such are more beautiful than cheap things can be, merely the love of elaboration in another shape, merely another form of the terror of simplicity? When we could not afford expensive things we sought to imitate them in cheaper wares. When this was manifestly impossible, the cheap things were abandoned to their inherent ugliness. It was wise to disregard them, for they could not be improved. Wall-papers heavy with gilding, lace curtains whose patterns we did not notice, stiff silks crude in color and ugly of fold,— these were of necessity beautiful because costly. Where these could not be had our walls went white and our windows bare. Effects of rare building materials might be imitated after a fashion. So we grained our woodwork and marbled our papers, and painted our oilcloths in parody of mosaic flooring. And up stairs, where this was not attempted, we gave up our woodwork, like our walls, to the despair of unvaried whiteness. Here, again, it will be seen, simplicity needed to be taught, and was well taught through the gospel of "sincerity." It was necessary to do away with the painted wood's pretence of natural grain, with the ghastly veining of glazed-paper marble, with the coarse machine-work that aped hand-carving, with the bas-reliefs and mouldings that were only glued on, with the marble mantels whose figure- and flower-sculpture and the frescoed walls whose figure- and flower-painting were alike the hideous record of untrained hands and unsensitive eyes. And it was necessary, besides abolishing all this, to show that beauty might be won from cheap materials as from simple shapes. We soon learned to paper our walls with twenty-five cent hangings of soft and gracious tints, to paint our pine doors in unison, to curtain our windows with cheesecloth or burlapping, to stain our floors and then soften them with rag rugs, to build our chairs and tables perfectly straight and plain; and, so doing, to make our rooms more satisfactory, more artistic, more beautiful in every way, than were the gaudy parlors of the aristocracy or the white walls and hair-cloth of the middle classes. But when we went on to say that cheap materials had some inherent moral value unshared by their costlier sisters, when we began to pride ourselves on having drawn beauty from simplicity to such an extent that we scorned the aid of richer fabrics, we almost made the new movement ridiculous. We have already begun to see the folly of such a mood, and the "æsthetico-economical school," as it has been called, no longer dares to arrogate all virtue to itself. Better pretty chintz than ugly satin, but better still, a thousand times, a beautiful brocade, an Oriental embroidery, an embossed velvet. And better a thousand times marble, rare woods, gold and bronze than their cheaper substitutes, if only, I repeat, style and workmanship be as good.

With color—to pass to our second dogma—the case has been similar. It is not too much to say that a few years ago we were absolutely destitute of the sense of color—apathetically cold to its vivid or its delicate charms, and protected by our apathy against its most violent offences. The middle-class parlor was white and black, with a raw and glaring Brussels carpet; and in more wealthy neighborhoods the dark-green dining-room, the bright-yellow drawing-room and crimson library of one house were varied in the next by the mere substitution of blue or crimson for the drawing-room, green for the library, and tan-color, perhaps, for the dining-room. It was necessary to begin our reform by preaching the folly of such absurd narrowness, by showing that there were a thousand available tints and combinations besides these five orthodox solid colors—by demonstrating that it was not well to furnish a whole room in one unvaried shade, or imperative that a color be glaring in order to be lovely. More than this. It was necessary to do away entirely with most of the colors in use, since they *were* glaring rather than simply bright, and since our eyes could not appreciate the difference. So the virtues of dead colors and half-tints and manifold slight contrasts and combinations of nearly allied shades were preached, and preached to our infinite benefit. It would have been hopeless to say, "Keep your bright colors, but purify and grade and combine and contrast them, and relieve or soften or intensify them with duller tints." We could not have done it. The trumpet-tones of red and yellow, the still more unmanageable force of vivid blue, the startling intensity of white, the strong voices of light green and deep purple were utterly beyond our control. They stunned and confused us, and we were wise to study the laws of harmony and educate our perceptive powers by means of the lower, softer, more easily managed harmonies of brown and gray and olive, russet, sage, cream, maroon and all dusky tints. Successful results were more easily achieved with them, and partial failures were not so shocking. Great, indeed, is the delight they have afforded to eyes accustomed to a glaring color in monotonous extension or in painful relief against gilded furniture and dead-white walls. But when we go on to claim for our *feuille-morte* coloring the monopoly of all artistic and decorative value—

yes, even when we accord it the lion's share of such value—we go very far wrong. The most highly developed color-sense has *always* sought the brightest colors, but knew how to get them of just the right kind. It has been well said that no color can be too intense if of the proper quality. What we fail to realize is, that between one bright tint and another bright tint of the same color there may be all the difference there is between richest beauty and distressing ugliness. Half-tints, on the contrary, are almost always good, and are more or less easy of combination. They never can sin as flagrantly as the pronounced colors, which so far surpass them in possibilities of radiant excellence. In color, as in other things, mediocrity is the safest, but not the most glorious, path. And in art, as in all things, the degradation of the very best results in the very worst.

· · ·

Two of our three self-imposed dogmas have now been noticed—the dogma that preaches a so-called "sincerity" in form, and the one that preaches the reticence of a low key in color. There still remains for consideration the third dogma, which demands that a line be drawn between decorative and representative art, and that the former be restricted to "conventional" design. All three dogmas are, of course, more or less connected with each other, but this last is held with the greatest tenacity and viewed as the most important. So it threatens to outlive the others, and have a more deadening effect upon our artistic future.

NOTES

1. Charles Eastlake, *Hints on Household Taste in Furniture, Upholstery, and Other Details* (London, 1868).

2. Giorgione (1477/78–1510) is considered the founder of the High Renaissance style in Venice and is known to have painted frescoes, which have for the most part vanished.

LOUIS SULLIVAN

Ornament in Architecture

I take it as self-evident that a building, quite devoid of ornament, may convey a noble and dignified sentiment by virtue of mass and proportion. It is not evident to me that ornament can intrinsically heighten these elemental qualities. Why, then, should we use ornament? Is not a noble and simple dignity sufficient? Why should we ask more?

If I answer the question in entire candor, I should say that it would be greatly for our æsthetic good if we should refrain entirely from the use of ornament for a period of years, in order that our thought might concentrate acutely upon the production of buildings well formed and comely in the nude. We should thus perforce eschew many undesirable things, and learn by contrast how effective it is to think in a natural, vigorous and wholesome way. This step taken, we might safely inquire to what extent a decorative application of ornament would enhance the beauty of our structures—what new charm it would give them.

If we have then become well grounded in pure and simple forms we will reverse them; we will refrain instinctively from vandalism; we will be loath to do aught that may make these forms less pure, less noble. We shall have learned, however, that ornament is mentally a luxury, not a necessary, for we shall have discerned the limitations as well as the great value of unadorned masses. We have in us romanticism, and feel a craving to express it. We feel intuitively that our strong, athletic and simple forms will carry with natural ease the raiment of which we dream, and that our buildings thus clad in a garment of poetic imagery, half hid as it were in choice products of loom and mine, will appeal with redoubled power, like a sonorous melody overlaid with harmonious voices.

I conceive that a true artist will reason substantially in this way; and that, at the culmination of his powers, he may realize this ideal. I believe that architectural ornament brought forth in this spirit is desirable, because beautiful and inspiring; that ornament brought forth in any other spirit is lacking in the higher possibilities.

That is to say, a building which is truly a work of art (and I consider none other) is in its nature, essence and physical being an emotional expression. This being so, and I feel deeply that it is so, it must have, almost literally, a life. It follows from this living principle that an ornamented structure should be characterized by this quality, namely, that the same emotional impulse shall flow throughout harmoniously into its varied forms of expression—of which, while the mass-composition is the more profound, the decorative ornamentation is the more intense. Yet must both spring from the same source of feeling.

I am aware that a decorated building, designed upon this principle, will require in its creator a high and sustained emotional tension, an organic singleness of idea and purpose maintained to the last. The completed work will tell of this; and if it be designed with sufficient depth of feeling and simplicity of mind, the more intense the heat in which it was conceived, the more serene and noble will it remain forever as a monument of man's eloquence. It is this quality that characterizes the great monuments of the past. It is this certainly that opens a vista toward the future.

To my thinking, however, the mass-composition and the decorative system of a structure such as I have hinted at should be separable from each other only in theory and for purposes of analytical study. I believe, as I have said, that an excellent and beautiful building may be designed that shall bear no ornament whatever; but I believe just as firmly that a decorated structure, harmoniously conceived, well considered, cannot be stripped of its system of ornament without destroying its individuality.

It has been hitherto somewhat the fashion to speak of ornament, without perhaps too much levity of thought, as a thing to be put on or omitted, as the case might be. I hold to the contrary—that the presence or absence of ornament should, certainly in serious work, be determined at the very beginnings of the design. This is perhaps strenuous insistence, yet I justify and urge it on the ground that creative architecture is an art so fine that its power is manifest in rhythms of great subtlety, as much so indeed as those of musical art, its nearest relative.

If, therefore, our artistic rhythms—a result—are to be significant, our prior meditations—the cause—must be so. It matters then greatly what is the prior inclination of the mind, so much so indeed as it matters what is the inclination of a cannon when the shot is fired.

If we assume that our contemplated building need not be a work of living art, or at least a striving for it, that our civilization does not yet demand such, my plea is useless. I can proceed only on the supposition that our culture has progressed to the stage wherein an imitative or reminiscential art does not wholly satisfy, and that there exists an actual desire for spontaneous expression. I assume, too, that we are to begin, not by shutting our eyes and ears to the unspeakable past, but rather by opening our hearts, in enlightened sympathy and filial regard, to the voice of our times.

Nor do I consider this the place or the time to inquire if after all there is really such a thing as creative art—whether a final analysis does not reveal the great artist, not as creator, but rather as interpreter and prophet. When the time does come that the luxury of this inquiry becomes a momentous necessary, our architecture shall have neared its final development. It will suffice then to say that I conceive a work of fine art to be really this: a made thing, more or less attractive, regarding which the casual observer may see a part, but no observer all, that is in it.

It must be manifest that an ornamental design will be more beautiful if it seems a part of the surface or substance that receives it than if it looks "stuck on," so to speak. A little observation will lead one to see that in the former case there exists a peculiar sympathy between the ornament and the structure, which is absent in the latter. Both structure and ornament obviously benefit by this sympathy; each enhancing the value of the other. And this, I take it, is the preparatory basis of what may be called an organic system of ornamentation.

The ornament, as a matter of fact, is applied in the sense of being cut in or cut on, or otherwise done: yet it should appear, when completed, as though by the outworking of some beneficent agency it had come forth from the very substance of the material and was there by the same right that a flower appears amid the leaves of its parent plant.

Here by this method we make a species of contact, and the spirit that animates the mass is free to flow into the ornament—they are no longer two things but one thing.

If now we bring ourselves to close and reflective observation, how evident it becomes that if we wish to insure an actual, a poetic unity, the ornament should appear, not as something receiving the spirit of the structure, but as a thing expressing that spirit by virtue of differential growth.

It follows then, by the logic of growth, that a certain kind of ornament should appear on a certain kind of structure, just as a certain kind of leaf must appear on a certain kind of tree. An elm leaf would not "look well" on a pine-tree—a pine-needle seems more "in keeping." So, an ornament or scheme of organic decoration befitting a structure composed on broad and massive lines would not be in sympathy with a delicate and dainty one. Nor should the ornamental systems of buildings of any various sorts be interchangeable as between these buildings. For buildings should possess an individuality as marked as that which exists among men, making them distinctly separable from each other, however strong the racial or family resemblance may be.

Everyone knows and feels how strongly individual is each man's voice, but few pause to consider that a voice, though of another kind, speaks from every existing building. What is the character of these voices? Are they harsh or smooth, noble or ignoble? Is the speech they utter prose or poetry?

Mere difference in outward form does not constitute individuality. For this a harmonious inner character is necessary; and as we speak of human nature, we may by analogy apply a similar phrase to buildings.

A little study will enable one soon to discern and appreciate the more obvious individualities of buildings; further study, and comparison of impressions, will bring to view forms and qualities that were at first hidden; a deeper analysis will yield a host of new sensations, developed by the discovery of qualities hitherto unsuspected—we have found evidences of the gift of expression, and have felt the significance of it; the mental and emotional gratification caused by these discoveries leads on to deeper and deeper searching, until, in great works, we fully learn that what was obvious was least, and what was hidden, nearly all.

Few works can stand the test of close, business-like analysis—they are soon emptied. But no analysis, however sympathetic, persistent or profound, can exhaust a truly great work of art. For the qualities that make it thus great are not mental only, but psychic, and therefore signify the highest expression and embodiment of individuality.

Now, if this spiritual and emotional quality is a noble attribute when it resides in the mass of a building, it must, when applied to a virile and synthetic scheme of ornamentation, raise this at once from the level of triviality to the heights of dramatic expression.

The possibilities of ornamentation, so considered, are marvelous; and before us open, as a vista, conceptions so rich, so varied, so poetic, so inexhaustible, that the mind pauses in its flight and life indeed seems but a span.

Reflect now the light of this conception full and free upon joint considerations of mass-composition, and how serious, how eloquent, how inspiring is the imagery, how noble the dramatic force that shall make sublime our future architecture.

America is the only land in the whole earth wherein a dream like this may be realized; for here alone tradition is without shackles, and the soul of man free to grow, to mature, to seek its own.

But for this we must turn again to Nature, and hearkening to her melodious voice, learn, as children learn, the accent of its rhythmic cadences. We must view the sunrise with ambition, the twilight wistfully; then, when our eyes have learned to see, we shall know how great is the simplicity of nature, that it brings forth in serenity such endless variation. We shall learn from this to consider man and his ways, to the end that we behold the unfolding of the soul in all its beauty, and know that the fragrance of a living art shall float again in the garden of our world.

ADOLF LOOS

Ornament and Crime

The human embryo in the womb passes through all the evolutionary stages of the animal kingdom. When man is born, his sensory impressions are like those of a newborn puppy. His childhood takes him through all the metamorphoses of human history. At 2 he sees with the eyes of a Papuan, at 4 with those of an ancient Teuton, at 6 with those of Socrates, at 8 with those of Voltaire. When he is 8 he becomes aware of violet, the colour discovered by the eighteenth century, because before that the violet was blue and the purple-snail red. The physicist points today to colours in the solar spectrum which already have a name but the knowledge of which is reserved for the men of the future.

The child is amoral. To our eyes, the Papuan is too. The Papuan kills his enemies and eats them. He is not a criminal. But when modern man kills someone and eats him he is either a criminal or a degenerate. The Papuan tattoos his skin, his boat, his paddles, in short everything he can lay hands on. He is not a criminal. The modern man who tattoos himself is either a criminal or a degenerate. There are prisons in which eighty per cent of the inmates show tattoos. The tattooed who are not in prison are latent criminals or degenerate aristocrats. If someone who is tattooed dies at liberty, it means he has died a few years before committing a murder.

The urge to ornament one's face and everything within reach is the start of plastic art. It is the baby talk of painting. All art is erotic.

The first ornament that was born, the cross, was erotic in origin. The first work of art, the first artistic act which the first artist, in order to rid himself of his surplus energy, smeared on the wall. A horizontal dash: the prone woman. A vertical dash: the man penetrating her. The man who created it felt the same urge as Beethoven, he was in the same heaven in which Beethoven created the *Ninth Symphony*.

But the man of our day who, in response to an inner urge, smears the walls with erotic symbols is a criminal or a degenerate. It goes without saying that this impulse most frequently assails people with such symptoms of degeneracy in the lavatory. A country's culture can be assessed by the extent to which its lavatory walls are smeared. In the child this is a natural phenomenon: his first artistic expression is to scribble erotic symbols on the walls. But what is natural to the Papuan and the child is a symptom of degeneracy in the modern adult. I have made the following discovery and I pass it on to the world: *The evolution of culture is synonymous with the removal of ornament from utilitarian objects.* I believed that with this discovery I was bringing joy to the world; it has not thanked me. People were sad and hung their heads. What depressed them was the realization that they could produce no new ornaments. Are we alone, the people of the nineteenth century, supposed to be unable to do what any Negro, all the races and periods before us have been able to do? What mankind created without ornament in earlier millenia was thrown away without a thought and abandoned to destruction. We possess no joiner's benches from the Carolingian era, but every trifle that displays the least ornament has been collected and cleaned and palatial buildings have been erected to house it. Then people walked sadly about between the glass cases and felt ashamed of their impotence. Every age had its style, is our age alone to be refused a style? By style, people meant ornament. Then I said: Weep not! See, therein lies the greatness of our age, that it is incapable of producing a new ornament. We have outgrown ornament; we have fought our way through to freedom from ornament. See, the time is nigh, fulfilment awaits us. Soon the streets of the city will glisten like white walls. Like Zion, the holy city, the capital of heaven. Then fulfilment will be come.

There were black albs, clerical gentlemen, who wouldn't put up with that. Mankind was to go on panting in slavery to ornament. Men had gone far enough for ornament no longer to arouse feelings of pleasure in them, far enough for a tattooed face not to heighten the aesthetic effect, as among the Papuans, but to reduce it. Far enough to take pleasure in a plain cigarette case, whereas an ornamented one, even at the same price, was not bought. They were happy in their clothes and glad they didn't have to go around in red velvet hose with gold braid like fairground monkeys. And I said: See, Goethe's deathchamber is finer than all Renaissance splendour and a plain piece of furniture more beautiful than any inlaid and carved museum pieces.[1] Goethe's language is finer than all the ornaments of Pegnitz's shepherds.

The black albs heard this with displeasure, and the state, whose task it is to halt the cultural development of the peoples, made the question of the development and revival of ornament its own. Woe to the state whose revolutions are in the care of the *Hofrats!* Very soon we saw in the Wiener Kunstgewerbemuseum (Vienna Museum of Applied Art) a sideboard known as "the rich haul of fish," soon there were cupboards bearing the name "the enchanted princess" or something similar referring to the ornament with which this unfortunate piece of furniture was covered. The Austrian state took its task so seriously that it is making sure the foot-rags used on the frontiers of the Austro-Hungarian monarchy do not disappear. It is forcing every cultivated man of 20 for three years to wear foot-rags instead of manufactured footwear. After all, every state starts from the premise that a people on a lower footing is easier to rule.

Very well, the ornament disease is recognized by the state and subsidized with state funds. But I see in this a retrograde step. I don't accept the objection that ornament heightens a cultivated person's joy in life, don't accept the objection contained in the words: "But if the ornament is beautiful!" Ornament does not heighten my joy in life or the joy in life of any cultivated person. If I want to eat a piece of gingerbread I choose one that is quite smooth and not a piece representing a heart or a baby or a rider, which is covered all over with ornaments. The man of the fifteenth century won't understand me. But all modern people will. The advocate of ornament believes that my urge for simplicity is in the nature of a mortification. No, respected professor at the school of applied art, I am not mortifying myself! The show dishes of past centuries, which display all kinds of ornaments to make the peacocks, pheasants and lobsters look more tasty, have exactly the opposite effect on me. I am horrified when I go through a cookery exhibition and think that I am meant to eat these stuffed carcasses. I eat roast beef.

The enormous damage and devastation caused in aesthetic development by the revival of ornament would be easily made light of, for no one, not even the power of the state, can halt mankind's evolution. It can only be delayed. We can wait. But it is a crime against the national economy that it should result in a waste of human labour, money, and material. Time cannot make good this damage.

The speed of cultural evolution is reduced by the stragglers. I perhaps am living in 1908, but my neighbour is living in 1900 and the man across the way in 1880. It is unfortunate for a state when the culture of its inhabitants is spread over such a great period of time. The peasants of Kals are living in the twelfth century. And there were peoples taking part in the Jubilee parade (of the Emperor Franz Joseph) who would have been considered backward even during the migration of the nations. Happy the land that has no such stragglers and marauders. Happy America!

Among ourselves there are unmodern people even in the cities, stragglers from the eighteenth century, who are horrified by a picture with purple shadows because they cannot yet see purple. The pheasant on which the chef has been working all day long tastes better to them and they prefer the cigarette case with Renaissance ornaments to the smooth one. And what is it like in the country? Clothes and household furniture all belong to past centuries. The peasant isn't a Christian, he is still a pagan.

The stragglers slow down the cultural evolution of the nations and of mankind; not only is ornament produced by criminals but also a crime is committed through the fact that ornament inflicts serious injury on people's health, on the national budget and hence on cultural evolution. If two people live side by side with the same needs, the same demands on life and the same income but belonging to different cultures, economically speaking the following process can be observed: the twentieth-century man will get richer and richer, the eighteenth-century man poorer and poorer. I am assuming that both live according to their inclinations. The twentieth-century man can satisfy his needs with a far lower capital outlay and hence can save money. The vegetable he enjoys is simply boiled in water and has a little butter put on it. The other man likes it equally well only when honey and nuts have been added to it and someone has spent hours cooking it. Ornamented plates are very expensive, whereas the white crockery from which the modern man likes to eat is cheap. The one accumulates savings, the other debts. It is the same with whole nations. Woe when a people remains behind in cultural evolution! The British are growing wealthier and we poorer . . .

Even greater is the damage done by ornament to the nation that produces it. Since ornament is no longer a natural product of our culture, so that it is a phenomenon either of backwardness or degeneration, the work of the ornamentor is no longer adequately remunerated.

The relationship between the earnings of a woodcarver and a turner, the criminally low wages paid to the embroideress and the lacemaker are well known. The ornamentor has to work twenty hours to achieve the income earned by a modern worker in eight. Ornament generally increases the cost of an article; nevertheless it happens that an ornamented object whose raw material cost the same and which demonstrably took three times as long to make is offered at half the price of a smooth object. Omission of ornament results in a reduction in the manufacturing time and an increase in wages. The Chinese carver works for sixteen hours, the American worker for eight. If I pay as much for a smooth cigarette case as for an ornamented one, the difference in the working time belongs to the worker. And if there were no ornament at all—a situation that may perhaps come about in some thousands of years—man would only have to work four hours instead of eight, because half of the work done today is devoted to ornament. Ornament is wasted labour power and hence wasted health. It has always been so.

Since ornament is no longer organically linked with our culture, it is also no longer the expression of our culture. The ornament that is manufactured today has no connexion with us, has absolutely no human connexions, no connexion with the world order. It is not capable of developing. What happened to Otto Eckmann's ornament, or van de Velde's?[2] The artist has always stood at the forefront of mankind full of vigour and health. But the modern ornamentalist is a straggler or a pathological phenomenon. He himself will repudiate his own products three years later. To cultivated people they are immediately intolerable; others become aware of their intolerable character only years later. Where are Otto Eckmann's works today? Modern ornament has no parents and no progeny, no past and no future. By uncultivated people, to whom the grandeur of our age is a book with seven seals, it is greeted joyfully and shortly afterwards repudiated.

Mankind is healthier than ever; only a few people are sick. But these few tyrannize over the worker who is so healthy that he cannot invent ornament. They force him to execute in the most varied materials the ornaments which they have invented.

Changes of ornament lead to a premature devaluation of the labour product. The worker's time and the material employed are capital goods that are wasted. I have stated the proposition: the form of an object lasts, that is to say remains tolerable, as long as the object lasts physically. I will try to explain this. A suit will change its form more often than a valuable fur. A lady's ball gown, intended for only one night, will change its form more quickly than a desk. But woe if a desk has to be changed as quickly as a ball gown because the old form has become intolerable; in that case the money spent on the desk will have been lost.

This is well known to the ornamentalist, and Austrian ornamentalists are trying to make the best of this shortcoming. They say: "We prefer a consumer who has a set of furniture that becomes intolerable to him after ten years, and who is consequently forced to refurnish every ten years, to one who only buys an object when the old one is worn out. Industry demands this. Millions are employed as a result of the quick change."

This seems to be the secret of the Austrian national economy. How often do we hear someone say when there is a fire: "Thank God, now there will be work for people to do again." In that case I know a splendid solution. Set fire to a town, set fire to the empire, and everyone will be swimming in money and prosperity. Manufacture furniture which after three years can be used for firewood, metal fittings that have to be melted down after four years because even at an auction sale it is impossible to get a tenth of the original value of the material and labour, and we shall grow wealthier and wealthier.

The loss does not hit only the consumer; above all it hits the producer. Today ornament on things that have evolved away from the need to be ornamented represents wasted labour and ruined material. If all objects would last aesthetically as long as they do physically, the consumer could pay a price for them that would enable the worker to earn more money and work shorter hours. For an object I am sure I can use to its full extent I willingly pay four times as much as for one that is inferior in form or material. I happily pay forty kronen for my boots, although in a different shop I could get boots for ten kronen. But in those trades that groan under the tyranny of the ornamentalist no distinction is made between good and bad workmanship. The work suffers because no one is willing to pay its true value.

And this is a good thing, because these ornamented objects are tolerable only when they are of the most miserable quality. I get over a fire much more easily when I hear that only worthless trash has been burned. I can be pleased about the trash in the Künstlerhaus because I know that it will be manufactured in a few days and taken to pieces in one. But throwing gold coins instead of stones, lighting a cigarette with a banknote, pulverizing and drinking a pearl create an unaesthetic effect.

Ornamented things first create a truly unaesthetic effect when they have been executed in the best material and with the greatest care and have taken long hours of labour. I cannot exonerate myself from having initially demanded quality work, but naturally not for that kind of thing.

The modern man who holds ornament sacred as a sign of the artistic superabundance of past ages will immediately recognize the tortured, strained, and morbid quality of modern ornaments. No ornament can any longer be made today by anyone who lives on our cultural level.

It is different with the individuals and peoples who have not yet reached this level.

I am preaching to the aristocrat, I mean the person who stands at the pinnacle of mankind and yet has the deepest understanding for the distress and want of those below. He well understands the Kaffir who weaves ornaments into his fabric according to a particular rhythm that only comes into view when it is unravelled, the Persian who weaves his carpet, the Slovak peasant woman who embroiders her lace, the old lady who crochets wonderful things with glass beads and silk. The aristocrat lets them be; he knows that the hours in which they work are their holy hours. The revolutionary would go to them and say: "It's all nonsense." Just as he would pull down the little old woman from the wayside crucifix and tell her: "There is no God." The atheist among the aristocrats, on the other hand, raises his hat when he passes a church.

My shoes are covered all over with ornaments consisting of scallops and holes. Work done by the shoemaker for which he was never paid. I go to the shoemaker and say: "You ask thirty kronen for a pair of shoes. I will pay you forty kronen." I have thereby raised this man to heights of bliss for which he will thank me by work and material infinitely better than would be called for by the additional price. He is happy. Happiness rarely enters his house. Here is a man who understands him, who values his work and does not doubt his honesty. He already sees the finished shoes in his mind's eye. He knows where the best leather is to be found at the present time; he knows which craftsman he will entrust the shoes to; and the shoes will be so covered in scallops and holes as only an elegant shoe can be. And then I say to him: "But there's one condition. The shoes must be completely smooth." With this I have cast him down from the heights of bliss to the pit of despondency. He has less work, but I have taken away all his joy.

I am preaching to the aristocrat. I tolerate ornaments on my own body, when they constitute the joy of my fellow men. Then they are my joy too. I can tolerate the ornaments of the Kaffir, the Persian, the Slovak peasant woman, my shoemaker's ornaments, for they all have no other way of attaining the high points of their existence. We have art, which has taken the place of ornament. After the toils and troubles of the day we go to Beethoven or to Tristan. This my shoemaker cannot do. I mustn't deprive him of his joy, since I have nothing else to put in its place. But anyone who goes to the *Ninth Symphony* and then sits down and designs a wallpaper pattern is either a confidence trickster or a degenerate. Absence of ornament has brought the other arts to unsuspected heights. Beethoven's symphonies would never have been written by a man who had to walk about in silk, satin, and lace. Anyone who goes around in a velvet coat today is not an artist but a buffoon or a house painter. We have grown finer, more subtle. The nomadic herdsmen had to distinguish themselves by various colours; modern man uses his clothes as a mask. So immensely strong is his individuality that it can no longer be expressed in articles of clothing. Freedom from ornament is a sign of spiritual strength. Modern man uses the ornaments of earlier or alien cultures as he sees fit. He concentrates his own inventiveness on other things.

NOTES

1. See Goethe's excerpt and biographical note in this volume; Loos is here praising the simplicity of his house in Weimar just as Muthesius does (see his excerpt in Part I of this volume).

2. Otto Eckmann (1865–1902) was one of the founders of the *Jugendstil* in Munich, described in note 4 of Muthesius's excerpt; see van de Velde's excerpt and biographical note in this volume.

KARL GROSZ

Ornament

Rich and varied are the treasures of ornament that the millennia have bequeathed to us. But have we taken possession of our inheritance? Have we "earned" these treasures, that we may truly "own" them?[1] Some will say Yes, as a matter of course; but some will demur; and there are others who will not hear of such an inheritance. They think themselves man enough to create ornament for their own age by their own unaided efforts.

One thing, at all events, is certain: that, where ornament is concerned, we are currently in a predicament. Not just at present, either, but for some time past. Let us look back one hundred years. The "Empire Style" of those days plucked tidbits from the inheritance of antiquity. A certain number of ornamental motifs was superficially imposed on every material, with a well-developed feeling for beauty, but without the creative force that had enabled the "Renaissance" to make the classical inheritance intellectually its own. Techniques have a creative power, and this has its own part to play in ornament: a truth that the Empire Style almost entirely forgot.

Then came the "Biedermeier Style," with its solid craftsmanship and its bourgeois principles.[2] But this, too, suffered in the absence of those creative talents that had decamped into High Art as far back as the early Renaissance, and no evolution of ornament took place. A ruthless upstart, the "Nineteenth-Century Industrial Style," now took command. The ancestral inheritance, with its treasures of ornament from successive millennia, became a quarry, which the Industrial Style plundered to gratify the whims of fashion. So far from "earning" those treasures, it stole them for its own nefarious dealings.

Alongside this Industrial Style there was an unassertive flowering of artistic talents which sought, in the "Works of Our Fathers" section of the Munich Exhibition of 1876, to revive the fine, old spirit of good ornament and to restore its treasures to the German lands by infusing them with true artistry. But the Industrial Style debased and counterfeited all this gold, and the true prospectors found little support.

The close of the century brought revolution and anarchy. Abandoning all hope of healthy evolution, the reformers overturned all historical barriers to give free rein to the artistic impulse. They began with ornament. Designers went back to Nature, which they sought to confine in new ornamental fetters. From Belgium came a concurrent attempt to solve the problem by means of abstract lines and forms. Both of these honest artistic endeavors were promptly purloined by the Industrial Style, in its fashionable craving for novelty; the result was the talentless travesty of ornament that held the market for awhile under the appellation of *Jugendstil*.[3] The artists' intentions were lost to view.

What were the artists' intentions? First of all, they wanted to create a new kind of ornamentation; but they soon realized that no reform could begin with ornament. Form is the main thing, and decoration comes later. Initially, therefore, all was form, plain and simple. This was natural and quite right. It was necessary to start from scratch, from a simple scale of notes, whether the aim was to appropriate all that was good in former periods, in a spirit of freedom and proper understanding, or to create new compositions. This stage—that of learning from scratch—is where we stand today; and we must be aware that, with the "outcry for ornament," we are now facing the prospect of a highly significant, but also a highly perilous phase for our movement.

Some things must never again have anything to do with ornament. Think of the shapes of our conveyances, notably the automobile, and of our weapons. Here, a sensitive concern with function finds fulfillment in pure, beautiful formal design. The same applies to many of our utilitarian objects, in which the artistry that permeates the form, and the quality of materials and workmanship, are such as to satisfy even the most exalted demands for luxury. In earlier times, of course, weapons, vehicles, utensils, buildings, and tools were ornamented; but this was simply to set them apart from the mass of everyday objects. Now, thanks to the Industrial Style, it is the mass that is swamped in cheap ornament; to stand out, one has only to seek refinement in simplicity. Such is the reversal that we have just experienced.

Now we yearn for enrichment, for ornament, once more. Experience teaches us, however, that all enrichment must be inseparable from quality; it must be a sign of exceptional value, and the utmost caution must be exercised in coining it into small change. The question arises at once: Must enrichment be ornament?

No!—The prime enrichment of a building is a good distribution of masses. A fine articulation, moldings, cornices, string courses, dressings, are enrichments that often suffice without any admixture of ornament. The same holds good for furniture. Anyone who has seen, on old pieces, how often the surface itself—from a simple plane to a rich array of moldings—creates a vigorous decorative effect, will not be tempted to mistake enrichment for ornament. In metalwork and ceramics, too, many opportunities arise wholly from the aesthetic that is implicit in the technique. If the evolution of our ornamental design is not to involve an unnatural hiatus, we must first cultivate this enrichment without ornament, so to speak, which the sensitive practitioner has always had at his fingers' ends.

The origin of ornament does not lie in the natural sense of beauty: it lies in the intensification of that sense into creative, artistic skill. Far back in the mists of time, when man first sought to add especial meaning to his implements by scratching natural representations onto them, ornament was born. Over the millennia, it evolved and passed from nation to nation until the Gothic age. The Renaissance was the first period in which there was a deliberate revival of an earlier style. The power of that rebirth was felt for centuries. But from the Empire Style onward, as I have said, this power of reviving earlier styles began to fail. We now face the question: What next?

In the course of a few decades, we have explored and studied the ornamental motifs of every existing style; we have attempted to derive ornaments directly from natural motifs, and to extract them from abstract forms and lines; but we have not really progressed.

The reason is probably that in all of these experiments we have concentrated too exclusively on the issue of ornament. Three things are required for success. First, the study of Nature, which we need in order to collect motifs that will make us as independent as possible of those used in the past, and also in order to acquire a sensitivity to form and color. Then, the study of the decorative effects of the products of every age and every nation. This is necessary in order to impress upon us the wealth of extant beauty; but it is not to be confused with the copying of ornamental motifs. It remains to be seen whether we possess the power to add some truly new ornamental effects, with an evolutionary potential of their own: at all events, such experiments prove tolerable only where a mature artistic sensibility lies behind them. Finally, the ornament must be integrated in such a way as to form an organic part of the given formal context. With this, as with all formal design, creative ability is an essential prerequisite; and it will take time for new types of application to crystallize.

The consequence for us today is this: we must seek stimulus and inspiration in the varied decorative effects achieved in the past; we must rework these in the light of our own study of Nature, and—most difficult of all—we must take the results and make them fit organically into the given formal context. This demands a great deal of study and talent, if we are not to relapse once more into feeble stylistic imitation. Anything that still has an antiquarian air has yet to be adequately reshaped to suit the age we live in and the people we are. Many things have lost their intuitive justification for us, and these are therefore no longer available to us as sources. We must learn to face facts. By all means, let the ablest among us conduct experiments; but we must be serious, and reject all frivolous ventures, whether artistic or technical. In this way, new ornamental values can in due course emerge for all to use.

So much for the artistic aspects of the question of contemporary ornament; but there is also an economic issue. Ornamental decoration, applied to objects created to satisfy mass needs, is a debasement of values. And yet the masses instinctively crave decorated things, and they must not be denied. Here, industry will attain its ends only by keeping in view one fundamental principle: that all decoration must possess both technical and artistic qualities. Then, the hierarchy of effects, from modest to ambitious, will simply be a matter of price: for even the simplest thing can be beautiful. Industry will never achieve healthy economic objectives if it tries to imitate elaborate decorative values on the cheap: this imposes on the ignorance of a mass public and ultimately undermines industry itself and its good name.

The noblest and truest objective, for all those branches of industry that work in three dimensions, will be the ennobling of form. Beauty of form satisfies even in the absence of decoration; in the past, the Industrial Style sought to smother bad form with cheap ornament. Quality, including technical quality, is essential if we are to pave the way for an ornamental design fit for the twentieth century.

If ornament is once more to become what it once was, and what it must enduringly remain—namely, a special distinction, something that causes an object to stand out from the mass—then it must be work of good quality. The very survival of applied art directly depends on this principle.

For the present, all this remains no more than a set of fine theories; they may seem nimble enough on paper, but the dead weight of commercial realities will reduce them to a snail's pace.

Let us maintain our optimism! The Werkbund has been set up for the specific purpose of holding together all those who, "in spite of everything," refuse to give up.[4] The problem of devising ornament to match our sensibilities is one to which the Werkbund will have to devote its particular attention.

NOTES

1. Goethe, *Faust*, I, "Nacht": "Was du ererbt von deinen Vätern hast, / Erwirb es, um es zu besitzen." (What your fathers have left you: earn it, that you may own it.)

2. On the Biedermeier Style see note 4 of the Muthesius excerpt in this volume.

3. On the *Jugendstil* see note 4 of the Muthesius excerpt.

4. The Deutscher Werkbund was an association of architects, designers, and industrialists. It was active from 1907 to 1934, and then from 1950; Muthesius was one of its founding members, along with Peter Behrens, Heinrich Tessenow, and others. It marked the end of the *Jugendstil* and the beginning of a new direction of German decorative arts toward industrial art.

OWEN JONES

"Ornament of Savage Tribes" and "Moresque Ornament"

CHAPTER I. ORNAMENT OF SAVAGE TRIBES

From the universal testimony of travellers it would appear, that there is scarcely a people, in however early a stage of civilisation, with whom the desire for ornament is not a strong instinct. The desire is absent in none, and it grows and increases with all in the ratio of their progress in civilisation. Man appears everywhere impressed with the beauties of Nature which surround him, and seeks to imitate to the extent of his power the works of the Creator.

Man's earliest ambition is to create. To this feeling must be ascribed the tattooing of the human face and body, resorted to by the savage to increase the expression by which he seeks to strike terror on his enemies or rivals, or to create what appears to him a new beauty [Plate 8].* As we advance higher, from the decoration of the rude tent or wigwam to the sublime works of a Phidias and Praxiteles, the same feeling is everywhere apparent: the highest ambition is still to create, to stamp on this earth the impress of an individual mind.[1]

From time to time a mind stronger than those around will impress itself

Plate 8. Female Head from New Zealand

*The tattooing on the head which we introduce from the Museum at Chester is very remarkable, as showing that in this very barbarous practice the principles of the very highest ornamental art are manifest, every line upon the face is the best adapted to develope the natural features.

on a generation, and carry with it a host of others of less power following in the same track, yet never so closely as to destroy the individual ambition to create; hence the cause of styles, and of the modification of styles. The efforts of a people in an early stage of civilisation are like those of children, though presenting a want of power, they possess a grace and *naïveté* rarely found in mid-age, and never in manhood's decline. It is equally so in the infancy of any art. Cimabue and Giotto have not the material charm of Raphael or the manly power of Michael Angelo, but surpass them both in grace and earnest truth.[2] The very command of means leads to their abuse: when Art struggles, it succeeds; when revelling in its own successes, it as signally fails. The pleasure we receive in contemplating the rude attempts at ornament of the most savage tribes arises from our appreciation of a difficulty accomplished; we are at once charmed by the evidence of the intention, and surprised at the simple and ingenious process by which the result is obtained. In fact, what we seek in every work of Art, whether it be humble or pretentious, is the evidence of mind,—the evidence of that desire to create to which we have referred, and which all, feeling a natural instinct within them, are satisfied with when they find it developed in others. It is strange, but so it is, that this evidence of mind will be more readily found in the rude attempts at ornament of a savage tribe than in the innumerable productions of a highly-advanced civilisation. Individuality decreases in the ratio of the power of production. When Art is manufactured by combined effort, not originated by individual effort, we fail to recognise those true instincts which constitute its greatest charm.

Plate 9. The ornaments on this Plate are from portions of clothing made chiefly from the bark of trees. Patterns No. 2 and 9 are from a dress brought by Mr. Oswald Brierly from Tongotabu, the principal of the Friendly Island group. It is made from thin sheets of the inner rind of the bark of a species of hibiscus, beaten out and united together so as to form one long parallelogram of cloth, which being wrapped many times round the body as a petticoat, and leaving the chest, arms, and shoulders bare, forms the only dress of the natives. Nothing, therefore, can be more primitive, and yet the arrangement of the pattern shows the most refined taste and skill. No. 9 is the border on the edge of the cloth; with the same limited means of production, it would be difficult to improve upon it. The patterns are formed by small wooden stamps, and although the work is somewhat rude and irregular in execution, the intention is everywhere apparent; and we are at once struck with the skilful balancing of the masses, and the judicious correction of the tendency of the eye to run in any one direction by opposing to them lines having an opposite tendency.

When Mr. Brierly visited the island one woman was the designer of all the patterns in use there, and for every new pattern she designed she received as a

Plate 9. The Ornament of Savage Tribes, I

reward a certain number of yards of cloth. The pattern No. 2 [Plate 9], from the same place, is equally an admirable lesson in composition which we may derive from an artist of a savage tribe. Nothing can be more judicious than the general arrangement of the four squares and the four red spots. Without the red spots on the yellow ground there would have been a great want of repose in the general arrangement; without the red lines round the red spots to carry the red through the yellow, it would have been still imperfect. Had the small red triangles turned outwards instead of inwards, the repose of the pattern would again have been lost, and the effect produced on the eye would have been that of squinting; as it is, the eye is centred in each square, and centred in each group by the red spots round the centre square. The stamps which form the pattern are very simple, each triangle and each leaf being a single stamp: we thus see how readily the possession of a simple tool, even by the most uncultivated, if guided by an instinctive observation of the forms in which all the works of Nature are arranged, would lead to the creation of all the geometrical arrangements of form with which we are acquainted. On the upper left-hand corner of pattern No. 2, the eight-pointed star is formed by eight applications of the same tool; as also the black flower with sixteen pointing inwards and sixteen pointing outwards. The most complicated patterns of the

Byzantine, Arabian, and Moresque mosaics would be generated by the same means. The secret of success in all ornament is the production of a broad general effect by the repetition of a few simple elements; variety should rather be sought in the arrangement of the several portions of a design, than in the multiplicity of varied forms.

The stamping of patterns on the coverings of the body, when either of skins of animals or material such as this, would be the first stage towards ornament after the tattooing of the body by an analogous process. In both there would remain a greater variety and individuality than in subsequent processes, which would become more mechanical. The first notions of weaving, which would be given by the plaiting of straws or strips of bark, instead of using them as thin sheets, would have equally the same result of gradually forming the mind to an appreciation of a proper disposition of masses [Plate 10]: the eye of the savage, accustomed only to look upon Nature's harmonies, would readily enter into the perception of the true balance both of form and colour; in point of fact, we find that it is so, that in savage ornament the true balance of both is always maintained.

After the formation of ornament by stamping and weaving, would naturally follow the desire of forming ornament in relief or carving. The weapons for defence or the chase would first attract attention. The most skilful and the bravest

would desire to be distinguished from their fellows by the possession of weapons, not only more useful, but more beautiful. The shape best fitted for the purpose having been found by experience, the enriching of the surface by carving would naturally follow; and the eye, already accustomed to the geometrical forms produced by weaving, the hand would seek to imitate them by a similar repetition of cuts of the knife. The ornaments on Plate 11 show this instinct very fully. They are executed with the utmost precision, and exhibit great taste and judgment in the distribution of the masses. Nos. 11 and 12 [Plate 11] are interesting, as showing how much this taste and skill may exist in the formation of geometrical patterns, whilst those resulting from curved lines, and the human form more especially, remain in the very first stage.

The ornaments in the woodcuts below [Plates 12, 13, 14] show a far higher advance in the distribution of curved lines, the twisted rope forming the type as it naturally would be of all curved lines in ornament. The uniting of two strands for additional strength would early accustom the eye to the spiral line, and we always find this form side by side with geometrical patterns formed by the interlacing of equal lines in the ornament of every savage tribe, and retained in the more advanced art of every civilised nation.

The ornament of a savage tribe, being the result of a natural instinct, is nec-

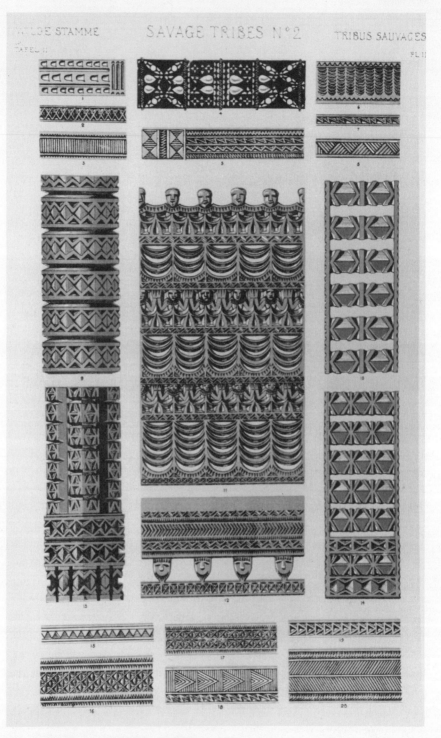

Plate 11. The Ornament of Savage Tribes, II

Plate 12. (top) Head of Canoe, New Guinea
Plate 13. (right) From the Side of the Canoe, New Zealand
Plate 14. (bottom) Head of Canoe, New Guinea

essarily always true to its purpose; whilst in much of the ornament of civilised nations, the first impulse which generated received forms being enfeebled by constant repetition, the ornament is oftentimes misapplied, and instead of first seeking the most convenient form and adding beauty, all beauty is destroyed, because all fitness, by superadding ornament to ill-contrived form. If we would return to a more healthy condition, we must even be as little children or as savages; we must get rid of the acquired and artificial, and return to and develope natural instincts.

The beautiful New Zealand paddle, Nos. 5–8, on Plate 15, would rival works of the highest civilisation: there is not a line upon its surface misapplied. The general shape is most elegant, and the decoration everywhere the best adapted to develope the form. A modern manufacturer, with his stripes and plaids, would have continued the bands or rings round the handle across the blade. The New Zealander's instinct taught him better. He desired not only that his

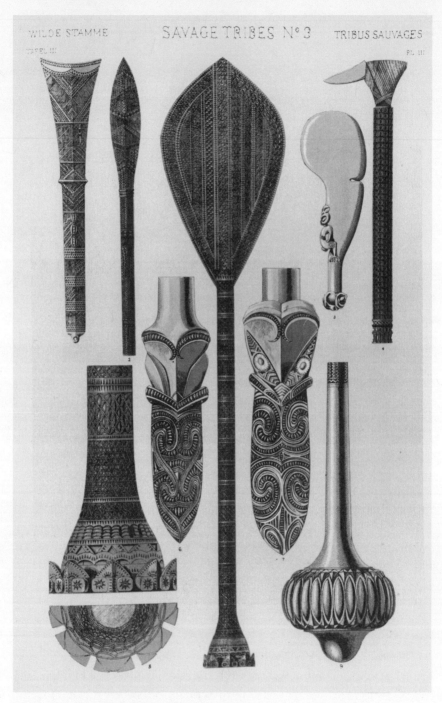

Plate 15. The Ornament of Savage Tribes, III

paddle should be strong, but should appear so, and his ornament is so disposed as to give an appearance of additional strength to what it would have had if the surface had remained undecorated. The centre band in the length of the blade is continued round on the other side, binding together the border on the edge, which itself fixes all the other bands. Had these bands run out like the centre one, they would have appeared to slip off. The centre one was the only one that could do so without disturbing the repose.

The swelling form of the handle where additional weight was required is most beautifully contrived, and the springing of the swell is well defined by the bolder pattern of the rings.* [Plates 16 and 17]

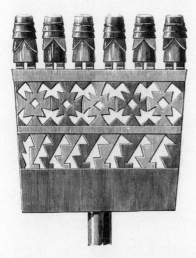

Plate 16. Handle of Paddle, British Museum

Plate 17. Club, Eastern Archipelago

*Captain Cook and other voyagers repeatedly notice the taste and ingenuity of the islanders of the Pacific and South Seas: instancing especially cloths, painted "in such an endless variety of figures that one might suppose they borrowed their patterns from a mercer's shop in which the most elegant productions of China and Europe are collected, besides some original patterns of their own." The "thousand different patterns" of their basketwork, their mats, and the fancy displayed in their rich carvings and inlaid shell-work, are, likewise, constantly mentioned. See *The Three Voyages of Captain Cook*, 2 vols. Lond. 1841–42; Dumont d'Urville's *Voyage au Pole Sud*, 8vo. Paris, 1841; Ditto, *Atlas d'Histoire*, fol.; Prichard's *Natural History of Man*, Lond. 1855; G. W. Earle's *Native Races of Indian Archipelago*, Lond. 1852; Kerr's *General History and Collection of Voyages and Travels*, London, 1811–17.

Our illustrations of the ornament of the Moors have been taken exclusively from the Alhambra, not only because it is the one of their works with which we are best acquainted, but also because it is the one in which their marvellous system of decoration reached its culminating point. [Plate 19 and 20] The Alhambra is at the very summit of perfection of Moorish art, as is the Parthenon of Greek art. We can find no work so fitted to illustrate a Grammar of Ornament as that in which every ornament contains a grammar in itself. Every principle which we can derive from the study of the ornamental art of any other people is not only ever present here, but was by the Moors more universally and truly obeyed.

We find in the Alhambra the speaking art of the Egyptians, the natural grace and refinement of the Greeks, the geometrical combinations of the Romans, the Byzantines, and the Arabs. The ornament wanted but one charm, which was the peculiar feature of the Egyptian ornament, symbolism. This the religion of the Moors forbade; but the want was more than supplied by the inscriptions, which, addressing themselves to the eye by their outward beauty, at once excited the intellect by the difficulties of deciphering their curious and complex involutions, and delighted the imagination when read, by the beauty of the sentiments they expressed and the music of their composition.

To the artist and those provided with a mind to estimate the value of the beauty to which they gave a life they repeated, *Look and learn.* To the people they proclaimed the might, majesty, and good deeds of the king. To the king himself they

Plate 18. *"There is no Conqueror but God."*
Arabic Inscription from the Alhambra

never ceased declaring that there was none powerful but God, that He alone was conqueror, and that to Him alone was for ever due praise and glory.

The builders of this wonderful structure were fully aware of the greatness of their work. It is asserted in the inscriptions on the walls, that this building surpassed all other buildings; that at sight of its wonderful domes all other domes vanished and disappeared; in the playful exaggeration of their poetry, that the stars grew pale in their light through envy of so much beauty; and, what is more to our purpose, they declare that he who should study them with attention would reap the benefit of a commentary on decoration.

Plate 19. Interlaced Ornaments (Moresque Ornament from the Alhambra)

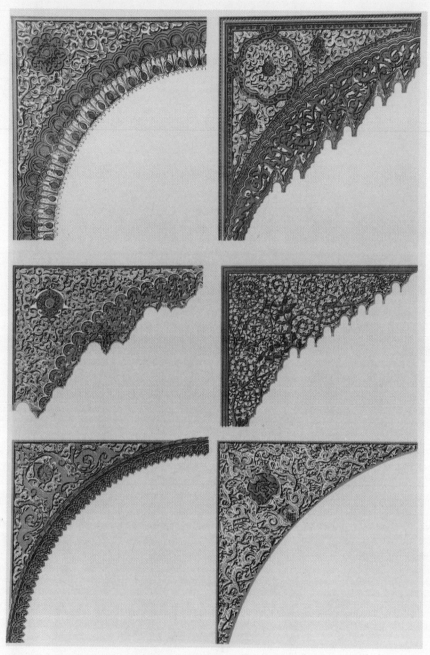

Plate 20. Spandrils of Arches (Moresque Ornament from the Alhambra)

We have endeavoured to obey the injunctions of the poet, and will attempt here to explain some of the general principles which appear to have guided the Moors in the decoration of the Alhambra—principles which are not theirs alone, but common to all the best periods of art. The principles which are everywhere the same, the forms only differ.

1.* The Moors ever regarded what we hold to be the first principle in architecture—to *decorate construction, never to construct decoration:* in Moorish architecture not only does the decoration arise naturally from the construction, but the constructive idea is carried out in every detail of the ornamentation of the surface.

We believe that true beauty in architecture results from that "*repose which the mind feels when the eye, the intellect, and the affections are satisfied, from the absence of any want.*" When an object is constructed falsely, appearing to derive or give support without doing either the one or the other, it fails to afford this repose, and therefore never can pretend to true beauty, however harmonious it may be in itself: the Mohammedan races, and Moors especially, have constantly regarded this rule; we never find a useless or superfluous ornament; every ornament arises quietly and naturally from the surface decorated. They ever regard the useful as a vehicle for the beautiful; and in this they do not stand alone: the same principle was observed in all the best periods of art: it is only when art declines that true principles come to be disregarded; or, in an age of copying, like the present, when the works of the past are reproduced without the spirit which animated the originals.

2. All lines grow out of each other in gradual undulations; there are no excrescences; nothing could be removed and leave the design equally good or better.

In a general sense, if construction be properly attended to, there could be no excrescences; but we use the word here in a more limited sense: the general lines might follow truly the construction, and yet there might be excrescences, such as knobs or bosses, which would not violate the rule of construction, and yet would be fatal to beauty of form, if they did not grow out gradually from the general lines.

There can be no beauty of form, no perfect proportion or arrangement of lines, which does not produce repose.

All transitions of curved lines from curved, or of curved lines from straight, must be gradual. Thus the transition would cease to be agreeable if the break at

---

*This essay on the general principles of the ornamentation of the Alhambra is partially reprinted from the "Guide Book to the Alhambra Court in the Crystal Palace," by the Author.

A were too deep in proportion to the curves, as at B.
Where two curves are separated by a break (as in this
case), they must, and with

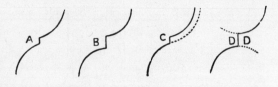

the Moors always do, run parallel to an imaginary line (C) where the curves
would be tangential to each other: for were either to depart from this, as in the
case at D, the eye, instead of following gradually down the curve, would run
outwards, and repose would be lost.*

3. The general forms were first cared for; these were subdivided by general
lines; the interstices were then filled in with ornament, which was again subdivided and enriched for closer inspection. They carried out this principle with
the greatest refinement, and the harmony and beauty of all their ornamentation derive their chief success from its observance. Their main divisions contrast and balance admirably: the greatest distinctness is obtained; the detail
never interferes with the general form. When seen at a distance, the main lines
strike the eye; as we approach nearer, the detail comes into the composition; on
a closer inspection, we see still further detail on the surface of the ornaments
themselves.

4. Harmony of form appears to consist in the proper balancing and contrast
of the straight, the inclined, and the curved.

As in colour there can be no perfect composition in which either of the three
primary colours is wanting, so in form, whether structural or decorative, there
can be no perfect composition in which either of the three primary figures is
wanting; and the varieties and harmony in composition and design depend on
the various predominance and subordination of the three.†

In surface decoration, any arrangement of forms, as at A [p. 313], consisting
only of straight lines, is monotonous, and affords but imperfect pleasure; but
introduce lines which tend to carry the eye towards the angles, as at B, and you

*These transitions were managed most perfectly by the Greeks in all their mouldings,
which exhibit this refinement in the highest degree; so do also the exquisite contours of
their vases.

†There can be no better example of this harmony than the Greek temple, where the
straight, the angular, and the curved are in most perfect relation to each other. Gothic architecture also offers many illustrations of this principle; every tendency of lines to run in
one direction is immediately counteracted by the angular or the curved: thus, the capping
of the buttress is exactly what is required to counteract the upward tendency of the straight
lines; so the gable contrasts admirably with the curved windowhead and its perpendicular
mullions.

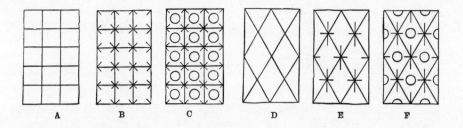

have at once an increased pleasure. Then add lines giving a circular tendency, as at C, and you have now complete harmony. In this case the square is the leading form or tonic; the angular and curved are subordinate.

We may produce the same result in adopting an angular composition, as at D: add the lines as at E, and we at once correct the tendency to follow only the angular direction of the inclined lines; but unite these by circles, as at F, and we have still more perfect harmony, *i.e.* repose, for the eye has now no longer any want that could be supplied.*

5. In the surface decorations of the Moors all lines flow out of a parent stem: every ornament, however distant, can be traced to its branch and root. They have the happy art of so adapting the ornament to the surface decorated, that the ornament as often appears to have suggested the general form as to have been suggested by it. In all cases we find the foliage flowing out of a parent stem, and we are never offended, as in modern practice, by the random introduction of an ornament just dotted down, without a reason for its existence. However irregular the space they have to fill, they always commence by dividing it into equal areas, and round these trunk-lines they fill in their detail, but invariably return to their parent stem.

They appear in this to work by a process analogous to that of nature, as we see in the vine-leaf; the object being to distribute the sap from the parent stem

---

*It is to the neglect of this obvious rule that we find so many failures in paper-hangings, carpets, and more especially articles of costume: the lines of papers generally run through the ceiling most disagreeably, because the straight is not corrected by the angular, or the angular by the curved: so of carpets; the lines of carpets are constantly running in one direction only, carrying the eye right through the walls of the apartment. Again, to this we owe all those abominable checks and plaids which constantly disfigure the human form— a custom detrimental to the public taste, and gradually lowering the tone of the eye for form of this generation. If children were born and bred to the sound of hurdy-gurdies grinding out of tune, their ears would no doubt suffer deterioration, and they would lose their sensibility to the harmonious in sound. This, then, is what is certainly taking place with regard to form, and it requires the most strenuous efforts to be made by all who would take an interest in the welfare of the rising generation to put a stop to it.

Owen Jones {313}

to the extremities, it is evident the main stem would divide the leaf as near as may be into equal areas. So, again, of the minor divisions; each area is again subdivided by intermediate lines, which all follow the same law of equal distribution, even to the most minute filling-in of the sap-feeders.

6. The Moors also follow another principle; that of radiation from the parent stem, as we may see in nature with the human hand, or in a chestnut leaf.

We may see in the example how beautifully all these lines radiate from the parent stem; how each leaf diminishes towards the extremities, and how each area is in proportion to the leaf. The Orientals carry out this principle with marvellous perfection; so also did the Greeks in their honeysuckle ornament. We have already remarked, in Chapter IV., a peculiarity of Greek ornament, which appears to follow the principle of the plants of the cactus tribe, where one leaf grows out of another. This is generally the case with Greek ornament; the acanthus-leaf scrolls are a series of leaves growing out one from the other in a continuous line, whilst the Arabian and Moresque ornaments always grow out of a continuous stem.

7. All junctions of curved lines with curved, or of curved with straight, should be tangential to each other; this also we consider to be a law found everywhere in nature, and the Oriental practice is always in accordance with it. Many of the Moorish ornaments are on the same principle which is observable in the lines of a feather and in the articulations of every leaf; and to this is due that additional charm found in all perfect ornamentation, which we call the graceful. It may be called the melody of form, as what we have before described constitutes its harmony.

We shall find these laws of *equal distribution, radiation from a parent stem, continuity of line,* and *tangential curvature,* ever present in natural leaves.

8. We would call attention to the nature of the exquisite curves in use by the Arabs and Moors.

As with proportion, we think that those proportions will be the most beautiful which it will be most difficult for the eye to detect;* so we think that those compositions of curves will be most agreeable, where the mechanical process of

---

*All compositions of squares or of circles will be monotonous, and afford but little pleasure, because the means whereby they are produced are very apparent. So we think that compositions distributed in equal lines or divisions will be less beautiful than those which require a higher mental effort to appreciate them.

describing them shall be least apparent; and we shall find it to be universally the case, that in the best periods of art all mouldings and ornaments were founded on curves of the higher order, such as the conic sections; whilst, when art declined, circles and compass-work were much more dominant.

The researches of Mr. Penrose have shown that the mouldings and curved lines in the Parthenon are all portions of curves of a very high order, and that segments of circles were very rarely used.[3] The exquisite curves of the Greek vases are well known, and here we never find portions of circles. In Roman architecture, on the contrary, this refinement is lost; the Romans were probably as little able to describe as to appreciate curves of a high order, and we find, therefore, their mouldings mostly parts of circles, which could be struck with compasses.

In the early works of the Gothic period, the tracery would appear to have been much less the offspring of compass-work than in the later period, which has most appropriately been termed the *Geometrical*, from the immoderate use of compass-work.

Here is a curve (A) common to Greek Art, to the Gothic period, and so much delighted in by the Mohammedan races. This becomes graceful the more it departs from the curve which the union of two parts of circles would give.

9. A still further charm is found in the works of the Arabs and Moors from their conventional treatment of ornament, which, forbidden as they were by their creed to represent living forms, they carried to the highest perfection. They ever worked as nature worked, but always avoided a direct transcript; they took her principles, but did not, as we do, attempt to copy her works. In this, again, they do not stand alone: in every period of faith in art, all ornamentation was ennobled by the ideal; never was the sense of propriety violated by a too faithful representation of nature.

Thus, in Egypt, a lotus carved in stone was never such an one as you might have plucked, but a conventional representation perfectly in keeping with the architectural members of which it formed a part; it was a symbol of the power of the king over countries where the lotus grew, and added poetry to what would otherwise have been a rude support.

The colossal statues of the Egyptians were not little men carved on a large scale, but architectural representations of Majesty, in which were symbolised the power of the monarch, and his abiding love of his people.

In Greek art, the ornaments, no longer symbols, as in Egypt, were still further conventionalised; and in their sculpture applied to architecture, they adopted a conventional treatment both of *pose* and relief very different to that of their isolated works.

In the best periods of Gothic art the floral ornaments are treated conventionally, and a direct imitation of nature is never attempted; but as art declined, they became less idealised, and more direct in imitation.

The same decline may be traced in stained glass, where both figures and ornaments were treated at first conventionally; but as the art declined, figures and draperies, through which light was to be transmitted, had their own shades and shadows.

In the early illuminated MSS. the ornaments were conventional, and the illuminations were in flat tints, with little shade and no shadow; whilst in those of a later period highly-finished representations of natural flowers were used as ornament, casting their shadows on the page.

NOTES

1. Phidias (490–430 BCE) and Praxiteles (400–330 BCE) were the foremost sculptors of the Classical and Late Classical periods of Greek art, representing the climax of figurative art for Jones.

2. Giotto (1267–1337) and Cimabue (1240–1302) were painters of the early Renaissance; Jones considers them less skilled than such painters of the High Renaissance as Raphael and Michelangelo.

3. Francis C. Penrose, *An Investigation of the Principles of Athenian Architecture*. (London, 1851).

GOTTFRIED SEMPER

The Textile Art
Considered in Itself and in Relation to Architecture

B. ON THE MANNER IN WHICH STYLE IS CONDITIONED BY THE TREATMENT OF THE MATERIAL[1]

§46. Preliminary Remarks

This is a subject that offers a wide range of benefits to a manufacturer who combines a thorough technical knowledge with scientific and artistic education, and for whom the growing receptiveness of the people for beauty, especially among the producers, is inseparable from true progress and the growth of industry—both generally as well as materially.

For my part, I have already declared my incompetence in taking up such a difficult task and *wish only to stimulate* discussion by making some suggestions on what in my opinion merits primary consideration in a future treatment of such a rich subject matter. Besides, the subject gives rise to questions that more directly relate to my own field and for which I believe I am better prepared.

All operations in the textile arts seek to transform raw materials with the appropriate properties into products, whose common features are great pliancy and considerable absolute strength, sometimes serving in threaded and banded forms as bindings and fastenings, sometimes used as pliant surfaces to cover, to hold, to dress, to enclose, and so forth.

§47. Bands and Threads. Primitive Products of This Kind

The most primitive products of this kind were borrowed, as it were, directly from the simplest operations of nature. Classed among them are stalks and raw stems, tree branches, animal sinews and entrails, for whose preparation a process already becomes necessary, namely, *twisting*, by which the product receives a form circular in section and fulfills better its purpose of strength and elasticity. In the next class are animal hides cut up for straps and, among other, less noteworthy products, threads made from resinous plant materials, long known to a few savage tribes and becoming important to us only in most recent times.

The style of these objects, insofar as it is dependent of the processes and tools used in their production, is simple to explain: some of these objects have or receive a circular sectional plane; others, like straps, may first be fashioned bandlike but then are twisted, giving them a *spiral shape.*

The rubber thread imitates the leather strap but can also be shaped as a smooth circular thread or assume a spiral form. Following the well-known properties of rubber, it has no specific style but is totally flexible.

The technical means and tools used in working these products have remained the same since time immemorial. Wall paintings at Thebes show that Egyptian saddlers had the same crescent-shaped knife that still serves our leather workers for cutting long spiral straps from a single hide. With such a strap cut from a cowhide, Dido won the piece of land in Carthage.

The decoration of the strap is partly dependent on its bandlike form and should be consistent with this form. Above all, it should remain surface decoration and not disrupt the intent of the strap; it should imitate its function as a band.

§48. Spun Yarn

Spun yarn is an artificial thread consisting of many natural threads. After natural threads have been properly prepared, the means of combing, plucking, squeezing, seizing, and twisting are used in its production. By combing, the threads are set as parallel as possible. With entangled and short raw materials, this operation is often replaced by carding, whereby the thread receives a somewhat feltlike appearance.

Since time immemorial the operations of plucking, squeezing, seizing, and twisting have been accomplished with the help of the clammy hand and the rotating spindle. In this, the new spinning machines have changed nothing in principle; they only duplicate and simplify production by replacing the hand, and by using machinery to bring in motion at one time many spindles and their parts substituting for the hand. The finest and strongest threads are still being produced in India, where the old methods of spinning have continued.

Every material requires its own method of processing. This influences the style of the spun yarn, which is, of course, particularly conditioned by the use for which it is made. Much can still be said on this important subject, about which only a specialist is able to speak in greater detail.

§49. Twisted Yarn

Twisted yarn is a product related to spun yarn, a strong artificial thread made up of two or more artificial threads. The necessary operations are fewer than those of spinning. Plucking, pressing, and seizing are unnecessary, and it needs only to be twisted, which is done more easily on a flywheel or a similar apparatus. Before the individual threads are to be twisted they are wound onto cylindrical spindles or rollers, then run through a ring, after which the twisting takes place. Following the same operation, several twisted threads can be bound onto a thicker rope. Threads of different materials, of unequal diameter, and different color can be twisted together, and even this process can vary, depending on the intention. One can, for instance, make a loose and strong yarn or manage double twists that run either with or against each other, and so on. For realizing the useful in the beautiful, this simple technique offers the richest material for stylistic consideration, a task that is reserved for an artistic-philosophical haberdasher. For this operation, too, we possess illustrations that are older than our written history.*

§50. The Knot

The knot is perhaps the oldest technical symbol and, as I have shown, the expression for the earliest cosmogonic ideas that arose among nations.

The knot serves, first of all, as a means of tying together two ends of cord, and its strength is chiefly based on the resistance of friction. The system that best promotes friction by lateral pressure when the two cords are pulled in opposite directions along their length is the strongest. Another condition occurs when pressure is exerted on the cords not in the direction of length but perpendicular to their extension, although even in this case the resultant of the tension is best considered as moving in the longitudinal direction of the chords. The weaver's knot is the strongest and most useful of all knots, perhaps also the oldest or at least the first that figured in the technical arts. The rope maker and sailor know a great number of knot systems, on which, unfortunately, I can only speak as a layman. Related to the description of these systems are other things that would be of interest to our interpretation, but these also must be left to more expert hands.

A very ingenious and ancient application of the knot led to the invention of the network, which even the most savage tribes know how to make and use for fishing and hunting. The mesh of the net, whose knot is illustrated here,† has the advantage that a damaged mesh does not affect the whole system and is easily mended. [Plate 21] This is, at the same time, the criterion for the network, which in other respects permits the most diverse variations but in this particular point remains the same under all conditions. Spanish hemp was considered the best for nets in antiquity. Cumean hemp was also famed in this regard. The

*See [J. Gardner] Wilkinson's often cited work on the Egyptians [*The Manners and Customs of the Ancient Egyptians* (1837)], vol. III, p. 144.

†Closer examination shows that it is identical with the weaver's knot.

Plate 21.

Plate 22.

ancients made nets in which wild boars were caught, but of such great fineness that a single man could carry enough of them on his back to surround an entire forest. Yet the same netting in a thicker mesh also served as a corselet, in which each thread, although fine in itself, was sewn together from three hundred to four hundred individual fibers. This industry appears to have prospered especially in Egypt.* The Egyptians also made decorative nets from glass-bead necklaces, of which several charming examples have survived. This ornament was also prevalent among Greek women, as well as among Etruscan and Roman women. In India the net serves as a rich motive for head coverings and necklaces that are admirable in the alteration of the mesh and in the distribution of the decorations and pendants. The Middle Ages† loved the network, and the Spanish have retained the time-honored value of delicate networks as adornments for the hair and as a very light wrap. [Plate 22]

In architecture, in ceramics, and generally in all the arts, the net is used for the decoration of surfaces, and is often applied in a structural-symbolic way as an adornment on projecting and bulging parts, for example, on the paunch of vases. For the archaeology of nets, compare the numerous writings and essays of Böttiger on the adornment of the ancients.‡

*Compare Pliny [*Natural History*] 19, 1 and Herodotus.

†In Ebener's *Trachten* and in the work, *Moyen-âge et Renaissance,* in the article "Costûmes," there are charming illustrations of medieval nets. The Museum for Practical Art and Science in Kensington contains Indian nets and adornments in the form of a net.

‡[C. A. Böttiger, *Die*] *aldobrandinische Hochzeit,* p. 150.

§54. Weaving

Could I do justice to this paragraph it would compose an entire book by itself! So much could be discussed here! Every salon, every new fashion show, every fair, every industrial exhibition attests to the perplexity of our artistic weaver's trade, forsaken by the Graces and drowning, as it were, in its own excessive resources. How inferior it is with regard to taste and invention when compared to what was and still is being produced today on the looms of the Hindus and the Kurds with far simpler and more limited means, and in centuries less industrial but with a greater understanding of art. We have sufficient professorships to teach the sciences in their application to the industrial arts; what is lacking altogether is a practical aesthetic for the manufacturer and especially for the weaver, who are ill-prepared for the artistic part of their industry and are therefore forced to turn to artists and draftsmen. These artists, however, have limited technical knowledge and, furthermore, are not up to date with artistic and general education. Only an industrialist familiar with all aspects of weaving, with mechanics, with dyeing, as well as with the business aspect of the trade, an industrialist who is at the same time a humanist, scholar, philosopher, and artist in the true sense, and who has at his disposal a textile collection well furnished and arranged according to the history of style as a teaching aid for his instruction—only he is competent to assume such a position. With all of these things, he will still have a hard time coping with the spirit of the time and his industrial colleagues.

For my part I would rather not express my views on this subject in a partial, disconnected way, which would only betray the lack of a most basic technical knowledge! Perhaps the best discussion of this is contained in Redgrave's already much cited "Supplementary Report on Design,"[2] although this discussion lacks coherence, is too incomplete and too rigidly schematic in its details. Style, as far as it is dependent on the purpose of a thing, can be more easily formulated into principles than can the speculative theory of form be deduced in those areas where the form must be considered as a function of the technical means that come into play.

One should have to deal systematically with all weavings from the simplest cross weave to the most elaborate polymite, the brocaded and high-warp weavings, outline their history, show for what materials and purposes they are suited, define their *means* and *limits* in an artistic and formal sense, indicate the course along which improvement is possible, identify the influence of machine fabrication on the style of the products, examine critically the taste of the time, and investigate how this taste influences artistic technique or is influenced by it. One should have to emphasize that what is better could but does not exist and prepare the ground for bringing it about, and not hold up the excellence passed down by history as the absolute model, thereby arrogantly disregarding the present and its inventions, but use it as an example of how the task had been solved correctly in times of true artistic understanding from the given facts *of those times,* so that we, in following *this* model, must enlist the *present* facts to bring about the solution to an analogous task. Finally, one should have to show that all technical, mechanical and economic means that we have invented and that give us an advantage over the past will lead to barbarity rather than indicate the progress of true industrial art or civilization, as long as we are generally unsuccessful in mastering these means artistically! All this, among many other things not touched upon, are the principles that a professor of weaving has to set out in theoretical and practical instruction.

§55. The Stitch, Embroidery, acu pingere, pinsere, pugere, γράφειν

Embroidery is an arrangement of threads that one affixes to a natural or artificially produced, soft and supple surface with the aid of a pointed instrument. [Plate 23] The elements of the designs produced in this way are called *stitches,* and are comparable with the units (*tesserae, crustae*) out of which the mosaic is assembled; embroidery is, in fact, *a kind of mosaic in threads,* by which its general character and its relation to *painting* and *sculpture* is determined. Just as with the mosaic both surface presentations and relief presentations are brought about (and it is unclear on which of the two is conferred the right of seniority),* so there are *relief embroideries* and *surface embroideries* that arise from different and totally unrelated principles.

This contrast is revealed in the form and organization of the stitches that are the generating elements in both kinds of embroidery. Two types of stitches are possible: (1) the flat stitch, (2) the cross stitch.

The limit or, if you wish, the abstract concept of the flat stitch is the *line;* the limit of the cross stitch is the *point.*

· · ·

Yet we scarcely need such historical documentation for conditions that are to some extent self-explanatory. I repeat my belief that sewing is older than

---

*The oldest mosaics are perhaps the wall decorations found at Warka, which also form relieflike projections. Among the Greek–Roman mosaics, it is the relief mosaic that exhibits the unmistakable, older Greek style. With the exception of the mosaic floor in the pronaos of the Temple of Zeus at Olympia and a few broken pieces of uncertain date, all the actual mosaic paintings are from the later Roman period. Compare [Désiré Raoul] Rochette, *Peintures antiques inédites* [*précédées de Recherches sur l'emploi de la peinture dans la décoration des édifices sacrés et publics, chez les Grecs et chez les Romains*], pp. 393ff.

weaving and that the former led to the idea of embroidery, which was carried out much earlier on leather and barks than on actual fabrics. The fabrics themselves and, for this reason, all the more their later, figurative designs are therefore of a later origin than embroidered integuments.

This question might seem insignificant to practice, yet to someone who realizes the close interrelation of every branch of art and who considers the artistic conception as the epitome of practice, it is not unimportant. Yet let us turn to other considerations that relate directly to practice and are more obvious.

I do not wish simply to reiterate the fact that the style of embroidery has to conform to the material on which and by which it is embroidered, that embroidery on red deerskin trousers or on a tobacco pouch made from yellow maple bark, for instance, must be different from embroidery on cashmere or on a white transparent muslin (although modern articles of this last class, of which the Swiss are especially proud, and numerous other examples of the unspeakable, tasteless acupiction of the most recent times fail altogether to recognize the limits of these distinctions), because the laws that prevail here belong more to the domain of style insofar as it is dependent on material and purpose and therefore were mentioned in the preceding discussion, which treated style in these two respects. I only wish to add with regard to these distinctions, which are also somewhat conditioned by the procedures used, that strong and coarse materials demand to be embroidered with relatively large stitches and with threads whose strength is consistent with the ground, and therefore for these a thick and full embroidery is appropriate, whereas for veillike, spun fabrics a

loose tendril-work, fine stripes (*viae*), sprigs, or something similar is befitting.*
If only we had a few fabrics from Cos to study the true veil style!

Yet let us leave this (and set aside the other mixed factors of style that are almost as numerous within the vast field of embroidery as the individual materials and means of application that exist and multiply daily), and let us focus, rather, on the *factor of free treatment,* which is a characteristic common to all hand embroidery in the flat-stitch manner and which almost elevates it to the standing of a free art. The strength of this style is the hand embroidery, subservient neither to strict symmetry nor to geometrical pattern—indeed, it should manifest its style in the *disregard of both within certain limits, manifest it in the free painterly arrangement insofar as the latter remains compatible with the other conditions of style.*

The freer the design of ornamental motives, the more a distribution of masses and of the balance of forms and colors arranged according to certain higher laws of taste becomes necessary; in this connection the material, spatial, and practical demands that each task entails are decisive for the *how* of the conception. Freedom within these limitations of style is the secret of high art that, although still very bound, sets its wings in motion for the first time in embroidery. One can argue that free art in the Orient never went beyond this point of unfolding, that it permanently adhered to the limits of the embroidery style. Yet if this is true, it is also equally correct to say that nowhere has the spirit of the embroidery style as such been grasped so perfectly as there, and that for this reason the free ornamentation of the Orient, in particular Indian and Chinese embroidery, remains a model for us and our art industry, on which we should

*It may be appropriate here to give a short excerpt from Redgrave's often cited report, in which he says the following about muslin curtains: "These fabrics should, of course, have a perfectly flat treatment, whether purely ornamental forms or flowers are used for their decoration. The best effect for borders is obtained by a symmetrical arrangement of flowing lines, which may be large in pattern, from the lightness of the material; while a diaper treatment, or small sprigs arranged with large and regular spaces over the central field, are the simple rules for their decoration. It would seem hardly possible to err much in designing for a fabric which admits of such small variation, the contrast of the thick work with the more filmy ground being the source of the ornamental form, and colour being rarely used; yet perhaps, in the whole Exhibition, there are not more glaring mistakes than are made in the decoration of these goods. In the Swiss muslins, the effort seems to have been directed rather to curious skill in workmanship than to taste in design, and some of the most costly goods are in the worst conceivable taste—immense cornucopias, pouring out fruits and flowers, palm-trees, and even buildings and landscapes being used as ornaments. Even when this only consists of flowers they are used imitatively and perspectively, foldings of the leaves, and in some cases the actual relief of fruits, being attempted. Al-

practice our taste and our feeling for style with regard to both their forms and the principle of coloring observed in them.

For the purpose of free ornamental embroidery, the tendril designs and, generally speaking, the vegetable motifs that are always capable of repetition without tiring are the happiest—an unexhausted and inexhaustible source of the most graceful and freshest inventions. Where, however, art goes beyond these motifs and introduces figurative, symbolic, or even tendentious themes, it should above all guard against provoking disgust through symmetrical and periodic repetitions of similar motifs, through a monotonous significance that is an unfailing way to turn one's stomach. Medieval embroidery and knitted materials, especially those that were made in the fourteenth and fifteenth centuries in Italy and in other European mills, are frequently afflicted with this error of style. We see groups of angels holding a chalice, Madonnas, and all the saints, as well as other mystical symbols scattered over the surface in regular intervals and constantly repeated and—instead of the old fabled beasts of Asia whose ornamental repetition we can put up with more easily. A small but powerful party would have us take up this Gothic nonsense again today, but we are not deceived by its in no way purely aesthetic tendencies and would stay with our Malakoff towers, sun temples, and other tapestry motifs that, even if not tasteful, are at least harmless. This tendentious monotony is absolutely reprehensible on hand embroidery, where it can be avoided, and on woven materials and tapestries, where it is unavoidable as soon as one wants to be tendentious.

The easier art of canvas embroidery is the most common and preferred with

---

though the same faults occur in the English manufacturers, these, on the whole, slightly incline to better taste . . . but [in general] there is a sad want of good design in this class."

Therefore worse than the English—that is strong! Certainly I agree in general with these final judgments on the achievements of the modern art of embroidery, in part but not in full with the author's view of the simplicity of the stylistic rules that are possible with them. I find, for example, that the size and use of a curtain as a finishing influences the character of the pattern, which should correspond both to this condition and to the seemingly opposing conditions that dictate the delicate, sheer material. The fine sprigs, therefore, are hardly appropriate in this place, just as the regular diaper decoration may be undesirable here, since it is completely out of character with freehand embroidery in the flat-stitch manner. It is more consistent with woven and printed materials, probably also with embroideries in the cross-stitch manner. Yet we will give further details on this in the text. [Quotation from R. Redgrave, "Supplementary Report on Design," *Reports by the Juries,* 730. The phrase "especially in some of the woven curtains from Nottingham, and in the fabrics exhibited by the *Utrecht Company* (Class, XIX., 265, p. 570)" is deleted from the next to last line of Semper's translated quotation, and "in general" is added by Semper.]

our ladies (particularly for wool embroidery). What is characteristic for the first-named embroidery is *without style* for wool embroidery, and just for that reason our eccentric taste chances upon depicting the most adventurous imitations of nature in the freest arrangement—the wildest, most naturalistic conceptions with a technique that wants, above all, to do just the opposite. It would be futile to become worked up over this; the design of embroidery patterns is in bad hands and it would be difficult for a real artist to succeed today, like that old, honest engraver Siebmacher,[3] who published a *true* pattern book for canvas embroidery.* Yet this master and his colleagues Altdorfer, Aldegrever, Pens, Beham, Virgilius Solis, Theodor de Bry, Jean Collaert, Etienne de Laulne, called Stephanus, Peter Woeriot, and the other *petits maîtres* already belonged to a time in which the practicing technician no longer designed his own compositions, as before. The art already had begun to separate itself from handicraft. Before this separation our grandmothers were indeed not members of the academy of fine arts or album collectors or an audience for aesthetic lecturers, but they knew what to do when it came to designing an embroidery. There's the rub!

NOTES

1. The text begins in Volume 1 of *Style in the Technical and Tectonic Arts,* with Part 2 of the fourth section. In Section 1 Semper introduces his projected treatise; in Section 2 he classifies artistic motives into four material operations, leading to the technical arts of textiles, ceramics, timber frameworks, and masonry. In Section 3 Semper begins his analysis of the art of textiles, which he divides into "general-formal" and "technical-historical" components. The fourth section starts the technical-historical analysis, the first part of which is entitled "On Style Conditioned by the Raw Material." The text continues with Part 2. [H. F. Mallgrave]

2. Redgrave's report was published in *Reports by the Juries* (London, 1852), 708–49. [H. F. Mallgrave]

3. The Nuremberg painter and engraver Johann Siebmacher (Sibmacher, Syber) was a famed German engraver of the late sixteenth century. He was involved with several publications; Semper was probably referring to *Schön Neues Modelbuch von allerley lustigen Mödeln nachzunehen Zuwürcken vñ Zustickē* (1597). Reynard's text, mentioned in Semper's footnote, was entitled *Ornements des anciens maîtres des xve, xvie, xviie et xviiie siècles, recueillis par O. Reynard* (Paris, 1841–6). [H. F. Mallgrave]

---

*Siebmacher's compositions were republished in part in Reynard's reproductions of the *petits maîtres*. A fashion journalist should use, or better still, even copy them for his subscribers, instead of the bad things that are now presented to them.

EUGÈNE-EMMANUEL VIOLLET-LE-DUC

from *Lectures on Architecture*

But what is style? I am not speaking now of style as applied to the classification of the arts by periods, but of style as inherent in the arts of all times; and to make myself better understood, I remark that independently of the style of the writer in each language, there is a style which belongs to all languages, because it belongs to humanity. This style is inspiration; but it is inspiration subjected to the laws of reason,—inspiration invested with a distinction peculiar to every work produced by a genuine feeling rigorously analysed by reason before being expressed; it is the close accord of the imaginative and reasoning faculties; it is the effort of the *active* imagination regulated by reason. I said in a previous page:—the *passive* imagination of a Greek presents the idea of a man on a horse; his active imagination suggests the combination of the two in a single being; reason shows him how to weld the torso of the one to the breast of the other: he creates a centaur, and this creation has *style* for us as well as for the Greek.

A distinguished writer lately remarked that in architecture, "style is first the period, next the man."* This definition appears to me to confound what are conventionally designated *the styles* with style. There are periods which have their style, but in which style is wanting. Such for instance is the Roman period under the last Emperors of the West. There is a Louis XIV. style, a Louis XV. style, and some have lately discovered even a Louis XVI. style. Nevertheless, one of the characteristics of Architectural Art at the close of the seventeenth and during the eighteenth century is the absence of style. "Terms should be defined," says Voltaire; and Voltaire is often right.[1] Style proper and style as an archælogical indication are two widely different things.

Style consists in a marked distinction of form; it is one of the essential elements of beauty, but does not of itself alone constitute beauty. Civilisation dulls those instincts of man which lead him to introduce style into his works, but it does not destroy them. These instincts come into play involuntarily. In a certain assembly you remark one person in particular. This person may not possess any of those striking characteristics which constitute beauty; the fea-

---

* *"Traité d'Architecture,"* by M. Léonce Raynaud, vol. ii. p. 86. [Paris, 1850]

tures may not be regular; yet, attracted by a mysterious influence, your gaze continually reverts to the individual in question. However unaccustomed to such observation you succeed in explaining to yourself the reasons which impel you to satisfy that instinctive attraction: the first thing that strikes you is a marked line,—a harmony between the frame and the muscles; it is an *ensemble* in some cases irregular, but which excites in you sympathy or antipathy. Your attention is engaged by a contour, by certain forms of the bones which are covered with muscles in harmony with those forms, the manner in which the hair grows on the brow, the junction of the limbs with the body, the concordance between the gestures and the thought; you have soon arrived at settled ideas as to the habits, taste, and character of that person. Though seen for the first time,—a stranger to whom you have never spoken,—you build up a whole romance on the individual in question. Of animated beings only those who have *style* possess this mysterious power of attraction. Individuals of the human race are so often spoiled by an artificial education, and by moral and physical infirmities, that it is rare to find one of them possessing style: the brutes, on the contrary, all exhibit this harmony,—this perfect conformity between the outward form and the instinct—the breath which animates them. Hence we may say that the brutes have style,—from the insect to the noblest of the quadrupeds. Their gestures are always true; their movements always plainly indicate a want or a definite purpose, a desire or a fear. Brutes are never affected, artificial, or vulgar; whether beautiful or ugly they possess style, because they have only simple feelings and seek their ends by simple and direct means. Man,— especially civilised man,—being a very complicated animal, and altered in character by an education which teaches him to resist his instincts, must make a retrospective effort,—shall I say,—to acquire style; and Alceste is right when he prefers to the sonnet of Oronte the lines:—

> "Si le roi m'avait donné
> Paris sa grand' ville."[2]

Every one is of Alceste's opinion; but this does not hinder the Orontes of their day from composing vapid sonnets, or architects from overlaying their buildings with ornaments devoid of reason and of style.

In the present day we are no longer familiar with those simple and true ideas which lead artists to invest their conceptions with style; I think it necessary therefore to define the constituent elements of style, and in so doing, carefully to avoid equivocal terms, and those meaningless phrases which are repeated with the profound respect that is professed by most people for what is incomprehensible. Ideas must be presented in a palpable form,—a definite embodiment,—if we would communicate them. Clearly to understand what style as regards form is, we must consider form in its simplest expressions. Let us therefore take one of the primitive arts,—one of the earliest practised among all nations, because it is among the first needed,—the art of the coppersmith, for example. It matters little how long it took man to discover the method of refining copper, and of reducing it to thin plates, so as to make a vessel with it fit to contain liquid. We take the art at the time when he had discovered that by beating a sheet of copper in a particular way he could so model it as to give it the form of a vessel. To effect this, all the workman needs is a piece of iron as a point of support, and a hammer. He can thus, by beating the sheet of copper, cause it to return on itself, and of a plane surface make a hollow body. He leaves a flat circular bottom to his vessel, so that it may stand firm when full. To hinder the liquid from spilling when the vessel is shaken, he contracts its upper orifice, and then widens it out suddenly at the edge, to facilitate pouring out the liquid; the most natural form therefore—that determined by the mode of fabrication—is this [Plate 24]. There must be a means of holding the vessel: the workman therefore attaches handles with rivets. But as the vessel must be inverted when empty, and has to be drained dry, he makes the handles so that they shall not stand above the level of the top of the vessel. Thus fashioned by methods suggested in the fabrication, this vessel has style: first, because it exactly indicates its purpose; second, because it is fashioned in accordance with the material employed and the means of fabrication suited to this material; third, because the form obtained is suitable to the material of which this utensil is made, and the use for which it is intended. This vessel has style, because human reason indicates exactly the form suitable to it. The coppersmiths themselves, in their desire to do better or otherwise than their predecessors, deviate from the line of the true and the good. We find therefore a second coppersmith, who wishes to alter the form of the primitive vessel in order to attract purchasers by the distinction of novelty; he gives a few extra blows of the hammer, and rounds the body of the vessel which had hitherto

Plate 24.
Primitive Form of Copper Vessel

Eugène-Emmanuel Viollet-le-Duc {329}

Plate 25 (top). *Modified Form of Copper Vessel*
Plate 26 (bottom). *Bad Form of Copper Vessel*

been regarded as perfect [Plate 25]. The form is in fact new, and all the town wish to have vessels made by the second coppersmith. A third coppersmith, perceiving that his fellow-townsmen are taken with the rounding of the base, goes still further, and make a third vessel [Plate 26], which is still more popular. This last workman, having lost sight of the principle, bids adieu to reason, and follows caprice alone; he increases the length of his handles, and advertises them as of the newest taste. This vessel cannot be placed upside down to be drained with-out endangering the shape of these handles; but every one praises it, and the third coppersmith is credited with having wonderfully improved his art, while in reality he has only deprived a form of its proper style, and produced an un-sightly and relatively inconvenient article.

This history is typical of that of style in all the arts. Arts which cease to express the want they are intended to satisfy, the nature of the material employed, and the method of fashioning it, cease to have style. The style of Architecture during the declining years of the Roman Empire and that of the eighteenth century consist in the absence of style. We may follow custom in saying, "The style of the arts of the Lower Empire," or of the reign of Louis XV.; but we cannot say: "The arts of the Lower Empire, or those of the reign of Louis XV., *have style*," for their defect (assuming it to be such) is that they dispense with style, since they show an evident contempt for the form really appropriate to the object and its use. If a Roman matron of the period of the Republic were to appear in a drawing-room filled with ladies dressed in hooped skirts, with powdered hair and a superstructure of plumes or flowers, the Roman lady would present a singular figure; but it is none the less certain that her dress would have *style*, while those of the ladies in hooped skirts would be in (the style of the period), but would not possess *style*. Here then we have, I think, an intelligible starting-point for the appreciation of style. Are we then to suppose that style is inherent in one form alone, and that women, for instance, if they wish their dress to have style, must dress themselves like the mother of the Gracchi? Certainly not. The satin and the woollen dress may both have style; but on the condition that the shape of neither is at variance with the forms of the body; that it does not ridiculously exaggerate the former nor hamper the movements of the latter; and that the cut of the dresses in each shows a due regard to the special qualities of the material. Nature invariably exhibits style in her productions, because however diversified they may be they are always subject to laws,—to immutable principles. The leaf of a shrub, a flower, an insect—all have style; because they grow, are developed, and maintain their existence according to laws essentially logical. We can subtract nothing from a flower, for each part of its organism expresses a function by taking the form which is appropriate to that function. Style resides solely in the true and marked expression of a principle and not in an immutable form; consequently, as nothing exists except in virtue of a principle, there may be style in everything. I have already remarked, and I repeat it lest it should be forgotten:—discussions on art turn on ambiguities. They tell you in the schools that Greek art has the impress of style; that that style is pure,—complete, namely, and without alloy; copy the Greek form therefore if you wish your art to have style. As well might it be said:—The tiger or the cat has style; disguise yourself therefore as a tiger or a cat if you would lay claim to style. Instead of this it should be explained why the cat and the tiger, the flower and the insect, have style, and the instruction should run thus:— Proceed as nature does in her works, and you will be able to invest with style all that your brain conceives. True, this is not easy amidst a complicated civilisation, greatly embarrassed to know what suits it,—subjected to traditions and prejudices through habit rather than from conviction,—swayed by fashion,— *blasé*,—sceptical and little inclined to accept the true expression of a principle, but it is not impossible.

NOTES

1. Voltaire, pen name of François-Marie Arouet (1694–1778), a major French philosopher and author, developed a practical philosophy of common sense, most famously embodied in his *Candide* (1759).

2. This is a line from Molière, *Le Misanthrope* (1666), Act I, scene II: "If the king had given me Paris the great city."

from *Prolegomena to a Psychology of Architecture*

VII. ORNAMENT

Only with difficulty have I been able to delay the discussion of ornament. It contributes enormously to the characteristics of horizontal development but even more to vertical development. Yet it seems to me that the theme
has to be treated as a coherent whole.

What is ornament? The answer to this question has been clouded by those
many critics who, like Bötticher in his *Die Tektonik der Hellenen* (The Tectonic
of the Hellenes), inquired into the canonical meaning of each part in an attempt to find a closed system or grappled with the question of the historical
origin of every form.

I am in a more fortunate position as I only need to know one thing: what is
the *effect* of ornament?

[Heinrich] Wagner (*Handbuch der Architektur*, 4.1: 31ff.)[1] makes the usual
distinction between decorative and constructional ornament. Of the former,
however, he can say no more than that it "should rationally animate dead surfaces and rigid articulations," whereas he gives to constructional ornament the
task "of elevating and embellishing the stylistically conditioned art-form of the
structural parts."

Not much can be done with this explanation.

Even the distinction between decorative and constructional ornament is of
dubious value. In applying it, one immediately runs into problems, for the de-
marcation between the two terms is so tenuous. In any case, it makes an inad-
visable starting point, so I shall take ornament as a single whole and suggest the
following provisional definition: *Ornament is an expression of excessive force of
form.* The heavy mass sprouts no flowers.

Let us evaluate the definition first with a Doric temple.

The whole lower half of the temple, from the capital downward, displays no
decorative forms; neither the stylobate nor the column shaft carries a decoration. In the case of the stylobate, we have the raw mass lying heavily on the

ground, scarcely achieving the simplest form; in that of the shaft, we expect the effort and concentrated strength that the fluting clearly expresses. A sculptured column would altogether lose the character of concentration. We shall speak later of the capital. What happens above the columns? The entablature, which is the load to be carried, is a massive horizontal member. If the load were greater, the columns would give way in the middle and the horizontal would dominate. But the reverse is true, for the vertical force is the more powerful one. At first, it penetrates the weight only slightly. The architrave remains an unbroken whole, and the effect of the thrust is seen only in the guttae over the column. With the overcoming of this first resistance, the load becomes lighter and the force breaks through. A tectonically independent life is apparent in the vertical parts of the triglyphs, which resume the fluting motif of the columns, and in the intervening metopes. The latter are the spaces created for developing the most refined figures, and when finally the mutules are filled in along the length of the entablature, they give the impression of the column's thrust gently ebbing away after having extended itself over the whole entablature. Now follows the highest achievement: gravity is subdued. The excess of upward force is seen in the *lifting** of the pediment and celebrates its greatest triumph in its sculptures—which, relieved of pressure, can develop freely.†

In conceding what has been said thus far, one might still find an inconsistency in the capital, which invites interpretation not as an excess of upward force but as a compression of the column. This, however, is incorrect. Bötticher found such an idea clearly presented in the painted rim of leaves that seem to buckle under the pressure; in replying, I beg to champion the firsthand impression. In no way do the leaves indicate a compression: they sprout from the echinus quite unconstrainedly. Indeed, what would be achieved if the weight of the whole entablature could only bend a few leaves? The motif would be absurdly

---

*Vischer once asked whether the gable rises or falls. It does both. It is lifted in the center, which is expressed in the ridge tiles. The sides slope downward, for the (sideward facing) *acroteria* bend back the force that gathers there. (The steeper the gable, the more pronounced these acroteria must be.) The Gothic, on the contrary, displays an excess of vertical force in the *crockets*.

†Perhaps it is also possible to establish a correspondence between the figures on the pediment and the number of triglyphs. I have not investigated this issue, but I note, for example, such a correspondence in the Temple of Aegina: eleven triglyphs and eleven figures. On the astonishing correspondence between architecture and composition in the Gigantomachy in Pergamon, see Brunn's essay (Berlin, 1885), p. 50. [Heinrich von Brunn, "Über die kunstgeschichtliche Stellung der pergamenischen Gigantomachie," *Jahrbuch der königlich Preußischen Kunstsammlungen* 5 (1884): 231–92, esp. p. 278.]

petty. In short, it seems to me that the leaves have nothing to do with the conflict of those powerful masses but are possible only because the load has not extinguished the free life of the column.

It is important to understand that compression can never have an aesthetic effect. Self-determination is the first requirement. Every form must be sufficient reason in itself; and so it is here. The column spreads out because it makes good sense to take the load on broad shoulders, not because it is crushed.* It still retains enough strength to contract once again (directly under the abacus). And it is precisely the extent to which it spreads out that guarantees its self-determination. It is just as wide as the abacus. But the abacus—and here we are astonished at the architectural sensitivity of the Greek architects—this abacus is a proportional representation of the whole entablature. That is, the column knows exactly what it has to support and acts accordingly.

With Ionic architecture, as we have already noted, a striving toward freer movement asserts itself. There is no longer a desire to carry such a heavy load. The column is unburdened and the lighter impression is principally achieved by having it discharge its excess of force into the volutes (which is not the case with the painted Doric column). In comparisons of the Doric and Ionic orders, I have often heard it said that the Ionic holds its head freely upright, whereas the Doric bends its head down. The ancients themselves seem to have had this impression, at least if one may refer to the telamones of Akragas as Doric and the caryatids of the Erechtheion as Ionic. I believe such a view is justified. Indeed, I have even known a person who had seen neither the telamones nor the caryatids characterize the Doric column with its echinus as very similar to someone spreading out his elbows and bending his head and likewise to describe the volutes of the Ionic column as the flowing hair of a fully upright figure.

We can illustrate the relation between the two styles in Goethe's apt phrase (from his essay on architecture of 1788): "It is human nature to continue ever further, even beyond one's goal; and thus it is only natural that the eye has constantly sought to find more slender proportions in the relation of the thickness of a column to its height and that the mind has derived from this a sense of *greater elevation and freedom*."[2]

Greater elevation and freedom! That is also the impulse that transformed the Romanesque style into Gothic forms. In these prolegomena, which are intended to be no more than hints, I cannot begin to analyze these decorations; but such an analysis is not difficult with the principles put forth. It becomes clear that all the fireworks of Gothic ornament were possible only because of

*Of course we are not denying some elastic deflection.

the enormous excess of force of form over matter. Ornament is the blossoming of a force that has nothing more to achieve. Thus it was a very correct feeling that transformed the capital into a lightly foliated ornament, for the Gothic pillar soared upward without dissipating any of its strength. The Italian Renaissance was equally sensitive when it later felt the need to insert a piece of entablature between the arch and a column so that the arch was not carried directly on the capital. The force of the column is broken like a stream of water that meets a barrier. It shows the profound architectural insight of [Filippo] Brunelleschi that he recognized this necessity. It also demonstrates that our thesis is well founded and correct in its essential points.

For this reason I hope that no one will demand further analyses here, and I would like to conclude this section* with a historical observation.

Mature cultures always demand a great excess of force of form over matter. The restful effect of compact masses of masonry becomes unbearable. The demand is for movement and excitement as we have already had occasion to observe. With respect to decoration, the result is an art that in its sensitivity nowhere allows quiet surfaces but demands of each muscle a pulsating life. Thus in the Gothic period, in Arabian architecture, and (under very different architectural conditions) in late Rome we find similar symptoms. People "enliven" every surface with niches, pilasters, and so on, as an outlet for the disquiet they feel in their own bodies, and that precludes them from taking any pleasure in tranquillity.

VIII. PRINCIPLES OF HISTORICAL JUDGMENT

We have seen how the general human condition sets the standard for architecture. This principle may be extended still further: any architectural style reflects the *attitude and movement of people* in the period concerned. How people like to move and carry themselves is expressed above all in their costume, and it is not difficult to show that architecture corresponds to the costume of

---

*Architecture has a secondary source of ornamentation in the so-called suspended ornaments, that is, rings, hangings, bands, and so on. These ornaments cannot actually be called architectonic, for they are a transposition of the way in which the *finished human form* is adorned. They work in the very same way: namely, through the sense of touch. Cinctured columns, for example, evoke the same feeling as a bare arm wearing a bracelet. After the masterly development of the principle of ornament that Lotze has given in the *Mikrokosmos* (2: 203ff.) [H. Lotze, *Mikrokosmos* (Leipzig, 1856–64)] I need not say anything further here.

its period. I would like to emphasize this principle of historical characterization all the more energetically because I am unable here to pursue the idea in any detail.

The Gothic style will serve as an example.

Lübke[3] saw it as the expression of spiritualism. Semper called it lapidary scholasticism. According to what principles has it been judged? The *tertium comparationis* is not exactly clear, even though there may be a grain of truth in both descriptions. We will find firm ground only by referring these psychological observations to the human figure.

The mental fact in question is the tendency to be precise, sharp, and conscious of the will. Scholasticism clearly reveals this aversion to anything that is imprecise; its concepts are formulated with the greatest precision.

Physically, this aspiration presents itself in precise movements, pointed forms, no relaxation, nothing bloated, and a will that is everywhere most decisively expressed.

Scholasticism and spiritualism can be considered the expression of the Gothic period only if one keeps in mind this intermediate stage, during which a psychological feeling is directly transformed into bodily form. The sophisticated subtlety of the scholastic centuries and the spiritualism that tolerated no matter divested of will can have shaped architectural form only through their bodily expression.

Here we find the Gothic forms presented in principle: the bridge of the nose becomes narrower; the forehead assumes hard vertical folds; the whole body stiffens and pulls itself together; all restful expansiveness disappears. It is well known that many people (especially university lecturers) like the feeling of rolling a sharply angled pencil between their fingers in order to sharpen their thoughts. A round pencil would not serve the same purpose. What does roundness want? Nobody knows. And the same is true with the Romanesque rounded arch; no definite will can be recognized. It ascends, but this upward impulse finds a clear expression only in the pointed arch.

The human foot points forward but does that show in the blunt outline in which it terminates? No. The Gothic age was troubled by this lack of the precise expression of a will, and so it devised a shoe with a long pointed toe (the crakow appears in the twelfth century; see [Hermann] Weiss, *Kostümkunde*, 4: 8).[4]

The width of the sole is a result of the body's weight. But the body has no rights; it is material, and no concessions are to be made to senseless matter. The will must penetrate every part.

This is why Gothic architecture dissolved the wall into vertical members, and the sole of the human foot becomes a shoe with three high heels, thereby eliminating the feeling of a broadly planted sole.

I shall not pursue how the principle of the gable can be seen in the pointed hats, how stiff, delicate, determined, and precise all of these movements are, or finally (as I have already noted) how the body itself appears to have been stretched out and made excessively slim;* I am satisfied if I have made my point.

It is astonishing to travel through history and observe how architecture everywhere imitates the ideal of man in the form and movement of the body and how great *painters* even created a suitable architecture for their figures. Do the architectural forms of Rubens not pulsate with the same life that animates his bodies?

I will conclude. It has not been my intention to give a complete psychology of architecture, but I hope to have made one idea manifest: an organic understanding of the history of forms will be possible only when we know with what threads our form imagination is bound to human nature.

The historian who has to evaluate a style has no organon for his definition of character but is directed only by an instinctive presentiment.

The ideal of "working exactly" is also present in the historical disciplines. Art history adopts such an ideal above all to avoid any corrupting contact with aesthetics; and often the historian simply strives to describe what happened and when, without comment. Little as I am inclined to underestimate the positive side of this tendency, I firmly believe that this cannot be the highest calling of scholarship. A history that seeks only to ascertain the chronology of what has taken place cannot be sustained; it would be particularly mistaken if it supposed itself thereby to have become "exact." One can work exactly only when it is possible to capture the stream of phenomena in fixed forms. Mechanics, for instance, supplies physics with such fixed forms. The humanities still lack any such foundation; it is only in psychology that it can even be sought. Psychology would also enable art history to trace individual events to general principles or laws. Psychology is certainly far from a state of perfection in which it could present itself as an organon for historical characteristics, but I do not believe this goal is unattainable.

Some may object to the idea of a psychology of art—one that infers from the impressions we receive the popular sentiments that generated these forms and proportions—by arguing that conclusions of this kind are without foundation,

---

*One should certainly not forget that paintings, and even more so sculptures, may not be safe historical sources for this observation.

for proportions and lines do not always mean the same thing but change with the human sense of form [*Formgefühl*].

This objection cannot be refuted so long as we have no psychological basis; yet as soon as the organization of the human body is shown to be the constant denominator within all change, we are safe from this charge, for the continuity of this organization also insures the continuity of the sense of form.

It is too well known to require comment that styles are not created at will by individuals but grow out of popular sentiments and that individuals can create successfully only by immersing themselves in the universal and by representing perfectly the character of the nation and the time. But even if the sense of form remains qualitatively unchanged, one should not underestimate the fluctuations in its intensity. There have been few periods in which every form has been purely understood, that is, experienced. These are the only periods that have created styles of their own.

But since the large forms of architecture cannot respond to every minute change in popular sentiment, a gradual alienation sets in, and the style becomes a lifeless schema maintained only by tradition. The individual forms continue to be used but without understanding; they are falsely applied and thus completely deprived of life.

The pulse of the age then has to be felt elsewhere: in the minor or decorative arts, in the lines of ornament, of lettering, and so on.*

Here the sense of form satisfies itself in the purest way, and here also the birthplace of a new style has to be sought.

This fact is of great importance for countering the materialist nonsense that finds it necessary to account for the history of architectural form through the mere compulsion of material, climate, and purpose. I am far from underestimating the significance of these factors, but I must insist that they can never divert a people's true vision of form into other paths. What a nation has to say, it always says; and if we observe its language of form where it speaks most freely and later rediscover the same forms, the same lines, and the same proportions in the high art of architecture, then we may rightly expect to hear no more of that mechanistic view.

And with that, the most dangerous adversary of a psychology of art will have quit the field.

---

*Since we started to print from cast-metal types, this easy flexibility has admittedly disappeared. Today we have become accustomed (in standard [German] type) to put Baroque uppercase letters in front of Gothic lowercase letters. See [Reinhold] Bechstein, *Die Deutsche Druckschrift* [*und ihr Verhältnis zum Kunststil alter und neuer Zeit* (Heidelberg: C. Winter, 1884)].

NOTES

1. Heinrich Wagner, "Die Anlage des Gebäudes," in Josef Durm et al. eds., *Handbuch der Architektur,* part 4, Halbband 1: "... *in sinniger Weise tote Flächen und starre Gliederungen beleben sollen.*" (Darmstadt, 1888–1923) [Mallgrave and Ikonomou]

2. Johann Wolfgang Goethe, "Zur Theorie der bildenden Künste: Baukunst," in *Goethes Werke* (Weimar: Hermann Böhlau, 1896), 47: 60–64: "*Es liegt in der menschlichen Natur immer weiter, ja über ihr Ziel fortzuschreiten; und so war es auch natürlich, daß in dem Verhältniß der Säulendicke zur Höhe das Auge immer das Schlankere suchte, und der Geist mehr Hoheit und Freiheit dadurch zu empfinden glaubte*" (p. 62. Wölfflin's emphasis). [Mallgrave and Ikonomou]

3. Wilhelm Lübke (1826–1893) was professor of art history in Zurich, Stuttgart, and Karlsruhe. He was the author of *Grundriß der Kunstgeschichte* (Outline of art history), 1860, among many other period studies. [Mallgrave and Ikonomou]

4. Hermann Weiss, *Kostümkunde: Handbuch der Geschichte der Tracht, des Baues und des Geräthes der Völker des Alterthums* (Stuttgart: Ebner & Seubert, 1862), 2: part 2, chap. 3, 557ff. [Mallgrave and Ikonomou]

ALOIS RIEGL

The Geometric Style

All art, and that includes decorative art as well, is inextricably tied to nature. All art forms are based on models in nature. This is true not only when they actually resemble their natural prototypes but even when they have been drastically altered by the human beings who created them, either for practical purposes or simple pleasure.

This intimate connection between art and nature, however, is more evident in some media than in others. It is most evident in sculpture, where the natural model is directly reproduced in all three physical dimensions. However, whenever artists abandon the third dimension and the realm of complete physical appearances—which is what happens when an image is rendered on a flat surface—then they begin to deviate more radically from natural prototypes, so that the connection between art and nature becomes obscured.

Let us take this point a little further. What we have just done is to describe the two major divisions of the decorative arts: sculpture in the round and surface decoration. Furthermore, we can already draw conclusions about their genetic relationship. If we ignore concrete examples for a moment and try in a purely deductive way to reason out abstractly which of them came first in the development, then we will find ourselves forced a priori—in the face of considerable opinion to the contrary—to conclude that three-dimensional sculpture is the earlier, more primitive medium, while surface decoration is the later and more refined. That is to say, once human beings acquired a mimetic instinct, there was nothing very complicated about modeling an animal reasonably well in wet clay, since the model—the living animal—already existed in nature. When, however, they first attempted to draw, engrave, or paint the same animal on a flat surface, they were involving themselves in a truly creative act. In this case, they could no longer copy the three-dimensional physical model; instead, they had to invent the silhouette or contour line freely, since it does not exist in reality.* Only after this creative act did art begin to acquire its endless

*Travelers often describe how Hottentotts and Australian aborigines fail to recognize their own image in a drawing or photograph: they can comprehend things physically, but not

representational possibilities. This turning away from three-dimensional corporeality toward two-dimensional illusion was a crucial step; it unleashed the imagination from the constraints of the strict observation of nature and allowed a greater freedom in the manipulation and combination of forms.

No matter how divorced from nature a freely invented decorative form may seem, the natural model is always discernible in its individual details. This is true of both sculpture and surface decoration. The snakelike feet of a Titan, for example, are based just as much on prototypes from nature as is the human upper torso, even though Titans as such do not actually exist in the real world. Similarly, the purely linear, three-pronged flowers found, for example, on Cypriote vases were obviously derived from lotus blossoms, regardless of whether the Cypriote potters who made the designs were conscious of their connection to a particular species of Egyptian flora or not.

Therefore, nature continued to provide models for art even after the third dimension was abandoned and the imaginary encircling line had become an element of representation. Even though they are not three-dimensional, animal figures rendered in terms of contour lines are still very much representations of animals. Ultimately, however, line became an art form in and of itself and was used without direct reference to any particular model in nature. Since, of course, not just any irregular scribble can claim to be an art form, linear shapes were made to obey the fundamental artistic laws of symmetry and rhythm. As a result, straight lines became triangles, squares, rhombuses, zigzag patterns, etc., while curved lines produced circles, undulating lines, and spirals. These are the shapes familiar to us from plane geometry; in art history, they are generally referred to as *geometric*. Consequently, the style based on the exclusive or predominant use of these patterns is called the Geometric Style.

Even if the forms of the Geometric Style do not seem to be based on real things, they are nevertheless not completely divorced from nature. The same laws of symmetry and rhythm that govern geometric shapes are apparent in the natural forms of humans, animals, plants, and crystals as well. In fact, it does not require any particular insight to perceive how the basic shapes and configurations of plane geometry are latent in natural things. Therefore, the proposition made at the beginning of the chapter about the intimate relationship between all art forms and the physical appearance of nature is also true of the Geometric Style. Geometric forms in art behave in respect to other art forms precisely in the same way that laws of mathematics do with regard to the laws

---

two-dimensionally—proof that the latter kind of perception presupposes an advanced stage of culture.

of natural living things. Nature, it seems, can claim as few examples of absolute perfection as humans can of their ethical behavior; after all, the kinds of things that make history, that immediately capture our attention and save us from the monotonous pace of everyday life tend to be the exceptions to abstract laws. The Geometric Style, strictly constructed in accordance with the highest laws of symmetry and rhythm, is from the standpoint of regularity the most perfect of styles; on our scale of values, however, it occupies the lowest rank. Our present understanding of how the arts developed associates the Geometric Style as a rule with cultures still at a relatively low stage of development.

Despite this limited aesthetic appreciation, interest in the Geometric Style has mounted considerably in the last two decades, first of all within archaeological circles. Excavations at the earliest burial sites on Cyprus, the pre-Homeric strata of Troy-Hissarlik, the Terramare burials of the Po River Valley, and the graves of prehistoric northern and central Europe, to name a few, have unearthed objects in the Geometric Style whose origins, according to very convincing evidence, date back to relatively early periods. This information has been supplemented by the research of ethnologists, who often discover the typical linear motifs of the Geometric Style adorning the utensils of modern primitive peoples. If, following the spirit of today's natural science, we are justified in assuming that contemporary primitive cultures are the rudimentary survivors of the human race from earlier cultural periods, then their geometric ornament must represent an earlier phase of development in the decorative arts and is therefore of great historical significance.

The few basic motifs of the Geometric Style occur in the same manner among practically all prehistoric and contemporary primitive cultures in Europe and Asia, in Africa as well as in America and Polynesia, although they may occur in different combinations and with varying preferences for a particular motif. Consequently, some scholars have concluded that the Geometric Style could not have been invented at one geographic location, from whence it spread throughout the world, but that it spontaneously came into existence within most, if not all of the cultures where it occurred. As a result, anyone who tried to argue that two pots with the same zigzag pattern but of disparate geographic provenance were somehow connected to each other—and it need not have been a very direct connection but only a distant relationship separated by a long chain of intermediaries—was considered rather naive and ignorant. The Geometric Style originated spontaneously throughout the entire world: this is the first doctrinaire proposition that is nowadays considered valid for the Geometric Style.

Once this was firmly established, it led immediately to the further conclusion that the impetus for the invention and development of the style must have been the same everywhere. The spirit of our scientific age, in its hectic pursuit of causal relationships, attempted straightaway to get to the bottom of whatever it was that had allowed the Geometric Style to spring spontaneously to life at so many different locations. Moreover, whatever it was, it had to be tangible and material; the simple suggestion that intangible psychological processes might have been involved would not have sufficed. Furthermore, this motivating something could not be sought in the open countryside: the abstract, linear patterns of the Geometric Style are, of course, not obvious in nature; releasing them from their latent existence in nature into an independent existence in art requires a conscious mental act whose intervention, however, was to be ignored at all costs. Therefore, the only tangible things left were the objects made by the human hand. Since this involved technical processes from the most primitive, nascent periods of the human race, then only the most primitive objects and the most fundamental products of the elementary drive for basic necessities made by human hands could come under consideration. The need to protect the body was believed to be one such drive. Very early on, so it seemed, humans must have sought refuge from the hostile outer world within the wickerwork fence, or protection against the weather from woven textiles.[1]

Because of the technical procedures they involve, wickerwork and textile weaving seem to be those very crafts which are especially limited to producing linear ornaments. Now, let us try to reconstruct how the linear patterns of the Geometric Style might have come into being had they first appeared to human eyes in the crisscrossing structure of a wickerwork fence or a coarsely woven garment. For example, a fortuitous interweaving of colored fibers might have prompted the creation of a zigzag line; the symmetry of its slanting bands and rhythmic repetition would surely have delighted the human beings who accidently produced it. Of course, should the question arise at this point as to the source of this delight and what might have caused it in primitive people, it would have to be fastidiously ignored; the conclusions made thus far apparently suffice. The reasoning goes like this: the human hand produced the first geometric ornaments in an unconscious, nonspeculative way, guided only by the necessities of a purely practical purpose. Once they were available, people were then capable of using them however they liked. For example, a zigzag line could be pressed into a cup of wet clay. Even though it was not necessitated by technique on a ceramic cup, like crisscrossed fibers in weaving, it was nevertheless just as appealing in ceramics, so that it began to be used even in techniques where it had not spontaneously originated. The geometric zigzag motif, originally the fortuitous product of a purely technical process, had thereby been promoted to an ornament and an artistic motif. The simplest and most important artistic motifs of the Geometric Style were originally generated by the techniques of wicker and textile weaving: this is the second absolute proposition about the Geometric Style considered valid today.

This second proposition overlaps with the first one regarding the spontaneous, independent generation of the style at different locations in the world, to the extent that the elementary need to protect the body must have come into force independently at a number of different places throughout the world and therefore could at the same time have prompted the spontaneous invention of weaving wickerwork fences and cloth at a number of different locations. In this manner, one proposition supports the other; together they present an even more convincing and harmonious picture of the formation of the Geometric Style and of the earliest, most primitive artistic activity.

It was Gottfried Semper who first traced the linear ornaments of the Geometric Style back to the techniques of weaving, wickerwork, and textiles. This conclusion, however, did not occur to him in isolation as we described above; it was related to the fundamental theory he sought to establish and demonstrate systematically in his book *Der Stil*: the theory of dressing as the origin of all monumental architecture. As a result, he was able to associate all flat decoration with the idea of a protective blanket and its trimmed, bound border, terms that are already linguistically connected with textiles. It is obvious in numerous passages in *Der Stil* that Semper originally conceived of the prototypes of blanket and border primarily as abstractions and not really in a concrete materialist way, for Semper would surely have been the last person to discard thoughtlessly truly creative, artistic ideas in favor of the physical-materialist imitative impulse; it was his numerous followers who subsequently modified the theory into its crassly materialist form. Nevertheless, the desire to fit things into a materialist context was evident, and in at least one place in *Der Stil*,* it is clear beyond a doubt that Semper is espousing the theory of the technical-materialist origin of geometric ornament, specifically in regard to the emergence of pattern from wickerwork and weaving.

Semper's theory was readily accepted in art historical circles. The historical, scientific spirit of our age, ever ready to probe in reverse the causal relationships of all phenomena, was more than charmed and satisfied by a hypothesis that could claim an origin so natural and so astonishingly simple for so eminent an intellectual sphere as that of art. Classical archaeology was especially enthusiastic, since it was groping for some way to deal with the protoclassical art that had been unearthed in Greece. Conze's work of twenty years ago is crucial in this respect.[2] This scholar, who is still the most distinguished exponent

---

*G. Semper, *Der Stil in den technischen Künsten; oder praktischer Ästhetik* (Munich, 1878–1879), 1:213, to which we shall return.

of the two propositions, applied Semper's theory to the vases of the Greek Geometric Style. His accomplishment loomed so large that there was no immediate demand to go beyond the general wording of the propositions. It was considered superfluous to examine the process any more closely or to discuss any other questions, such as which of the various weaving techniques might have been involved or which geometric motifs should be properly associated with them, etc. Only recently, as we shall see later, have there been any attempts to delve somewhat more deeply into these problems. However, the propositions concerning the spontaneous generation of the Geometric Style at various locations from weaving techniques not only went unchallenged by these efforts but actually began to receive greater support.

Let us now test the validity of the currently accepted view about the origin of the Geometric Style.

. . .

Wickerworking and textile weaving are considered to be the oldest mechanical skills, while the rectilinear, geometric shapes count as the oldest decorative or artistic forms. Since their versatility and ease of execution make straight-sided geometric shapes especially well suited as patterns in simple woven objects, it seemed most natural to relate both phenomena in causal terms and to declare that the rectilinear geometric figures were not originally the result of artistic invention but were generated spontaneously by technology.

The rectilinear geometric ornaments, however, are not the only ones found on the earliest proto- and early Greek vases: there are also curvilinear forms such as undulating lines, circles, and spirals, etc., whose origin cannot be as convincingly attributed to the weaving techniques as it can for the rectilinear ornaments. Consequently, a number of other crafts had to be called into action. This resulted in what has increasingly become over the past twenty years a fundamental method of classical archaeology: it consists of taking motifs whose origins could not be traced back systematically beyond a certain point and matching them up with the techniques from which, unaided by conscious, artistic invention, they had been spontaneously generated. This is the theory of the technical-materialist origin of primal art forms, which archaeology has elevated to a position of unlimited authority. Within this theory, the origin of rectilinear geometric ornaments from weaving is a mere subcategory, just as the rectilinear geometric ornaments themselves comprise but a fraction of all of the basic ornamental motifs that have come to our attention. Almost as if they had been looking directly over the shoulders of prehistoric people in their first moments of artistic inspiration, as though they had witnessed the actual materials and tools, archaeologists proceeded to point out the specific technique, be it weaving, metalworking, or stonecutting, that was responsible for each of the individual decorative motifs on the earliest vases. An enormous amount of energy was squandered on these investigations, a wide variety of combinations investigated, and as was to be expected, a wide variety of techniques suggested for one and the same motif. And just as it had been a German, Häckel, who developed Darwin's theory most systematically and authoritatively, so it was the German archaeologists who once again strode staunchly in the forefront.[3] How far they strayed from the ideas of the actual father of the theory, Gottfried Semper, is revealed by the following excerpt from *Der Stil* 2: 87:

> The rule that the decorative aspects of a vessel are directly related to the material and mode of manufacture leads to problematic uncertainties regarding the original technique and medium of many common decorative forms. This is due to interactions among the various media, which were already influencing and modifying one another at an early stage. Therefore, it is difficult to determine whether the consistent rendering of bands of zigzag ornaments, waves, and scrolls in painted and incised technique on the earliest ceramic vessels was derived from the same shallowly engraved embellishments on the oldest bronze utensils and metal weapons, or vice versa, or whether such patterns originally had no relation to either material. . . . *The conscious recognition and artistic exploitation of the limitations and possibilities* inherent in the various materials available for artistic activity *does not begin until an advanced stage of art.*

This is the cautious wording of an author who, as both artist and scholar knew and understood better than most others of his century the technical procedures involved in the creation of art as a larger, mutually interactive process. According to Semper, as quoted above, technology played its formative role at a more advanced stage of artistic development and not at the very inception of artistic activity. This is precisely my conviction. Nothing is further from my mind than to deny the important role that technical processes play in the evolution and further development of certain ornamental motifs, and it will always remain Gottfried Semper's most valuable achievement to have opened our eyes in this respect. Should this point become obscured or insufficiently emphasized in what follows, it is only because I have set myself the special task of refuting the exaggerated claims made for technology in regard to a particular stage of development, namely the one in which the very earliest art forms were created. I do not intend to dispute the value and significance of the materialist movement in art of the last twenty years, or even less to criticize the theory of Darwin and his followers. It is clear that the theory of the technical-materialist origin of all primitive art forms represented a necessary phase of archaeological scholarship, which, as things stood, had to be worked through. This is confirmed not only by the prominence of its first pioneers, Semper and Conze, but also no less by the fact that the theory enjoyed immediate and widespread dissemination throughout all of Germany and far beyond. Nevertheless, it is now time to admit that we have gone too far in this direction as regards art, and that serious concerns, which I will elaborate shortly, compel us to discredit this tendency to use technical-materialist premises to account for the earliest art works made by human beings.

. . .

We now know beyond a doubt that there were groups of human beings who developed a highly remarkable form of art even though they never possessed a textile technology, except for sewn animal skins. They were apparently able to protect their bodies, to meet the elemental need generally considered to be the impetus for textile art, supposedly the first and earliest technique, without resorting to wickerwork enclosures and woven clothing. These groups of people lived in caves and clothed themselves with the skins of the animals they hunted. Their low cultural standard can be gauged from the fact that they sucked the marrow from the bones of the animals they killed and left the uneaten meat to rot in the caves. We are confronted by a form of cannibalism. The many needles of animal and fish bone that have been discovered show that these cave dwellers were able to sew skins together using the sinews of animals, as the grooves often found on leg bones serve to demonstrate. One might be tempted to interpret the zigzag pattern as the spontaneous product of the sewn seam, were it not for evidence that proves that the cave dwellers were capable of far greater and much more accomplished things, for these quasi cannibals with their roughly hewn, unpolished axes, practiced a genuine and unquestionable form of sculpture.

The carvings [Plate 27] and the engraved reliefs [Plate 28] on animal bones that have been discovered at several locations in western Europe, especially in the caves of Aquitaine, and whose authenticity has been largely established beyond any doubt by the very precise and conscientious excavations and records of Lartet and Christy, have already been known and published for a number of decades.*

---

*Consult in particular E. A. Lartet and H. Christy, *Reliquiae Aquitanicae; Being Contributions to the Archaeology and Palaeontology of Périgord and the Adjoining Provinces of Southern France* (London, 1875); furthermore, the *Dictionnaire archéologique de la Gaule, époque celtique,* Commission de la Topographie des Gaules (Paris, 1875), from which Plates 28 and 29 have been taken; and the concise summary of the enlightened A. Bertrand, *La Gaule avant les gaulois d'après les monuments et les textes* (Paris, 1884), the source of Plate 27.

Plate 27. Carved Reindeer Bone Spear Thrower from Laugerie-Basse

Plate 28. Engraved Reindeer Bone from La Madeleine

· · ·

The best place at present to get an overall impression of the art of the cave dwellers is in the collection of the Musée des antiquités nationales in the old castle at Saint-Germain-en-Laye, where almost all of the objects found to date are exhibited either in the original or in plaster casts. The material involved is almost exclusively animal bone, mostly reindeer, and the main technique is carving or engraving. It is very enlightening to observe the relationship that exists between the techniques of carving and engraving on these earliest of artworks. There are many fully round objects, such as handles of weapons or knives carved in the shape of a reindeer [Plate 27].* There are even frequent repetitions of the same motif. Then comes a whole series of developmental phases during which the sculptural characteristics gradually disappear: at first, three-dimensional sculpture becomes flattened, then various degrees of high relief are followed by low relief, finally resulting in pure engraving [Plate 28], which is frequently combined with low relief as one merges into the other.

This corresponds exactly to the natural development established at the beginning of the chapter in a purely speculative way. The earliest works of art are sculptural; consequently, all artistic activity begins with the direct reproduction of the actual physical appearance of natural things in response to an imitative impulse that has been spurred into action by a psychic process to be described

*The well-conceived way in which the forelegs conform to the shape of the animal's torso without ruining the naturalistic effect deserves considerable attention, according to Lartet, moreover, this piece remained unfinished.

below. Since things in nature, however, are only seen from one side, relief sculpture began to satisfy the same purpose; it renders just enough of the three-dimensional appearance of a thing to convince the human eye. Subsequently, two-dimensional representation was established and led to the idea of the outline. Finally, sculptural qualities were abandoned all together and replaced by drawing.

The most important part of the whole process is undoubtedly the appearance of the outline, which captures the image of any entity in nature on any given surface. This is the moment when line, the basic component of all drawing, all painting, and in fact, all art that is restricted to two dimensions, was invented. And this was the step that the cave dwellers of Aquitaine had already taken, even though they had never seen the interwoven threads of textile art or felt the need for them. Technical factors surely played a role as well, even within the process described above, but it was by no means the leading role that the supporters of the technical-materialist theory of origin assumed. The impetus did not arise from the technique but, on the contrary, from the particular artistic impulse. First came the desire to create the likeness of a creature from nature in lifeless material, and then came the invention of whatever technique was appropriate. A carved reindeer on the hilt of a dagger certainly does not make it any easier to handle. Therefore, it must have been an immanent artistic drive, alert and restless for action, that human beings possessed long before they invented woven protective coverings for their bodies, and that impelled them to carve bone handles in the shape of reindeer.

Before proceeding to describe the nature of this drive in more detail, however, we should take another look at the evolution of two-dimensional decoration from sculpture in order to show that there is nothing at all outlandish about our assertion.

. . .

The techniques employed by the cave dwellers of Aquitaine are not, strictly speaking, peculiar to the so-called applied arts and crafts but are much more characteristic of so-called fine art, namely figurative sculpture. This fact reveals how senseless and unjustifiable it is from the scholarly point of view to make such a distinction. The same is true for content, since as we have seen, cave art consists mostly of reproductions of creatures from nature, not insignificant, "purely ornamental" two-dimensional designs. The animals depicted on the various implements were either a source of food or a source of danger: reindeer, horses, bison, goats, cattle, bear, and fish. We also find the human figure, both engraved and in the round, but rendered much more awkwardly than the animals: an ubiquitous phenomenon in primitive art.

The objects discovered in the caves of Dordogne, therefore, overwhelmingly contradict the general assumption that the purely practical technique of weaving represents the first creative activity, since they are executed specifically in the kind of techniques where the subject and artistic content are already determined before the material is worked. The reason for shaping the material into an animal, whether in three or two dimensions, was purely artistic and decorative. The intention was specifically to decorate the tools. It is the urge to decorate that is one of the most elementary of human drives, more elementary in fact than the need to protect the body. This is not the first time such a proposition has been made; Semper himself expressed it several times.* It is thus even more difficult to understand why, in the face of all this evidence, the origin of creative activity is still believed to postdate the invention of the techniques used to create protection for the body. Do we not still encounter Polynesian tribes today who do without any form of clothing, while they tattoo their bodies from head to toe, thereby making full use of linear decorative motifs?† Unfortunately, we have no way of knowing whether the cave dwellers of Aquitaine tattooed their skin as well; there is, at any rate, no evidence for it on their representations of human figures. We know for certain, however, that they wore jewelry. Otherwise, what would have been the purpose of the large number of perforated cattle and bear teeth found in caves partially engraved with animals except to be strung on a sinew or strip of raffia and worn around the neck? Here people are already following the elementary artistic principle of arranging things in rows and, moreover, without any inspiration from crisscrossed fibers, since the cave dwellers apparently had not felt the need to invent and practice the technique of weaving. The same goes for symmetry. Already Lartet and Bertrand noted symmetrically arranged ornaments in relief on a tool that Lartet believed was used for scooping out marrow.‡ [Plate 29] However, there are also ornaments on the objects produced by the Aquitanian cave dwellers, which are based on pure rhythm and abstract symmetry. In other words, there are also examples of the linear motifs of the Geometric Style.

*He states in the same passage cited above from *Der Stil* (1:213): "The art of covering the nakedness of the body (*excluding the painting of the body itself* [Riegl's emphasis]) is presumably a later invention than the use of protective surfaces for shelters and spatial enclosures." *Der Stil* contains the statement: " . . . the adornment of the body itself for cultural, philosophical reasons initially activates the sense of beauty" (2:466).

†Semper's statement in *Der Stil* (1:92), contradicts what was quoted above: "The motifs on the skin of these people consist of painted or tattooed *threads* . . . " He mitigates this contradiction by explaining that tattooing might not be characteristic of a primitive, but of a more advanced state of culture. This assumption, once again, only makes sense within the context of Semper's frequently expressed idea about the perfect original state of the human

Plate 29. Marrow Spoon of Graved Decoration from Laugerie-Basse

Zigzag lines occur on engraved reindeer bones [Plate 29].* They are arranged in rhythmic variations of the so-called fish-bone pattern, which include sets of three dashes alternating with each other, networks of crossed lines (the pattern supposedly most closely connected to weaving), and crosses arranged on their sides in rows, as well as many others. They have obviously not been copied from nature but are purely decorative patterns intended to adorn a given surface. Their creation was guided by the same desire to decorate, or *horror vacui,* that informed the animal images. It is important to note, however, that these geometric "patterns" are far fewer in number than the animal images. Whoever agrees that this preference for animal images is not accidental must concede that they predate geometric patterns and acknowledge

---

race. How does this idea, however, fit in with the theory of evolution and its accompanying technical-materialist theory of the origin of art?

‡Bertrand, *La Gaule avant les gaulois* (66): " . . . porte des ornements en relief disposés symétriquement et d'un très bon goût." See also Lartet and Christy, *Reliquiae Aquitanicae.*

*Publications to date have naturally devoted considerably less attention to geometric decoration than to the astonishing carvings. Plate 29 is a relatively good example of the ones published in the *Dictionnaire archéologique de la Gaule;* however, the patterns on the objects not yet published are far better and much stronger than the perfunctory zigzag in Plate 29.

that the creative drive in primitive people initially expressed itself primarily in sculpture. How then did these patterns come into being? The cave dwellers were obviously not familiar with the crisscrossed fibers and threads of the weaving technique that are supposed to have provided the model. But there is really no need to assume this familiarity in the first place, since we have already described how the cave dwellers' experience with sculpture might have led them to invent the line, which is the basic component of all two-dimensional drawing and surface decoration. The invention of line apparently took place during the natural course of an essentially artistic process. Consequently, the cave dwellers were already well acquainted with lines. All they needed to do was to arrange them according to the principles of rhythm and symmetry with which, as we have likewise seen, they were just as familiar. Anyone who can string bear's teeth into a necklace can do the same with engraved lines. The Geometric Style of the cave dwellers of Aquitaine, therefore, was not the material product of a handicraft but the pure fruit of an elementary artistic desire for decoration.

All of art history presents itself as a continuous struggle with material; it is not the tool—which is determined by the technique—but the artistically creative idea that strives to expand its creative realm and increase its formal potential. Why should this situation, which obtains throughout the history of art, have been any different during its initial stages?

The surviving cultural data concerning the artistic activity of the earliest, apparently semicannibal people does not require us in any way to assume a technical-materialist origin for art, and especially for decorative motifs of the Geometric Style: in fact, the evidence directly contradicts such an origin.

In light of this conclusion, it is no longer necessary to speculate about how, for example, one geometric motif or another arose spontaneously from one of the weaving techniques and then was applied to another material in a different technique. We have already seen that weaving by itself could not satisfactorily account for the origin of all geometric ornaments in every case, and that other techniques had to be pressed into service, especially metalworking, which presupposes a relatively advanced level of culture. We will be examining specific examples of this kind of scholarship in the following chapters.

· · ·

The question still remains as to why purely geometric "patterns" or linear decorations have survived so persistently on textile products like weaving and wickerwork right into our own time. It is no doubt because these patterns are best suited to textile technique, or better said, because it is more difficult in these techniques to go beyond angular, linear patterns. As is well known, weaving in particular finally did succeed in creating roughly rounded shapes: the human artistic impulse has always aimed unswervingly at transcending technical limitations. At the same time, however, the geometric patterns that could be executed with less effort remained continuously in use, particularly in minor arts. The late antique weaving workshops in Egypt are a good example. There was no curvilinear form that the Egyptians could not execute, and yet it is always the Gamma, the Tau, and other geometric patterns that decorate hems and simple borders, especially on the less prominent parts that served mainly as binding or neutral trimming. This was not because they were throwbacks to the erstwhile primary, weaving motifs but simply because they were the easiest and simplest motifs to represent.

Rectilinear geometric motifs arranged according to the principles of rhythm and symmetry do indeed seem to be most appropriate for the simpler types of textile art. This does not at all imply, however, that these patterns were originally peculiar to textile technology alone, which then, so to speak, gave birth to them. No one today is in a position to say whether the earliest linear ornaments, as they appear, for instance, on the tools of Aquitanian cave dwellers, were first incised on bones, carved into wood or fruit rinds, or tattooed on the skin.

Contrary to current opinion, I do not find it at all unnatural that the geometric decoration of the so-called Bronze Age should have succeeded the figurative carvings and engravings of the Stone Age.* Once the possibilities of line and of its various rhythmic and symmetrical combinations on a plane were recognized, it is easy to understand why they were particularly singled out for surface decoration: they were simply easier to create than the silhouettes of animals or human beings. Moreover, figurative shapes could still be executed in sculpture. However, the simpler, more easily-rendered ornaments readily sufficed as decoration for the countless tools and vessels required by advancing civilization, especially for ceramic examples. These included the geometric mo-

---

*Hjalmar Stolpe seems to have discovered an analogous process in the ornament of certain Polynesian island people: first, human figures carved out of wood are increasingly stylized. Finally, the various parts of the figures, which have been reduced to geometric lines, are used as independent motifs that can be repeated and rhythmically arranged in rows. Stolpe's article first appeared in the Swedish journal *Ymer* and then, translated into German, in *Mittelheilungen der Wiener Anthropologischen Gesellschaft* pamphlets 1 and 2, (1892). Stolpe's tendency to concentrate on narrow, isolated aspects of ornament for his studies and to temporarily ignore large, universal issues seems to me to be the only sensible thing to do in a field like ethnology where only a small amount of rather unsystematic work has been done in regard to art. For this reason, the results of his research, as recorded in the article I have cited, are quite admirable.

tifs, which were first incised and then sketched in paint on ceramic vases. It was not until the next great stage of artistic development that the Geometric Style was abandoned or at least relegated to cheap, mass-produced objects. One of the distinguishing characteristics of this next stage is the introduction of ornamental vegetal motifs. What is extremely enlightening to note in the context of our present discussion is that once plants were established in the repertory of decorative motifs, they—the lotus especially—were immediately geometricized, and clearly because of the technical and artistic advantages inherent in two-dimensional shapes. Animal and human images were occasionally reduced to the Geometric Style even earlier than vegetal motifs. The works produced by the cave dwellers, which we examined earlier, however, prove beyond a doubt that these geometric stylizations were not simply a result of technical necessity or inability; these works aimed unmistakably to capture as much as possible the actual appearance of animals and human beings in the silhouette. Originally, human beings and animals were consciously stylized into linear patterns, just as geometric ornaments were conscious combinations of lines arranged according to the principles of symmetry and rhythm. That is why it is incorrect, as one is often inclined to interpret geometricized figures like those of the Dipylon vases or the art of primitive peoples as the vestigial remains of a supposedly primal geometric style arising from textile technique. On the contrary, geometricized figures, no less than pure geometric shapes, were the result of an artistic process that had already progressed beyond any primary state, a process that was by no means primitive.

NOTES

1. [Riegl often refers to "die textilen Techniken" (textile techniques), which for him always include the weaving of the wickerwork fence (*geflochtener Zaun, Pferch, Ruthenzaun*), baskets (*Korb*), and cloth (*Gewand*, etc.). "Flechterei" (wickerwork) sometimes refers exclusively to basketry or basket weaving, but is often meant to include the weaving of both fences and baskets, as distinct from "Weberei" (weaving), which is strictly the weaving of cloth. More so than in German, the English word "weaving" is specifically associated with cloth production, as is the word "textile" with cloth or fabric. When Riegl uses these terms, however, he is most often referring to the larger concept: by "weaving," he usually means the process of crisscrossing and interweaving that is common to the wickerworking of both fences and baskets, and the weaving of cloth. With the word "textile," used both as a noun and an adjective, he is usually referring to the products or qualities of that process, whether they involve the use of branches, wicker, bast, fibers, or spun threads. I have attempted to keep the terminology as clear as possible without unnecessary wordiness and repetition, but the reader should be alerted to the fact that "weaving" is most often understood as the larger, more inclusive process.] [E. Kain—Tr.]

2. Here Riegl is referring to A. Conze, "Zur Geschichte der Anfänge griechischer

Kunst," parts 1 and 2, *Sitzungsberichte, Kaiserliche Akademie der Wissenschaften, Wien,* Philosophische und Historische Classe, vol. 64 (1870): 505–34, esp. 522–23, 529; vol. 73 (1873): 221–50, esp. 228, 240. [D. Castriota]

3. Biologist and philosopher Ernst Heinrich Philipp August Haeckel (1834–1919) was the first German advocate of Darwin's theory of evolution.

HENRI FOCILLON

II. Forms in the Realm of Space

Space as defined by form. The space of ornament and its variations. Respect for or cancellation of the void: "the system of the series" and "the system of the labyrinth." Hybrids. Motion in an imaginary space.

A work of art is situated in space. But it will not do to say that it simply exists in space: a work of art treats space according to its own needs, defines space, and even creates such space as may be necessary to it. The space of life is a known quantity to which life readily submits; the space of art is a plastic and changing material. We may find it difficult to admit this, so completely are we influenced by the rules of Albertian perspective.[1] But many other perspectives exist as well, and rational perspective itself, which constructs the space of art upon the model of the space of life, has, or will presently be seen, a far greater propensity than we think to strange fictions and paradoxes. It is an effort to admit that anything which may elude the laws of space is still a legitimate treatment of space. Perspective, moreover, pertains only to the plane representation of a three-dimensional object, and this problem is but one of many others with which we are confronted. Let us note at once, however, that it is impossible to consider every one of these problems *in abstracto,* or to reduce them to a certain number of general solutions which would condition each particular application. Form is not indiscriminately architecture, sculpture, or painting. Whatever exchanges may be made between techniques—however decisive the authority of one over the others—form is qualified above all else by the specific realms in which it develops, and not simply by an act of reason on our part, a wish to see form develop regardless of circumstances.

There is, however, one art that seems to be capable of immediate translation into various different techniques: namely, ornamental art, perhaps the first alphabet of our human thought to come into close contact with space. It is, too, an art that takes on a highly individual life—although one that is oftentimes drastically modified by its expression in stone, wood, bronze, or brushstroke. It commands, moreover, a very extensive area of speculation; it is a kind of observatory from which it is possible to discern certain elementary, generalized aspects of the life of forms within their own space. Even before it becomes formal rhythm and combination, the simplest ornamental theme, such as a curve or *rinceau* whose flexions betoken all manner of future symmetries, alternating movements, divisions, and returns, has already given accent to the void in which it occurs, and has conferred upon it a new and original existence. Even if reduced merely to a slender and sinuous line, it is already a frontier, a highway. Ornament shapes, straightens, and stabilizes the bare and arid field on which it is inscribed. Not only does it exist in and of itself, but it also shapes its own environment—to which it imparts a form. If we will follow the metamorphoses of this form, if we will study not merely its axes and its armature, but everything else that it may include within its own particular framework, we will then see before us an entire universe that is partitioned off into an infinite variety of blocks of space. The background will sometimes remain generously visible, and the ornament will be disposed in straight rows or in quincunxes; sometimes, however, the ornament will multiply to prolixity, and wholly devour the background against which it is placed. This respect for or cancellation of the void creates two orders of shapes. For the first, it would seem that space liberally allowed around forms keeps them intact and guarantees their permanence. For the second, forms tend to wed their respective curves, to meet, to fuse, or, at least, from the logical regularity of correspondences and contacts, to pass into an undulating continuity where the relationship of parts ceases to be evident, where both beginning and end are carefully hidden. In other words, what I may call "the system of the series"—a system composed of discontinuous elements sharply outlined, strongly rhythmical, and defining a stable and symmetrical space that protects them against unforeseen accidents of metamorphosis—eventually becomes "the system of the labyrinth," which, by means of mobile syntheses, stretches itself out in a realm of glittering movement and color. As the eye moves across the labyrinth in confusion, misled by a linear caprice that is perpetually sliding away to a secret objective of its own, a new dimension suddenly emerges, which is neither a dimension of motion nor of depth, but which still gives us the illusion of being so. In the Celtic gospels, the ornament, which is constantly overlaying itself and melting into itself, even though it is fixed fast within compartments of letters and panels, appears to be shifting among different planes at different speeds.

It must be obvious that, in the study of ornament, these essential factors are not less important than are pure morphology and genealogy. My statement of the situation might appear entirely too abstract and systematic, were it not henceforth evident that this strange realm of ornament—the chosen home of metamorphoses—has given birth to an entire flora and fauna of hybrids that are subject to the laws of a world distinctly not our own. The qualities of permanence and energy implicit in this realm are extraordinary; although it welcomes both men and animals into its system, it yields nothing to them—it incorporates them. New images are constantly being composed upon the same figures. Engendered by the motions of an imaginary space, these figures would be so absurd in the ordinary regions of life that they would not be permitted to exist. But the more stringently the fauna of the formal labyrinth are held in captivity so much the more zeal do they show in increasing and multiplying. These hybrids are found not only in the abstract, but boldly defined frameworks of the art of Asia and of Romanesque art; they recur too in the great Mediterranean cultures, in Greece and Rome, where they appear as deposits from older civilizations. I need mention here but one example. In the grotesque ornament that was restored to fashion by the men of the Renaissance, it is evident that the charming exotic plants shaped like human beings have undergone, by being transplanted into a very large space and as it were brought back into the open air, a formal degeneration. They have lost their powerful, paradoxical capacity for *life*. Upon the light walls of the loggias their elegance seems dry and fragile. No longer are these ornaments untamed, no longer endlessly distorted by metamorphoses, no longer capable of tirelessly spawning themselves over and over again. They are now merely museum pieces, torn from their natal surroundings, placed well out in the open upon an empty background, harmonious, and dead. Be it background, visible or concealed; support, which remains obvious and stable among the signs or which mingles in their exchanges; plan, which preserves unity and fixity or which undulates beneath the figures and blends with their movements—it is always the question of a space constructed or destroyed by form, animated by it, molded by it.

·   ·   ·

I have spoken already of ornamental space. This important department of art is by no means one that commands all possible approaches, but it is one that has for many centuries and in many countries translated men's meditations on form. Ornamental space is the most characteristic expression of the high Middle Ages in the western world. It is an illustration of a philosophy that renounces development in favor of involution, that surrenders the concrete world for the frivolities of fantasy, the sequence for the interlace. Hellenistic art had disposed about man a limited, exact space. It was a space, whether urban or rural, whether of a street corner or of a garden, that was still a "site," bucolic to a certain extent, and rich with elegantly combined accessories that served as a frame for trivial myths and for romantic fables. But as they hardened and became fixed forms incapable of renewal, the accessories themselves tended gradually to schematize the entire environment in whose topography they had once been but scattered landmarks. The vine-branches and the arbors of Christian pastorals completely overran their landscape. They reduced it to a void. Ornament, resuscitated from primitive civilizations, dispensed with the dimensions of an environment that was degenerate and spineless; the ornament was, moreover, its own environment and its own measure. I have tried to show that the space of the interlace is neither flat nor motionless. It moves, since metamorphoses do occur under our eyes, not by distinct stages, to be sure, but within a complex continuity of curves, spirals, and entwined stems. It is not flat, since, like a river losing itself in subterranean regions and later reappearing above ground, the ribbons that compose these unstable figures pass beneath one another, and their outward, visible form upon the plane of the image can be explained only by a secret activity on the plane below. This perspective of the abstract is, as I have said, notable in Irish manuscripts. But in that painting it is discernible in far more than the mere play of the interlaces. Alternately light and dark combinations, like those on a checkerboard, or irregular polyhedrons similar to isometric views of ruined cities or to visionary town-plans, will, without the least suggestion of any shadow, occasionally give us the importunate, if fugitive illusion of a glittering relief. This is also the case with the meanders that are partitioned off by light or dark folds. Romanesque mural painting, chiefly in the western districts of France, retained some of these types of treatment in the composition of the borders. However rarely such treatments may occur in the figures themselves, at least the great monochrome compartments that make up the figures never juxtapose two equivalent values without inserting a different value between—although this is perhaps due simply to a necessity for optical harmony. But it seems to me that this practice, if followed with absolute constancy, would apply to the structure of the ornamental space whose curious perspective I have outlined above. Figures painted on walls can no more allow the illusion of projection and recess than the requirements of stability can authorize an excessive number of openings in the wall. And yet when we observe a wall in its entirety, whatever purely tonal differences in ornament we may see still do suggest a certain relationship between the various parts of the wall. This relationship—if I may be allowed to indicate by a contradiction in terms the curious optical contradiction resulting from these differences—may be called flat modelling. Here, then, is further confirmation of the idea that ornament is not a mere abstract graph evolving within any given space whatsoever. What ornamental form does is to create its own modes of space, or better, since our conceptions of form and space are so inseparably united, what they do is to create *one another* within the realm of ornament, with identical freedom respecting the object and according to identically reciprocal laws.

But however true it is that these terms are closely and dynamically united in the normative and classic state of every possible ornamental style, cases nevertheless exist where space remains only an ornament, while the object occupying it—as, for example, the human body—tends to emancipate itself. There are likewise other cases where the form of the object retains its ornamental value, while the space surrounding it tends to acquire a rational structure. The frequently troublesome concept of *background* in painting is a case in point, whenever, that is, nature and space are no longer an extension beyond man, or a periphery around him that both prolongs and penetrates his being, but are instead an entirely separate entity with which he is not in accord. In this respect, Romanesque painting occupies an intermediate position. Here colored stripes, flat tones, scattered shapes, cloths hung across porticoes, all serve to cancel out the backgrounds. But the figures take their places logically, without isolation from the backgrounds, for, even if they are not strictly ornamental, that is, not held tightly within well-defined architectural frames, they are nevertheless primarily mere monograms and arabesques. There are, obviously, exceptions to this qualification: it does not apply, despite their elegance of profile, to the figurines in thirteenth-century Parisian Psalters. These figurines do not stem from some remote, impossible world, but are adapted to a wholly terrestrial life whose exigencies their beautifully articulated limbs and accurate proportions obey; and, even though more often than not, they are completely isolated within decorative architectural frames, they seem to step forward (in the fullest sense of the word) from backgrounds strewn with stars or embroidered with *rinceaux*. In spite of the difference in his manner, a similar observation could be made regarding Jean Pucelle and his little imaginary gardens, which contain elements strictly of this world, as well as fictions of an enchanting vivacity, both of which, however, are cut up like a grillwork of wrought iron and hung out upon a standard over the empty margins. In a painted manuscript, as on a painted wall, the space continues to struggle against any purely make-believe emptiness, even while, at the very same moment, the form begins to assume a slight relief.[2] On the other hand, examples of exactly the opposite are often met with in Italian Renaissance art. The work of Botticelli displays several very striking instances.[3] He knows and practices—sometimes, of course, merely as a virtuoso—every device that permits the likely construction of linear and aerial space, but the beings who move within that space itself he does not completely define. They preserve a sinuous and *ornamental* line, certainly not that of any ornament known and classified in an index, but a line that might be described in the undulations of a dancer who, even in merely maintaining the physiological equilibrium of his body, is purposely seeking to compose such or such a figure. This unique—almost feudal—privilege long remained the property of Italian art.

NOTES

1. Focillon is referring to the method of constructing one-point linear perspective, first accurately set out by Leon Battista Alberti in *De pictura,* a manuscript dating from c. 1434.

2. Jean Pucelle (active c. 319–34) was a French illuminator who displayed an innovative approach to three-dimensional space.

3. Sandro Botticelli (1444/5–1510) was a foremost painter of late fifteenth-century Florence.

Biographical Notes on Authors

Jean Le Rond d'Alembert (1717–1783) was a prominent French scientist, mathematician and a rationalist *philosophe,* committed to the dissemination of scientific knowledge. D'Alembert achieved his widest recognition as co-editor, with Denis Diderot, of the *Encyclopedia,* twenty-eight volumes of Enlightenment philosophy. From about 1746 until 1758, d'Alembert served as editor of the *Encyclopedia*'s mathematical and scientific articles, and he contributed introductions to several of the earlier volumes, including a preliminary discourse explaining the various branches of human knowledge. A member of the Académie Française, d'Alembert also wrote a six-volume *Histoire des membres de l'Académie* (1785–87), in addition to other writings on physics, mathematics, and musical theory.

Samuel (or Siegfried) Bing (1838–1919) was born in Germany. He was instrumental in the creation and promotion of both Japanese taste and the Art Nouveau style in late-nineteenth-century Paris. In 1888 he founded the journal *Le Japon artistique;* an 1893 commission from the French government to study artistic culture in the United States resulted in his writing of *La Culture artistique en Amérique* of 1896 and inspired Bing's interest in contemporary design. In 1895 he opened his Paris gallery "L'Art Nouveau," a name that became synonymous with the style of the artists and designers whose works he exhibited there. Bing's patronage included such artists as Henry van de Velde, Toulouse-Lautrec, and Pierre Bonnard, and he showed the designs of Louis Comfort Tiffany, William Morris, and Liberty & Co. Bing eventually established his own manufacturing company, whose designs were featured in a pavilion at the Paris Exposition Universelle of 1900.

R. G. (Robin George) Collingwood (1889–1943) was a lecturer in history and professor of metaphysical philosophy at Oxford University. Collingwood made an influential contribution to the aesthetic philosophy of the twentieth century with his *Principles of Art* of 1938. Extensively reworking his earlier publication, *Outlines of a Philosophy of Art* (1925), Collingwood there responded to the changes in art, drama, poetry, and literature that he saw occurring in his own time. Drawing distinctions among art, craft, magic, and amusement, Collingwood saw art as defined by its imaginative vision—the ability to bring emotion and sensation into the consciousness, after it ceased to be an immediate experience. In contrast, he argued that "craft" entails only skill, technique, and the use of a set procedure with a predetermined result. Collingwood's avowal of art as an expressive, imaginative activity, and his dismissal of the importance of technique, were influential concepts in the development of twentieth-century art.

Le Corbusier (1887–1965) is the pseudonym of Charles-Edouard Jeanneret, a controversial architect, artist, and theorist. Active mostly in France, the Swiss-born Le Corbusier was a visionary figure in the development of modern architecture. Extremely versatile, he designed furniture and decorative art, in addition to streamlined buildings, and revolutionary urban plans (such as La Cité Nouvelle in Marseilles); he also wrote more than fifty books. His charismatic character and stimulating writings made him a leading figure of the Modernist movement of the 1920s. Later, his stance became more skeptical, as he explored the social and cultural implications of design, often shifting theoretical positions. Although many of his most ambitious urban and housing projects were never realized, the influence of his designs established his enduring importance within the history of twentieth-century architecture and design.

Walter Crane (1845–1915) was a British illustrator, painter, and designer active in the mid-1860s on. Crane's greatest successes were his illustrations for children's books and his ornamental and pattern designs done in the Japanese-influenced manner of the aesthetic movement. He designed wallpapers for Jeffrey & Co. and produced pottery designs for such British companies as Pilkington and Wedgwood. Influenced by John Ruskin's theories, Crane fully embraced the value of the useful arts, maintaining as William Morris did, that the dignity of the craftsman was evident in his work, and was thus conveyed to the user. As such, Crane was dedicated to the improvement of artistic education in England, and was the author of several influential treatises on art. His writings include *The Claims of Decorative Art; Of the Decorative Illustration of Books; Line and Form;* and *An Artist's Reminiscences.*

Denis Diderot (1713–1784), French writer, philosopher, and critic, is best known for his work on the *Encyclopedia,* a major organ of Enlightenment philosophy in the eighteenth century. Before beginning the *Encyclopedia,* Diderot worked as a teacher and translator, and his public espousal of atheistic materialism earned him a brief prison sentence. Released from prison to work with Jean Le Rond d'Alembert, he was soon joined as well by Voltaire, Montesquieu, and Rousseau among others. Originally conceived as a simple translation of Ephraim Chamber's *Cyclopaedia* (1728), the publication was soon recast as an ambitious summation of rational knowledge. Diderot worked on the *Encyclopedia* for twenty years; it was ultimately published in twenty-eight volumes as *Encyclopedia or Rational Dictionary of the Sciences, Arts, and Crafts* (Encyclopédie, ou Dictionnaire Raisonné des Sciences, des Arts et des Metiers [1751–72]). He also wrote fiction, including *Rameau's Nephew* and *Jacques le fataliste et son maître.*

Norbert Elias (1897–1990), German-born sociologist, is best known for his principal work, *The Civilizing Process: The History of Manners* (Über den Prozess der Zivilisation), a detailed study of the changing codes of behavior in western Europe beginning in the late Middle Ages. Early in his career, Elias studied medicine, philosophy, and sociology, and he taught at the universities of Heidelberg and Frankfurt. With the rise of Nazism, he fled to France and later to England. Written in 1939, *The Civilizing Process* expresses Elias's influential theory that the civilization of western Europe developed through a complex, evolutionary process. In his work, he examines the gradual changes in European social behavior and personality and argues that they are related to the formation of states and the power structures within them. Other works by Elias include *The Established and the Outsiders, The Society of Individuals,* and *The Germans.*

Henri Focillon (1881–1943) was a French art historian, whose academic posts included the Sorbonne, the Institut d'Art et du Moyen Age, and Yale and Harvard universities. Focillon is considered to be one of the most influential French art theorists of the twentieth century. He developed a system of formal analysis to account for the evolution of style in art in general. As such, his interests were wide-ranging, and he made no distinction between the fine and decorative arts, applying his methodology and theories to painting, engraving, drawing, stained glass, sculpture, and architecture. In 1934 Focillon proposed his model for structuring diverse material in *The Life of Forms in Art,* which drew on the theories of Adolf von Hildebrand, Heinrich Wölfflin, and Alois Riegl. Focillon also produced studies in subjects ranging from classical antiquity and Asian art, to Italian Renaissance painters, French nineteenth-century painting, and medieval art.

Johann Wolfgang von Goethe (1749–1832), German poet, statesman, scientist, historian, and philosopher, profoundly influenced eighteenth-century European culture. Perhaps now best known as the author of poetry and dramas like *Faust,* Goethe was also a widely published aesthetic theorist, writing on optics as well as ideals of beauty. As a young man, steeped in the intellectual atmosphere of the romantic *Sturm und Drang*— the German reaction to neoclassical rationalism—Goethe came to see classical Greek culture as the ideal reconciliation of the rational and irrational aspects of human nature. He expressed these beliefs most notably in his short-lived journal *Propyläen* (1798). Ultimately, Goethe came to accept the legitimacy of more than one authentic style, taking a renewed interest in Gothic art, exploring the arts of the orient, and continuing to stress the symbolic and passionate aspects of all true art.

Walter Gropius (1883–1969) was a German-born architect, who founded the Bauhaus, the innovative school of allied arts, in Weimar, Germany, in 1919. Gropius's program at the Bauhaus encouraged cooperation between the arts and technology, and it was celebrated for achievements in functionalist architecture and for experimental use of materials. Gropius was director of the school from 1919 until 1928, when it was moved to Dessau, Germany, into buildings he designed. In 1934 Gropius emigrated to England and later settled in the United States, where he practiced architecture in partnership with Marcel Breuer, and became chairman of the School of Architecture at Harvard University. Gropius's work was based on the belief that well-designed places could integrate the individual with society; he expounded his views in such writings as: *The New Architecture and the Bauhaus; Rebuilding Our Communities;* and *Architecture and Design in the Age of Science.* Gropius's works in architecture include the Fagus Works, Alfeld, Germany; model factory and office, Cologne; Harvard Graduate Center; and the U.S. Embassy in Athens.

Karl Grosz (1869–19/) was a designer and sculptor from Dresden. He was trained at the Munich School of Applied Art, and in 1898 he began teaching at the Dresden School of Applied Art. He made a name for himself as a designer, especially of furniture and of complete interiors. He participated in the Secession Exhibition in Munich, as well as in other exhibitions in Dresden in 1901, 1908, and 1912. He was firmly allied to the revival of craft, and his many writings reflect his espousal of the tenets of the German Werkbund established by Hermann Muthesius.

Adolf von Hildebrand (1847–1921) was a German sculptor, theorist, and writer. His figural sculptures owed much to Renaissance Florentine art, and he spent much of his career in Florence. During Hildebrand's early travels in Italy, he made friends with philosopher and art theorist Konrad Fiedler and the painter Hans Reinhard von Marées, both of whose "ideal-formalist" theories of art were to be of great importance to him. It was at Fiedler's encouragement that Hildebrand published his only work in art theory, *The Problem of Form in Painting and Sculpture.* Based on conversations between Hildebrand and Fiedler, the book was begun in 1876 and finally published in 1893. Hildebrand's ideas exerted considerable influence on many art scholars, most notably Heinrich

Wölfflin, whose studies in the human psychological response to form developed out of Hildebrand's formalist theories.

Owen Jones (1809–1874) was a British architect and designer whose work and ideas contributed to a design reform movement in England. He was involved in the planning of the Great Exhibition of 1851, and his outstanding legacy was the 1856 publication of the influential *The Grammar of Ornament,* a lavishly illustrated volume with examples of historic ornament. Jones felt strongly that nineteenth-century design should reflect its own distinctive character and not simply be derived from past styles. He developed his own theory of ornament, based on geometry, which he published as thirty-seven principles of ornamental design in the introduction to *Grammar of Ornament.* As architect, Jones was influenced by his knowledge of Islamic and Spanish design. During his career he created elaborate interior schemes for such buildings as Joseph Paxton's Crystal Palace, and he produced pattern designs for several manufacturers.

Friedrich August Krubsacius (1718–1789) was a German architect and theorist. From the late 1740s on, he was the favored architect of Graf von Brühl, the most important architectural patron in Saxony, before becoming Court Master Builder to the Elector of Saxony in 1755. In 1764 Krubsacius accepted an influential post as professor at the Dresden Kunstakademie. During a trip to Paris, he encountered French neoclassical architectural theory and classical antiquity, which influenced his own designs and writings, such as his 1759 *Reflections on the Origin, Growth, and Decline of Decoration in the Fine Arts* (Gedanken von dem Ursprunge, Wachsthum und Verfalle der Verzierungen in den schönen Künsten) and a survey of landscape architecture, published in Johann Christoph Gottsched's *Handlexikon der schönen Wissenschaften und freyen Künste* (1760).

Adolf Loos (1870–1933), Austrian architect, theorist, and writer, was one of the most influential pioneers of the Modern movement in Northern Europe. Radically polemical in his views, Loos was an early advocate of the functionalist aesthetic, and was sharply critical of the reigning Vienna Secession style early in his career. During a three-year stay in the United States, Loos encountered the leading American architects and was influenced by Sullivan's suggestion to abandon ornament. This led him to develop a radical aesthetic puritanism. His aversion to superfluous ornament is expressed in his much-quoted "Ornament and Crime," in which Loos postulated that human progress was marked by the gradual shedding of ornament. His influential essays were published as *Spoken into the Void: Collected Essays 1897–1900* (Ins Leer gesprochen) and *Trotzdem, 1900–1933.*

Karl Philipp Moritz (1757–1793) was a German-born writer whose brief career produced one of the earliest autobiographical novels as well as major works on language, art, and aesthetics. He briefly studied theology, attempted an acting career, taught grammar school, and edited a newspaper. In 1785 appeared his important, "On the Concept of Self-Sufficient Perfection" (Über den Begriff des in sich Vollendeten); he then traveled to Italy, where he was befriended by Goethe, wrote his autobiographical fiction, *Andreas Hartknopf* (1786) and *Anton Reiser* (1785–90), and produced such key writings on aesthetics as *Über die bildende Nachahmung des Schönen* (1788). Upon returning to Germany in 1789, Moritz was appointed professor of aesthetics and archaeology at the Academy of Arts in Berlin. The preparatory notes for his *Preliminary Ideas on the Theory of Ornament* (Vorbegriffe zu einer Theorie der Ornamente), in which he linked his concept of beauty to a theory of ornament, were posthumously published with that title in 1793.

William Morris (1834–1896) is considered the founder of the Arts and Crafts movement, and his influence continued well into the early twentieth century. A prolific writer and ardent Socialist, Morris was profoundly influenced by Ruskin, whose writings addressed Morris's most consuming interests: Gothic architecture and the pivotal relation between the fulfilled worker and successful work. Abandoning his training as an architect, Morris studied painting among the pre-Raphaelites and in 1861 co-founded the firm Morris, Marshall, Faulkner & Co. (from 1875 on Morris & Co.), which produced stained glass, furniture, and extremely popular wallpaper and textile designs. His Kelmscott Press, founded in 1888, published numerous writings on art and politics.

Hermann Muthesius (1861–1927) was a German architect, theorist, and critic. Appointed technical attaché to the German Embassy in London (1896–1903), Muthesius was profoundly affected by the work of such British country-house architects as Philip Webb, R. Norman Shaw, and Edwin Lutyens. In his three-volume *Das Englische Haus*, Muthesius introduced many tenets of English design reform to German architects. Like Morris, Muthesius promoted conscientious craftsmanship but did not forswear the machine; he also took an active interest in new methods of construction and in the use of new materials. He expressed his views in his 1902 treatise *Stilarchitektur und Baukunst*, and his criticism of the craft system in Germany helped to establish the Deutscher Werkbund, a nationalist forum for design. In 1914, Muthesius's advocation of industrial design brought him into an escalated confrontation with fellow Werkbund members, most notably Henry Van de Velde.

A. W. N. (Augustus Welby Northmore) Pugin (1812–1852), architect, writer, and designer, was a key figure in the nineteenth-century Gothic revival in Britain. His designs for churches, furniture, metalwork, ceramics, textiles, stained glass, wallpaper, and illustrated publications helped to establish the style of Gothic revival, and provided it with a theoretical basis. Largely because of Pugin's *Contrasts* and *The True Principles of Christian or Pointed Architecture* (1841), the Gothic style became recognized as the most suitable architectural style for Christian (especially Catholic) churches. His writings also influenced the reform-minded tendencies of Ruskin and were later adopted by members of the Arts and Crafts movement. Although the great majority of his architectural commissions were for churches, his best-known work is the interior of the Houses of Parliament, where he collaborated with architect Charles Barry.

Alois (also Aloïs) Riegl (1858–1905), an Austrian art historian, was considered one of the founding fathers of the Viennese School of art history. Influenced by the works of Karl Schnaase as well as by G. W. F. Hegel's philosophy of history, Riegl conceived of a systematic art history, in which artistic form evolves in response to internal aesthetic requirements. The driving force behind artistic creation, according to Riegl, was *Kunstwollen*, artistic volition; art, he believed, did not arise out of a human impulse toward naturalism, as some historians claimed, nor did it result by chance from the use of certain materials and tools. Riegl's early work was written in response to Semper's belief in the technical origins of artistic creativity; and his influential *Problems of Style* (Stilfragen [1893]) was the first to argue for a continuous, independent history of ornament from antiquity to the Middle Ages. In his later writings, including *Late Roman Art Industry* (Die spätrömische Kunstindustrie [1901]) and *The Group Portraiture of Holland*

(*Das holländische Gruppenporträt* [1902]), Riegl explored how a culture's world-view conditioned the different forms of its artistic expression.

Pedro Rioux de Maillou, who was active from the 1870s to the 1910s, was a relatively little-known French art critic. He was clearly an active member of the Union Centrale des arts décoratifs, helping to edit for instance V. Poterlet's *Les Arts du bois, des tissus et du papier* (Paris, 1883), published by the Union; he was also secretary of the Executive Committee for the Seventh Exposition at the Palais de l'industrie in 1882. His topics ranged from the decorative arts to travel accounts as well as souvenirs, and his writings appeared in such journals as the *Revue des arts décoratifs* and *L'Art*.

John Ruskin (1819–1900) was a British writer, artist, philanthropist, and collector. Ruskin had a great influence on the contemporary art and architecture of the nineteenth century, along with the emerging field of art history. His early writings promoted contemporary landscape painters, pre-Raphaelite artists, as well as architects working in the medieval Gothic style. In two of his numerous books, *The Seven Lamps of Architecture* and *The Stones of Venice*, Ruskin argued that the Gothic style was superior to others because of its relation to nature and its spiritual and moral dimensions. His more controversial writings attacked the industrialization of England, caused by what he perceived as the materialism of his age. His late espousal of Socialism alienated some of his early public, and he eventually moved into the academic sphere, accepting a position as the first Slade Professor of Art at Oxford University.

Gottfried Semper (1803–1879) was a German architect, teacher, and writer. His lasting influence on nineteenth-century architecture and theory was the result of his writings on form, technique, and style in the visual arts. In the 1850s, Semper contributed to the preparations for the Great Exhibition of 1851 in London, and as a result he began an unprecedented historical study of the "industrial arts," tracing the routes of their style back to the exigencies of function, technique, and materials. In *Style in the Technical and Tectonic Arts* (Der Stil in den technischen und tektonischen Künsten, 2 vols., 1860–63), he discusses the development of textile, pottery, carpentry, masonry, and metalwork, arguing that craftsmen created ornamental forms predating those of architecture. Often seen as a purely materialistic theorist, Semper intended to write a third volume of *Style*, focusing on the role of human creativity in the development of form, but never did. Semper's emphasis on function and materials is also seen to have influenced the later emergence of modern architecture.

Georg Simmel (1858–1918) was a prominent German sociologist and neo-Kantian philosopher. His works on sociological methodology made a significant contribution to the acceptance of sociology as a social science in Germany, particularly his major early work *Sociology*. A professor of philosophy at the universities of Berlin (1885–1914) and Strasbourg (1914–1918), Simmel took up all the major themes of the twentieth century in his penetrating and unorthodox studies of modern society. His works showed the variety of his interests; they include *The Philosophy of Money*, *The Sociology of Religion*, and *The Conflict of Modern Culture*, along with other works on human sexuality and gender. Simmel also wrote on metaphysics and aesthetics in the last decade of his life, investigating how men and women in modern society used art as an expression of individuality.

Louis Henri Sullivan (1856–1924) was at the forefront of the progressive architecture movement in Chicago in the 1890s. Considered by many to be the father of Functionalism,

Sullivan originated the phrase "form follows function," by which he meant that architecture should visually reflect its use and its environment. Opposed to the historical eclecticism of his time, Sullivan also stressed that ornament should be integrated into form, rather than simply applied. He produced highly original designs for architectural ornament, drawing on the materials and techniques of the industrial age to sheath his steel-framed skyscrapers with delicate ornament, mass-produced in terra-cotta slabs. Sullivan expressed his influential ideas in many writings, including *The Autobiography of an Idea* and *Kindergarten Chats* and a series of articles that were later revised for publication in book form.

Henry van de Velde (1863–1957), Belgian designer, architect, painter, and writer, was one of the leading artists associated with Art Nouveau. Van de Velde began as a painter but after being inspired by the ideals of the Arts and Crafts movement, he began working as an illustrator, architect, and designer of a variety of household furnishings. After his work was displayed in Samuel Bing's new gallery L'Art Nouveau in Paris, Van de Velde's sinuous designs became synonymous with Art Nouveau style, or *Jugendstil*, as it was known in Austria and Germany. In his writings, Van de Velde argued that ornament was not to be applied to form but was to grow organically from it; he also held that ornament must reflect artistic originality and therefore was critical of industrial design. In 1925 Van de Velde returned to Belgium, accepting a position as architecture professor at the University of Ghent.

Mariana Griswold Van Rensselaer (1851–1934) was a prominent American critic of architecture, landscape design, and the visual arts in the late nineteenth and early twentieth centuries. As a young woman, she traveled extensively with her family in Europe; fluent in English, French, and German, Van Rensselaer read both contemporary and historic works on art and design. Active as a critic beginning in the late 1870s, Van Rensselaer is best known for her highly regarded 1888 biography of the architect Henry Hobson Richardson. She also wrote prolifically for many journals including *Century Magazine, Harper's Weekly, North American Review, Lippincott's, Garden and Forest,* and *American Architect and Building News.*

Eugène-Emmanuel Viollet-le-Duc (1814–1879) was a promoter of Gothic revival in nineteenth-century France. Viollet-le-Duc's architectural career focused on the rebuilding and restoration of medieval churches, including the abbey church of the Madeleine, Vézelay, Amiens Cathedral, and, in Paris, the Sainte-Chapelle, the Abbey of Saint-Denis, and Notre-Dame. Viollet-le-Duc's scholarly studies of medieval architecture, especially his *Dictionnaire raisonné de l'architecture française du XIe au XVIe siècle* and *Lectures on Architecture* (Entretiens sur l'architecture), substantially enhanced the knowledge of medieval buildings of his time. These writings affected contemporary attitudes to both authentic restoration and contemporary design, particularly because of his enthusiasm for the use of new materials like iron to create innovative effects and to solve engineering problems.

Heinrich Wölfflin (1864–1945) was a Swiss art historian who devoted his career to the interpretation of the visual, formal character of works of art. Teaching mainly in Germany, Wölfflin like Riegl explored the hidden dynamics linking art and culture, developing and codifying the notion of period style. Focusing on Renaissance and Baroque art, Wölfflin hypothesized the existence of a polarity of styles, a more linear, closed, realistic depiction of visual form versus a more painterly and looser representation. In his

1886 doctoral dissertation, *Prolegomena to a Psychology of Architecture* (Prolegomena zu einer Psychologie der Architektur), Wölfflin adopted a psychological approach to the analysis of art, explaining that the viewer empathetically feels the visual energy and movement of a building in his or her own body. In his most influential work, *Principles of Art History,* he suggested that fluctuations of style throughout the history of art could be succinctly explained through five artistic polarities or principles, which he believed governed all stylistic development.

Frank Lloyd Wright (1867–1959) continues to be one of the most widely admired and best-known American architects. Early in his career Wright worked for the architect Louis Sullivan in Chicago, and he established his own practice there in 1893. From the beginning of his long career, Wright's work reflected an interest in human-centered and site-centered design and the influence of both Japanese architecture and the Arts and Crafts movement. Wright's innovative ideas were expressed in his designs of public and private buildings and dwellings, including the Willits House, the Robie House, Larkin Building, and Unity Temple, as well as in his writings on architecture; these include a 1927–28 series of articles for the *Architectural Record,* and the widely read *The Disappearing City, The Future of Architecture,* and *The Natural House.*

Select Bibliography

PRIMARY SOURCES

Alberti, Leon Battista. *Leon Battista Alberti, On the Art of Building in Ten Books.* Trans. and ed. by J. Rykwert, N. Leach, and R. Tavernor. Cambridge, Mass., 1988.

Benton, T. and C. Benton, eds., with D. Sharp. *Form and Function: A Source Book for the History of Architecture and Design, 1890–1939.* London, 1975.

Bing, Samuel, "Wohin treiben wir?" *Dekorative Kunst* (Munich) 1 (1897–98): 1–3, 68–71, 173–177.

Blanc, Charles. *Grammaire des arts décoratifs.* Paris, 1882.

———. *L'Art dans la parure et dans les vêtements.* Paris, 1875.

Bode, W. von. "Aufgaben unserer Kunstgewerbemuseen." *Pan* 2 (1896): 121ff.

Bötticher, Karl. *Architektonische Formenschüle in Ornament Erfindungen.* Potsdam, 1847.

———. *Die Tektonik der Hellenen.* 2 vols. Potsdam, 1844–52.

Bourgoin, J. *Théorie de l'ornement.* Paris, 1873.

Christie, A. H. *Traditional Methods of Pattern Designing.* Oxford, 1910.

Collingwood, R. G. *The Principles of Art.* Oxford, 1977.

Conrads, Ulrich, ed. *Programs and Manifestoes on 20th-Century Architecture.* Trans. by M. Bullock. Cambridge, Mass., 1975.

Le Corbusier (Jeanneret, Charles-Edouard). *The Decorative Art of Today.* Trans. and intro. by J. I. Dunnett. Cambridge, Mass., 1987.

Crane, Walter. *The Bases of Design.* London, 1898.

———. *The English Revival of the Decorative Arts.* London, 1892.

———. "Of Ornament and Its Meaning." In *Ideals in Art. Papers—Theoretical, Practical, Critical.* London, 1905, pp. 102–109.

D'Alembert, J. Le Rond. *Preliminary Discourse to the Encyclopedia of Diderot.* Trans. by R. N. Schwab. Indianapolis, 1963.

Day, Lewis Foreman. *The Application of Ornament.* London, 1888.

———. *Nature in Ornament.* London, 1892.

Diderot, Denis. *Diderot. Oeuvres Complètes: Encyclopédie I.* Ed. by J. Lough and J. Proust. Paris, 1976.

Doordan, D. P., ed. *Design History: An Anthology.* Cambridge, Mass., 1995.

Dresser, Christopher. *The Art of Decorative Design.* London, 1862.

———. *Development of Ornamental Art in the International Exhibition.* London, 1862.

———. *Modern Ornamentation.* London, 1886.

———. *Principles of Decorative Design.* London, 1873.

Eitelberger, R. von. *Denkschrift über den Bau und die Organisation des Museums für Kunst in Wien.* Vienna, 1867.

Elias, Norbert. *The Civilizing Process: The History of Manners.* Trans. by E. Jephcott. Oxford, 1994.

Endell, August. "The Beauty of Form and Decorative Art." *Dekorative Kunst* (Munich) 1 (1897–98): 75–77, 119–125.

Falke, J. von. *Aesthetik des Kunstgewerbes, ein Handbuch für Haus, Schule und Werkstätte.* Stuttgart, 1883.

———. *Geschichte des modernes Geschmacks.* Leipzig, 1866.

———. *Die Kunst im Hause.* Vienna, 1871.

———. *Die Kunst-Industrie der Gegenwart: Studien auf der Pariser Welt-Ausstellung 1867.* Leipzig, 1868.

Ferri, Gaetano. *Corso elementare di ornato tratto dal naturale a semplice contorno per uso della gioventù studiosa.* Macerata, 1854.

Focillon, Henri. *The Life of Forms in Art.* Trans. by C. B. Hogan and G. Kubler. New Haven, 1942.

Goethe, J. von. "Kunst und Handwerk." In *Kunsttheorische Schriften und Übersetzung.* Vol. 1. Berlin, 1973, pp. 159–162.

Gombrich, E. H. *The Sense of Order: A Study in the Psychology of the Decorative Arts.* Oxford, 1979.

Goodyear, W. H. *The Grammar of the Lotus.* London, 1891.

Grabar, Oleg. *The Mediation of Ornament.* Princeton, 1992.

Greenhalgh, P. *Quotations and Sources on Design and the Decorative Arts.* Manchester, 1993.

Grosz, Karl. "Ornament." *Jahrbuch des Deutschen Werkbundes* (Jena) 1912: 60–64.

Guillaume, E. *L'Histoire de l'art et de l'ornement.* Paris, 1886.

Haüselman, J. *Anleitung zum Studium der dekorativen Künste.* Leipzig-Zurich, 1887.

———. *Studien und Ideen über Ursprung, Stil, und Wesen des Ornaments.* 2nd ed., Zurich, 1887.

Havard, Henry. *Dictionnaire de l'ameublement et la décoration depuis le XIII siècle jusqu'à nos jours.* 4 vols. Paris, 1887–90.

Hermann, W., trans. and ed. *In What Style Should We Build? The German Debate on Architectural Style.* Santa Monica, Calif., 1992

Hildebrand, Adolf von. "Handarbeit—Maschinenarbeit." In *A. von Hildebrand: Gesammelte Schriften zur Kunst.* Ed. by H. Bock. Köln, 1969, p. 498.

———. *The Problem of Form in Painting and Sculpture.* Trans. by M. Meyer and R. M. Ogden. New York, 1907.

Hogarth, W. *The Analysis of Beauty.* Ed. by J. Burke. Oxford, 1953.

Hume, David. "On the Rise and Progress of the Arts and Sciences." In *Of the Standard of Taste and Other Essays.* Ed. and intro. by J. Lenz. Indianapolis, 1965, pp. 72–94.

Jones, Owen. *The Grammar of Ornament.* London, 1856.

———. *Lectures on Architecture and the Decorative Arts.* London, 1863.

———. *On the True and the False in the Decorative Arts: Lectures Delivered at Marlborough House.* London, 1863.

Krubsacius, Friedrich August. "Betrachtungen über den wahren Geschmack der Alten in der Baukunst und über desselben Verfall in neuern Zeiten." *Neuer Büchersaal der schönen Wissenschaften und freyen Künste.* Vol. 4. Leipzig, 1747, p. 419ff.

———. *Gedanken von dem Ursprung, Wachstum und Verfall der Verzierungen in den schönen Künsten.* Leipzig, 1759.

Laborde, Léon. *De l'Union des arts et de l'industrie.* 2 vols. Paris, 1856.

Lang, Konrad. *Schön und praktisch. Eine Einführung in die Aesthetik der angewandten Künste.* Esslingen, 1908.

Lethaby, William Richard. *Form in Civilization: Collected Papers on Art and Labour.* London, 1922.

Loos, Adolf. *Spoken into the Void: Collected Essays, 1897–1900.* Trans. by J. O. Newman and J. H. Smith. Cambridge, Mass., 1982.

———. *Trotzdem, 1900–1930.* Vienna, 1931.

Mallgrave, H. F. and E. Ikonomou, trans. and eds. *Empathy, Form and Space: Problems in German Aesthetics, 1873–93.* Santa Monica, Calif., 1994.

Moritz, Karl Philipp. *Karl Philipp Moritz, Werke.* Ed. by Horst Günther. 3 vols. Frankfurt, 1981.

———. *Vorbegriffe zu einer Theorie der Ornamente* (Preliminary Ideas on the Theory of Ornament). Intro. by H.-W. Kruft. Nordlingen, [1793] 1986 reprint.

Morris, William. *Collected Works,* with an Introduction by his Daughter May Morris. 24 vols. London, 1910–15.

———. *The Unpublished Lectures of William Morris.* Ed. by E. D. Lemire. Detroit, 1969.

———. *William Morris, News from Nowhere and Selected Writings and Designs.* Ed. by A. Briggs. Harmondsworth, 1962.

Muthesius, Hermann. "Die Bedeutung des Kunstgewerbes." *Dekorative Kunst* 10 (1907): 177–192.

———. "Der Weg und das Ziel des Kunstgewerbes." *Kunstgewerbe und Architektur* (Jena) 1907: 1–28.

Odescalchi, Baldassare and Raffaele Erculi. *Il movimento artistico-industriale in inghilterra, nella Francia e nel Belgico.* Rome, 1880.

Panofsky, Erwin. "The Concept of Artistic Volition." *Critical Enquiry* 8 (1981): 7–33.

Pfnor, Rodolphe. *Ornamentation usuelle de toutes les époques.* Paris, 1866–68.

Pica, Vittorio. *L'arte decorative all'esposizione di Torino del 1902.* Bergamo, 1903.

Posener, J., ed. *Anfänge des Funktionalismus. Von Art und Crafts zum Deutschen Werkbund.* Berlin, 1964.

Probst, H., ed. *Walter Gropius. Ausgewählte Schriften.* 3 vols. Berlin, 1988.

Pugin, A. Welby. *The True Principles of Pointed or Christian Architecture.* 2nd ed., London, 1853.

Redgrave, Richard. "Supplementary Report on Design." In *Reports by the Juries.* Vol. 2, London, 1852, pp. 708–749.

Riegl, Alois. *Altorientalische Teppiche.* Leipzig, 1891.

———. *Historische Grammatik der bildenden Künste. 1897–99.* Ed. by K. M. Swoboda and O. Pächt. Graz, 1966.

———. *Late Roman Art Industry.* Trans. by R. Winkes. Rome, 1985.

———. *Problems of Style. Foundations for a History of Ornament.* Trans. by E. Kain, notes by D. Castriota, preface by H. Zerner. Princeton, 1992.

———. *Volkskunst, Hausfleiss und Hausindustrie*. Berlin, 1894

Riegl, Alois, and G. Delio. *Konservieren, nicht restaurieren. Streitschriften zur Denkmalpflege um 1900*. Ed. by G. Märsch. Braunschweig, 1988.

Rioux de Maillou, P. "Les Arts décoratifs et les machines." *Revue des Arts Décoratifs* 15 (1895): 225–231, 267–273.

Rouaix, Paul. *Dictionnaire des Arts Décoratifs*. Paris, nd.

Rozoi, M. *Essai philosophique sur les écoles gratuites de dessin pour les arts méchaniques*. Paris, 1769.

Ruskin, John. "Modern Manufacture and Design." In *The Two Paths: Being Lectures on Art, and Its Application to Decoration and Manufacture*, delivered 1858–59. New York, 1859.

———. *The Seven Lamps of Architecture*. London, 1849.

Schlosser, Julius von. *Stilgeschichte und Sprachgeschichte der bildenden Kunst*. Munich, 1935.

Schmarsow, August. "Die reine Form in der Ornamentik aller Künste." *Zeitschrift für Aesthetik und allgemeine Kunstwissenschaft* 17 (1924): 1–17, 129–145, 209–234, 305–320.

———. "Von Wesen des Ornaments." *Innendekoration* (1925): 49ff.

Semper, Gottfried. *Der Stil in den technischen und tektonischen Künsten, oder praktischen Aesthetik*. (Style in the Technical and Tectonic Arts). 2 vols. Frankfurt, 1860–63.

———. "Science, Art, and Industry: Proposals for the Development of a National Taste in Art at the Closing of the London Industrial Exhibition." In *Gottfried Semper: The Four Elements of Architecture and Other Writings*. Trans. by W. Herrmann and H. F. Mallgrave, with intro. by H. F. Mallgrave. Cambridge, 1989, pp. 130–167.

———. *Über die formelle Gesetzmässigkeit des Schmuckes und dessen Bedeutung als Kunstsymbol*. Zurich, 1856.

Shaw, Henry. *The Encyclopedia of Ornament*. London, 1842.

Simmel, Georg. *The Sociology of Georg Simmel*. Trans., ed., and intro. by K. H. Wolff. New York, 1950 (2nd ed. 1964), pp. 338–344.

Sombart, Werner. *Kunstgewerbe und Kultur*. Berlin 1908.

Stickley, Gustav. *Craftsman Homes*. New York, 1909.

Stohmann, Lisbeth. *Kunst und Gewerbe: Forderungen, Leistungen, Aussichten diesem Berufen*. Leipzig, 1899.

Sullivan, Louis. *Kindergarten Chats*. New York, 1947.

———. *A System of Architectural Ornament According with a Philosophy of Man's Powers*. New York, 1924.

Van de Velde, Henry. "A Chapter on the Design and Construction of Modern Furniture." *Pan* (Berlin) 3 (1897): 260–264.

———. *Henry Van de Velde. Zum neuen Stil*. Ed. by H. Curjel. Munich, 1955.

———. *Kunstgewerbliche Laienpredigten*. Leipzig, 1902–07.

———. *Die Renaissance im modernen Kunstgewerbe*. Berlin, 1901.

Van Rensselaer, Mariana Griswold. "Decorative Art and Its Dogmas." In *Accents as Well as Broad Effects: Writings on Architecture, Landscape, and the Environment, 1876–1925*. Ed. by D. Gebhard. Berkeley, 1996, pp. 110–121.

Viollet-le-Duc, Eugène-Emmanuel. *De la Décoration appliquée aux édifices*. Paris, 1880.

———. *Dictionnaire raisonné du mobilier français de l'époque carlovingienne à la renaissance*. 6 vols. Paris, 1858–75.

———. *Dictionnaire raisonné de l'architecture Française du XIe au XVIe siècle*. 10 vols. Paris, 1854–1868.

———. *Lectures on Architecture*. Trans. by B. Bucknall. 3 vols. London, 1877.

Vitruvius Pollio. *The Ten Books of Architecture*. Trans. by M. H. Morgan. New York, 1960.

Waagen, G. F. *Das Deutsche Gewerbe-Museum in Berlin*. Berlin, 1868.

Waentig, Heinrich. *Wirtschaft und Kunst. Eine Untersuchung über Geschichte und Theorie der modernen Kunstgewerbebewegung*. Jena, 1909.

Winckelmann, J. *Reflections on the Imitation of Greek Works in Painting and Sculpture*. Trans. by E. Heyer and R. C. Norton. La Salle, Ill., 1987.

Wölfflin, Heinrich. *Prolegomena zu einer Psychologie der Architektur*. Munich, 1886.

Wornum, Ralph N. *Analysis of Ornament. The Characteristics of Styles*. London, 1882.

———. "The Exhibition as a Lesson in Taste." In *The Crystal Palace Exhibition: Illustrated Catalogue*. London, 1851, pp. i–xxii.

Worringer, Wilhelm. *Abstraction and Empathy: A Contribution to the Psychology of Style*. Trans. by M. Bullock. New York, 1963.

———. "Entstehung und Gestaltungsprinzipien in der Ornamentik." In *Kongress für Aesthetik und Allgemeine Kunstwissenschaft*. Stuttgart, 1914, pp. 222–31.

Wright, Frank Lloyd. "The Art and Craft of the Machine." In *Frank Lloyd Wright Collected Writings. Vol. 1 (1894–1930)*. Ed. by B. B. Pfeiffer. New York, 1992, pp. 58–69.

SECONDARY SOURCES

Ackerman, James. "Style." In *Art and Archeology*. Englewood Cliffs, N.J., 1963, pp. 164–186.

Alsop, Joseph. *The Rare Art Traditions: The History of Art Collecting and Its Linked Phenomena*. Princeton, 1982.

Appadurai, A. *The Social Life of Things: Commodities in Cultural Perspective*. Cambridge, 1986.

Atterbury, Paul. *Pugin: A Gothic Passion*. London, 1994.

Auslander, Leora. *Taste and Power: Furnishing Modern France*. Berkeley, Calif., 1996.

Backemeyer, S. and T. Gronberg, eds. *W. R. Lethaby, 1857–1931: Architecture, Design, and Education*. London, 1984.

Baltrusaîtis, J. *Anamorphoses ou magie artificielle des effets merveilleux*. Paris, 1969.

———. *Reveils et prodiges*. Paris, 1988.

Bandman, G. "Ikonologie des Ornaments und der Dekoration." *Jahrbuch für Aesthetik* 4 (1959): 232–254.

———. "Der Wandel der Materialbewertung in der Kunsttheorie des 19. Jahrhunderts." In *Beiträge zur Theorie der Künste im 19. Jahrhundert*. Vol. 1. Ed. by H. Koopman and J. A. Schmoll. Frankfurt am Main, 1971, pp. 129–157.

Bauer, Hermann. *Kunstgeschichte und Kunsttheorie im 19. Jahrhundert*. Berlin 1963.

———. *Rocaille: Zur Herkunft und zum Wesen eines Ornament-Motivs*. Berlin, 1962.

Bayer, H., ed. *Bauhaus 1919–1928*. Boston, 1952.

Bazin, G. *Histoire de l'histoire de l'art de Vasari à nos jours*. Paris, 1986.

Bell, Quentin. *The Schools of Design*. London, 1963.

Boe, Alf. *From Gothic Revival to Functional Form: A Study in Victorian Theories of Design*. Oslo, 1951.

Bois, Yve-Alain. *Painting as Model*. Cambridge, Mass., 1990.

———. *Susan Smith's Archeology*. New York, 1989.

Börsch-Supan, E., et al., eds. *Gottfried Semper und die Mitte des 19. Jahrhunderts*. Basel, 1976.

Bryson, Norman, M. A. Holly, and K. Moxey. *Visual Theory: Painting and Interpretation*. New York, 1991.

Burkhardt, Lucius. *Le Design au-delà du visible*. Trans. by J-L. Evard. Paris, 1991.

Carmagnola, Fulvio. *Della mente e dei sensi*. Milan, 1994.

Collins, Peter. *Changing Ideals in Modern Architecture, 1750–1950*. London, 1965.

Coomaraswany, Ananda. "Ornament." *The Art Bulletin* 21 (1939): 376ff.

Crook, J. Mordaunt. *The Dilemma of Style: Architectural Ideas from the Picturesque to the Post-Modern*. Chicago, 1987.

Dahle, T. N. *Bauhaus und Werkbund*. Stuttgart, 1984.

Damisch, H. "Ornamento." In *L'Enciclopedia Einaudi*. Vol. 10. Turin, 1980, pp. 219–232.

Debes, Dietmar. *Das Ornament, Wesen und Geschichte: ein Schriften Verzeichnis*. Leipzig, 1956.

Derrida, Jacques. *La Verité en peinture*. Paris, 1978.

Dittmann, Lorenz. *Stil, Symbol, Strukturr—Studien zu Kategorien der Kunstgeschichte*. Munich, 1967.

Döhmer, Klaus. *In welchem Stil sollen wir bauen? Architektheorie zwischen Klassizismus und Jugendstil*. Munich, 1976.

Dormer, P., ed. *The Culture of Craft*. Manchester, 1997.

Duncan, Carol. *The Aesthetics of Power. Essays in Critical Art History*. Cambridge, 1993.

Ehresmann, Donald L. *Applied and Decorative Arts, A Bibliographical Guide to Basic Reference Books, Histories and Handbooks*. Littleton, Co., 1977.

ffrench, E. *The Crystal Palace Exhibition: Illustrated Catalogue*. New York, 1970.

Fortov-Smalov, Paula. *Das ägyptische Ornament*. Prague, 1963.

Frank, I. "Alois Riegl (1858–1905) et l'analyse de style des arts plastiques." *Littérature* 105 (1997): 66–77.

———. "Das körperlose Ornament im Werk von Owen Jones und Alois Riegl." In *Rhetorik des Ornaments*. Ed. by I. Frank and F. Hartung. Berlin, 2000.

Fumerton, Patricia. *Cultural Aesthetics: Renaissance Literature and the Practice of Social Ornament*. Chicago, 1991.

Goldstein, C. *Teaching Art: Academics and Schools from Vasari to Albers*. Cambridge, 1996.

Grabar, Oleg. *The Formation of Islamic Art*. New Haven, 1974.

Harries, Karsten. *The Bavarian Rococo Church: Between Faith and Aestheticism*. New Haven, 1983.

———. *The Ethical Function of Architecture*. Cambridge, Mass., 1997.

Harrison, Charles, ed. *Art in Theory: 1900–1990*. Oxford, 1992.

Hofmann, Werner. "L'Émancipation des dissonances." *Gazettes des Beaux-Arts* ser. 6, 108 (1986): 220–230.

Iversen, Margaret. *Alois Riegl: Art History and Theory*. Cambridge, Mass., 1993.

Jencks, Charles. *What Is Post-Modernism?* London, 1986.

Kemp, W. *The Desire of My Eyes: The Life and Work of John Ruskin*. Trans. by J. van Heurck. New York, 1990.

Kirkham, P. *Ray and Charles Eames: Designers of the Twentieth Century*. Cambridge, Mass., 1995.

Koopman, H. and J. Schmoll. *Beiträge zur Theorie der Künste im 19. Jahrhundert*. 2 vols. Frankfurt am Main, 1971.

Krauss, Rosalind. *The Optical Unconscious*. Cambridge, Mass., 1993.

Kristeller, P. O. "The Modern System of the Arts." In *Renaissance Thought II. Papers on Humanism and the Arts*. New York, 1965, pp. 163–227.

Kroll, Frank Lothar. *Das Ornament in der Kunsttheorie des 19. Jahrhunderts*. Hildesheim, 1987.

Kruft, Hanno-Walter. *Geschichte der Architekturtheorie*. Munich, 1985.

———. "Die Arts-and-Crafts-Bewegung und der deutsche Jugenstil." In *Von Morris zum Bauhaus*. Ed. by G. Bott. Hanau, 1977, pp. 25–39.

Landes, David. *The Unbound Prometheus: Technological Change and Industrial Development in Western Europe from 1750 to the Present*. London, 1969.

MacCarthy, Fiona. *The Simple Life: C. R. Ashbee in the Cotswolds*. Berkeley, 1980.

———. *William Morris: A Life for Our Times*. London, 1994.

Mahsun, C. A., ed. *Pop-Art: A Critical Dialogue*. Ann Arbor, Mich., 1989.

Mallgrave, Harry Francis. *Gottfried Semper: Architect of the 19th Century*. New Haven, 1996.

Margolin, V., ed. *Design Discourse: History, Theory, Criticism*. Chicago, 1984.

Middleton, Robin. "Viollet-le-Duc's Academic Ventures and the *Entretiens sur l'architecture*." In *Gottfried Semper und die Mitte des 19. Jahrhunderts*. Ed. by E. Börsch-Supan et al. Basel, 1976, pp. 239–254.

Mitchell, J. W. *Picture Theory: Essays on Verbal and Visual Representations*. Chicago, 1994.

Mundt, Barbara. *Die deutschen Kunstgewerbemuseen im 19. Jahrhundert*. Munich, 1974.

———. *Historismus. Kunstgewerbe zwischen Biedermeier und Jugendstil*. Munich, 1981.

Naylor, Gillian. *The Arts and Crafts Movement*. London, 1971.

———. *Bauhaus Revisited*. London, 1985.

Olin, Margaret. *Forms of Representation in Alois Riegl's Theory of Art*. University Park, Penn., 1992.

The Oxford Companion Guide to the Decorative Arts. Ed. by H. Osborne. Oxford, 1985.

Pächt, O. "Art Historians and Art Critics, VI: Alois Riegl." *Burlington Magazine* 105 (1963): 188–195.

Papanek, Victor. *Design for the Real World: Human Ecology and Social Change*. London, 1984.

Parry, Linda, ed. *William Morris*. London, 1996.

Pevsner, Nikolaus. *Academies Past and Present.* New York, 1973.

———. *An Enquiry into Industrial Art in England.* New York, 1937.

———. *Pioneers of Modern Design.* New York, 1951.

———. *Studies in the Art, Architecture, and Design Victorian and After.* Princeton, 1986, pp. 38–107.

Pfabigen, A., ed. *Ornament und Askese im Zeitgeist des Wiener Jahrhundertwende.* Vienna, 1985.

Pfeiffer, B. B., ed. *Frank Lloyd Wright. Collected Writings. Vol. I (1894–1930).* New York, 1992.

Piel, Friedrich. *Die Ornament-Groteske in der italienischen Renaissance; zu ihrer kategorialen Struktur und Entstehung.* Berlin, 1962.

Pirovano, Carlo, ed. *History of Industrial Design 1750–1850.* Milan, 1990.

Ploegaerts, Leon and Pierre Puttemans. *L'Oeuvre architecturale de Henry van de Velde.* Paris, 1987.

Podro, Michael. *Manifold in Perception.* Oxford, 1972.

———. *The Critical Historians of Art.* New Haven, 1982.

Preziosi, D., ed. *The Art of Art History: A Critical Anthology.* Oxford-New York, 1998.

Reed, Christopher, ed. *Not at Home: The Suppression of Domesticity in Modern Art and Architecture.* London, 1996.

Rukschcio, B. and R. Schachel. *Adolf Loos, Leben und Werk.* Salzburg, 1982.

Rykwert, Joseph. "Ornament Is No Crime." In *The Necessity of Artifice. Ideas in Architecture.* New York, 1982, pp. 92–101.

———. "Semper and the Conception of Style." In *Gottfried Semper und die Mitte des 19. Jahrhunderts.* Ed. by E. Börsch-Supan et al. Basel, 1976, pp. 67–81.

Sauerländer, Willibald. "Alois Riegl und die Entstehung der autonomen Kunstgeschichte am Fin de Siècle." In *Fin-de-siècle: Zur Literatur und Kunst der Jahrhundertwende.* Frankfurt am Main, 1977, 125–139.

Scheffer, Jean-Marie. *L'Art de l'âge moderne. L'Esthètique et la philosophie de l'art du XVIIIe siècle à nos jours.* Paris, 1992.

Schueling, H. *Zur Geschichte der ästhetischen Wertung: Bibliographie der Abhandlung über dem Kitsch.* Giessen, 1971.

Scott, Katie. *The Rococo Interior: Decoration and Social Spaces in Early Eighteenth-Century Paris.* New Haven, 1995.

Sembach, Klaus-Jurgen. *Henry van de Velde.* Trans. by M. Robinson. New York, 1989.

Shattuck, Roger. *The Innocent Eye.* New York, 1984.

Silverman, Deborah. *Art Nouveau in Fin-de-Siècle France: Politics, Psychology, Style.* Berkeley, 1989.

Smith, P. *Craft Today.* New York, 1987.

Snodin, M. and M. Howard. *Ornament: A Social History Since 1450.* New Haven, 1996.

Stansky, Peter. *Redesigning the World: William Morris, the 1880s, and the Arts and Crafts.* Princeton, 1985.

Stanton, Phoebe. *Pugin.* London, 1971.

Summer, David. "Art Historical Description." *Critical Enquiry* 15 (1987): 376ff.

Todorov, Tzvetan. *Thèories du symbole*. Paris, 1977.

Troy, Nancy J. *Modernism and the Decorative Arts in France: Art Nouveau to Le Corbusier.* New Haven, 1991.

Tzeng, Shai-shu. *Imitation und Originalität des Ornamentdesigns.* Munich, 1993.

Varnedoe, K. and A. Gopnik, eds. *High-Low Art.* New York, 1990.

Walker, John. *Art in the Age of Mass Media.* 2nd ed., London, 1994.

Wingler, H. M. *The Bauhaus: Weimar, Dessau, Berlin, Chicago.* Trans. by W. Jabs and B. Gilbert, and ed. by J. Stein. Cambridge, Mass., 1969.

———, ed. *Kunstschulreform, 1900–1933.* Berlin, 1977.

Zerner, Henri. "Review of Gombrich: *A Sense of Order,* The Sense of Sense." *New York Review of Books,* Vol. 26, no. 11 (June 28, 1979): 8–21.

Original Sources and Permissions

The publisher would like to thank the following individuals and publishers who have kindly given their permission to reproduce the texts listed below.

Jean Le Rond d'Alembert, *Preliminary Discourse to the Encyclopedia of Diderot*, trans. by Richard N. Schwab, Indianapolis: The Bobbs-Merrill Company, 1963, pp. 40–43. Reprinted by permission of Prentice-Hall, Inc., Upper Saddle River, NJ.

Samuel Bing, "Wohin treiben Wir? III" (Where Are We Going?), 1 *Dekorative Kunst* (Munich), 1 (1897–98): 173–177. Translated by David Britt for this volume.

R. G. Collingwood, "Art and Craft," in *The Principles of Art*, reprint Oxford: Clarendon Press, [1938] 1977, pp. 15–29. Reprinted by permission of Oxford University Press.

Le Corbusier (Charles-Edouard Jeanneret), "Type-Needs: Type-Furniture" and "The Decorative Art of Today" [1925], in *The Decorative Art of Today*, trans. and intro. by J. I. Dunnett, Cambridge, Mass.: MIT Press, 1987, pp. 69–101.

Walter Crane, "The Importance of the Applied Arts and Their Relation to Common Life," in *The Claims of Decorative Art*, London: Lawrence and Bullen, 1892, pp. 106–118.

Denis Diderot, "Art," in *French Thought in the Eighteenth Century. Rousseau, Voltaire, Diderot*, presented by R. Rolland, A. Maurois, and E. Herriot, intro. by G. Brereton, New York: David McKay Co., 1953, pp. 292–302.

Norbert Elias, "On the Use of the Knife at Table," and "On the Use of the Fork at Table" in *The Civilizing Process: The History of Manners*, trans. by Edmund Jephcott, Oxford: Blackwell Publishers, 1994, pp. 99–105.

Henri Focillon, "Forms in the Realm of Space," in *The Life of Forms in Art*, trans. by C. B. Hogan and G. Kubler, New Haven: Yale University Press, 1942, pp. 19–21, 29–31.

J. von Goethe, "Kunst und Handwerk" (Art and Handicraft), in *Kunsttheoretische Schriften und Übersetzung*, vol. 1 (vol. 19 Beliner Ausgabe), Berlin: Afbau-Verlag, 1973, pp. 159–62. Translated by David Britt for this volume.

Walter Gropius, "Manifesto of the Staatliche Bauhaus in Weimar," in Hans M. Wingler, *The Bauhaus, Weimar, Dessau, Berlin, Chicago*, trans. by Wolfgang Jabs and Basil Gilbert, Cambridge. Mass.: MIT Press, 1978, p. 31.

Karl Grosz, "Ornament," *Jahrbuch des Deutschen Werkbundes* (Jena) 1912: 60–64. Translated by David Britt for this volume.

Adolf von Hildebrand, "Handarbeit—Maschinenarbeit" (Hand Work—Machine Work), in *A. von Hildebrand: Gesammelte Schriften zur Kunst*, ed. by H. Bock, Köln, 1969, 498. Translated by David Britt for this volume.

Owen Jones, "General Principles," "Ornament of Savage Tribes," and "Moresque Ornament," in *The Grammar of Ornament*, London: Day and Son, 1856, pp. 5–8, 13–17, 65–70.

Friedrich August Krubsacius, *Gedanken von dem Ursprung, Wachstum und Verfall der*

Verzierungen in den schönen Künsten (Reflections on the Origin, Growth, and Decline of Decoration in the Fine Arts), Leipzig, 1759, pp. 9–16. Translated by David Britt for this volume.

Adolf Loos, "Ornament and Crime" [1910], in *Programs and Manifestoes on 20th-Century Architecture*, ed. Ulrich Conrads, trans. by Michael Bullock, Cambridge, Mass.: MIT Press, 1975, pp. 19–24.

P. Rioux de Maillou, "Les Arts décoratifs et les machines" (The Decorative Arts and the Machine) *Revue des Arts Décoratifs* 15 (1895): 225–31, 267–73. Translated by David Britt for this volume.

Karl Philipp Moritz, "Über den Begriff des in sich selbst Vollendenten" (On the Concept of Self-Sufficient Perfection); "Anwendung des Begriffs vom Isolieren auf die Verzierungen" (Application of the Idea of Isolation to Decoration); "Borromino": "Über Verzierungen" (On Ornament); "Die Arabesken in Raffaels Logen" (The Arabesques in the Loggia of Raphael), from *Vorbegriffe zu einer Theorie der Ornamente*, now in *Karl Philipp Moritz. Werke*, ed. by H. Günther, Frankfurt am Main: Insel Verlag, 1981, vol. 2, pp. 543–48, 919–20, 395–96, 430–32, 449–51. Translated by David Britt for this volume.

William Morris, "The Revival of Handicraft"; "The Arts and Crafts of To-day," in *Collected Works*, intro. and ed. by May Morris, London: Routledge/Thoemmes Press, 1910–1915, 1992 reprint, vol. 22, pp. 331–41, 356–374.

Hermann Muthesius, "Die Bedentung des Kunstgewerbe" (The Significance of Applied Art), *Dekorative Kunst* 10 (1907): 177–192. Translated by David Britt for this volume.

A. Welby Pugin, "On Metal-work," in *The True Principles of Pointed or Christian Architecture*, 2nd ed. London: J. Weale, 1853, reprint 1969, pp. 19–25, 29–30.

Alois Riegl, *Historische Grammatik der bildenden Künste* (1897–99), ed. by K. M. Swoboda and O. Pächt, Graz: Hermann Böhlaus Nachf, 1966, pp. 207–18. Translated by David Britt for this volume.

Alois Riegl, "Introduction," "The Geometric Style," in *Problems of Style. Foundations for a History of Ornament*, trans. by Evelyn Kain, notes by D. Castriota, preface by H. Zerner, Princeton, 1992, pp. 3–13, 14–40. © 1992 by Princeton University Press. Reprinted by permission of Princeton University Press.

John Ruskin, "The Lamp of Sacrifice"; "The Lamp of Truth"; "The Lamp of Life"; "The Lamp of Beauty," in *The Seven Lamps of Architecture*, reprint New York: E. P. Dutton, 1910, pp. 24–27, 52–56, 105–09, 117–18, 118–25, 173–75, 177–79.

John Ruskin, "Modern Manufacture and Design," in *The Two Paths: Being Lectures on Art, and Its Application to Decoration and Manufacture*, New York, 1859, pp. 78–98, 108–12.

Gottfried Semper, *Über die formelle Gesetzmässigkeit des Schmuckes und dessen Bedeutung als Kunstsymbol* (Concerning the Formal Principles of Ornament and Its Significance as Artistic Symbol), Zurich: Monatschrift des wissenschaftlichen vereins, 1856, pp. 5–25. Translated by David Britt for this volume.

Gottfried Semper, "Science, Art, and Industry: Proposals for the Development of a National Taste in Art at the Closing of the London Industrial Exhibition"; "On the

Manner in Which Style Is Conditioned by the Treatment of the Material," in *Gottfried Semper: The Four Elements of Architecture and Other Writings,* trans. by W. Herrmann and H. F. Mallgrave, with intro. by H. F. Mallgrave, Cambridge: Cambridge University Press, 1989, pp. 133–39, 215–19, 226–34. Reprinted with permission of Cambridge University Press.

Gottfried Semper, "Introduction," in *Der Stil in den technischen und tektonischen Künsten, oder praktische Aesthetik,* 2nd ed., Munich: F. Bruckmann, 1870, vol. I, pp. 1–11. Translated by David Britt for this volume.

Georg Simmel, "Adornment," in *The Sociology of Georg Simmel,* trans., ed., and with intro. by K. H. Wolff, New York: The Free Press/(Simon & Schuster) Macmillan Publishing, 1950, 2nd ed. 1964, pp. 338–44. Reprinted with the permission of The Free Press, a Division of Simon & Schuster. © 1950 renewed 1978 by The Free Press.

Louis Sullivan, "Ornament in Architecture" in *Kindergarten Chats* (revised 1918 as *Kindergarten Chats and Other Writings* New York: Schulz, 1947, pp. 187–90. (Originally published in *Engineering Magazine,* August, 1892.)

Mariana Griswold Van Rensselaer, "Decorative Art and Its Dogmas," in *Accents as Well as Broad Effects: Writings on Architecture, Landscape, and the Environment, 1876–1925,* ed. by David Gebhard, Berkeley: University of California Press, 1996, pp. 110–21. (Originally published in *Lipincott's Magazine* 25 (February 1880): 213–20.)

Henry van de Velde, "Allgemeine Bemerkungen zu einer Synthese der Kunst" (Observations Toward a Synthesis of Art) [also printed as "Aperçus en vue d'une synthèse d'art" 1895, Brussels], German edition in H. Curjel, ed., *Henry van de Velde. Zum Neuen Stil,* Munich, 1955, pp. 36–56. Translated by David Britt.

Eugène-Emmanuel Viollet-le-Duc, "Lecture VI," in *Lectures on Architecture,* trans. by Benjamin Bucknall, vol. I, London, 1877, reprint New York: Dover Publications, 1987, pp. 177–81.

Heinrich Wölfflin, "Ornament," and "Principles of Historical Judgment," in *Empathy, Form and Space: Problems in German Aesthetics, 1873–1893,* intro. and trans. by Harry Francis Mallgrave and Eleftherios Ikonomou, Santa Monica: The Getty Center for the History of Art and the Humanities, 1994, pp. 178–185. © 1994 by The Getty Center for the History of Art and the Humanities. All rights reserved. [Originally published as *Prolegomena zu einer Psychologie der Architectur,* Inaugural-Dissertation der hohen philosophischen Fakultät der Universität München, Munich, 1886.]

Frank Lloyd Wright, "The Art and Craft of the Machine" in B. B. Pfeiffer, *Frank Lloyd Wright Collected Writings. Vol. 1 (1894–1930),* New York: Rizzoli, 1992, pp. 59–69.

Index

Page numbers in *italics* refer to illustrations.

Bacon, Francis, 140, 147, 148n1

Baroque art, 246, 262n1

Bauhaus, 23; "Manifesto of the Staatliche Bauhaus in Weimar," 83

Bayeux Tapestry, 53, 59n

Bazaar de l'Hotel de Ville, Paris, 215, 218n4

beauty, 5, 132, 136–37, 179, 182, 246, 254; Bing on, 23, 71–73; Corbusier on, 23–24, 84–89, 137; d'Alembert on, 27–29; Greek concept of, 136; Moritz on, 21–22, 24, 30–34; Morris on, 22–23, 61–70, 170–76; Muthesius on, 74–82; in nature, 42, 62–63; and ornament, 42–46, 47–60, 64–66, 91–104, 156, 245, 247, 266–70, 276–83, 297, 298, 305, 312–13, 327; Pugin on, 35–41; Ruskin on, 7–8, 22, 42–46, 47–60; and self-sufficient perfection, 30–34; uses of, 21–89; van de Velde on, 199–200; Wright on, 201–2, 206–7

Beidermeier Style, 80, 82n4, 295

Bing, Samuel, 13, 135, 249; "Where Are We Going?" 23, 71–73

Blenheim Palace, 64, 70n

Bloch, Ernst, 14

body: ornament on, 91–103, 111, 114, 118, 288, 299, 299, 302, 343, 350 and n; painting, 93–94; tattooing, 93–94, 111, 114, 118, 288, 299, 299, 302, 350 and n

bolts, 35, 36, 37

bone, ornament, 92–93, 98, 99, 347–48, 348, 349, 351, 351, 353

Borelli, Giovanni Alfonso, 256, 257n3

Borromini, Francesco, 259–60, 262n1

Botticelli, Sandro, 360, 361n3

Bramante, Donato, 262, 263n7

brick, 157–58, 224

bronze, 346

Bronze Age, 353

Buffon, Georges Louis Leclerc de, 147, 149n9

Burke, Edmund, 4

Byzantine ornament, 53, 233, 302, 308

calligraphy, 252

cannibalism, 347

capitalism, 13, 132, 170, 171

Caradosso, 100, 104n7

Carolingian Period, 234

carpet, 40, 166, 252, 282, 313n

carved reindeer bone spear thrower (Laugerie-Basse), 347, 348, 349

cast iron, 7, 35–36, 153–54, 207, 215; mullion, 153, 153; railings, 35–36, 36

cave dwellers, ornament of, 347–48, 348, 349–51, 351, 352–54

Cellini, Benvenuto, 100, 104n7

Celts, 93, 357, 359

Certosa of Pavia, 265, 270n4

chandeliers, 217

Chartres Cathedral, 52

Chevreul, Michel-Eugène, 98, 104n, 274 and n

Chicago Universal Exhibition (1892), 188, 193n8

China, 125, 163, 220, 291, 307n; architecture, 219; ornament, 99, 101, 102, 233–35, 324

Chippendale, Thomas, 207, 212n3

Chodowiecki, Daniel Nikolaus, 78, 82n2

Cimabue, 300, 316n2

clay. See pottery/ceramics

clothing, 49, 76, 118, 179; ancient, 24–25, 95–103; English, 57 and n; ornament, 95–103, 228, 251, 293, 294, 300, 301, 302, 313n, 323, 330–31, 347

club, Eastern Archipelago, 307, 307

Colbert, Jean-Baptiste, 140, 148nn2,3

Colleoni Chapel, Bergamo, 265, 270n4

Collingwood, R. G.: "Art and Craft," 236–42; Principles of Art, 136–37

color, 207, 282, 297, 312; Jones on, 271–75; Van Rensselaer on, 282–83

commerce, 67–69, 132, 180–82, 184; Morris on, 67–69, 176. See also industry; machine production

Cook, Captain, 307n

co-operative tradition, 65–70

function (continued)

    and ornament, 247; Pugin on, 6–7, 35–41; Riegl on, 25, 105–15; Ruskin on, 7–8, 22, 42–46, 47–60; Semper on, 11, 24–25, 91–104, 222; Simmel on, 25; theory of, 24–26, 91–128; uses of beauty, 21–89

Functionalism, 13, 24

furniture, 35, 46, 64, 66, 76, 180, 260, 280; Corbusier on, 84–89, 214 and n., 215, 216; and machine production, 187–91, 206–7, 292; ornament, 296; wood, 187–91, 206–7; Wright on, 206–7

gaslight, 164

Geometric Style, 226–29, 251; Riegl on, 340–55

geometry, 98; Diderot on, 144–45; and ornament, 98, 226–29, 303, 315, 340–55

Germany, 5, 6, 11, 15n5, 249, 255, 295, 298n4, 346, 347; applied art in, 74–82; Bauhaus, 83

Ghiberti, Lorenzo, 269, 270n6

Giorgione, 281, 283n2

Giotto, 265, 270n3, 300, 316n2

glass, 1, 52, 66, 141, 166, 195, 224; stained, 52, 316

Goethe, Johann Wolfgang von, 5, 78, 82n2, 131–32, 133, 150–52, 289, 294n1, 334; "Art and Handicraft," 150–52

gold, 120, 224

Goltzius, Hendrick, 255, 257n2

Gombrich, E. H., 2

Goodyear, W. G., *The Grammar of the Lotus*, 230–31

Gothic style, 6, 38–39, 45, 52, 53, 75, 231, 251, 280, 297, 315–16, 325; architecture, 45, 160, 199, 221, 264–66, 312n, 332, 334–35, 336–37; pattern papers, 39, *39*, 40

Grabar, Oleg, 2

graphic arts, 79

Great Britain, 6, 16n16, 35, 45, 46, 53, 57–59, 64, 81, 151, 180, 205, 248, 278, 281; Crystal

Palace exhibition (1851), 5, 11, 16n15, 132, 163, 166, 168nn2,3; 19th century reform of decorative arts, 6–10, 131–34, 202

Greece, ancient, 43, 91–94, 162, 203, 214, 218n3, 236, 327, 358; architecture, 43, 51, 91, 102, 103, 106, 107, 219, 257, 280, 308, 312n, 315, 332, 333n, 334; art, 50, 51, 106–7, 109–12, 160, 209, 230–33, 246, 254–55, 257, 316n1, 358; ornament, 50–53, 91–103, 230–33, 249, 254–55, 267–70, 308, 312n, 314, 315, 318, 320, 322n, 342, 344; pottery, 53, 106, 107, 345; vegetal motifs, 230–33, 314

Gropius, Walter, 23; "Manifesto of the Staatliche Bauhaus in Weimer," 83

Grosz, Karl, 248–49; "Ornament," 295–98

grotesques, 262 and n2

Haeckel, Ernst, 346, 355n3

handicraft. *See* craftsmanship

handle of paddle, British Museum, 307, *307*

Heine, H., 240, 242n2

Heraldic Style, 229, 232

Hildebrand, Adolf von, 133; "Hand Work —Machine Work," 177

Hindus, 99, 101, 321

hinges, 35, *36*

"historicism," 25

history of decorative art, 1–18; emergence of, 10–13; theory, 1–18

Hogarth, William: *Analysis of Beauty*, 246, 256

Horace, 261 and n

Hottentotts, 340n

Ideal, 71, 72, 106, 189, 197, 249, 337; asymmetrical, 246; and machine production, 189, 191, 201–12; of simplicity, 205–6; Wright on, 201–12

illuminated manuscripts, 316, 360

imagination, 111–12, 114

imitation, 77, 150, 297; of nature, 29, 30, 112; of painting, 208

materials and technique (continued)
Maillou on, 184–93; Morris on, 132, 133, 169–76; Muthesius on, 76–77; Pugin on, 6–7, 35–41, 153–55; Riegl on, 135–37, 226–35; Ruskin on, 7–8, 57–59, 132, 133, 156–61; Semper on, 135–37, 162–68, 219–25, 249–50, 317–26; theory of technique, 135–37, 219–42; van de Velde, 194–200; Wright on, 201–12. *See also* bone; glass; iron; metal; pottery; skin; stone; textiles; wood

mechanical arts, 3–5, 16n10, 21, 30, 131, 135; d'Alembert on, 27–29; Diderot on, 139–41. *See also* machine production

Mendelssohn, Moses, 30, 34n1

metal, 1, 35–41, 76, 77, 118, 150, 160, 163, 180, 192, 195, 196, 207, 216, 218, 237, 238; function of, 35–41, *36–40*; ornament, 35–41, *36–40*, 153, *153*, 154, 269, 292, 296, 329–30, *329–30*, 345, 346; Pugin on, 35–41, 153–55; *repoussé*, 225 and n; Semper on, 222–25. *See also specific metals*

Michelangelo, 47, 51, 59 and n, 300, 316n2

Michelet, Jules, 185–86; *Nos fils,* 185, 193n2

Middle Ages, 3, 16n10, 46, 65, 67, 112, 120, 126, 158, 166, 171, 175, 207, 231, 234, 288, 320, 325, 358, 360

Mies van der Rohe, L., 13

Migration Period, 234

Modernism, 2, 13–15, 17n30, 18n52, 24, 131, 248, 252

Montaigne, Michel de, 147, 149n7

Moorish ornament. *See* Arabesque ornament

Moritz, Karl Philipp, 2, 5, 15n6, 24, 26nn1,2, 30–34, 245, 246–47, 251, 259–63; "On the Concept of Self-Sufficient Perfection," 21–22; *Preliminary Ideas on the Theory of Ornament,* 5, 30–34, 246, 252n4, 259–63

Morris, William, 2, 6, 7, 8–10, 13, 17nn19, 29, 30, 22–23, 25, 132, 133, 134, 183, 248; "The Arts and Crafts of To-day," 10, 22, 61–70; "The Lesser Arts," 10, 23; "The

Revival of Handicraft," 169–76; Wright on, 201–8

mosaic, 179, 302, 322 and n

mullion: cast-iron, 153, *153;* stone, 153, *153*

museums, 11, 200

music, 3, 4, 163, 196–97, 241–42, 288, 294

muslin curtains, 323, 324 and n., 325

Muthesius, Hermann, 23, 74–82, 249, 298n4; "The Significance of Applied Art," 23, 74–82

nails, 35, 36, *37*

Naturalism, 198, 232

Nature, 28, 29, 71, 72, 97, 98, 106, 110, 112–14, 178, 255; and art, 340–41; beauty in, 42, 62–63; imitation of, 29, 30, 112; and ornament, 42, 62, 230–35, 256–57, 287, 297, 313–14, *314,* 315–16, 325, 340, 341, 354, 357–59

nets, 319–20

New Guinea: head of canoe, 303, *305;* plaited straw from, 302, *303*

New Holland (Australia), 92, 93

New Zealand, 305; female head from, 299, *299;* paddle, 305, *306,* 307; side of canoe, 303, *305*

nineteenth century, 1, 5–13, 14, 15, 24, 25, 73, 78, 131, 245, 247; British reform of decorative arts, 6–10, 131–34, 202

Notre Dame, Paris, 35

objects, types of. *See* architecture; clothing; fresco; furniture; jewelry; painting; sculpture; utensils; vessels

Oriental ornament, 99, 101, 102, 233–35, 249, 314, 324

ornament and style, 2, 5, 12, 13–15, 18nn46,52, 22, 26n3, 69, 73, 111, 136, 243–361; absence of, 294; ancient, 24–25, 35, 52–54, 92–103, 230–35, 246, 254–62, 308, 312n, 314, 315, 318, 320, 322n, 331, 341–54; Arabesque, 6, 93, 233–34, 249, 261–62, 302, 308–16, *308–15,* 335;

Shelley, Percy, 209–10, 212n5

Sheraton, Thomas, 207, 212n3

Siebmacher, Johann, 326 and n3

silver, 154

Simmel, Georg, 14, 25, 26; "Adornment," 116–21; *Sociology*, 25

simplicity, 218; ideal of, 205–6

skin, ornament on, 91–103, 111, 114, 118, 288, 299, 299, 302, 343, 350 and n

Socialism, 9, 10, 13, 171, 176 and n2, 186, 199

society, 57n-58n, 175, 193, 199, 281; and eating techniques, 122–28; Morris on, 175–76

South Sea Islands, 92, 93, 307n

space, ornamental, 356–61

spandrils of arches (Moresque ornament from the Alhambra), 308, *310*

Spranger, Bartholomaus, 255, 257n2

spun yarn, 318

stained glass, 52, 316

steel, 207, 211, 216, 236

Stickley, August, 13

stone, 35, 76, 77, 118, 153, 157–58, 160, 163, 167, 196, 217, 222, 224, 239, 345, 356; mullion, 153, *154;* Semper on, 223–24

Stone Age, 353

store fronts, 44

stucco, 281

style. *See* ornament and style

Sullivan, Louis, 13; "Ornament in Architecture," 284–87

symmetry, 226, 254, 255, 341; and ornament, 54–56, 95–97, 226, 343, 350, 354

tapestries, 53, 59n, 229, 325. *See also* textiles

tattooing, 93–94, 111, 114, 118, 288, 299, *299,* 302, 350 and n

technique. *See* materials and technique

terminology, 1–5, 14, 18nn49,51, 214 and n

terra-cotta, 109, 207, 224

textiles, 1, 3, 40, 66, 143, 146, 166, 171, 195, 215, 222, 250; and architecture, 317–26;

embroidery, 322–23, *323,* 324–26; ornament on, 95–103, 228–29, 300, *301,* 302, 347, 351–54; Semper on, 223–24, 250, 317–26, 344, 350; wickerwork, 302, *303,* 307n, 343–45, 347, 352, 354n

theory of decorative art: history of, 1–18; and function, 24–26, 91–128; and style, 249–52, 299–361; and technique, 135–137, 219–42. *See also specific authors*

Third German Applied Art Exhibition, Dresden, 74, 79, 82n1

tiles, 224; ancient paving, 40, *40*

Tintoretto, 48, 49, 59n

Titian, 48, 50, 51, 59n, 70n

twentieth century, 1, 13–15, 131, 136, 245

twisted yarn, 318–19

typewriter, 87n

United States, 6, 9, 248, 287, 291

upholstery, 40–41, 171, 280

utensils, eating, 26, 30–31, 49, 76, 118–19, 163, 346; Elias on, 122–28; primitive, 346, 351, *351*

Vallgren, Ville, 72, 73n2

van de Velde, Henry, 13, 134, 194–200, 249, 291; "Observations Toward a Synthesis of Art," 194–200

Van Rensselaer, Mariana Griswold, 248; "Decorative Art and Its Dogmas," 276–83

Vatican, Rome, 260–62 and n2, 263n7

vegetal ornament, 51, 230–35, 256–57, 313–14, *314,* 315–16, 324n, 325, 341, 354, 357–59

Venice, 46, 48, 49, 281, 283n2

Venturi, Robert, 18n52

vessels, 53, 66, 106, 109–11, 141, 223–24, 259; copper, 329–30, *329–30;* ornament, *329–30,* 346, 353, 354. *See also* pottery/ ceramics

Vienna, 11, 12, 14

Villa Borghese, 151, 152n2